THE THEFT ACTS 1968 AND 1978

AUSTRALIA AND NEW ZEALAND
The Law Book Company Ltd.
Sydney : Melbourne : Perth : Brisbane

CANADA
The Carswell Company Ltd.
Agincourt, Ontario

INDIA
N. M. Tripathi Private Ltd.
Bombay
and
Eastern Law House Private Ltd.
Calcutta *and* Delhi
M.P.P. House
Bangalore
and
Universal Book Traders
New Delhi

ISRAEL
Steimatzky's Agency Ltd.
Jerusalem : Tel Aviv : Haifa

PAKISTAN
Pakistan Law House
Karachi

THE THEFT ACTS
1968 AND 1978

By

EDWARD GRIEW, MA., LL.B.

of Gray's Inn, Barrister
Emeritus Professor of Law,
University of Nottingham

SIXTH EDITION

LONDON
SWEET & MAXWELL
1990

First Edition	1968
Second Edition	1974
Third Edition	1978
Fourth Edition	1982
Fifth Edition	1986
Sixth Edition	1990

Published by Sweet & Maxwell Ltd.,
South Quay Plaza, 183 Marsh Wall, London E14 9FT
Computerset by
MFK Typesetting Ltd., Hitchin, Hertfordshire
Printed in Scotland by
Thomson Litho

A CIP catalogue record
for this book is available
from the British Library

PREFACE TO THE SIXTH EDITION

This edition aims to reflect the relevant law and literature available up to the end of June 1990. I have also, as usual, reconsidered the whole text in terms of organisation, soundness (or at least plausibility) of argument and quality of statement. This process always throws up passages for revision in alarming quantity.

Chapter 6 (Introduction to the Fraud Offences) has been introduced for the sake of placing the deception offences briefly in the wider context of the criminal law concerned with fraud. The other main structural change is the creation of a distinct part of Chapter 2 (Theft) to deal in an orderly way with the theft of intangible property, and particularly of things in action, and more particularly of bank credits. This very important topic has undergone significant development since the previous edition. A large part of the same chapter has had to be substantially reorganised and rewritten in the light of major additions to the unhappy case law on appropriation (especially *Dobson* v. *General Accident*, etc.). This central topic, as will be seen, remains quite beyond my capacity to expound both simply and accurately. The passage begins with a plea of not guilty. Among other new passages I may perhaps single out brief excursions on overcharging as deception (at § 7–27: stimulated by *Silverman*) and on the stubborn "original thief or subsequent handler?" conundrum (at § 14–52: in the light of the Privy Council's crack at the problem in *Yip Kai-foon*).

Finally, I draw attention to a very small matter for the sake of making a point and acknowledging a debt. It will be found that cases (other than those reported in the Law Reports) are now wherever possible cited in the footnotes by reference to the Criminal Appeal Reports. Contrary to modern practice in the case of Cr.App.R., but in accordance with the useful convention otherwise applying to consecutively numbered series, the year given in round brackets is the year of decision rather than the year of publication (if that is different). In this connection I am grateful to the editorial department of Sweet and Maxwell, who are entirely innocent of the pedantic decision but have been kindly involved in its tedious execution.

Edward Griew
July 1990

Theft Acts 1968 and 1978
© Crown copyright

CONTENTS

vii

CONTENTS

TABLE OF CASES

xi

xiii

TABLE OF STATUTES

Chapter 1

PRELIMINARY AND MISCELLANEOUS

1. ABBREVIATIONS

THROUGHOUT this book the following abbreviations will be used: 1–01
    "The Act," unless the context otherwise requires, means the Theft Act
1968. References to sections and Schedules, except in §§ 6–05 to 6–08 and in
Chapters 8, 9 and 12 and unless otherwise indicated, are references to
sections of and Schedules to that Act.
    "The Bill," except in § 6–05, means the Theft Bill introduced in the House
of Lords in December 1967. This Bill became the Theft Act 1968.
    "The Committee" means the Criminal Law Revision Committee.
    "The draft Bill," except in § 6–05, means the Draft Theft Bill annexed to
the Committee's *Eighth Report.*
    "The *Eighth Report*" means the Committee's *Eighth Report: Theft and
Related Offences* (Cmnd. 2977).
    "The *Thirteenth Report*" means the Committee's *Thirteenth Report: Sec-
tion 16 of the Theft Act 1968* (Cmnd. 6733).

Two invaluable works will be referred to in abbreviated form: 1–02

    "Smith, *Theft*"means J. C. Smith, *The Law of Theft* (6th ed. 1990).
    "Williams, *Textbook*" means Glanville Williams, *Textbook of Criminal
Law* (2nd ed. 1983).

Parties will be found referred to much of the time in the conventional   1–03
modern manner: "D" is the person whose possible criminal liability is under
discussion; "P" is the victim of D's conduct.

2. THE BACKGROUND TO THE ACTS

The Theft Act 1968

Before the passing of the Act, the law of theft and related offences was   1–04
largely contained in the Larceny Act 1916. That statute enshrined most of
the indictable offences of dishonesty. It stated, but did not reform, the
complex law of larceny and other common law offences; and it consolidated,
but did not rationalise, numerous accretions to the statute book in the form
of special offences of larceny and other crimes.
    In March 1959 Mr. R. A. Butler, the Home Secretary, asked the newly
created Criminal Law Revision Committee

1

"to consider, with a view to providing a simpler and more effective system of law, what alterations in the criminal law are desirable with reference to larceny and kindred offences and to such other acts involving fraud or dishonesty as, in the opinion of the committee, could conveniently be dealt with in legislation giving effect to the committee's recommendations on the law of larceny."

There was then no talk of a general codification of a revised criminal law. But this reference of "larceny and kindred offences" to the Committee was well justified; the law in this area was generally acknowledged to be in an unsatisfactory state. It is not necessary now to conduct a post-mortem on the old law, but an indication of some of its outstanding deficiencies will be given as necessary in the introductory passages to later chapters of this book.

The subject occupied the Committee for seven years. Their *Eighth Report: Theft and Related Offences* was presented to Parliament in May 1966. The draft Bill annexed to this Report, slightly amended, was the basis of the Theft Bill introduced in the House of Lords in December 1967. After further amendments during its passage, that Bill received the Royal Assent in July 1968. The Act came into force on January 1, 1969.

The Theft Act 1978

1–05   It was, before long, a matter of general agreement that section 16(2)(*a*) of the Act required replacing. The highly unsatisfactory nature of that provision justified special amending legislation in advance of a general review of fraud offences promised by the Law Commission.[1] Proposals for such legislation were made by the Committee on a reference from the Home Secretary. The outcome was the Theft Act 1978, which came into force on October 20, 1978.[2]

3. THE CONTENTS OF THIS BOOK

1–06   The texts of the Acts are printed in the Appendices. Most of their provisions are examined in detail in the ensuing chapters. But some provisions of the 1968 Act are not dealt with elsewhere in this chapter or in those that follow. In particular:

(a) Section 14. This is a jurisdictional provision concerned with offences of theft or robbery committed outside England and Wales in relation to mail bags or postal packets in the course of transmission between different jurisdictions in the British postal area (as defined in section 14(2)). Section 14(1) renders the offender amenable to justice in England and Wales.

(b) Section 26(1). This empowers a justice of the peace to issue a search warrant for stolen goods.

---

[1] See Law Com. No. 76, *Report on Conspiracy and Criminal Law Reform* (1976), para. 1.15; *Thirteenth Report*, para. 3.

[2] The background to the 1978 Act is more fully treated below, at §§ 6–04 to 6–08 and §§ 12–02 to 12–05.

(c) Section 31(1).[3] This mainly concerns the liability of a person to answer incriminating questions in certain non-criminal proceedings and the effect of such answers in the event of the prosecution of that person or of his or her spouse for an offence under the Act (or under the 1978 Act: see s.5(2) thereof).

4. HUSBAND AND WIFE

The spouse as offender

The Theft Acts apply in relation to the parties to a marriage as if they were not married (s.30(1)), so that a husband can commit any offence under the Acts against his wife or in connection with her property, and vice versa. Any argument to the effect that if the parties were not married the victim would have no interest in the property that is the subject-matter of the alleged offence is defeated by the same subsection, which requires any interest derived from the marriage to be treated as if it subsisted independently of the marriage.   **1–07**

The subsection does not, of course, affect general doctrines of the criminal law relating to husband and wife. The defence of marital coercion will be as available to a wife on a prosecution under the Acts as on other prosecutions[4]; and husband and wife will no more be able to conspire together to commit an offence under the Acts than they are able to conspire to commit other offences.[5]

The spouse as prosecutor

Section 30(2) assimilates the position of the married to that of the unmarried in another respect and is not limited to offences under the Acts. It provides that "a person shall have the same right to bring proceedings against that person's wife or husband for any offence (whether under this Act or otherwise) as if they were not married."   **1–08**

The prosecution of spouses

Section 30(2) is subject to a restriction on some prosecutions imposed, in respect of prosecutors generally, by section 30(4).[6] This provides that certain proceedings are to be instituted only by or with the consent of the Director of Public Prosecutions save in special cases. The proceedings in respect of which the limitation is imposed are proceedings against a person "for any offence of stealing or doing unlawful damage to property which at the time of the offence belongs to that person's husband or wife, or for any   **1–09**

[3] Considered in *Khan* v. *Khan* [1982] 2 All E.R. 60.
[4] Criminal Justice Act 1925, s.47; Williams, *Criminal Law—General Part* (2nd ed.), pp. 764–768.
[5] Criminal Law Act 1977, s.2(2)(a).
[6] The subsection operated to render the proceedings a nullity in *Withers* [1975] Crim.L.R. 647.

attempt, incitement or conspiracy to commit such an offence." The phrase "belongs to" in this passage is to be interpreted in accordance with section 5(1) (s.34(1)), which is discussed in the chapter on theft.[7]

1–10   The restriction on prosecution does not apply—

(i) if the accused spouse is charged with committing the offence jointly with the other spouse (an example would be a case in which a wife is alleged to have stolen with her husband partnership property belonging to him and his partner); or

(ii) "if by virtue of any judicial decree or order (wherever made)" the spouses "are at the time of the offence under no obligation to cohabit"[8] (s.30(4), proviso (a)).

The restriction would, on the other hand, appear to apply (unless the case falls within either of these exceptions) even where the marriage is at an end before the institution of proceedings, for the subsection is expressed in terms of marriage "at the time of the offence."

Subsection (4) does not in general prevent the arrest without warrant, or the issue or execution of a warrant for the arrest, of a person for any offence, or the remand in custody or on bail of a person charged with any offence.[9] But the spouse-victim cannot himself or herself arrest without warrant for an offence within the subsection, and a warrant of arrest cannot be issued on an information laid by him or her without the Director's consent (subs.(5)[10]).

5. MODE OF TRIAL. THE TRIBUNAL OF FACT

Mode of trial

1–11   Most offences under the two Theft Acts are triable either way.[11] The exceptions are referred to in the relevant chapters.

The tribunal of fact

1–12   It follows that it would seem appropriate, throughout most of this book, to refer equally to juries and to magistrates, either by mentioning both in terms or by gathering up both in a single phrase—the "tribunal (or trier) of fact." Either course, however, would be tedious. Moreover, a great deal of the

---

[7] See below, §§ 2–21 to 2–29.
[8] See *Woodley* v. *Woodley* [1978] Crim.L.R. 629 (proviso applied to divorce judge's committal order suspended on terms that husband did not molest wife or approach within 200 yards of her home).
[9] Prosecution of Offences Act 1985, s.25(2)(a).
[10] Added by the Criminal Jurisdiction Act 1975, s.14(4) and Sched. 5, and amended by the Prosecution of Offences Act 1979, s.11(1) and Sched. 1.
[11] Magistrates' Courts Act 1980, Sched. 1, para. 28.

case law is expressed in terms of the way in which a trial judge should deal with the jury; and the issues which are for determination by magistrates as judges of fact are precisely those which are conventionally described as "jury issues." So the general method of this book, when discussing the function of the tribunal of fact or the way in which it ought to be directed or advised, will be to refer to the jury, and to the judge directing the jury, alone. It is hoped that this will not be misunderstood, even by magistrates and their clerks who are well aware that they are dealing with the great majority of the Theft Act cases coming before the courts. Clerks to justices will no doubt understand that they are to advise their benches in much the way that the Crown Court judge is to direct the jury; stipendiary magistrates will direct themselves in the same way. For "jury" read also "magistrate(s)" whenever the context permits.

6. VERDICTS

Criminal Law Act 1967, s.6(3) and (4)

The Criminal Law Act 1967, s.6, contains provisions, of general applica-   **1–13** tion to trial on indictment (but not to summary trial), which it is convenient to mention here rather than repeatedly throughout the book.

Provision for alternative verdicts

Section 6(3) of the Criminal Law Act 1967 confers important powers on a jury who find an accused person not guilty of an offence with which he is specifically charged. If "the allegations in the indictment amount to or include (expressly or by implication) an allegation of another offence" within the trial court's jurisdiction, the jury may find him guilty of that other offence; or they may find him guilty of an offence of which he could be found guilty if he were specifically indicted for that other offence. For the purposes of section 6(3) an allegation of an offence always includes an allegation of an attempt to commit it (section 6(4)).

The offence of which the jury may convict by virtue of section 6(3) is commonly called the "lesser offence" (as opposed to the "major offence" charged). This language has been judicially frowned upon as not being justified by the terms of the subsection. But it is convenient shorthand; and the provision may be expected to achieve in practice convictions of offences less serious than those charged.[11a]

"Included" allegations

An allegation of a lesser offence may be found to be *expressly* included in   **1–14**

[11a] The trial judge is not invariably obliged to tell the jury of the possibility of conviction of a less serious offence: see *Maxwell* [1990] 1 W.L.R. 401; [1990] 1 All E.R. 801, and cases there cited.

the allegations in an indictment by applying "the red pencil test"—that is, by "striking out all the averments which have not been proved"[12] and seeing whether what is left amounts to an allegation of the lesser offence.

It was formerly understood that an allegation of a lesser offence was included *by implication* in the allegation of a major offence only where the lesser offence was "an essential ingredient of the major offence"—as theft, for example, is an essential ingredient of robbery.[13] This was a clear, soundly-based rule. But it was overthrown by the controversial decision of the House of Lords in *Wilson*.[14] This held that an allegation of one offence may be included by implication in the allegation of another even though the former is not a necessary element of the latter. Specifically, an allegation of inflicting grievous bodily harm includes an allegation of assault occasioning actual bodily harm even though "inflicting" does not require an assault. The explanation seems to be that an allegation of grievous bodily harm "includes" (in one sense of that term) an allegation of actual bodily harm, as the greater includes the less; and that an assault is one way, no doubt the commonest way, of inflicting bodily harm and is therefore "included" (in another sense of that term) in "inflicting" as being an example of it; " 'inflicting' can . . . include 'inflicting by assault.' "[15] This shift from one sense of "includes" to another is not explicitly noticed in the opinion of Lord Roskill, with which the other lords agreed; it must be regarded as a serious flaw in the reasoning.

1–15   The application of section 6(3) to indictments for Theft Act offences is not always clear in the light of the *Wilson* decision, as the following discussion shows. The headings refer to the offences charged.

Theft (s.1). An allegation of theft does not by implication include an allegation of handling (*s.22*) by receiving[16] or by any other means. This surely remains true since *Wilson*, even though handling by receiving stolen goods is a way of stealing those goods.[17] Precisely because the handling will almost inevitably be a theft, there must be a strong argument that a conviction of handling on a theft charge would be inconsistent with acquittal of the theft itself.

1–16   *Robbery (s.8(1)); assault with intent to rob (s.8(2)).* Robbery involves theft as an essential ingredient. On a charge of robbery, therefore, the jury may find the accused not guilty of robbery but guilty of theft.[18] The other

---

[12] *Lillis* [1972] 2 Q.B. 236 at 241–242.
[13] *Springfield* (1969) 53 Cr.App.R. 608; *Lillis* [1972] 2 Q.B. 236 at 241.
[14] [1984] A.C. 242. The decision and its reasoning caused astonishment; see J. C. Smith [1984] Crim.L.R. 37; Emmins, *ibid.* at 152; Glanville Williams [1984] C.L.J. 290.
[15] [1984] A.C. 242 at 261.
[16] Compare *Woods* [1969] 1 Q.B. 447.
[17] See below, § 14–49.
[18] Similarly, a conviction of conspiracy to steal should be available on a charge of conspiracy to rob (where all that is not proved is the agreement to use force); but see to the contrary, unconvincingly, *Barnard* (1979) 70 Cr.App.R. 28 at 33.

ingredient of robbery is the use of force on any person or the putting or seeking to put any person in fear of being then and there subjected to force. One charged with robbery could not formerly be convicted of assault with intent to rob, for robbery may be committed without an assault (by a mere seeking to put in fear).[19] But as an assault will occur in most robberies, the alternative verdict may now be possible by analogy with *Wilson*. There cannot be conviction of a mere assault, however, on a charge of robbery or of assault with intent to rob, as "common assault and battery" are now summary offences and not within the jurisdiction of the Crown Court, as section 6(3) requires.[19a]

Burglary (s.9). One way of committing burglary is to enter a building as a **1–17** trespasser and to steal (or attempt to steal) therein or to inflict (or attempt to inflict) on any person therein any grievous bodily harm (section 9(1)(*b*)). An allegation of entering a building as a trespasser and stealing therein includes an allegation of theft. If the trespass is not proved, the allegation of it may be struck out, as may the word "therein" and even the date alleged, to reveal an express allegation of theft committed wheresoever and whensoever.[20]

An allegation of entry followed by theft has been held, applying *Wilson*, to include by implication an allegation of entry with intent to steal[21]; and an allegation of entry followed by inflicting grievous bodily harm includes by implication an allegation of assault occasioning actual bodily harm.[22]

It seems, notwithstanding *Wilson*, that on an indictment (under section 9(1)(*a*)) charging burglary by entering a building as a trespasser with intent to commit an offence mentioned in section 9(2) (say, theft or rape), it is not possible to acquit of the burglary and convict of an attempt to commit the intended offence (still less of the intended offence itself); an allegation of entry with intent to steal, for instance, does not imply an allegation of conduct that has got as far as an attempted theft.[23]

Aggravated burglary (s.10). A person charged with aggravated burglary **1–18** may be convicted of burglary as described in the indictment or of any offence of which he could be found guilty on an indictment charging burglary so described.

Handling (s.22). Many (maybe most) persons guilty of handling stolen **1–19** goods are also guilty of theft. But a handling charge does not imply an

---

[19] *Tennant* [1976] Crim.L.R. 133 (as to assault); compare *Springfield* (1969) 53 Cr.App.R. 608. (Otherwise, if force or an actual putting in fear is expressly alleged?)
[19a] Criminal Justice Act 1988, s.39; *Mearns* [1990] Crim.L.R. (708); *Savage*, [1990] Crim.L.R. 709. (This is so although a count for common assault might have been added under s.40.)
[20] *Lillis* [1972] 2 Q.B. 236. But before leaving to the jury the possibility of a conviction of theft, the judge should ensure that the defendant "has had the opportunity of fully meeting that alternative": see *per* Lord Roskill in *Wilson* [1984] A.C. 242 at 261; and see the criticism of *Lillis* by J. C. Smith [1972] Crim.L.R. 459.
[21] *Whiting* (1987) 85 Cr.App.R. 78, regarding *Hollis* [1971] Crim.L.R. 525, to the contrary, as no longer good law.
[22] *Jenkins* (decided with *Wilson*) [1984] A.C. 242.
[23] Compare *Lyttle* [1969] Crim.L.R. 213 (charge, in effect, of entry with intent to rape).

allegation that the accused intended to deprive the victim permanently of the goods, which is essential for theft; nor is theft a way of committing handling, so as to be implied by an allegation of handling in the sense apparently intended in *Wilson*. So a verdict of theft is not possible on a handling indictment.

Attempt or preliminary act charged; complete offence proved

1–20   Section 6(4) of the Criminal Law Act 1967 goes on to provide for the situation in which an indictment charges a mere attempt or an assault or other act preliminary to an offence, but in which it is proved that the accused was in fact guilty of the completed offence. In such a case the accused can be convicted of the attempt[24] or other preliminary offence charged, or the court can discharge the jury so that an indictment for the completed offence can be preferred. An example under the present Act might arise from a charge of assault with intent to rob under section 8(2) where the jury find that the accused in fact committed the full offence of robbery.

Summary trial

1–21   There is no power on summary trial to acquit of the only offence charged but to convict of an attempt to commit it or of some other offence. So a failure to anticipate a difficulty of proof and to charge an alternative offence, or an attempt, can lead to an unmerited acquittal or to duplication of proceedings. This was illustrated in *Bogdal* v. *Hall*[25]: charges of obtaining unemployment benefit girocheques by deception failed for want of proof that the particular girocheques were received; attempts in the form of the making of fraudulent claims were proved but not separately charged.

Provision in the Theft Acts

1–22   Only in one case do the Theft Acts themselves provide for conviction of one offence on the charge of another: a person charged on indictment with theft may be found guilty of taking a conveyance.[26]

Nowhere do the Acts provide for conviction of the offence charged where some other offence, but not the offence charged, is found to have been committed. Yet the Court of Appeal has on one occasion allowed a conviction of theft to stand on the ground that, if that offence was not committed, the appellant was guilty of obtaining a pecuniary advantage by deception, so that (as the court asserted) no miscarriage of justice had occurred.[27] To convict a person of an offence not proved to have been committed because he has committed an offence with which he has not been charged surely requires statutory warrant. The decision should be regarded as an aberration.

---

[24] Similarly on summary trial, for the attempt does not merge in the completed offence: *Webley* v. *Buxton* [1977] Q.B. 481.
[25] [1987] Crim.L.R. 500.
[26] s.12(4).
[27] *McHugh* (1976) 64 Cr.App.R. 92.

7. INTERPRETATION[28]

The Theft Act 1968, as has been judicially observed in several cases, "is an   **1–23**
Act designed to simplify the law."[29] There is no controversy about this. The
Act greatly reduced the number of offences employed to cover the range of
conduct penalised; it employs, on the whole, simpler, more modern and less
technical language than was formerly used; and it removed a good many
"technicalities and subtleties"[30] that had marred the old law.

Two further points ought to be beyond controversy. First, the Act's aim of
simplifying the law should not be frustrated by gratuitous subtlety in its
interpretation. The courts for their part may be expected to reject a subtle
reading in favour of a simple reading where both are truly available, and
they will be right to do so. Still, it is a practitioner's proper function to take a
subtle point on behalf of his client when the need arises; and a commentator
will occasionally feel bound to suggest an analysis of the Act that appears to
be available, even if he regards it as unattractive on the ground of undue
subtlety or of policy.

Secondly, judicial exegesis should be clear and consistent. If a series of
decisions is unrelated and incoherent, the result will be uncertainty and
obscurity rather than simplicity. This, unhappily, has been the tendency of
much of the case law on the Act. Previous relevant authority has been too
often ignored or apparently contradicted without adequate explanation, so
that the case law has tended to become increasingly confused; and judgments have been casually and obscurely phrased, and decisions therefore
hard to interpret. If the Act is to be kept simple, decisions upon it require
internal clarity and collective consistency.

Questions of civil law

Closely associated with the view of the Act as one designed to simplify the   **1–24**
law is the proposition (which does not follow from it) that it ought to be
capable of being understood by a lay person. From this proposition proceeds
the notion (which also does not follow) that the Act should receive a plain
person's interpretation; and the feeling seems to be that, the plain person
being no lawyer, there is something disreputable about construing it in a
lawyerly way.[31] This, it is thought, contributes to the defects in the case law
mentioned above. It also leads to an insupportable doctrine concerning the
relation between the criminal law in this Act and other principles of law. In
the case of *Baxter*,[32] Sachs L.J. elaborated the statement that the Act is one
"designed to simplify the law" by saying that

---

[28] Brazier [1974] Crim.L.R. 701.
[29] *Baxter* [1972] 1 Q.B. 1 at 13, *per* Sachs L.J.
[30] *Bonner* (1970) 54 Cr.App.R. 257 at 264–265, *per* Edmund Davies L.J.
[31] Close kin to this is a tendency to resort to the ordinary person's supposed conception of theft
as a factor in interpreting the elaborate provisions on that offence: see especially, below,
§ 2–28.
[32] See n. 29, above; compare *Nordeng* (1975) 62 Cr.App.R. 123 at 128 (and commentary by J.
C. Smith [1976] Crim.L.R. at 195).

"it uses words in their natural meaning and is to be construed thus to produce sensible results; when [the] Act is under examination this court deprecates attempts to bring into too close consideration the finer distinctions in civil law as to the precise moment when contractual communications take effect or when property passes."

To the same effect was the suggestion of Lord Roskill in *Morris*[33] that

"it is on any view wrong to introduce into this branch of the criminal law questions whether particular contracts are void or voidable on the ground of mistake or fraud or whether any mistake is sufficiently fundamental to vitiate a contract. These difficult questions should so far as possible be confined to those fields of law to which they are immediately relevant and I do not regard them as relevant questions under the 1968 Act."

1–25　　The major difficulty with this benignly-intentioned approach is that the Act inevitably defines offences against property in terms of the categories of the civil law (see, for instance, ss.4, 5, 9 and 15). Words by means of which reference to those categories is made (such as "things in action," "ownership," "possession," "proprietary right or interest," "trespasser") do not have "natural" meanings but technical ones. This is helpful, not harmful; it makes for certainty in the criminal law. The Act should of course be read sensibly; but that does not mean that there is a painless plain person's route to its meaning. There are bound, in particular, to be cases in which the practitioner cannot do his full duty without an adequate grasp of relevant principles of the civil law. And the courts should be prepared to make careful application of those principles, for two reasons: as an indispensable means of fixing the boundaries of criminal liability with adequate certainty; and to avoid incongruous and even unjust conflict between the respective demands on citizens of the civil and criminal law.[34]

A valuable corrective to the judicial statements quoted above is the case of *Walker*,[35] decided by the Court of Appeal a few days after the decision in *Morris*. P had bought a video recorder from D. He found it to be defective and returned it to D for repair. He later issued a summons to recover the price and this was served on D. D resold the recorder and was charged with theft of it. D's resale could be theft only if P had still a "proprietary right or interest" in the recorder at the time of the resale.[36] This depended on civil law principles relating to the rejection of goods by buyers which the trial judge had failed to apply or to explain to the jury. D's conviction was inevitably quashed. The law of contract and of property applies in all courts and in all contexts. There is in truth, as the Court of Appeal insisted, "no distinction between the civil law and the criminal law."[37]

---

[33] [1984] A.C. 320 at 334.
[34] See J. C. Smith [1972 B] C.L.J. 197, *passim* and especially at 197–198; Williams [1977] Crim.L.R. 127 at 128 *et seq.*
[35] (1983) 80 L.S. Gaz. 3238; [1984] Crim.L.R. 112.
[36] See ss.1(1) and 5(1).
[37] See also, *e.g. Shadrokh-Cigari* [1988] Crim.L.R. 465, referring to a doctrine of equity; *Dobson* v. *General Accident Fire and Life Assurance Corp. plc* [1990] Q.B. 274 at 289, *per* Bingham L.J., as to need to resort to civil law on, in effect, questions of ownership.

"Ordinary words"

There has, in fact, been a judicial tendency to leave the interpretation of **1–26** particular statutory words to the lay tribunal. The relevant doctrine is that an "ordinary word" does not need judicial explanation; its "natural" or "ordinary" meaning is known to the jury. This view has been pervasive, though it is not always given effect.[38] Its application has sometimes been very puzzling, as when for a time the identification of an "obligation" was said to be a matter for the jury although the word means "legal obligation."[39] And generally—and especially in relation to the central word "dishonestly"[40]— the doctrine has proved controversial.[41] It may be contended that there is much to be said for the criminal law's being able to reflect community values, as represented by justices and juries, and to respond to changes in those values; and that there is a real difficulty about tying down the meaning of words by judicial pronouncement. The present book, however, will be found to reflect the belief that a person's liability to conviction should not depend upon the accidental composition of the bench or jury that tries him when it might depend upon a proposition of law[42]; that the prevailing view makes unjustified assumptions about the existence of clear community norms in a morally and socially plural society, and also about the existence of generally apprehended "natural meanings" of words[43]; and that it is the business of the judiciary, gradually by a course of decisions, to help the lay tribunal to as consistent an application of the criminal law as can reasonably be achieved.

---

[38] As to the impact of the doctrine in Theft Act cases, see D. W. Elliott [1976] Crim.L.R. 707.
[39] See below, § 2–34.
[40] See below, §§ 2–127 *et seq.*
[41] See Williams [1976] Crim.L.R. 472 and 532; and, as to the issue of dishonesty, see the references in § 2–131, nn. 37, 38.
[42] Compare, in other contexts, Criminal Law Revision Committee, *Fourteenth Report: Offences against the Person* (1980: Cmnd. 7844), para. 7; *Pearlman* v. *Harrow School* [1979] Q.B. 56 at 66–67, *per* Lord Denning M.R.
[43] There are several references in Theft Act cases to the "natural meaning" of words: *e.g. Baxter*, n. 29, above; *Treacy* [1971] A.C. 537 at 543, *per* John Stephenson J.; *D.P.P.* v. *Turner* [1974] A.C. 357 at 364, *per* Lord Reid. Nevertheless, it is thought that scepticism about this notion is permissible. In one case the jury asked for and were granted the use of a dictionary, probably to look up the word "dishonestly." The conviction was quashed; the jury should have been told to apply the "ordinary meaning" of the word, which was said to be "quite clear"; *Swift* (C.A. No. 1396/B/79), unreported.

Chapter 2

THEFT

1. DEFINITION AND BACKGROUND

2–01   SECTION 1(1) provides that a person

> "is guilty of theft if he dishonestly appropriates property belonging to
> another with the intention of permanently depriving him of it";

and section 7 provides a maximum penalty of 10 years' imprisonment on
conviction on indictment of this offence.[1] The basic definition in section 1(1)
requires quite extensive examination. This can conveniently be conducted,
for the most part, by way of a treatment of the words and phrases employed
in section 1(1), as defined or partially explained in sections 2 to 6, which
"have effect as regards the interpretation and operation of [section 1]"
(section 1(3)). The five following parts of this chapter concern, respectively,
"property" (which section 4 understands in wide terms, while also restricting
the scope of theft in relation to land); "belonging to another" (artificially
and extensively defined by section 5); "appropriates" (partially defined by
section 3(1)); "with the intention of permanently depriving the other of it"
(the subject of an ill-drafted marginal gloss in section 6); and "dishonestly"
(to the understanding of which section 2 makes a limited negative contribution, declaring certain conduct not to be dishonest). Important principles
relating to the theft of intangible property, which presents peculiar problems, are gathered together towards the end of the chapter.

2–02   By way of preface, however, a brief reference to the offences replaced by
the modern offence of theft may be useful.

Historically, *larceny* was an offence against another's possession of goods;
and it involved a violation of that possession by "taking and carrying away"
his goods without his consent, with the intention of permanently depriving
him of them. Such a "taking" could not occur where there was a consensual
delivery; nor could it occur where the offender was himself already in
possession, for instance as a bailee. But one who induced a delivery by fraud
was regarded as "taking" without consent because the fraud was treated as
negativing the victim's apparent consent; and a bailee became capable of
larceny (by conversion of the goods bailed) by a statutory extension of the
offence. The element of "carrying away" (or "asportation") required some
physical removal of the goods, however slight. Another important limitation
on the scope of larceny was the requirement that the intention to deprive the

---

[1] Proposed to be reduced to seven years: see White Paper, *Crime, Justice and Protecting the
Public*, Cm. 965 (1990), para. 3.14.

victim permanently should exist at the moment of the taking, though this rule was somewhat mitigated by intellectual ingenuity on the part of the judges.

Embezzlement was an offence of statutory origin designed to deal with the dishonest misappropriation by a servant of any chattel, money or valuable security delivered to the servant on account of his employer; for such misappropriation could not be larceny if it occurred before the property was reduced into the employer's possession.

Fraudulent conversion was another statutory creation. Its main *raison d'être* was the fact that, whereas a bailee could by statute be guilty of larceny by misappropriating the property bailed, one who had ownership of property could not, even though he had been entrusted with it otherwise than for his own beneficial enjoyment. The offence covered absconding trustees, club treasurers and the like. Unlike larceny and embezzlement it extended to any kind of property.

In the notion of a fraudulent conversion of any property the model was found for a single new offence of theft to replace the three crimes mentioned above. Or rather to replace a great many crimes, for under the old law there was a large number of different forms of larceny with different maximum penalties. There is now one offence of theft—though robbery, which is no mere aggravated theft but rather theft-plus-force, is preserved as a distinct crime and is separately treated in Chapter 3.

2. "PROPERTY"

" 'Property' includes money and all other property, real or personal, includ- 2–03
ing things in action and other intangible property" (s.4(1)); and wild creatures, tamed or untamed, are to be regarded as property (s.4(4)). Section 4 provides specially for land and wild creatures by limiting the circumstances in which they can be stolen. These special cases will be dealt with below.

Reduced to its shortest form, without any change in its meaning, section 4(1) reads: " 'Property' includes ... all ... property." Such a statement might be thought unworthy of the draftsman of the Act. It had a point, however, as a plain indication to those accustomed to the former law that the new theft was, in respect of its subject-matter, much wider than the old larceny. Only things capable of being "taken and carried away"—in effect, money and other tangible personalty—could formerly be stolen. The draftsman made his point emphatically by mentioning land and intangible forms of property as capable now of being stolen.

Land; and things growing wild thereon

Land can be stolen, but only by certain persons in certain particular ways. 2–04

A person who appropriates "land, or things forming part of land and severed from it by him or by his directions," is not guilty of theft unless he falls within one of the exceptional cases mentioned below, or unless what he appropriates is an incorporeal hereditament (s.4(2)).[2]

Land is not defined in the Act. Any difficulty that exists concerns the meaning of the phrase "things forming part of land." Problems can arise in connection with (i) things annexed to the land and (ii) materials deposited on the land.

(i) As to *things annexed to the land*, "the general maxim of the law is, that what is annexed to the land becomes part of the land; but it is very difficult, if not impossible, to say with precision what constitutes an annexation sufficient for this purpose."[3] There is no difficulty with houses and similar permanent structures or with things that are clearly integral parts of such structures.[4] In the case of anything resting on or attached to land or to a building thereon, the tests to be applied are those applied in the law relating to fixtures: whether such a thing forms part of the land depends in part upon the degree of annexation and in part upon the object of annexation.[5] In *Billing* v. *Pill*[6] the floor of an army hut built in seven sections was secured to concrete foundations by bolts let into the concrete. It was held that although the foundations formed part of the realty, the hut, in the light of the evidence as to the temporary object of its attachment to the land, did not. On the other hand "blocks of stone placed one on top of another without any mortar or cement for the purpose of forming a dry stone wall would become part of the land,"[7] at least if the wall was not purely temporary.

(ii) *Materials deposited on land*, such as sand and cinders, will not form part of the land if they lie in heaps on the ground; but if they are spread on the land they are likely to be found to have become part of the soil.[8]

When land can be stolen

2–05   Section 4(2) provides that land can exceptionally be stolen in the following situations.

(a) A trustee or personal representative or one authorised[9] to sell or dispose of land belonging to another[10] can steal the land or anything forming

---

[2] The most important incorporeal hereditaments are easements, *profits à prendre* and rent-charges. See Megarry and Wade, *The Law of Real Property* (5th ed.), Chap. 15.
[3] *Holland* v. *Hodgson* (1872) L.R. 7 C.P. 328 at 334, *per* Blackburn J.
[4] See *per* Lord Goddard C.J. in *Billing* v. *Pill* [1954] 1 Q.B. 70 at 75.
[5] See, as to the meaning of fixtures, Megarry and Wade, *op. cit.*, pp. 730–734; Halsbury, *Laws of England* (4th ed.), Vol. 27, p. 111.
[6] [1954] 1 Q.B. 70.
[7] *Holland* v. *Hodgson* (1872) L.R. 7 C.P. 328 at 335, *per* Blackburn J. Compare *Skujins* [1956] Crim.L.R. 266 (a decision of quarter sessions); farm gate held to form part of the realty.
[8] As in *Morgan* v. *Russell & Sons* [1909] 1 K.B. 357.
[9] "by power of attorney, or as liquidator of a company, or otherwise. ..."
[10] See s.5(1)(2). Land held on trust, for instance, will belong to the beneficiaries.

part of it by dealing with it in breach of the confidence[11] reposed in him (s.4(2)(*a*)).

(b) A person not in possession[12] of land can in general steal something forming part of the land: he can appropriate it by severing it or causing it to be severed, or after it has been severed[13] (s.4(2)(*b*)). To come on to a person's land and take the tiles from his roof (severing) is obviously as much theft as to take the books from his shelves; and one may steal another's pasture by grazing cattle on his land[14] (causing to be severed).

The general rule that a person not in possession of land can steal by severance is subject to a large exception, provided by section 4(3), in relation to things growing wild. Save in one class of case, no one steals if he picks mushrooms[15] growing wild or if he picks flowers, fruit or foliage from a plant[16] growing wild. The excepted case is that in which the picking is done "for reward or for sale or other commercial purpose."

This piling of exception upon exception is confusing. We may approach these provisions in another way by observing that the Act makes a series of distinctions:

(i) One who is in possession of land and one who is not. The former cannot steal by severing (unless he is a tenant and he severs a fixture: see exception (c), below). The latter can, but in respect of him a distinction is drawn between—

(ii) Mushrooms and plants growing wild, and anything else "forming part of the land" (including cultivated plants). The latter can always be stolen by one not in possession of the land. As to "plants growing wild" the Act makes a third distinction:

(iii) Severing and picking.[17] Uprooting a plant, even one growing wild, will be "severing"; if the plant belongs to anyone and the severing is dishonest, it will be theft. But taking individual blooms from a wild shrub or a basketful of wild berries or a quantity of wild holly will be mere "picking" and cannot be theft, subject to one final distinction:

(iv) Commercial and non-commercial purpose. Even the picking of wild mushrooms or flowers, fruit or foliage from wild plants may be theft if done "for reward or for sale or other commercial purpose." So whether you steal when you pick wild flowers may depend on your motive: if you desire to decorate your house[18] or your friend, it is not theft; if you are picking for pay or to sell in the market, it is.[19] This distinction is contrary to the general

---

[11] The word "confidence" is purposely used in preference to "trust," which might have been understood in a technical sense. It would seem that an agent authorised to sell land will commit theft if, for instance, he dishonestly sells to his own nominee at an undervalue for the purpose of making a profit by then selling to a sub-purchaser on his own account.

[12] The phrase "not in possession" no doubt includes a member of the household of one in possession.

[13] After it has been severed it will surely not form part of the land.

[14] *McGill* v. *Shepherd* (1976: Victoria), unreported, cited by Williams and Weinberg, *Property Offences* (2nd ed.), p. 94.

[15] Includes any fungus.

[16] Includes any shrub or tree.

[17] The uprooting of any wild plant, or the picking, uprooting or destroying of a protected plant, may be a summary offence under s.13 of the Wildlife and Countryside Act 1981.

[18] If you desire to decorate your shop-window for the sake of the aesthetic effect, this may be construed as a "commercial purpose." The phrase is very vague.

[19] So long as the other elements of theft are present: there must be someone to whom the wild plants belong, and your act must be dishonest.

principle that theft does not depend upon motive, or even upon a view to gain (s.1(2)). It may also present disproportionate problems of proof. The burden is on the prosecution to prove the commercial purpose; and this will no doubt usually be very hard to do—save, for instance, where a known market trader is caught in the act of amassing a large quantity of flowers, fruit or foliage.

2–06   (c) The third exceptional case in which an appropriation of land or things forming part thereof may be theft is that in which a tenant[20] in possession appropriates a fixture[21] or structure let to be used with the land (s.4(2)(c)).

Some cases that are not theft

2–07   The following, in conclusion, are examples of cases in which appropriation of land or things forming part of land will not be theft:

(i) D is a lessee of land. He removes and sells ore or plants from the land. If he is "in possession of the land" (which he may not be; he may have sub-let it), he is not guilty of theft, for he is not within exception (b) above, and the thing taken is not a "fixture or structure" within exception (c).

(ii) D is in possession of land under a mere licence. He severs and appropriates a fixture. He is not within either exception (b) or exception (c) and so does not steal. It is odd perhaps that the licensee should have this advantage over the tenant.

(iii) D "squats" on P's land, or extends his fences so as to take in part of P's land, or forcibly turns P off his land. He does not steal, because exception (b) concerns only the severance of things forming part of the land.

Wild creatures

2–08   From the terms of section 4(4) it is clear that "a wild creature" means "a creature wild by nature." This was the language of the Larceny Act[22] and cases decided under the old law therefore remain relevant for the classification of some creatures as wild or otherwise. The last of those cases amusingly illustrated the ambiguity of the word "wild." The case concerned mussels on the sea shore. The prosecution's concession that they were wild creatures was both inevitable and mildly incongruous.[23]

Wild creatures that have been tamed or are ordinarily kept in captivity can be stolen as readily as any other property.

As to creatures at liberty, the problem was whether by means of the law of theft to protect the owner of, or the person having sporting rights over, the land on which they may be taken or killed. More tersely: should poaching be theft? The Committee recommended[24] that it should be theft when done "for reward or for sale or other commercial purpose," and the Bill so

[20] For the meaning of "tenancy" in this provision, see the text of s.4(2) in Appendix 1.
[21] See note 5, above.
[22] Larceny Act 1916, s.1(3) proviso (*b*).
[23] *Howlett* [1968] Crim.L.R. 222.
[24] *Eighth Report*, para. 52.

provided. This would have been a substantial departure from the pre-existing law and would have rendered the offender liable to very much greater penalties than those provided under other statutes controlling poaching. In the end the relevant provision was excluded from the Bill during its passage.

The result is that if a wild creature is "not tamed nor ordinarily kept in **2–09** captivity," it cannot normally be stolen. The rationale of this is that, although P may own the land on which the creature is and Q may have sporting rights over the land, no one owns the creature until it is killed or taken.[25] But when it has been reduced into someone's possession (and so long as it has not subsequently been lost or abandoned), or when someone is in course of reducing it into possession, it can be treated as the proper subject of theft. Section 4(4) provides accordingly, treating a wild creature and the carcass of a wild creature in identical terms. So it is not theft to kill and take game on P's land, unless, for instance, the creature is taken from P's snares (even from another poacher's snares) or from a hut in which P has put the product of his own day's shooting.

Fish and deer. Schedule 1 to the Act preserves in a modified form certain **2–10** provisions of the Larceny Act 1861 concerning the unlawful taking or destroying of fish in water which is private property or in which there is any private right of fishery. Other provisions, originally preserved by Schedule 1, relating to the taking or killing of deer, have been superseded by the Deer Act 1980, s.1. This creates summary offences of (1) entering any land, without the consent of the owner or occupier or other lawful authority, in search or pursuit of any deer with the intention of taking, killing or injuring it; (2) on any land, (a) intentionally taking, killing or injuring any deer (or attempting to do so), or (b) searching for or pursuing any deer with the intention of taking, killing or injuring it, or (c) removing the carcass of any deer, without the consent of the owner or occupier of the land or other lawful authority.

"Money"

A question about the legal meaning of "money" is invariably a question as **2–11** to the classes of assets referred to by the word in a particular context.[26] The Theft Act concerns the appropriation (or the obtaining by deception: s.15) of particular items of property,[27] some of which are singled out for mention as "money." All that the word seems to include in this context is current coins and bank notes (including, of course, foreign coins and notes).[28] So, if a person deals dishonestly with a cheque for £x, he can be convicted on a

[25] See *Blades* v. *Higgs* (1865) 11 H.L.C. 621.
[26] See F. A. Mann, *The Legal Aspect of Money* (4th ed.), Chap. I.
[27] See below, § 2–20.
[28] That is, coins and notes issued by the authority of the law and currently capable of serving as universal means of exchange in their country of origin: adapting language of Mann, *op. cit.* p. 8.

charge of stealing "£x in money" only if he cashes the cheque and appropriates the cash as property belonging to another.[29] It is tempting to give the
word "money" a wider meaning than this. After all, it is rightly observed in a
different connection that according to "the ordinary language and usage of
mankind, when a man says, 'I have so much money at my bankers,' he
considers and treats it as his money"[30]; so that, even when a testator's
reference to his "money" is to be construed in a "strict sense," it is allowed to
include what he has on current and deposit account.[31] It is one thing,
however, to permit a testamentary gift of "money" to pass the benefit of a
bank account. It is quite another thing to suppose that a person's bank
account is "money" for Theft Act purposes. The "property" in which a
bank's customer can have a "proprietary right or interest" (s.5(1)) is a thing
in action—namely, the debt owed to him by the bank when the account is in
credit.[32] If, say, £74.74 is credited to the account, the property available to
be stolen is not, strictly, "the sum of £74.74" but a "chose (or thing) in
action."[33]

"Things in action and other intangible property"[34]

2–12   "Things in action" are "all personal rights of property which can only be
claimed or enforced by action and not by taking physical possession."[35] They
include intangible things such as a debt,[36] a right under a trust and, it seems,
any obligation owed in law by one person to another and capable of being
enforced by that other[37]: the creditor, the beneficiary and the obligee have
"property" that can be stolen.

It was for a long time believed that the category, "things in action,"
embraced all kinds of personal property other than things in possession
(moveable chattels, including money as defined above).[38] But it is now clear
that there are some kinds of intangible property that are not things in action.
Patents and applications for patents are declared by statute not to be things
in action.[39] Another kind was revealed in *Attorney-General of Hong Kong* v.
Nai-keung,[40] where a company had export quotas issued by a government

---

[29] *Davis* (1988) 88 Cr.App.R. 347 (below, § 2–39); *Brady* v. *Inland Revenue Commissioners*
[1989] S.T.C. 178 (obtaining payment by cheque is not obtaining "money" for Theft Act
purposes).
[30] *Manning* v. *Purcell* (1855) 7 De G.M. & G. 55, *per* Turner L.J. at 67.
[31] *Re Collings* [1933] Ch. 920.
[32] *Foley* v. *Hill* (1848) 2 H.L.C. 28; *Space Investments Ltd.* v. *Canadian Imperial Bank of
Commerce Trust Co. (Bahamas) Ltd.* [1986] 1 W.L.R. 1072; [1986] 3 All E.R. 75 (as to trust
funds deposited with bank). Lord Goddard C.J. made the same point for Larceny Act
purposes in *Davenport* (1954) 38 Cr.App.R. 37 at 41.
[33] *Attorney-General's Reference (No. 1 of 1983)* [1985] Q.B. 182 at pp. 187–188. See also *Kohn*
(1979) 69 Cr.App.R. 395; *Golechha* (1989) 90 Cr.App.R. 241 at 246.
[34] See below, § 2–138, as to theft of such property generally; § 2–140, as to theft of bank credits.
[35] *Torkington* v. *Magee* [1902] 2 K.B. 427, *per* Channell J. at 430; adopted in *Kohn* (1979) 69
Cr.App.R. 395.
[36] But not the mere appearance of a debt, created by a fraudulent entry in an account:
Thompson (1984) 79 Cr.App.R. 191.
[37] See, *e.g.*, below, § 2–141.
[38] *Colonial Bank* v. *Whinney* (1885) 30 Ch.D. 261, *per* Fry L.J. at 285; Crossley Vaines,
Personal Property (5th ed.), pp. 11–13.
[39] Patents Act 1977, s.30(1).
[40] (1987) 86 Cr.App.R. 174.

department. The quotas conferred an expectation of a licence to export textiles to the amount of the quotas but no enforceable right to such a licence. There was a flourishing market in such quotas. The quotas (although not things in action) were held to be "intangible property" and therefore capable of being stolen by a dishonest director of the company who sold them at an undervalue for his own benefit.

Nothing, in truth, turns for theft purposes on whether a species of intangible property is a "thing in action." There is no doubt that, for example, intangibles such as shares and copyrights are property; there is no need to classify them further.

The tempting possibility of convicting a dishonest person of theft of **2–13** intangible property can lead to too energetic an attempt to identify available property. The potential difficulties of analysis and, it is submitted, the dangers, are illustrated by *Baruday*.[41] D, an insurance broker, acted as the agent of P, a large employer, in relation to workers' compensation policies with I, insurers. Premiums were paid in advance on the basis of estimates of P's wages bill; on subsequent adjustment P might be entitled to some return of premiums from I. D had a monthly running account with I on which he was constantly in debit. I credited to this account the amount of certain "return premiums."[42] D failed to pass on these credits to P by payment or by credit in account. The Supreme Court of Victoria upheld D's convictions of theft of things in action. The Crown had contended that the things in question were the debts due from I to P; but any such debts were discharged by the accounting with P's agent, D. Still, the court held that I's "creation of the credit [in favour of D] involved the creation of a 'thing in action' " which was "property belonging to [P]," and that D's "retention" of that property was an appropriation of it. This, with respect, makes the notion of a "thing in action" work altogether too hard. On I's discharge of its indebtedness the only relevant thing in action seems to have been P's claim against D himself. The credit allowed by I in its accounting with D was not itself "property" of any kind; it was not, and it did not create, any right of action against I (which was, in any case, D's creditor, not his debtor). There was no "property" for D to "retain." D became P's debtor. But the Theft Act does not make a thief of a debtor who dishonestly decides not to discharge his indebtedness and therefore conceals it.

Cheques and other instruments

If D dishonestly draws a cheque on P's cheque form in his own favour, or **2–14** draws such a cheque in E's favour and delivers it to E, he thereby steals the cheque form (whether or not he also steals P's right against his bank). It is

---

[41] [1984] V.R. 685. (Victoria's Crimes Act 1958 contains provisions in relevant respects identical to those of the Theft Act 1968.)
[42] The headnote refers to "cheques" received by D from I; but all indications in the judgment are of credits in account rather than cheques. If cheques had been received, theft convictions might have been based on the equivalent of s.5(3) of the English Act (see § 2–30, below); no reference to things in action need have been made.

immaterial whether the cheque is met, or whether it is drawn within the limits of P's credit or overdraft facility.[43] Some courts have regarded the cheque not simply as a piece of paper but as itself a thing in action, on the ground that a cheque is an instrument embodying a right in the person entitled to it to receive payment of the amount for which it is drawn.[44] But this analysis, with respect, will not do. The property stolen[45] must be property belonging to P and the thing in action created in the payee's favour by the transaction of drawing and delivering a cheque is not a thing that has ever belonged to the drawer. It is both simpler and more accurate to say that D has stolen P's cheque form—that is, a piece of paper.[46] Such a charge, of course, hardly expresses the gravamen of D's conduct, which is better conveyed by a charge of stealing P's bank credit, if such a charge can readily be proved.[47]

Excluded or doubtful things

2–15   Nothing that is not "property" can be stolen. There are some categories of things that are not, or are possibly not, "property."

Electricity

   The fact that section 13 of the Act creates a separate offence of abstracting electricity suggests that electricity is not intended to be property for the purpose of theft. This has been confirmed by the Divisional Court in *Low* v. *Blease*.[48]

The human body and its parts[49]

2–16   *Dead bodies.* There could be no larceny of a corpse at common law; for, it was consistently asserted, there could be no property in a dead body. Whatever the credentials of this principle,[50] it no doubt survives to limit the modern law of theft, at least to the extent that there can be no theft of a buried corpse. Nor, it is thought, does the theft sanction protect the possession of anyone having the right to possess the body for a limited purpose— such as the executor who has the right to possession of it until burial,[51] or a

---

[43] *Kohn* (1979) 69 Cr.App.R. 395 at 410. There may be theft of the cheque although in part it represents payment of a debt owed by P to E: see *Sobel* [1986] Crim.L.R. 261. See also *Shadrokh-Cigari* [1988] Crim.L.R. 465, below, § 2–27 (banker's drafts).
[44] *Ibid.* at 409–410; *Duru* (1973) 58 Cr.App.R. 151 at 160.
[45] Or, as in *Duru*, above, obtained by deception.
[46] Compare *Davis (Gary)* (1988) 88 Cr.App.R. 347 at 350–351 (see § 2–39, below).
[47] There is no difficulty about D's intention of permanently depriving P of the form: see below, § 2–106. In *Kohn*, above, there were convictions of stealing both cheque and bank credit in respect of the same transaction; but in *Wille* (1988) 86 Cr.App.R. 296, counts in respect of cheques were, surely more properly, withdrawn from the jury as superfluous.
[48] [1975] Crim.L.R. 513.
[49] P. Matthews [1983] C.L.P. 193; A. T. H. Smith [1976] Crim.L.R. 622.
[50] See P. Matthews, *op. cit.* p. 197.
[51] *Williams* v. *Williams* (1882) 20 Ch.D. 659.

licensed anatomist who is authorised to have possession of it for a "statutory period" for teaching or research purposes.[52] "Property" within the Act is probably limited to that which is capable of being owned or of indefinite lawful possession. If this is right, the law is unsatisfactory; the cadaver store of a university anatomy department should be within the protection of the Act.

A body may perhaps become capable of ownership by "the lawful exercise **2–17** of work or skill" which gives it "some attributes differentiating it from a mere corpse awaiting burial." Such an operation, it has been suggested, would give "a right to permanent possession" and render the body "the subject of property."[53] This principle cannot apply to a dissected corpse, which, after dissection, can be retained "for the purpose only of its decent disposal."[54] But it would apply to a mummified corpse preserved as a museum piece and (*a fortiori*) to a part of a body, such as a skeleton, lawfully preserved after dissection. Sections 5 and 6 of the Anatomy Act 1984 provide that, under licence granted in the interests of education and research, and in accordance with the deceased's permission, a person may be authorised to possess parts of bodies after dissection is concluded. No time limit is imposed upon such possession. There seems here to be a source of "property."

Parts of bodies removed after death for therapeutic purposes under section 1 of the Human Tissue Act 1961 ought certainly to be recognised as property, and so as capable of being stolen, before transplantation occurs.

Parts and products of living bodies. It seems that specimens of urine and **2–18** blood provided to the police can be stolen.[55] Blood and sperm banks must surely be protected by the law of theft. Nor need the status of "property" be denied to parts of living donors removed for transplantation or of ova removed for *in vitro* fertilisation. The case of an ovum fertilised *in vitro* is, to say the least, more doubtful.

Trade secrets and other confidential information

It is probably a good guess that few of the people responsible for the Act **2–19** contemplated trade secrets (secret industrial processes, for example) as "property" within the meaning of section 4(1) or as capable of being stolen. During the debates on the Bill, however, Lord Wilberforce took a wide view of the word "property" as including "things like business secrets."[56] He did

---

[52] Anatomy Act 1984, ss.2–4.
[53] *Doodeward* v. *Spence* (1908) 6 C.L.R. 406, *per* Griffith C.J. at 414. (The case was an action of detinue relating to the long-preserved corpse of a still-born two-headed child. Barton J., while agreeing with the Chief Justice's judgment holding that the action would lie, did not regard this curiosity as a "corpse" within the meaning of the general rule.)
[54] Anatomy Act 1984, s.5.
[55] *Welsh* [1974] R.T.R. 478; *Rothery* [1976] R.T.R. 550 (pleas of guilty).
[56] H.L. Deb., Vol. 259, col. 1309.

not pursue in detail the analysis required to demonstrate that the law of theft has become an effective weapon against modern forms of industrial espionage. Probably it has not. One can in popular parlance describe a person who "bugs" a private conversation or photocopies a confidential document as "stealing" a secret. But to achieve that result in law would involve reading the Act in a very robust way for the purpose of producing a dramatic new offence not hinted at by the Committee. The Act is not in fact the appropriate instrument to deal with this specialised kind of mischief.[57] The short way of disposing of an argument to the contrary is to deny that trade secrets are "property" within the Act. They should be treated in the same way as the confidential information contained in the proof copy of an examination paper; such information has been held to be incapable of being stolen because it is not "property."[58] But even if a secret were property, it would be peculiarly difficult to steal, for a reason that will be stated later in this chapter.[59]

"Property" means a particular asset

2–20 The word "property" in the definition of theft refers to particular assets. For that alone can be stolen which can be the subject of "possession or control" or of a "proprietary right or interest" (section 5(1)) and which can be "appropriated" with the intention of "depriving" another of it. So a dishonest act cannot be theft simply because (as its doer knows) it must in the ordinary course of events lead to the diminution of another's net wealth; nor does it become theft when that result occurs.

These observations are stimulated by *Navvabi*,[60] in which theft convictions were sought on a novel basis. D issued cheques which his bank account would be unable to meet. But they were backed by a banker's card, so that his bank was bound to honour them. The Court of Appeal quashed D's convictions of theft. There was held to be no appropriation of "that part of the bank's funds to which the sum specified in the cheque corresponded." The decision was expressed as turning on the meaning of "appropriation."[61] But the reason for denying theft in this kind of case is more fundamental. When the guaranteed cheque is delivered to the payee, there *is* no "part" of the bank's "funds" corresponding to the sum specified. The bank's obligation to pay does not attach to particular property. When the cheque is collected by the payee's bank (the common procedure), no "funds" are "transferred by the [paying] bank to the [payee]."[62] Rather, the transaction features in a general accounting between the banks. No particular asset of the paying bank is diminished. The element of "property" is not satisfied;

[57] Compare the Supreme Court of Canada in *Stewart* v. *R.* (1988) 50 D.L.R. (4th) 1 at 12–13, reversing *Stewart* (1983) 149 D.L.R. (3rd) 583; R. G. Hammond (1984) 100 L.Q.R. 252. In *Stewart* v. *R.*, at 12, Lamer J. pointed out the difficulty of defining a category of "confidential information."
[58] *Oxford* v. *Moss* (1978) 68 Cr.App.R. 183.
[59] Below, § 2–139. If a secret is written on a piece of paper and the paper is taken, a charge of theft naturally presents no difficulty.
[60] (1986) 83 Cr.App.R. 271.
[61] *Ibid.* at 276.
[62] *Pace* the language *ibid.*

there is no need to discuss appropriation. Only if the payee obtains cash for an open cheque is particular property of the paying bank affected. *Navvabi* was not such a case; but it is submitted, and the decision suggests, that the drawer of the guaranteed cheque does not appropriate the cash later paid to the payee.

3. "BELONGING TO ANOTHER"

Generally

In order that property may be stolen it must "belong to another" in the sense in which that phrase is defined in section 5.[63] **2–21**

When D picks P's pocket and extracts money, or when he removes valuables from P's house, it is obvious that the *actus reus* of a theft has occurred; but even in such simple cases the property does not necessarily "belong" to P in the loosest sense of the word "belong." P may be carrying Q's money for him or have Q's valuables on loan or for safe keeping. Yet clearly D steals from P, and whether P owns the property or not it is necessary to regard the property, for the purpose of the law of theft, as belonging to P as well as to Q. Indeed the law of property and the remedies which protect property rights tend to be concerned less with absolute ownership than with grades and classes of possessory or proprietary interests (using "proprietary," as section 5(1) does, to include equitable interests, such as those which arise under a trust); and it is such interests, including as the most common case the interest of one in possession of property, that are protected by the law of theft.

Moreover, even in the many cases in which ownership can in practice be talked about and an owner accurately identified, experience under the old law showed that to exclude from the ambit of theft all cases in which D himself was already the owner of the property or became the owner by the transaction alleged to involve a dishonest appropriation—to say that an owner could not steal, or that one could not both become owner and steal as a result of the same transaction—was unsatisfactory in a number of ways.[64]

The phrase "belonging to another" must therefore be given a meaning much wider than that which it bears in common speech. Section 5 provides accordingly.

Possession or control; proprietary right or interest

A very wide range of cases is covered by the provision in section 5(1) that property "shall be regarded as belonging to any person having possession or **2–22**

[63] In *Edwards* v. *Ddin* (1976) 63 Cr.App.R. 218 at 221, s.5 was said to be "not definitive of" the expression "belonging to another." This statement was unexplained and is believed to be incorrect.
[64] It led among other things to multiplicity of offences (special provisions being made for some appropriations by owners); to artificial reasoning and impure doctrine (some owners being speciously treated as non-owners in order to secure convictions of larceny); and to the acquittal of a number of persons whom a law of theft should arguably catch.

control of it, or having in it any proprietary right or interest (not being an equitable interest arising from an agreement to transfer or grant an interest)."

(i) *Possession or control*

The word "possession" in English law is a veritable chameleon, changing its meaning with every change in the context in which it occurs. If it had been used alone in section 5(1) there might have been much room for argument as to its meaning in this context; whereas the addition of the words "or control" ensures that some cases doubtfully of possession are in fact to be treated as equivalent to cases of possession. For instance, if D seizes goods from the hands of P, a customer handling them in a shop, there is clearly a theft from P, who has control if not possession, and there is no need to discover whether P has yet acquired a proprietary right by purchase.

2–23   *Things on P's land.* It is submitted that P can always be treated as having "control" of property lying on land that he occupies, even if he does not know of it. In *Woodman*,[65] a company had sold all the scrap metal on the site of its disused factory but retained control of the site. The company did not know that the purchasers had left some of the metal on the site. One who entered the site and removed the metal was properly convicted on an indictment describing the metal as belonging to the company. The language of the judgment was perhaps unduly cautious; a person in control of a site was described as "prima facie" having control of articles on it in "ordinary and straightforward cases."[66]

    The point is not of significance except in the case of property abandoned by its former owner. If property on P's land has not been abandoned it can be described (by amendment if necessary) as belonging to its named owner,[67] if known, or to "a person unknown." Abandoned property, on the other hand, may belong to P or to no one. The leading case on the relative claims of D and P to property found by D on P's land holds that D's claim prevails unless P had, expressly or impliedly, manifested an intention to exercise control over such property on the land.[68] An exception was asserted where D is a trespasser; and the exception was said to be reflected in a case of larceny where D scavenged for lost golf balls and was convicted of stealing from the golf club.[69] Such a scavenger no doubt steals under the present law. But the club's "control" of the balls within the meaning of section 5(1) can hardly depend on the fact of trespass. So the better view appears to be that P, as occupier, has "control" (which he is taken to intend to exercise at least

---

[65] [1974] Q.B. 754.
[66] *Ibid.* at 758.
[67] If to the Crown as owner of treasure trove, the fact that the property is treasure trove must be proved beyond reasonable doubt in the criminal proceedings: *Hancock* (1989) 90 Cr.App.R. 422.
[68] *Parker* v. *British Airways Board* [1982] Q.B. 1004.
[69] *Hibbert* v. *McKiernan* [1948] 2 K.B. 142.

against a trespasser) of anything on his land. But if he has manifested no "intention to exercise control" over particular property, or a particular class of property, the taking of such property by D (not being a trespasser) is not an appropriation because not adverse to any interest of P; and on that ground it would not be theft.[70]

Theft by owner. One result of the protection of possession is that an owner **2–24** can steal his own property. D may, for instance, have pledged his goods with P; or he may have entrusted goods to P for repair so that P has acquired an artificer's lien entitling him to retain possession until the repair bill is paid. If in either of these cases, in order to defeat P's possessory rights, D dishonestly takes the goods from P's possession, he may be convicted of theft. The Court of Appeal has in fact gone further than this in *Turner (No. 2)*,[71] where P, having repaired D's car, left it in the road near his (P's) garage. D came and took the car away. The possible existence of a lien was disregarded. D was nevertheless held rightly convicted of theft if he acted dishonestly, for P had "possession or control" (presumably as a bailee at will). The decision goes very far and its correctness is not clear. Once P's possible lien is ignored, D did nothing in relation to the car that he was not perfectly entitled to do. Attention should perhaps have been concentrated, therefore, on the question whether D "appropriated" the car[72] rather than on the question whether it "belonged to" P.

(ii) *Proprietary right or interest*

Something of the scope of theft is indicated by the inclusion among the **2–25** possible victims of the offence of "any person . . . having . . . any proprietary right or interest" in the property appropriated. The phrase clearly includes the owner of an estate in land or of any interest therein; a beneficiary under an express trust; the owner of a thing in action (the creditor in respect of a debt, for instance); a partner in respect of partnership property; and so on.[73] If D's act of appropriation is done with the intention of defeating P's right or interest in the property, it will properly be described as an appropriation of property "belonging to" P—even though other people may have other, and larger, rights in the same property. D himself may have a proprietary right or interest and still be guilty of theft: a part-owner or a partner, for example, may dishonestly appropriate property, as by selling it or by absconding with it, so as to defeat his co-owner or his partners[74]; and a dishonest sale by a trustee of trust property for his own purposes will be a theft of property belonging to the beneficiaries.

[70] For the case where P does have an interest in the property of which D claims to have been unaware, see below, § 2–100.
[71] (1971) 55 Cr.App.R. 336.
[72] As to which, see below, § 2–55.
[73] But the interest must be a proprietary one. A copyright owner has been held not to have a proprietary interest in material infringing the copyright, notwithstanding the Copyright Act 1956, s.18; *Storrow and Poole* [1983] Crim.L.R. 332 (Judge Lowry Q.C.); see now the Copyright, Designs and Patents Act 1988, ss.99, 100, 114.
[74] *Bonner* (1970) 54 Cr.App.R. 257.

2–26 *Beneficial interests under trusts.* Two express provisions make it perfectly clear that, in general, beneficial interests in property held on trust are "proprietary interests" within the meaning of section 5(1). First, section 5(2) provides that the persons to whom property subject to a trust is to be regarded as belonging include "any person having a right to enforce the trust." The purpose of this subsection is to ensure that a misappropriation of property held on trust for a charitable object shall not fail to be theft merely because no particular person has a beneficial interest in the property. Charitable trusts are enforced under the Charities Act 1960, s.28, by (among others) the Attorney-General. The terms of subsection (2) are in fact wide enough to cover all trusts: but most are already covered by subsection (1).

Secondly, subsection (1) itself troubles to exclude from those to whom property is to be regarded as belonging a person who has in it "an equitable interest arising only from an agreement to transfer or grant an interest." Since land cannot be stolen save in cases not material to this point, the exclusion will mainly affect dealings in shares and similar property. D contracts to transfer shares to P and receives money from P; he then transfers them to Q; he does not steal the shares, for P has only an equitable interest arising from the agreement to transfer.[75]

The provision just referred to excludes one, but only one, variety of trust imposed by operation of law. The apparent implication is that beneficiaries under trusts of all descriptions (unless expressly excluded) are persons to whom property belongs within the meaning of section 5(1).

2–27 *Possible constructive trusts.* Divisions of the Court of Appeal have, nevertheless, differed in their readiness to recognise the versatile institution of the constructive trust as a source of "proprietary interests" protected by the law of theft. In *Shadrokh-Cigari*,[76] on the one hand, the court applied to banker's drafts the recently-stated principle that one who transfers money to another under a mistake of fact retains an interest in that money under a constructive trust.[77] About a quarter of a million U.S. dollars had been transferred in error to the account of a boy, R, with P bank. R's guardian, D, prevailed upon R to authorise the bank to issue banker's drafts drawn in favour of D for the bulk of this sum. D then applied the drafts to his own purposes. He thus stole the drafts[78]; P bank had retained an equitable interest in them, having issued them on the mistaken assumption that the funds in the account could be properly dealt with as authorised by R.[79]

Such a response to a development in the law of trusts offers the prospect of a relatively active role for the criminal courts in the control of dishonest behaviour. Consider, for example, the application to the law of theft of a

---

[75] There is difficulty also, on the same ground, in finding a theft from P in a third party's dishonest dealings with shares that P has contracted to buy from O: see *per* Lord Keith of Kinkel in *Tarling* v. *Government of the Republic of Singapore* (1978) 70 Cr.App.R. 77 at 137. But see J. C. Smith [1979] Crim.L.R. at 225: there may be "property belonging to" P (an enforceable right against O: *cf.* above, § 2–12) other than an equitable interest in the shares.
[76] [1988] Crim.L.R. 465.
[77] *Chase Manhattan Bank N.A.* v. *Israel-British Bank (London) Ltd.* [1981] Ch. 105.
[78] That is, the pieces of paper: see above, § 2–14.
[79] An alternative basis of D's conviction was section 5(4): see below, § 2–38.

more general principle that has been accepted in at least one English civil case: "the receiving of money which consistently with conscience cannot be retained is, in equity, sufficient to raise a trust in favour of the party from whom or in whose account it was received."[80] If the circumstances in which D receives money make it inconsistent with conscience for him to retain it, a conscientious jury ought to be able to find that he acts dishonestly according to the standards of ordinary decent people[81] when, aware of the circumstances, he prefers to apply the money to his own purposes rather than restore it.

The court's response was very different, on the other hand, in *Attorney-* **2–28** *General's Reference (No. 1 of 1985).*[82] D was the manager of a tied public house. He was obliged, by the terms of his contract of employment with P (the brewers), to obtain from P all liquor to be sold in the public house and to pay all the takings of the house into P's bank account. D bought beer from other sources, sold it in the public house and kept the proceeds for himself. D was clearly liable to account to P for at least the profit he had made; but he could be guilty of theft only if he became a constructive trustee for P of the proceeds or the profit element in them. The immediate point of interest in the judgment is the court's opinion that a trust of the kind suggested would not in any case fall within section 5(1) so as to create a "proprietary interest" within that subsection. Even if D was a constructive trustee, his keeping all the proceeds of his improper sales would be "so far from the understanding of ordinary people as to what constitutes stealing" that it "should not amount to stealing."[83] It might not, indeed, be stealing because D might believe that he was entitled, as against P, to keep those proceeds.[84] But it is submitted that the interpretation of "proprietary interest" in section 5(1) as not including an interest under one variety of trust amounts to a rewriting of the Act which the court ought not to undertake. The court wants the Act to produce acceptable results. That motive justifies a call for parliamentary, rather than an act of judicial, legislation.

Secret profits. The Court of Appeal did not in fact consider that D became **2–29** a constructive trustee on the facts of *Attorney-General's Reference (No. 1 of 1985).*[85] Its reasons were (a) that the making of a secret profit by the use of a "fiduciary position" does not give rise to a trust; and (b) that in any case no separate profit element was identifiable as property to which a trust could attach. Proposition (a) is extremely surprising in its width, and especially in its application to a case in which the profit derives from the use of another's

---

[80] Story, *Commentaries on Equity Jurisprudence* (2nd ed., 1839), para. 1255; applied in *Neste Oy* v. *Lloyds Bank plc* [1983] 2 Lloyd's Rep. 658 (cited by Goff and Jones, *The Law of Restitution* (3rd ed.), p. 77).
[81] See below, § 2–129.
[82] [1986] Q.B. 491. The decision was accepted without criticism by the House of Lords in *Cooke* [1986] A.C. 909 (see especially *per* Lord Mackay at 934).
[83] [1986] Q.B. 491 at 507.
[84] See § 2–120, below.
[85] Note also the failure to find a trust in *Lewis* v. *Lethbridge* [1987] Crim.L.R. 59 (below, § 2–31).

property, facilities and time.[86] And proposition (b) seems to confuse the existence of a trust (surely attaching, if it exists, to the proceeds of sale as a whole) and the extent of P's interest under it.

Property received subject to an obligation

2–30   D may receive property in circumstances which render him bound, as between himself and another person, to deal with it in a particular way. A dishonest application of such property ought to be theft. D may, of course, be a bailee of goods. Or he may become owner of the property (as he almost always will when money is paid to him) but receive it as a trustee. In such cases the bailor or any beneficiary under the trust is a person with a "proprietary right or interest" in the property, and the property therefore "belongs to" him by virtue of section 5(1). Exhaustive examination of civil law principles might in fact reveal that a person has a "proprietary interest" in property whenever the use of that property is dictated by an obligation owed to him.[87] If so, no further provision would strictly be necessary to render such property capable of being stolen by the person holding it. The Act nevertheless makes such provision by section 5(3):

> "Where a person receives property from or on account of another, and is under an obligation to the other to retain and deal with that property or its proceeds in a particular way, the property or its proceeds shall be regarded (as against him) as belonging to the other."

It is this provision, rather than section 5(1), that is in practice commonly referred to where an obligation such as it mentions exists. The Committee itself gave as its illustration of section 5(3) the case of the treasurer of a holiday fund; his misapplication of the fund or part of it is said to be theft from "the persons to whom he owes the duty to retain and deal with the property as agreed."[88] The duty is surely that of a trustee.

To what kind of obligation does section 5(3) refer?

2–31   It must be stressed that it is not enough that D, when he receives money or other property, falls under some contractual obligation, or that a relationship of debtor and creditor is thereby created. D must be under an obligation which prescribes the application of *that* property or its proceeds.

---

[86] As to the difficult general question, whether and in what circumstances the making of secret profits, or of profits from the use of another's property, gives rise to a constructive trust and to potential theft liability, see A. T. H. Smith [1977] Crim.L.R. 395; P. St. J. Smart (1986) 136 New L.J. 913; Williams, *Textbook*, pp. 753–756; Arlidge and Parry, *Fraud*, paras. 4.03–4.05; *Tarling* v. *Government of the Republic of Singapore* (1978) 70 Cr.App.R. 77, *per* Lord Wilberforce at 111 (on which see J. C. Smith [1979] Crim.L.R. at 225–226). The Court of Appeal, rather surprisingly, could find "no distinction in principle" ([1986] Q.B. 491 at 505) between a case like that under consideration and the case of a bribe received by a servant or agent. The court relied on *Lister & Co.* v. *Stubbs* (1890) 45 Ch.D. 1 for the proposition that a bribe is not held on trust for the employer or principal. This tends to confirm the orthodoxy of the proposition; but for the modern status of the authority, see the literature cited above.
[87] See Williams, *Textbook* (1st ed.), pp. 713–723. But see § 2–28, above.
[88] *Eighth Report*, p. 127 (notes on draft Bill).

In *Hall*,[89] for example, D was a travel agent who had received deposits and payments from clients in respect of air trips to be arranged by him. He paid the sums into his firm's general trading account but arranged no trips and could not repay any of the money. His conviction of theft was quashed. There had not been proved such a special arrangement between him and any of the clients as would give rise to an obligation within section 5(3).

In *Lewis* v. *Lethbridge*[90] D, on behalf of a particular charity, obtained sponsorship for a runner in the London Marathon. He did not pay the charity the amount collected from the sponsors. There being nothing in the facts (including the rules of the charity) to justify a finding that D was obliged to maintain a fund consisting of the money collected or its proceeds,[91] D was merely a debtor; his conviction of theft had to be quashed.

If D is under a duty to P to collect money and to account to P for the money   **2–32**
less D's commission or other reward, the circumstances may be such as to oblige D to maintain a distinct fund representing his receipts. If so, D, dishonestly pocketing more than he is entitled to, will be guilty of theft of the excess.[92] Or the receipt of money by D as P's agent may create in D the obligation of a debtor only, so that a failure to account to P for what he receives cannot be theft.[93]

Similarly, if D sells P's goods on his behalf, he may owe P a fiduciary duty in relation to the proceeds of sale; or, once again, his resulting obligation to P may merely be that of debtor to creditor. In the former case only can there be any question of theft if he dissipates all his assets without paying P what he should.

The circumstances of the individual transaction, including most obviously the terms of any agreement between D and P, may plainly reveal the nature of D's obligation. If they do not, the obligation may be difficult to classify. "The cases . . . do not show that there is any general principle to determine whether the agent holds property or money in trust"[94]—which is what, in truth, the prosecution must show. One reason for this is that in the civil cases referred to the nature of the principal's remedy against the agent (whether personal, as against a debtor, or proprietary) "is not normally of consequence."[95]

The following generalisation, however, may be helpful. It seems that   **2–33**
section 5(3) will be satisfied where, having received money or other property from P, or on account of P, D has an obligation to P to preserve a fund or

---

[89] [1973] Q.B. 126.
[90] [1987] Crim.L.R. 59.
[91] *Sed quaere*: why does payment to one collecting for a charity not give rise to such an obligation—in fact, to a trust? Compare *Jones* v. *Attorney-General, The Times*, November 10, 1976 (cited by M. Stallworthy and P. Luxton (1988) 51 M.L.R. 114 at 120).
[92] Compare *Lord* (1905) 60 J.P. 467 (debt collector); *Messer* [1913] 2 K.B. 421 (taxi-driver).
[93] *e.g. Stanley Robertson* [1977] Crim.L.R. 629 (Judge Rubin Q.C.).
[94] *Bowstead on Agency* (13th ed.), p. 128.
[95] *Ibid.* p. 129. See now 15th ed., pp. 160–162, 192 (not repeating the statement quoted in the text).

corpus consisting of or representing[96] that money or other property, which fund or corpus is to be maintained except so far as it may or must be dealt with "in a particular way"—that is, in the manner required by the transaction with P, or by transfer to P or at his direction, or as justified by an accounting with P.

A legal obligation is required; the function of the judge

2–34   The "obligation" referred to in section 5(2) is, of course, a legal obligation.[97] The decision whether on the facts of a particular case such an obligation arose is one that must be made by the judge, applying the general law. The judge, however, does not know the facts of a contested case until the jury return their verdict. His direction to the jury must therefore be hypothetical in form. He will tell them that if they find certain facts, then the case is one in which a legal obligation arose to which section 5(3) applies. This was laid down by the Court of Appeal in *Mainwaring and Madders*.[98] The approach seems inevitable; a jury can hardly know without firm guidance whether given facts raise an obligation within the meaning of the subsection. In earlier cases, however, the court had stated that the matter was, or was at least sometimes, one for the jury's decision.[99] These remarkable statements should now be regarded as aberrations which the court has renounced.[1]

It is submitted that the guidance given in *Mainwaring* is unhappy in one respect. It contemplates that the judge will refer to section 5(3) in his direction. But if on given facts the application of the subsection is a matter of law, why should the jury be troubled with the mention of the subsection at all? Its application means that the property appropriated by D (whether what he originally received or its proceeds) is to be regarded, for purposes of his theft liability, as "belonging to" P. Section 5(3), that is to say, provides, for a special kind of situation, an artificial interpretation of one of the terms in the basic definition of theft. It is surely enough to tell the jury that a finding of certain facts will mean that the property D dealt with (dishonestly appropriated, as the prosecution allege) was property belonging to P. The judge ought to shield the jury from legal complexities whenever he possibly can.[2]

---

[96] As its "proceeds"—which must be generously interpreted to include the case where D is at liberty to set aside money which is the equivalent in value of the money received; this commonplace situation cannot be intended to be excluded. Liberal interpretation may also be needed where D mixes in a cash box or a bank account sums received from various persons for a common purpose and is entitled to do so. If proprietary interests in mixed funds are ignored (that is, if, as usual, only s.5(3) is alluded to, and not s.5(1) and (2)), it may be necessary to regard the whole of the fund as the "proceeds" of each contribution. For otherwise (ignoring proprietary interests), who is the victim if D misappropriates a part only of the fund?

[97] *D.P.P.* v. *Huskinson* [1988] Crim.L.R. 620 (no basis in relevant legislation for legal obligation to apply housing benefit to payment of rent).

[98] (1981) 74 Cr.App.R. 99.

[99] *Hayes* (1976) 64 Cr.App.R. 82; *Hall* [1973] Q.B. 126 at 132 (as to transactions not wholly in writing).

[1] The renunciation was achieved by a remarkable (more politely, perhaps, an indulgent) interpretation of the earlier cases; see 74 Cr.App.R. at 106.

[2] See *A Criminal Code for England and Wales* (Law Com. No. 177), Vol. 1, para. 3.43; *Shadrokh-Cigari* [1988] Crim.L.R. 465.

Further examples of the application of section 5(3)

The following are some further cases within section 5(3):   **2–35**
(a) P employs D to carry out repairs to P's house and advances £50 to D, not simply on account of the total cost of the job but specifically for the purpose of buying necessary materials. D may have an obligation to use the money in that way.[3] If so, a dishonest use of the £50, or any part of it, will be theft.[4]

(b) P1, P2 and D share a flat. The gas account is in the name of P1. P1 and P2 give D cheques so that, adding her own share, D may pay the gas bill. D, having no bank account, cashes the cheques with her employer. She spends the proceeds on Christmas presents and pays only a third of the gas bill. The proceeds of the cheques are to be regarded as belonging to P1 and P2. D may be convicted of theft.[5]

(c) P sends D a cheque which goes astray in the post. D applies to P for a substitute payment, which is made on the understanding that if the cheque turns up it will be returned to P. D steals the cheque, if, when it arrives, he dishonestly cashes it or pays it into his bank for collection.[6]

(d) D dishonestly sells P's goods without authority and misappropriates the proceeds. The proceeds constitute a fund over which P has a proprietary claim and which therefore "belongs to" him by virtue of section 5(1). D also receives the proceeds "on account of" P with a clear obligation to retain them for him.[7]

Secret profits and bribes—not received by D "on account of" P

D, a servant or agent, who takes a bribe or who makes a secret profit by an   **2–36**
abuse of his position or by an unauthorised use of the property of P, his employer or principal, will be bound to account to P for the amount of the bribe or the profit. But the existence of this duty to account for what is received does not mean that it is received "on account of" P within the meaning of section 5(3). In *Powell* v. *McRae*[8] C gave £2 to D, a turnstile operator at Wembley Stadium, as an inducement to let C into the stadium to see an all-ticket match. The bribe was held not to belong to D's employers for theft purposes. And in *Attorney-General's Reference* (*No. 1 of* 1985),[9] where D, the manager of a tied public house, made prohibited sales of his own beer on the premises, he did not receive the proceeds of sale "on account of" his employers. In the light of these decisions it is doubtful

---

[3] Or at least to preserve, and use in that way, an equivalent fund.
[4] Compare *Hughes* [1956] Crim.L.R. 835; but, by contrast, *Jones* (1948) 33 Cr.App.R. 11 and *Bryce* (1955) 40 Cr.App.R. 62 show the need for great caution.
[5] *Davidge* v. *Bunnett* [1984] Crim.L.R. 297.
[6] *Wakeman* v. *Farrar* [1974] Crim.L.R. 136.
[7] So also with money obtained by the fraudulent cashing of a cheque intended for P or drawn without authority on P's account: compare *Gale* (1876) 2 Q.B.D. 141; *Davenport* (1954) 38 Cr.App.R. 37.
[8] [1977] Crim.L.R. 571.
[9] [1986] Q.B. 491 (above, § 2–28); following *Cullum* (1873) L.R. 2 C.C.R. 28. See also *Eighth Report*, para. 57(iii); *Kenatley* [1980] Crim.L.R. 505 (Judge Mendl).

whether the reference to property received "on account of another" in section 5(3) adds anything to the scope of the phrase "belonging to another" as the latter is elaborated in section 5(1).

Doubts about two cases

2–37   In *Brewster*[10] contracts between insurance companies and D, a broker, provided that premiums collected by D would vest in the companies. In practice, though, the companies permitted brokers to use money they collected for their own business purposes and to stand indebted to the companies for the amounts in question. The Court of Appeal held that this did not affect the nature of D's obligation, he having acted dishonestly. The case appears to be a rather special one of an obligation to maintain a specific fund reviving in the event of D's becoming dishonest. Until he becomes dishonest there is surely no such obligation (for the purposes of a civil action). So is not D convicted effectively as a dishonest debtor? (It is not suggested that a similar objection would apply if D could be proved dishonest from the outset.)

Finally, the curious and much discussed case of *Meech*[11] should be mentioned. D agreed with P to cash a cheque that P had obtained from Q. He paid the cheque into his bank, intending to draw cash to pay P. He then learnt that P had obtained the cheque by fraud. He drew the appropriate sum from his account and, with help from E and F, contrived the appearance of a robbery so as to have an excuse for not being able to pay the money to P. The Court of Appeal held that D was guilty, at the time of the bogus robbery, of stealing the proceeds of property that he had received from P under an obligation within section 5(3). The argument that P could never have enforced the so-called "obligation"[12] was met by holding that the question was to be looked at from D's point of view. He had "assumed an 'obligation' " which he thought was a legally binding one, and was therefore "under an obligation" within the meaning of section 5(3).[13] This is hardly acceptable. One cannot be guilty of an offence[14] just because he mistakenly believes an essential element of the offence to exist. D argued further that, as at the time of the appropriation he knew the truth, he was not then under an "obligation." This argument was rejected. The court had in any case already stated that the crucial time is "the time of the creation or the acceptance of the obligation."[15] But it has been correctly objected that, reading section 1(1) and 5(3) together, the obligation must plainly exist at the time of the appropriation.[16]

Property "got" by another's mistake[17]

2–38   Section 5(4) provides:

[10] (1979) 69 Cr.App.R. 375.
[11] [1974] Q.B. 549.
[12] Questioned by Glanville Williams [1977] Crim.L.R. at 337.
[13] [1974] Q.B. 549 at 555.
[14] As opposed to an attempt to commit it.
[15] [1974] Q.B. 549 at 555.
[16] J. C. Smith [1973] Crim.L.R. 777, and *Theft*, para. 76; Williams, *loc. cit.*, n. 12, above.
[17] Glanville Williams [1977] C.L.J. 62, for detailed discussion. For further discussion, see Parry, *Offences against Property*, paras. 1.34–1.36.

"Where a person gets property by another's mistake, and is under an obligation to make restoration (in whole or in part) of the property or its proceeds or of the value thereof, then to the extent of that obligation the property or proceeds shall be regarded (as against him) as belonging to the person entitled to restoration, and an intention not to make restoration shall be regarded accordingly as an intention to deprive that person of the property or proceeds."

The subsection was intended to cover a case like *Moynes* v. *Coopper*.[18] A wages clerk, not having been told that D had had an advance on his wages, gave D a wage packet containing his full wages without deduction. D was held not guilty of larceny when, opening the packet, he realised the error but kept the excess. Section 5(4) was passed primarily to reverse this result. D has "got" his full wages by his employer's mistake; he has an obligation to make restitution ("restoration") of the value of part of the payment; to that extent the money received is now to be regarded as belonging to the employer; dishonestly spending or banking the money, having formed the intention not to repay the excess, will be theft. D's mere retention of the money, indeed, with the dishonest intention not to repay his employer, may be enough to constitute theft. D has "come by [the money] ... without stealing it" and he seems now to be guilty of an "assumption of a right to it by keeping ... it as owner," which section 3(1) declares to be an appropriation. The point is no doubt academic in the case of money, with which D will probably "deal ... as owner" (*e.g.* by banking it) as soon as he decides to "keep" it; moreover, the exact time of the theft is unlikely to be material.[19]

The subsection applied

Section 5(4) was applied on interesting facts in the case of *Davis*.[20] **2–39** Because of an administrative error, D had received from the local authority housing benefit cheques to which he was not entitled. At one time he was entitled to benefit but received a double payment in the form of two

[18] [1956] 1 Q.B. 439.
[19] But as to payment into a bank account, see below, § 2–40.
[20] (1988) 88 Cr.App.R. 347. The close analysis to which Mustill L.J. submitted s.5(4) in this case deserves careful study. But one passage (at 351–352) is questionable. The Lord Justice takes the draftsman to have contemplated three possible "conditions" in which property, "got" by mistake, may be "by the time the defendant comes to commit his dishonest appropriation": it may still exist; it may have been exchanged for money or goods ("proceeds") which are still traceable; it may have "ceased to exist ... or ... gone out of reach of recovery." He supposes the subsection to refer to an obligation to restore "property," "proceeds" or "value" in these situations respectively. This, with respect, seems to be a misreading. The analysis cannot work for the case of "value," where, as the passage seems to mean, the property has been disposed of and there are no traceable proceeds. There would be nothing to steal. It is submitted that the obligation to restore "the property or its proceeds or ... the value ... thereof" must be an obligation existing, because of the mistake, *when the property is first "got."* In some cases D will be obliged to restore the property itself (or its proceeds if he should happen to convert them). In other cases, typically of mistaken payment or overpayment, his only obligation from the outset is to repay a sum equivalent to (the value of) what has been wrongly received. In all these cases, what was originally got by mistake, or any property into which it is converted, can be stolen by an appropriation dishonestly made with knowledge of the mistake.

cheques. When he ceased to be entitled to benefit he continued to receive (single) benefit cheques. His appeal concerned, in part, alleged thefts of "money" which he had obtained by cashing some of the cheques with a shopkeeper.

The later (single) cheques—the pieces of paper, rather than the things in action they created in D's favour—were plainly property that he got by mistake; so charges of theft of these cheques would have presented no difficulty. But D was charged with stealing "money," not cheques.[21] The Court of Appeal was clear that the cash into which D converted the cheques was their "proceeds" within the meaning of section 5(4). D was "under an obligation to make restoration" of these proceeds, which he could therefore be convicted of stealing.

In the double payment case, the two cheques (whenever each may have arrived in relation to the other) were to be treated as "got" by mistake, just as though the whole excessive payment had been made by a single cheque. D was under an obligation to restore their proceeds "in part." The proceeds were a single pool of cash which "to the extent of that obligation" was to be regarded as belonging to the local authority. D could be convicted of stealing cash to that amount without its being necessary to attribute the amount stolen to either cheque.[22]

Mistaken payments and bank accounts

2–40   Situations involving bank accounts require separate analysis. Two cases may be imagined. (i) D receives a payment in error (or an overpayment) by the crediting of his bank account through the banks' direct debit system. (ii) D has in error been paid cash (or too much cash) or been given a cheque (or a cheque for too large a sum), and he banks the cash or cheque before he discovers the error. To the extent of the overpayment the thing in action represented by the bank account[23] will, in case (i), be property "got" by mistake[24]; in case (ii) it will be "the proceeds" of such property. In either case the thing in action will be regarded (as against D) as property belonging to the person making the mistake—assuming, of course, that the mistake gives rise to an obligation to restore the "value" of the overpayment. This, at any rate, describes the situation where the account is in credit on completion of the banking transaction[25] (or, perhaps, later as a result of further transactions); for only if it is in credit does D have property, in the form of a thing in action (a creditor's right against the bank), to which section 5(4) can apply. Similarly, for theft to be possible, there must still be credit available to be stolen when, D having learned of the error and formed "an intention not to

---

[21] See above, § 2–14.

[22] Such an approach "may not be effective, if the proceeds . . . take more than one form, and if the prosecution is forced to identify which form is the one to have been stolen" (88 Cr.App.R. at 353).

[23] For bank credits as "property," see below, § 2–141.

[24] *Attorney-General's Reference (No.* 1 of 1983) [1985] Q.B. 182.

[25] Note that, although the amount of a cheque delivered to a bank for collection may be credited to the account at once, the credit is not usually effective, so as to give the customer any right against the bank, before the cheque is cleared.

make restoration," an alleged appropriation occurs. Whether D appropriates by simply forming that intention is uncertain.[26] The idea that theft may be committed by a mere decision not to pay a debt is one to be avoided if possible. A way of avoiding it may be to argue that the phrase in section 3(1), "keeping as owner," refers only to property that D ought to "restore" to P; that there is no question of restoring the bank credit itself, but only the "value" of the amount paid in error—an equivalent sum; and that an appropriation must be sought in some use of the account—perhaps a use that reduces the credit in the account (or any outstanding overdraft facility) to below the amount that ought to be paid to P.

A legal obligation is required; the overpaid punter

The "obligation" referred to in section 5(4) is a legal obligation.[27] Where **2–41** D decides to disregard a merely moral obligation to restore property got by P's mistake, the court has to resort to some other ground for holding that the property belonged to P if D is to be convicted. This was done in *Gilks*.[27] D, a punter, had won £10.62 by bets in P's betting shop. But P's manager paid D £117.25, wrongly thinking that D had backed one more winning horse than he had. D took the money knowing that he had been overpaid. His conviction of theft was upheld. He had no legal obligation to restore the overpayment of £106.63, as it had been made under a wagering contract.[28] So section 5(4) could not apply. But the Court of Appeal affirmed the trial judge's ruling that "the property in the £106.63 never passed to [D]."[29] On this basis D appropriated property belonging at all times to P without recourse to section 5(4). This is not satisfactory. The court eschewed elaborate argument to defend its proposition that the mistake made by P (or rather his manager[30]) was of a kind to prevent property in the money from passing; they referred only to a long-doubted Larceny Act case that was readily distinguishable.[31] The better view, it is submitted, is that D did obtain ownership of all the money paid.[32] That is surely what would have been held if a quasi-contractual right to recover the overpayment had existed and section 5(4) could have applied.

Some difficulties[33]

We have seen that the Court of Appeal in *Shadrokh-Cigari*[34] has applied **2–42**

[26] The point was left open in the *Attorney-General's Reference*, above, n. 24.
[27] *Gilks* (1972) 56 Cr.App.R. 734.
[28] *Morgan* v. *Ashcroft* [1938] 1 K.B. 49 (though the case and its generally-assumed consequence are both questioned by Williams, *loc. cit.*, n. 17, above, at 72–73).
[29] 56 Cr.App.R. at 737.
[30] It would be unsatisfactory if the case turned upon a want of authority in the manager to make an overpayment. The manager should be equated with P.
[31] *Middleton* (1873) L.R. 2 C.C.R. 38: 10s. due to D from post office; clerk, consulting document referring to E, handed D £8 odd; held, property did not pass (*sed quaere*).
[32] See also Williams, *loc. cit.* n. 17, above; Smith, *Theft*, para. 88; Parry, *Offences against Property*, para. 1.54; Heaton [1973] Crim.L.R. 736 at 739. In favour of the decision, see Williams and Weinberg, *Property Offences* (2nd ed.), p. 90.
[33] For a critical discussion, see Stuart (1967) 30 M.L.R. 609, especially at 622–623.
[34] [1988] Crim.L.R. 465.

in the context of theft a principle recognising P, the payer of money under a mistake, as retaining a beneficial interest in the money. If the money is converted into other property or paid into a larger fund, P's interest in the money will become an interest in that property or fund, subject only to the limits of a beneficiary's tracing remedy. Nor is there any reason why these principles should apply only to money (and to instruments giving rise to money claims, as in *Shadrokh-Cigari* itself), and not to property generally. It seems to follow that in almost any case within section 5(4) the property or proceeds referred to in that subsection will "belong to" the transferor of the property anyway by virtue of section 5(1). It might be thought an argument against the reasoning of *Shadrokh-Cigari* that it renders subsection (4) substantially redundant. But that reasoning is not the first to suggest that the reference in section 5(1) to "any proprietary . . . interest" added more to the scope of theft than was generally realised when the Act was drafted and passed.[35] In any event there is no question of subsection (4)'s ceasing to be invoked, its references to mistake and to an obligation to make restoration being so helpfully specific compared to the language of section 5(1).

2–43   A case of property "got" by mistake, under whichever provision it is analysed, is capable of presenting difficult problems in the law of trusts, restitution or quasi-contract. Whether a person is obliged "to make restoration" of property may, for instance, turn on difficult distinctions between mistakes of fact and mistakes of law. It is not clear that such distinctions should be relevant to criminal liability. Again, difficult problems attending claims in equity in respect of money paid under a mistake may infect the law of theft either via section 5(1) (if indeed "proprietary interest" includes any proprietary claim available against a constructive trustee) or via section 5(4) (for the subsection is not expressed to be limited to common law obligations). Problems in the law of tracing[36] cannot necessarily be kept out of the criminal courts.

2–44   There has been controversy as to the potential of section 5(4) as the basis of theft liability in deception cases. There is no difficulty where D induces P to make a payment in circumstances giving P a quasi-contractual right to recover money paid under a mistake of fact. If, for example, D falsely states facts which (if true) would have the effect that money was due under an existing contract, and P pays that money, the money will no doubt be "got" by mistake and a duty to make restoration of it will exist; section 5(4) will apply. So it will where a payment by P to D does not transfer ownership in the money concerned because it is made under a contract *void* for fundamental mistake induced by D's fraud; but in such a case the money "belongs to" P without resort to section 5(4).[37]

The controversial case is that where P pays money or delivers property to D under a contract which is itself *voidable* because of D's fraud. Whether section 5(4) can contribute to D's liability for theft is perhaps academic in

---

[35] Compare the comments on section 5(3), above, § 2–30.
[36] See Goff and Jones, *The Law of Restitution* (3rd ed.), Chap. 2.
[37] As in *Williams* [1980] Crim.L.R. 589 (but see commentator's note as to the court's remarkable view that the contract was void).

view of authority treating D's receipt of the property as theft without reference to the subsection.[38] It will suffice to note the argument that, although D no doubt "gets" the money or other property "by another's mistake," yet he has no obligation to make restoration unless and until the contract is avoided by a disaffirming act on P's part, and that on that ground section 5(4) does not apply to such a case.[39]

Corporations sole

Property belonging to a corporation sole is to be regarded as belonging to   **2–45**
the corporation notwithstanding a vacancy in the corporation (s.5(5)).

The property appropriated must belong to another

The fact that D dishonestly tries to get his hands on property does not   **2–46**
necessarily mean that he is guilty of an offence. There can, for instance, as one singularly optimistic prosecution has shown, be no theft or attempted theft of the property of a testatrix by inducing her to revoke one will (effectively) and make another, or by steps taken under the latter will on her death. The executors named by the revoked will were suggested as the intended victims of theft; but they never had a proprietary interest in the property.[40]

It must still belong to P at the time of the appropriation

A point more likely to cause difficulty is that property that has undoubt-   **2–47**
edly belonged to P must still belong to him (in some sense within s.5) at the time of the alleged theft. The point may require the application of principles of the law of contract, sale and agency.[41] It may be illustrated by reference to simple retail transactions.[42] Ownership ("the property") in goods passes to a buyer at the time the parties intend it to pass.[43] In the case of a supermarket or cash-and-carry store the courts attribute to the parties the intention that ownership shall pass only on payment. This applies no less to goods (such as meat and vegetables) wrapped and priced by an assistant within the store, but to be paid for at the check-out, than to goods with which the customer serves himself from the shelves. Accordingly, where a customer leaves the store without paying for goods so wrapped and priced, he removes goods that still belong to the store.[44] Conversely, once the property in the goods has passed under a valid contract and the buyer has taken delivery, there is no question of theft by any further act of the buyer. A motorist who fills his

---

[38] See below, §§ 2–49, 2–91.
[39] Smith, *Theft*, para. 89; Parry, *Offences against Property*, para. 1.58. *Kaur* v. *Chief Constable for Hampshire* (1981) 72 Cr.App.R. 359, is consistent with this view.
[40] *Tillings and Tillings* [1985] Crim.L.R. 393 (Mann J.).
[41] This uncomfortable fact is discussed above, § 1–24.
[42] On theft from shops, see A. T. H. Smith [1981] Crim.L.R. 586.
[43] Sale of Goods Act 1979, s.17.
[44] *Davies* v. *Leighton* (1978) 68 Cr.App.R. 4.

tank with petrol at a garage and then decides not to pay does not steal the petrol when he drives away[45]; property in the petrol has passed to him under the sale transaction and the garage retains neither possession nor a proprietary interest.[46] A plainer case is that of the diner who decides at the end of his meal not to pay for it; he cannot steal the food in his stomach, as the Divisional Court had once solemnly to hold.[47]

2-48 There may be a question as to the validity of a contract of sale and therefore as to whether ownership passed under it. In *Kaur* v. *Chief Constable for Hampshire*[48] a supermarket cashier mistook the price of goods and undercharged D (who knew the correct price). But the mistake was not regarded as rendering the contract a nullity. On that basis ownership passed to D on payment. The justices had found her to be dishonest; but it was held that she did not appropriate property belonging to the store when she took the goods from the premises.[49]Another stage in the history of goods sold may be a revesting of the ownership in the seller on the buyer's rejection of them. Then the seller does not by re-selling the goods, even dishonestly, appropriate property that any longer belongs to the first buyer. A jury dealing with a case of this kind plainly needs clear guidance on the legal effect of the buyer's acts.[50]

Appropriation by act causing property to cease to belong to P

2-49 If D takes delivery of goods from P under a voidable contract of sale induced by D's fraud and the property in the goods passes to D on delivery, D may thereby appropriate the goods; and if he does so, the appropriation is of property "belonging to" P, although it ceases to belong to him by the very act of appropriation.[51] D also by deception obtains property belonging to P within section 15(1). It is enough to satisfy either section 1(1) or section 15(1) that the property belonged to P "up to the time" of the appropriation or obtaining, as the case may be.[52] The point was first decided by the House of Lords in *Lawrence* v. *Metropolitan Police Commissioner*,[53] where D, a taxi-driver, was charged with theft of an excessive sum taken in advance by way of fare from his passenger's proffered wallet. Even if property in the money so taken passed to D, the act of taking it could nevertheless be theft.

---

[45] He can be convicted of making off without payment: Theft Act 1978, s.3 (see Chap. 12).
[46] *Edwards* v. *Ddin* (1976) 63 Cr.App.R. 218; Sale of Goods Act 1979, s.18, r. 5(1). To the like effect, *Stewart, The Times*, December 14, 1982.
[47] *Corcoran* v. *Whent* [1977] Crim.L.R. 52.
[48] (1981) 72 Cr.App.R. 359 (pair of shoes, each with a different price, taken from a rack intended for shoes at the higher price; cashier read and charged the lower price). For discussion of this case and its implications, see J. C. Smith [1981] Crim.L.R. 259; and a controversy between Professors Williams and Smith at [1981] Crim.L.R. 666 and 677; [1982] Crim.L.R. 64.
[49] For the possibility of theft at an earlier stage, see below, § 2-76, n. 14.
[50] *Walker* [1984] Crim.L.R. 112; (1983) 80 L.S.Gaz. 3238; above, § 1-25.
[51] *Dobson* v. *General Accident Fire and Life Assurance Corporation plc* [1990] Q.B. 274.
[52] *Ibid. per* Bingham L.J. at 290.
[53] [1972] A.C. 626.

4. "APPROPRIATES"

General and theoretical

In *Morris*,[54] in a controversial leading case on this element in theft, Lord   **2–50**
Roskill feared that "a trail through a forest of decisions ... will tend to
confuse rather than to enlighten." It is widely agreed that the case itself
greatly added to the existing confusion; and later decisions (whether notic-
ing that the authorities are irreconcilable or newly interpreting them in
gallant attempts at reconciliation) have made the forest yet more im-
penetrable. It is seemly to apologise for what now follows but permissible to
claim that neither its length nor its difficulty is entirely the author's fault.

The main uncertainty affects this question in particular: In what circumstances, if any, can theft be committed by doing something which P permits,
consents to, or authorises? Since P's consent or authority may be induced by
deception, that question involves a famous "overlap" problem: When, if
ever, may the same act constitute both theft and the offence of obtaining
property by deception contrary to section 15(1)? The problem of the overlap
between sections 1 and 15 will be addressed at the end of this part of the
chapter.

Appropriation of intangible property (including bank credits)

The definition of theft assumes that one may "appropriate" a thing in   **2–51**
action or other intangible property. The theft of intangibles, and especially
of bank credits, has proved to be an important and complex subject. It is best
dealt with in a separate part of the chapter, where the main consideration of
the appropriation of such property will therefore be found.[55]

The notion of "appropriation"; and the statutory "definition"

A person appropriates property, in the non-technical sense of the word,   **2–52**
when he takes it to (or for) himself or makes it his own. This may have been
the conception of the Committee. The Committee gave two kinds of explanation. First, they said that the expression "dishonestly appropriates" meant
the same as "fraudulently converts to his own use or benefit, or the use or
benefit of any other person" in the Larceny Act 1916, section 20(1)(iv) (the
word "appropriates" being preferred as a shorter expression and as less of a
"lawyers' word").[56] They referred to appropriation as "the familiar concept
of conversion."[57] The *word* "conversion," however, though long used both

---

[54] *Morris*; *Anderton* v. *Burnside* [1984] A.C. 320 at 333. (These consolidated appeals will be
  referred to hereafter as *Morris*.)
[55] Below, §§ 2–138 to 2–150.
[56] *Eighth Report*, para. 35.
[57] *Ibid.* para. 34.

in criminal law[58] and in the law of tort, does not represent a single *concept* of settled meaning. As to the criminal context, the offences of larceny as a bailee and fraudulent conversion were concerned with misappropriations by those lawfully in possession of property with the consent of the owner or entrusted with ownership or possession of property for particular purposes. But these offences covered only part of the ground now covered by theft; and the meaning[59] of conversion in relation to them was never fully worked out. On the other hand, appropriation in criminal law appears not to be a replica of its tort counterpart. In *Rogers* v. *Arnott*,[60] decided under the Larceny Act, the act of a bailee in attempting to sell a borrowed tape recorder was held to be a criminal conversion although it would not in itself have founded liability in tort; and in *Bonner*[61] the Court of Appeal had no doubt that a partner who absconds with partnership property must be held to "appropriate" that property even if in the circumstances he would not be liable to his co-partner in tort.[62] It is submitted that this refusal to equate conversion in crime and in tort is right and inevitable.

2–53   Secondly, the Committee, although expressing the hope and belief "that the concept of 'dishonest appropriation' will easily be understood even without the aid of further definition,"[63] nevertheless offered such aid in a provision enacted as section 3(1):

> "Any assumption by a person of the rights of an owner amounts to an appropriation, and this includes, where he has come by the property (innocently or not) without stealing it, any later assumption of a right to it by keeping or dealing with it as owner."

The subsection does not read like a definition and was described by the Committee as a "partial definition."[64] But it is not clear what it was intended to leave unsaid. The House of Lords, as will be seen below, has held that an assumption of any of the rights of an owner may be an appropriation[65]; but the decision to this effect was expressed as an interpretation of section 3(1) itself and not by way of giving content to an assertion that the subsection was "not exhaustive."[66]

Consistency between civil and criminal law

2–54   Notwithstanding the broad terms of section 3(1), Professor Glanville

[58] Larceny Act 1916, ss.1(1) proviso, 20(1)(i) and (iv), 21 ("converts or appropriates").
[59] See Smith and Hogan, *Criminal Law* (1st ed.), pp. 358–360; *Russell on Crime* (12th ed.), pp. 966–969.
[60] [1960] 2 Q.B. 244; compare now, *Pitham and Hehl* (1976) 65 Cr.App.R. 45 (below, § 2–70).
[61] (1970) 54 Cr.App.R. 257.
[62] Co-ownership is a defence to an action founded on conversion except as specified in the Torts (Interference with Goods) Act 1977, s.10(1). S.10(1)(*a*) restated the only pre-existing exceptions as understood at the time of *Bonner*. Para. (*b*) added a further significant exception. The same Act made other modifications of the scope of conversion as a tort. It can hardly be the case that it thereby also casually modified the scope of theft.
[63] *Eighth Report*, para. 34.
[64] *Ibid.* See also *per* Lord Lane C.J. in *Morris* [1983] Q.B. 587 at 596.
[65] *Morris* [1984] A.C. 320; below, § 2–65.
[66] *Ibid.* at 331. The rest of the relevant passage, it has been observed, "treats it as if it were exhaustive": *Philippou* (1989) 89 Cr.App.R. 290 at 299.

Williams has powerfully urged that theft cannot be committed (a) "by a person who has or obtains an indefeasible title to the property when he commits the act charged as an appropriation" or (b) "by an act that is not wrongful (under the general law) against the person to whom the property belongs."[67] His arguments in favour of consistency between, on the one hand, what is permitted by the civil law and achieved by its transactions and, on the other hand, what may be done and enjoyed without attracting the sanctions of the criminal law are recommended for careful study. It is thought that his general thesis ought to be found persuasive in principle.

Professor Williams refers to decisions, encountered earlier in this chapter, **2–55** which are, or are possibly, against his thesis. The conviction in *Turner (No. 2)*[68] seems to have rested solely on a finding that D did not, as he claimed, believe that he was entitled to repossess his own car from outside the garage where it had been repaired. But if he was so entitled, the repossession should probably have been held to be no appropriation.[69] When *Gilks*[70] took up from the betting shop counter the excessive sum he was paid as winnings, he took what, according to civil law, could not be recovered from him. It may seem odd, then, that his taking of it was theft. The appearance of oddity is made possible by the even odder view that although Gilks could keep the money he did not become owner of it. The judgment in *Turner (No. 2)* is very obscure and *Gilks* has been demonstrated to be unsatisfactory in a number of ways.[71] So these cases (in neither of which was the word "appropriates" discussed) do not contribute convincingly to a denial of Williams's suggested principles. And it is submitted that *Bonner*,[72] where it was held that a partner's dishonest taking for himself of partnership property would be theft although not conversion, presents no problem; for the act seems plainly "wrongful" as a breach of the statutory obligation to hold and apply partnership property exclusively for the purposes of the partnership.[73]

Duration of appropriation; successive appropriations

Duration. Is theft over as soon as anything has been done that qualifies as **2–56** an appropriation? Or does the activity of stealing last beyond the first

---

[67] [1977] Crim.L.R. 127 and 205; *ibid.* at 327; *Textbook*, Chap. 35. Compare Arlidge and Parry, *Fraud*, paras. 1.10–1.15; Parry, *Offences against Property*, paras. 1.154–1.159, arguing that conduct that is lawful as a matter of civil law is not theft because not "dishonest"; *McHugh and Tringham* (1988) 88 Cr.App.R. 385 at 393: "The word 'appropriation' connotes a misappropriation."

[68] Above, § 2–24. See on this case Smith, *Theft*, para. 63, and [1972B] C.L.J. 197 at 215–217; Williams, *Textbook*, pp. 749–751; Parry, *Offences against Property*, paras. 1.156–1.157.

[69] See *Meredith* [1973] Crim.L.R. 253 (Judge da Cunha), where D, without reference to the police, removed his car from a police pound; a charge of theft was said to be improper (possibly overlooking *Turner*, but to satisfactory effect).

[70] Above, § 2–41.

[71] See Williams [1977] Crim.L.R. at 205–207, and [1977] C.L.J. 62 at 72–73; Smith, *Theft*, para. 88, and [1972] Crim.L.R. 586–590.

[72] Above, § 2–52.

[73] Partnership Act 1890, s.20(1); and see now the Torts (Interference with Goods) Act 1977, s.10(1)(*b*).

moment of appropriation? The answer given in the context of robbery, where it may be necessary to decide whether force was used "at the time of" stealing, is that an appropriation is not a merely momentary event.[74] This answer gives the law of theft a useful flexibility for a number of purposes.[75] The offence of handling stolen goods, on the other hand, cannot be committed "in the course of the stealing"; in this context, therefore, there is a temptation to limit the duration of the theft so as to extend the scope of the handling offence. The cases on robbery and handling are in consequence not easy to reconcile.[76]

2–57   *Successive appropriations.* It is clear that a person may appropriate the same property more than once. He may, for instance, find goods and keep them, thinking the owner untraceable (this is an appropriation but not dishonest, according to s.2(1)), and, when he learns who the owner is, steal by a subsequent appropriation (as s.3(1) confirms). But this does not mean that one can steal the same property more than once as a principal offender.[77] Where D bought stolen goods in France and conveyed them to England, his only theft was committed outside the jurisdiction and he could not be convicted here.[78] His original appropriation of the goods, however long exactly it lasted, was certainly over before he arrived within the jurisdiction.

2–58   There may also, it has been said, be different appropriations of the same goods by different persons during the same incident—as in a burglary in which several people take part.[79] But this seems to introduce an unnecessary complication. If D1 enters a building and takes possession of goods pursuant to an agreement with D2, D2 is all along guilty as a secondary party. But if D2 has nothing to do with the burglary until he himself later (by coincidence) enters, finds D1 already at work and joins in the removal of the same goods, he then becomes a party to a continuing appropriation. There seems to be no need to refer to separate theft offences.

Theft by taking possession

2–59   Most cases, happily, present no legal difficulty. D simply appropriates property by taking possession of it. But one kind of property requires a particular kind of acquisitive conduct: in order to steal something forming part of the land, one not in possession of the land must sever it or cause it to be severed.[80]

---

[74] *Hale* (1978) 68 Cr.App.R. 415.
[75] *e.g.* powers of arrest: see Tunkel [1978] Crim.L.R. 331. For the suggestion that an appropriation of a bank credit may last from the relevant act of the thief to the debiting of the account, see below, § 2–148. As to the pleading notion of one "continuous" theft by successive appropriations of different things, see below, § 2–153.
[76] See below, §§ 3–08, 14–45.
[77] Williams [1978] Crim.L.R. 69.
[78] *Figures* [1976] Crim.L.R. 744 (Mr. Recorder Waud).
[79] *Gregory* (1981) 77 Cr.App.R. 41.
[80] s.4(2)(*b*).

A person may take possession of something when he finds it lying lost and   **2–60**
takes it up. Whether this is an appropriation depends upon his state of mind.
If he intends to seek the owner, there is no appropriation: he has not
assumed possession for himself. If he decides to keep the thing for himself,
there is an appropriation (which may or may not be dishonest).[81] The same
possibilities exist where goods belonging to P are brought to D by a third
party and D assumes possession. It does not matter whether the third party is
guilty or innocent of any offence in relation to the goods. D's receipt of them
is an appropriation unless he intends to restore them to P. If he dishonestly
does not intend to do so, he commits theft—and if the goods are stolen and D
knows or believes this, he is also guilty of handling.[82]

Theft by one in possession

Section 3(1) is at pains to provide that where a person   **2–61**

"has come by . . . property (innocently or not) without stealing it, any later
assumption of a right to it by keeping or dealing with it as owner"

is an appropriation. This passage was hardly necessary; but it was valuable as
a message to pre-Theft Act practitioners, to whom it made clear that certain
gaps that existed under the old law had been filled. Among the persons
covered by the provision is he who finds property and takes possession of it,
but is not then guilty of theft either (i) because he intends to restore it to its
owner or (ii) because he does not believe that the owner can be found,[83] and
who subsequently decides (in case (i)) not to restore the property to its
owner or (in case (ii)) to hold on to the property although the owner turns
out to be known or traceable. Such a person is within the reach of the law of
theft, as is he who receives stolen goods intending to take them to the victim
or the police but who changes his mind. So too is one who takes property
when too drunk to steal and who when sober decides to deal with it as his
own; and the person who has "come by" property as a result of an error and,
discovering some time later the fact that he has it or that it was not intended
for him or is not what he was intended to have, decides nevertheless to keep
it.

Agents, bailees and custodians

The agent in possession of his principal's goods for sale who sells them   **2–62**
below the authorised price, intending to keep the proceeds[84]; the coal
merchant's employee who takes a sack of coal from the coal lorry for his own
use; the hirer of a camera who sells it as his own; the borrower of a library

---

[81] s.2(1)(c).
[82] s.22. See below, § 14–49.
[83] See s.2(1)(c).
[84] Compare cases of dishonest dealings with intangible property: *e.g. Kohn* (1979) 69
Cr.App.R. 395 (principal's bank credit); *Attorney-General of Hong Kong* v. *Nai-keung*
(1987) 86 Cr.App.R. 174 (transferable export quotas).

book who gives it as a birthday gift to his friend; the cashier at the supermarket check-out who deliberately rings up too low a price for goods on the
till and "sells" them to a customer for the reduced price[85]: each of these
people, having lawful possession or custody of the property of another,
appropriates it by assuming in it the rights of an owner—in the language of
the second part of section 3(1), having "come by . . . property . . . without
stealing it," he commits a "later assumption of a right to it by . . . dealing with
it as owner."

"Keeping . . . as owner"

2–63   One who has come by property without stealing it may later steal it by
dishonestly "keeping or dealing with it as owner." A "dealing" will involve a
positive act. A "keeping," on the other hand, may be constituted by a mental
act (a decision) and an omission to do what ought to be done with the
property. Suppose, for instance, that D finds goods. Thinking that the
owner is not traceable, he keeps them. This is not theft.[86] He then hears who
the owner is, but he decides not to give them up. His keeping them is then
theft. Although no doubt in practice such a theft is most likely to be revealed
when D deals with the property in some active way or expressly refuses to
give it up, it seems to be technically complete on the occurrence of the
dishonest non-restoration (assuming that D has an opportunity to restore).
But there can be no "keeping . . . as owner" during a period of indecision
about what to do with the property.[87] Apart from any other consideration,
while D remains undecided he does not have the intention of permanently
depriving P.

The exception for the bona fide purchaser

2–64   One person who is clearly within section 3(1) is nevertheless expressly
saved from liability for theft by section 3(2). This is the bona fide transferee
for value of property who discovers after the transfer that his transferor's
title was defective and nevertheless keeps or deals with the property. C
steals property from P and sells it to D, who neither knows nor suspects that
it is stolen. He later learns the truth. But he does not restore the property to
P. Indeed, he deals with it as his own. This is not theft.

An assumption of any of the rights of the owner

2–65   The controversial case of *Morris*[88] concerned the criminal liability of a

---

[85] In *Bhachu* (1976) 65 Cr.App.R. 261, however, the only appropriation identified by the Court
of Appeal was that of the shopper (to which the cashier was naturally held to be a party) in
taking the goods from the shop.
[86] s.2(1)(c).
[87] *Broom* v. *Crowther* (1984) 148 J.P.Rep. 592.
[88] [1984] A.C. 320.

person who takes goods from the shelf of a self-service store and substitutes for the price label on them a label showing a lower price, intending to buy the goods for that lower price at the till. Does he steal the goods? If so, when? The decision of the House of Lords was that he does steal the goods, the appropriation and therefore the theft being complete when he switches the price labels with that dishonest intention. Notwithstanding the opening words of section 3(1) itself, it was declared that the requirement of an appropriation was satisfied by "an assumption . . . of *any* of the rights of the owner. . . ."[89] It did not matter that the dishonest shopper had not yet assumed *all* the rights of an owner.

This view of appropriation was perhaps already implicit in a number of cases before *Morris*.[90] And it has since been expressly applied, on the authority of *Morris*, to determine the time at which a theft of credit in a bank account, by a dishonest dealing with the account, is complete: an appropriation, and therefore theft, occurs when a cheque drawn on the account is presented or an instruction to debit the account is transmitted to the bank. Presenting the cheque or sending the instruction is the exercise of one of the rights of the owner of the account.[91] This has great significance, in particular in relation to jurisdiction, in a case where an act is done in one country affecting an account at a bank in another country. The theft is committed where the act is done.[92] **2–66**

In a case like *Morris* the appropriation of the property will precede the deprivation of P which D intends. The store whose price label is changed will be "deprived" of the goods only when D buys them at the till for the price he has put on them. (There must then be a "deprivation" within the meaning of the Act; for the purchase will involve an offence of obtaining property by deception, which itself requires an intention of permanently depriving the victim.[93]) The necessary intention in theft was probably understood until recently to be an intention of depriving P of the property by the act of appropriation itself. Under *Morris* there may be an appropriation now with the intention of depriving P in the future. The former understanding may have been a legacy of larceny, which, except when committed by a bailee, required a taking of possession of movable property. The extended reading employed, though not explicitly referred to in *Morris*, is bold, but not impossible in the more flexible context of the modern offence. **2–67**

Inchoate transactions

Changing the price label upon goods is merely a step towards the intended **2–68**

[89] *Ibid.* at 331–332, claiming support in the language of the latter part of s.3(1), and in ss.2(1)(*a*) and 3(2). For doubts, see Smith, *Theft*, para. 36. Compare *Stein* v. *Henshall* [1976] V.R. 612.
[90] See cases mentioned in § 2–70, below; *Pilgram* v. *Rice-Smith* (1977) 65 Cr.App.R. 142 (theft at supermarket food-counter when the assistant, in league with the customer, wraps goods and understates their price on the wrapper); also *Easom* [1971] 2 Q.B. 315 (below, § 2–114: examining property to see whether it contains something worth stealing treated as an appropriation). The doctrine of *Morris* also supports the assertion that most cases of handling stolen goods are also cases of theft: see below, § 14–49.
[91] *Governor of Pentonville Prison, ex p. Osman* (1988) 90 Cr.App.R. 281.
[92] But perhaps also, where the account is in due course debited, at the place where the account is held: see below, § 2–148.
[93] s.15(1).

offence of obtaining the goods by deception. It will probably not suffice to constitute an attempt to commit that offence; for an attempt requires "an act more than merely preparatory" to the offence intended.[94] So the identification of a complete theft at the point when the label is changed operates to supplement the law of inchoate offences. The suspect shopper may, strictly, be apprehended at that point. But a conviction of theft on the strength of what he has so far done will in effect deprive him of the defence which the law of attempt is carefully designed to give him—namely, that he might still have changed his mind and abandoned his dishonest purpose. It is therefore suggested that (in justice, in addition to any practical consideration) he should be allowed to reach the till and be dealt with for the obtaining, or the attempt to obtain, by deception that he there commits.

Cases like *Morris* are by no means the only ones in which the courts have held theft to be complete at relatively early stages of the intended transactions. It is instructive to consider a range of situations in which theft has been allowed to encroach upon, and even to go beyond, the law of attempt.

Attempting to take property

2-69   There is, of course, no question of confining theft to cases where the criminal activity is in a real sense successful. A thief caught in possession of property a few seconds after seizing it has stolen and not merely attempted to steal. And there is no reason why the same should not be true of one who has gripped property so as to achieve effective control of it, but has not removed it. It seems that the courts will go as far as possible along this path. In *Corcoran* v. *Anderton*[95] a youth was held guilty of robbery (which involves theft) when he was party to an attack on a lady in which her handbag was wrested from her grasp—even though the bag fell to the ground and was never in his or his companion's control. The decisive circumstance may have been that the lady was made to lose control, if only momentarily. This, it is suggested, rendered the case a borderline one and possibly justified the court in finding a complete appropriation.[96] On the other hand, merely grasping property in an unsuccessful attempt to loosen it from P's control, or to part it from something to which it is attached, should perhaps be regarded as a mere attempt.[97]

Offering P's goods for sale

2-70   A theft of P's goods is held to be complete when D dishonestly offers to

---

[94] Criminal Attempts Act 1981, s.1(1).
[95] (1980) 71 Cr.App.R. 104.
[96] Too often one senses the prosecution being rescued from the consequences of a poor choice of charge. A more apt charge here was surely assault with intent to rob (s. 8(2)). For another example see *Monaghan* (below, § 2–71).
[97] But Eveleigh L.J., in a supporting judgment in *Corcoran* v. *Anderton*, regarded D's "*seeking to overcome [P's] efforts to retain [the bag]*" as an appropriation: (1980) 71 Cr.App.R. 104 at 108. (Italics supplied.) And a dictum in *Hale* (1978) 68 Cr.App.R. 415 at 418 assumes that the theft of a car occurs as soon as the thief opens the car door.

sell them to E, having no authority to do so.[98] It has been objected that the offer alone, not being a conversion of the goods, ought not to be theft.[99] It is submitted that this objection in itself ties theft too closely to the technicalities of conversion. Yet it does seem odd to describe as a complete theft an offer which E may in the event refuse; if E refuses, D will have achieved nothing at all. And it is thought that there can certainly be no theft where D does not intend to deliver the goods to E even if E accepts his offer and pays the price agreed. D's mere reference to the goods as a device to support his fraud on E can hardly be an appropriation; and in any case D has no intention of depriving P of the goods.[1]

Act preparatory to theft from a till

A striking case of a preparatory act treated as theft is *Monaghan*.[2] A **2-71** shop-assistant received £3.99 from a customer and put it in her till (as she was supposed to do). But she did not ring the sum up because she had a proved intention to remove an equivalent sum later. She was arrested before proceeding further and charged with theft of "the sum of £3.99." Her conviction was upheld on appeal. It is submitted that this goes too far. It cannot be known whether in the end the defendant would have removed any money. She had not yet got as far as attempting to do so within the meaning of a general law of attempt which provides ample opportunity for a late change of mind. Her conviction denies her that opportunity. Moreover, it is difficult to see what property she appropriated, since (it may be assumed) she mixed the sum she received with the employer's other money in the till. Her wrong was one of omission—namely, "omitting a material particular from an account," which is an offence of false accounting under section 17 of the Act.

Acts done with the consent or authority of the owner
The conflict between Lawrence and Morris

The following statement in the opinion of Lord Roskill in *Morris*[3] (effec- **2-72** tively giving the decision of the House of Lords) has occasioned great difficulty:

> "In the context of section 3(1), the concept of appropriation . . . involves not an act expressly or impliedly authorised by the owner but an act by way of adverse interference with or usurpation of [the owner's] rights."

The first part of this statement must be set alongside the decision of the

---

[98] *Pitham and Hehl* (1976) 65 Cr.App.R. 45; compare *Rogers* v. *Arnott* [1960] 2 Q.B. 244 (larceny as a bailee).
[99] Williams [1977] Crim.L.R. 127 at 131–132; for further argument, see *Textbook*, pp. 763–765.
[1] Even with the assistance of s.6(1); it is thought that D does not intend to "treat the thing as his own to *dispose* of." For fuller argument, see the 4th edition of the present work, §§ 2–56, 2–76; and for the contrary view of the hypothetical case, see Smith, *Theft* (5th ed.), paras. 25, 26.
[2] [1979] Crim.L.R. 673.
[3] [1984] A.C. 320 at 332.

House of Lords in *Lawrence* v. *Metropolitan Police Commissioner*.[4] In that case P was an Italian newly arrived in England. He hired D, a taxi-driver, to drive him from Victoria to Ladbroke Grove. The lawful fare for the journey was 10s. 6d. (53p). P gave D a £1 note, but D said that this was not enough and himself took £6 more from P's still open wallet. P offered no resistance to this act. D was charged with theft of about £6 and convicted. It was regarded as clear by the House of Lords, and in fact conceded on D's behalf, that there had been an appropriation of the £6. The argument relevant here was that P consented to that appropriation, which could not therefore be theft because the words "without the consent of the owner" should be implied in section 1(1).

The House of Lords responded by firmly declaring that to obtain a conviction of theft it need not be proved "that the taking was without the consent of the owner": the omission of words equivalent to the phrase "without the consent of the owner" in the repealed definition of larceny was deliberate.[5] And it is clear that the House's reason was not that the words were unnecessary because an absence of consent is inherent in the concept of appropriation itself; for it was also said that an appropriation may occur "even though the owner has permitted or consented to the property being taken."

2–73   The statements in *Lawrence* and *Morris* appear to be flatly inconsistent. It may be noticed that that in *Morris*, although relevant to answering the certified question in that case,[6] was not necessary for the decision that D was guilty of theft at least by the time he had switched the price labels, which is all that needed to be decided in order to uphold the conviction. The statement may therefore be regarded as *obiter*. At all events, the view has since been taken that "whatever *Morris* did decide it cannot be regarded as having overruled the very plain decision in [*Lawrence*'s case] that appropriation can occur even if the owner consents."[7] Nor were the propositions in *Lawrence* expressed to apply only to cases, such as *Lawrence* itself, in which the owner's consent is induced by deception.[8] The statement in *Morris* about "authorised" acts is open to general question.

Evidence in the Act; and a hint of a principle

2–74   Some evidence for the view that acts that are in some sense authorised

---

[4] [1972] A.C. 626.
[5] [1972] A.C. 626 at 630–631. Larceny required a taking and carrying away of goods "without the consent of the owner."
[6] Which asked at what stage, if any, an appropriation had occurred.
[7] *Per* Parker L.J. in *Dobson* v. *General Accident Fire and Life Assurance Corp. plc* [1990] Q.B. 274 at 285 (for this case, see below, § 2–90); and to the same effect, *Philippou* (1989) 89 Cr.App.R. 290 at 299–300. In *Dobson* Parker L.J. (at 286) was resigned, if necessary, to not applying *Morris* because of the difficulty of reconciling it with *Lawrence*. Bingham L.J. (at 288–289) had similar difficulty. He takes P in *Lawrence* to have "permitted . . . his money to be taken" and explains the recognition by the House of Lords in *Morris* ([1984] A.C. at 331) that there was an appropriation in *Lawrence* as based on the fact that P "had not in truth consented to the taxi driver taking anything in excess of the correct fare." This is a very desperate act of reconciliation. The judgments in *Dobson* and *Philippou* do much to undermine the authority of *Morris*.
[8] Deception cases are considered separately below, §§ 2–86 *et seq.*

may amount to theft is to be found in the Act itself. Section 2(1)(*b*) provides that if D believes that he would have P's consent to his appropriation if P knew of it and of its circumstances, the appropriation is not to be regarded as dishonest. And the same, it has been pointed out, must be true of an appropriation by one who believes that he actually has such consent.[9] The provision seems to contemplate that there can be consent to an appropriation. On the other hand, it must be the case that if one who merely believes he has consent does not commit theft, neither does he who actually does have consent. But in this proposition, as in section 2(1)(*b*), the consent referred to is "a true consent, honestly obtained,"[10] involving knowledge of the circumstances of the appropriation. It is submitted that, if consent is to exclude theft, P must know that D intends to deprive him permanently of the property and must consent to appropriation on this basis; and secondly, it must be more than apparent consent obtained by fraud or a mere submission induced by coercion.[11]

Consent and facilitation

A case where acquiescence in D's act should not prevent that act from being an appropriation is that where P learns that D proposes to steal his goods and instructs Q to "assist" D by facilitating his access to the goods in the guise of an accomplice. Suppose that D comes and takes the goods and is promptly arrested. Whether he appropriates them when he takes possession should not turn on the nature of the "assistance" given to him. If he is simply afforded easy access to the goods, it would seem that he steals them when he takes them[12]; his act is obviously in no sense authorised. If, on the other hand, Q actually hands D the goods on P's instructions, D's physical act is in a sense authorised; yet it should be no less theft. P may be said to consent to D's receipt of the goods; but D can hardly claim either a gift or a bailment. P consents to the bare receipt only; he is by no means consenting to being permanently deprived of the goods.[13]

2–75

Theft in self-service shops

The context of Lord Roskill's statement in *Morris* was, in effect, the

2–76

---

[9] *Lawrence* v. *Metropolitan Police Commissioner* [1972] A.C. 626 at 632.
[10] *Per* Kerr L.J. in *Attorney-General's Reference (No. 2 of 1982)* [1984] Q.B. 624 at 641; referring to *Lawrence* [1971] 1 Q.B. 373 at 377, *per* Megaw L.J.
[11] Where D compels P by duress to part with possession of property (*e.g.* by physical violence or the threat of it, by imprisonment, or by a threat to prosecute for some actual or pretended crime), D is plainly guilty of theft (and of robbery in a case of violence) if he intends to deprive P permanently. In some cases, however, the duress may induce a voidable contract under which ownership passes and not mere possession. Even if this should occur, a conviction of theft should be available; and for this purpose appeal can be made, if necessary, to the analogy of delivery under a contract of sale voidable for fraud: see below, § 2–90. For a case of theft by duress, see *Chapman* [1974] Crim.L.R. 488.
[12] Compare *per* Ackner L.J. in *Greater London Metropolitan Police Commissioner* v. *Streeter* (1980) 71 Cr.App.R. 113 at 119.
[13] See on this subject, Williams [1977] Crim.L.R. 327 at 330–335; I. D. Elliott (1977) 26 I.C.L.Q. 110 at 121 *et seq.* and 144 *et seq.*; J. C. Smith [1982] Crim.L.R. 64–66; *Theft*, para. 44. Whether or not the argument in the text is persuasive, D will be guilty at least of attempt to steal when he receives the goods from Q.

question whether the taking of goods from the shelf of a self-service shop could be an appropriation. In the Court of Appeal in *Morris* Lord Lane C.J. had asserted that it could[14]—even, apparently, that an honest shopper "appropriates" an article "when he takes [it] from the shelf determining to buy it." Lord Roskill rejected this view. He approved the decision in *Eddy* v. *Niman*,[15] in which D removed goods from a supermarket shelf and put them in the trolley provided by the store. His intention to steal the goods was proved. But he changed his mind and left without the goods. His acquittal by the magistrates was upheld by the Divisional Court because the only acts done were acts consented to by the store. In an earlier case Lord Roskill had approved of the conviction of theft in *McPherson*,[16] simply on the basis that in that case D had taken whisky from a supermarket display stand with the intention of leaving the store without paying[17]; but now he found an appropriation not simply in her taking of the whisky but in her doing so and then concealing it in her shopping bag.[18]

2–77   Is it true that the taking of goods from a supermarket shelf, intending to escape without paying for them, is an act "authorised" by the shop? Authority to remove the goods is surely given to honest shoppers only. It is submitted that the shoppers in both *McPherson* and *Eddy* v. *Niman* assumed the rights of an owner when they took possession of goods intending not to pay for them.[19] The concealment of the goods in the former case merely facilitates proof of the guilty intention; the repentance in the latter case is powerful mitigation but need not be regarded as preventing or undoing theft. The fact that in *Eddy* v. *Niman* the shopper did not appear to be doing anything untoward should have been irrelevant if his intention could be otherwise proved, as was the case.[20]

Express authorisation, not induced by deception

2–78   In *Fritschy*[21] P instructed D to collect a quantity of Krugerrands from bullion dealers in England and take them to Switzerland. When D collected

---

[14] [1983] Q.B. 587. Lord Lane (at 597) therefore thought that there should have been a conviction in *Kaur* v. *Chief Constable of Hampshire* (1981) 72 Cr.App.R. 359 (see above, § 2–48), on the basis of a dishonest appropriation when D took the shoes from the rack. Lord Roskill ([1984] A.C. at 334) was "disposed to agree that [the case] was wrongly decided," but did not say when, in his view, an appropriation occurred.
[15] (1981) 73 Cr.App.R. 237.
[16] [1973] Crim.L.R. 191.
[17] *Anderton* v. *Wish* (1980) 72 Cr.App.R. 23n, *per* Roskill L.J. at 25. This view was justified by the *McPherson* judgment: *per* Lord Lane C.J. in *Morris*, in the Court of Appeal, [1983] Q.B. 587 at 597; *per* Parker L.J. in *Dobson* v. *General Accident etc.* [1990] Q.B. 274 at 284.
[18] [1984] A.C. at 333.
[19] See also *Greenberg* [1972] Crim.L.R. 331 and *McHugh* [1977] Crim.L.R. 174 (petrol pump cases); and *per* Bingham L.J. in *Dobson* v. *General Accident etc.* [1990] Q.B. 274 at 287.
[20] Webster J. in that case (at 241) had required for an appropriation "some overt act . . . inconsistent with the owner's rights." But Lord Roskill himself in *Morris* ([1984] A.C. 320 at 334) thought "that the act need not necessarily be 'overt.' " To demand that it be overt is, indeed, to confuse evidence with substance.
[21] [1985] Crim.L.R. 745. To the like effect, *Grundy (Teddington) Ltd.* v. *Fulton* [1981] 2 Lloyd's Rep. 666.

the coins, he dishonestly intended to deal with them as his own. But everything he did within the jurisdiction was authorised by P. His conviction of theft was therefore quashed, the statement in *Morris* being applied. The case has subsequently been distinguished from the shopping cases and from *Lawrence* as being one of express authorisation, of "more than mere consent."[22] Conviction of theft where D has used no deception[23] and has acted only as instructed would certainly depend on a broad notion of appropriation, as including any taking of possession of property with the secret purpose of making it one's own. This conception could yet be adopted if the topic comes to be thoroughly reviewed.[24] For the time being *Fritschy* remains authoritative.[25]

"Adverse interference with or usurpation of" the owner's rights?

"[T]he concept of appropriation . . . involves . . . an act by way of adverse   **2–79**
interference with or usurpation of . . . rights."[26] This statement in *Morris*, already quoted above,[27] appears to be more than merely the positive equivalent of the negative statement, "an authorised act is not an appropriation." For it is used to explain why, for instance, a switching of price labels by "a shopper with some perverted sense of humour, intending only to create confusion," would not be an appropriation of the goods.[28] The dictum has been criticised as thoroughly obscure.[29] So, with respect, it is; and it is hardly needed to protect the mischievous label-switcher from theft liability, since he does not intend to deprive the owner of the labelled goods.

Yet it may be worth making the point that whether an act (such as moving, damaging or even destroying goods[30]) is an appropriation does depend on the state of mind with which it is done. Although an appropriation and an intention of depriving the victim are separate elements of theft, the existence of the former may clearly depend upon the existence of the latter. Theft seems to require an intention to acquire power, or to assert rights, over the property beyond the mere doing of the physical act itself. There is needed something akin to the intention to exercise dominion over goods that

---

[22] *Dobson* v. *General Accident etc.* [1990] Q.B. 274 at 286, *per* Parker L.J.

[23] A charge of obtaining property by deception was withdrawn from the jury in *Fritschy*. But there was certainly a deception in *Skipp* [1975] Crim.L.R. 114 (below, § 2–92), which Parker L.J. in *Dobson* v. *General Accident* sought to distinguish in the same way as *Fritschy*.

[24] Compare *McHugh and Tringham* (1988) 88 Cr.App.R. 385 at 394: "[E]ven an express authority, which is either obtained by the actor with a view to abuse, or is actually abused, can scarcely render innocuous what would otherwise be a misappropriation."

[25] *Meech* [1974] Q.B. 549 (above, § 2–37) is also often cited for the proposition that appropriation must be an unauthorised act. It was held that the money was not appropriated when it was withdrawn from the bank with a dishonest intent. The reason given was that performance of D's obligation (by payment to P) did not become impossible until the money was divided up at the scene of the fake robbery. No reference was made to authority or consent; and the reasoning in the judgment is weak throughout.

[26] *Morris* [1984] A.C. 320 at 332.

[27] § 2–72.

[28] [1984] A.C. 320 at 332.

[29] For an elaborate critique, see *per* Brooking J. (dissenting) in *Roffel* [1985] V.R. 511 at 527 *et seq*. Leigh (1985) 48 M.L.R. 167, at 169–170, reads "adverse interference . . . or usurpation" disjunctively; but the context suggests that they may be merely rhetorical alternatives.

[30] Many cases of unlawful damage under the Criminal Damage Act 1971 are also cases of theft, and some are charged as such: see J. N. Spencer (1978) 42 J.Cr.L. 125 at 126.

distinguishes a conversion of them from a mere trespass.[31] The statement in *Morris* may perhaps be supported as an attempt to convey some such idea; but it would be unwise to claim that that statement or any in this paragraph can serve to *define* "appropriation."

A "combination" of acts?

2–80   On Lord Roskill's analysis in *Morris*, it was the combination of removal from the shelf and the switching of the labels which "*evidenced*" adverse interference or usurpation[32]; and this leads later in his opinion to the general notion of a dishonest act, not itself an appropriation, combining with later acts to "*bring about*" an appropriation "within section 3(1)."[33] The idea that (as it was also expressed) "[i]t is the doing of one or more acts which individually or collectively *amount to* . . . adverse interference . . . or usurpation . . ."[34] was seized upon in *Philippou*[35] as a way of escape from the conflict between *Morris* and *Lawrence*. The controller of a company was charged with theft of the company's bank account by transferring the credit in it to Spain for his own advantage. It was argued that the use of the account was authorised (by himself) and therefore no theft under the doctrine relating to authorised acts asserted in *Morris*.[36] The response of the Court of Appeal was to find a "composite transaction" consisting of D's instruction to the bank to transfer money to Spain and the use of the money to buy Spanish property for another company owned and controlled by D. The court seems to say that the latter component shows the former to be dishonest and thus renders it "adverse."

2–81   It is submitted that this purported application of the *Morris* opinion involves a complex of confusions. On one reading, evidence of appropriation (the event showing the crucial act to be dishonest) is confused with the appropriation itself, by being treated also as a "component" of it. This confusion is involved if the *Philippou* judgment is indeed an application of the *Morris* idea of appropriation as a "combination" of acts. If it is not involved, it seems that the *Morris* opinion is being misread or misapplied. Another confusion is that between the theft elements of appropriation and dishonesty; for the dealing with the bank account is treated as (or as a component of) an appropriation only because it is revealed by the rest of the evidence as a dishonest act. It has been pointed out that the *Morris* opinion itself "appears to run together" the two elements,[37] which the Act itself shows to be separate.[38] The judgment in *Philippou* certainly does not advance understanding of appropriation. Nor, on the other hand, is the

---

[31] See Clerk and Lindsell on *Torts* (16th ed.), para. 22–12; and compare above, § 2–60.
[32] [1984] A.C. 320 at 332.
[33] *Ibid.* at 334.
[34] *Ibid.* at 333. (Emphasis is supplied in text at nn. 32–34.)
[35] (1989) 89 Cr.App.R. 290.
[36] See above, § 2–72.
[37] *Per* Parker L.J. in *Dobson* v. *General Accident Fire and Life Assurance Corpn. plc* [1990] Q.B. 274 at 283.
[38] See, most obviously, the opening words of s.2(1): "[An] appropriation . . . is not to be regarded as dishonest . . . if . . . ."

Morris notion of a combination of acts helpful. It may amount to no more than this truism: that if one act is not an appropriation, because it is authorised or merely mischievous, some other is needed before there is an appropriation. If it amounts to more than this, it too confuses evidence with substance.

Theft of company assets by company controller[39]

There can be no doubt that the director of a company having authority to deal with property of the company for the company's purposes can commit theft by dealing with it "dishonestly and in fraud of the company."[40] But theft of company assets by a person who wholly owns and controls the company requires further discussion. If he transfers company assets to himself or applies such assets to his own purposes, he undoubtedly deals with "property belonging to another," namely, the company. But it may seem somewhat unreal to describe him as stealing from the company. The true losers must always be other parties, normally loan or trade creditors or the revenue. If a sole trader transfers the assets of his unincorporated business beyond the reach of his creditors with intent to defraud them, he commits no theft. Indeed, he may commit no offence at all save in the event of a bankruptcy order, when the transfer becomes retrospectively an offence under the Insolvency Act 1986, s.357. It is odd that the sole trader who has turned himself into a "one-man company" should be in a different position; but it seems that he is.

2–82

In *Attorney-General's Reference (No. 2 of 1982)*[41] two men arranged large loans and overdrafts for companies they had established and then drew massively on the bank accounts for private purposes. Argument in the Court of Appeal on charges of theft from the companies was conducted on the footing that the only issue (the existence of appropriation being conceded) was whether the men had acted dishonestly. The opinion of the court reduced this to the question whether the men may have believed that they were entitled in law to act as they did.[42] It had been argued, in effect, that, as the defendants wholly owned and controlled the companies, their acts and knowledge were the companies' acts and knowledge and that those acts could not therefore be theft. But the doctrine of identification between a company and its controllers was rejected in its suggested application to acts done in fraud of the company itself.[43] More particularly, the court rejected an argument based on section 2(1)(b)—that is, that the defendants' knowledge being the company's knowledge, they were not dishonest because they believed they had the company's consent.[44]

2–83

[39] Sullivan [1983] Crim.L.R. 512; [1984] Crim.L.R. 405 (replying to Dine [1984] Crim.L.R. 397); Arlidge and Parry, *Fraud*, paras. 4.26 *et seq*.
[40] *Attorney-General of Hong Kong* v. *Nai-keung* (1987) 86 Cr.App.R. 174 (for facts, see above, § 2–12). For consideration of opinions apparently to the contrary in *Tarling* v. *Government of the Republic of Singapore* (1978) 70 Cr.App.R. 77, see J. C. Smith [1979] Crim.L.R. at 224.
[41] [1984] Q.B. 624.
[42] See s.2(1)(a).
[43] Citing *Belmont Finance Corp. Ltd.* v. *Williams Furniture Ltd.* [1979] Ch. 250; distinguishing *Tesco Supermarkets Ltd.* v. *Nattrass* [1972] A.C. 153.
[44] See below, § 2–124.

2–84   Subsequent cases have had to be decided in the light of the dictum in *Morris* requiring, for an appropriation, "not an act expressly or impliedly authorised by the owner, but an act by way of adverse interference with or usurpation of [the owner's] rights."[45] The dictum was followed by the majority of the Supreme Court of Victoria in *Roffel*,[46] in holding that the effective controller of a company who drew on the company's bank account for his own purposes did not thereby appropriate the company's property because the company (through him) had consented to his acts. And the *Morris* dictum also clearly influenced the Court of Appeal in *McHugh and Tringham*[47] in framing the following speculative proposition:

> "Where the actor is beneficially entitled to the entire issued share capital (or at least the entire voting share capital) of the company it may be that his act is not an appropriation because—(a) his act is equivalent to an act of the company, and his intent is the intent of the company, so that there can be no circumstance in which any of his acts is unauthorised; and/or (b) since he has the irresistible power to determine what policies the company shall pursue, there is nothing which he himself may do in the company's name which could in practice be unauthorised."

But the facts of the case did not oblige the court to determine the correctness of this proposition. It is in any case weakened by the court's not referring to *Attorney-General's Reference (No. 2 of 1982)*[48]; and it is further weakened by the fact that, as has been seen, *Morris* was shortly to be invoked to quite other effect in *Philippou*,[49] in which a company controller's use of the company's bank account was held to be an appropriation and theft.

2–85   The majority in *Roffel* took the view that D's consent to his own act may be the company's consent even if the transaction is *ultra vires* the company or an infringement of fundamental company law principles. Resort to the *ultra vires* doctrine may in any case be more problematical than formerly, in the light of recent company law reform.[50] But there remains much force in the view, which has been strongly championed,[51] that a company controller's transfer to himself of company assets, being an unauthorised reduction of capital, is an act to which the company cannot consent. This argument could yet prove to be decisive if the continuing debate about appropriation should see consent re-emerge as a determinative factor.

---

[45] [1984] A.C. 320 at 332; above, § 2–72.
[46] [1985] V.R. 511; von Nessen [1986] Crim.L.R. 154.
[47] (1988) 88 Cr.App.R. 385 at 393.
[48] Above, § 2–83.
[49] (1989) 89 Cr.App.R. 290 (above, § 2–80); apparently decided in ignorance of *McHugh*.
[50] Companies Act 1985, s.35(1) (as substituted by Companies Act 1989, s.108(1)): "The validity of an act done by a company shall not be called into question by reason of anything in the company's memorandum." But see *ibid.* s.35(3), requiring a special resolution to ratify an act that would be beyond the company's capacity but for s.35(1).
[51] See works cited in n. 39, above; judgment of Brooking J. (dissenting) in *Roffel* [1985] V.R. 511.

Obtaining by deception as theft[52]

In *Lawrence* v. *Metropolitan Police Commissioner* (the facts of which **2–86** have already been mentioned[53]) the Court of Appeal regarded the additional £6 taken from P's wallet as having been obtained by deception and also appropriated. The court went so far as to say "that in any case where the facts would establish a charge under section 15(1) they would also establish a charge under section 1(1)."[54] Viscount Dilhorne, for the House of Lords, confirmed that in some cases the same facts may justify conviction of both offences.[55] Yet in some subsequent cases in which property has been obtained by deception, the Court of Appeal has regarded theft as committed only at some later time although from the outset D had the intention necessary for theft. It will be convenient to refer first to cases of obtaining *ownership with possession* by deception, secondly to the fraudulent obtaining of *ownership without possession*, and then to the cases of obtaining *possession only* in which theft has been denied.

Obtaining ownership with possession

It seems that in *Lawrence* the Court of Appeal regarded D as having **2–87** obtained *ownership* in the £6 by fraud. This appears from their having taken the view that under the old law D's offence would have been obtaining by false pretences.[56] That offence occurred where, under the influence of D's fraud, P intended to part with ownership of property. Such a case could not be one of larceny, and the offence of obtaining by false pretences was created by statute precisely because of the impotence of the law of larceny in this respect. The problem, on the Court of Appeal's view of the facts in *Lawrence*, was not so much whether D appropriated the £6 as whether when he did so it was property belonging to another.

The Committee did not intend every case of obtaining property by decep- **2–88** tion to be also a case of theft and apparently contemplated that the old offence of obtaining by false pretences would be replaced only by the offence under section 15(1).[57] There were two ways of achieving this. One was to argue that an appropriation cannot occur when ownership passes to D. But no one doubted in *Lawrence* that there had been an appropriation. The other way was to argue that when by deception I obtain ownership of property, my appropriation is of property which, by virtue of the transaction

---

[52] See Smith, *Theft*, paras. 37 *et seq.*; Williams [1977] Crim.L.R. at 133 *et seq.*, 207 *et seq.*; *Textbook*, pp. 803 *et seq.*; Parry, *Offences against Property*, paras. 1.80 *et seq.* For controversy between Smith and Williams, see [1981] Crim.L.R. 666 and 677; [1982] Crim.L.R. 64 (and a related letter, *ibid.* at 391).
[53] Above, § 2–72.
[54] [1971] 1 Q.B. 373 at 378. A person is guilty of an offence under s.15(1) if by deception he dishonestly obtains ownership, possession or control (see s.15(2)) of property belonging to another with the intention of permanently depriving the other of it.
[55] [1972] A.C. 626 at 633.
[56] [1971] 1 Q.B. 373 at 378.
[57] *Eighth Report*, paras. 38, 90. (A case involving land must in any case be an exception: see s.4(2)).

so induced, has come to belong not to my victim—he retains no "proprietary right or interest" in it—but to me only; on that analysis the case would not be one of theft. This argument was never without its difficulties. Suppose (to take facts less ambiguous than those in *Lawrence*) that D deceives P into making him a gift of money, which P does by placing cash in D's hands. The transfer of ownership[58] here is of course effected by the transfer of possession. To say in this case that D has committed an offence under section 15 but not under section 1 is, in effect, to say (i) that what is "obtained" by the transaction of gift is property owned or possessed by P ("belonging to" P), but (ii) that what is "appropriated" by the closing of D's hands around the notes or coins is property that P has already ceased either to own or to possess (not "belonging to" P). This way of achieving the envisaged degree of separation between the offences involves some strain.

2–89 The argument was unsuccessfully advanced for the appellant in *Lawrence*. The Court of Appeal, as seen above, treated ownership in the money as having passed and offences under both section 1 and section 15 as having been committed. The view of the House of Lords, in the opinion of Viscount Dilhorne, is less easy to interpret. The appellant's counsel had stressed (correctly, it is thought) that if ownership in the £6 did not pass, that was the end of the matter. Viscount Dilhorne stated that it had not been established that P consented "to the acquisition by [D] of the £6" or "to the taking of the £6." But he went on to deal with the appellant's argument in this way:

> "Mr. Back Q.C. . . . contended that if Mr. Occhi consented to the appellant taking the £6, he consented to the property in the money passing from him to the appellant and that the appellant had not, therefore, appropriated property belonging to another. He argued that the old distinction between the offence of false pretences and larceny had been preserved. I am unable to agree with this."[59]

"This" must surely mean "this argument as a whole." His lordship went on at once to remark on the occurrence of the words "belonging to another" in both section 1(1) and section 15(1) and to express the view that in both contexts the phrase

> "signifies no more than that, at the time of the appropriation or the obtaining, the property belonged to another. . . . The short answer to [D's contention] is that the money in the wallet which he appropriated belonged to another, to [P]."[59]

Viscount Dilhorne's opinion, itself read as a whole, seems to mean: "It does not appear that ownership in the £6 passed; but even if it did, the conviction of theft stands."

2–90 It has since been recognised in *Dobson* v. *General Accident Fire and Life Assurance Corp. plc*[60] that theft and obtaining property by deception may

---

[58] It is assumed that the deception does not induce a mistake so fundamental as to prevent a transfer of ownership; see *Williams* [1980] Crim.L.R. 589; *Davies* (1981) 74 Cr.App.R. 94.
[59] [1972] A.C. 626 at 632.
[60] [1990] Q.B. 274.

coincide when ownership in goods passes on delivery under a contract of sale that is voidable because of the buyer's fraud. D agreed to buy a gold watch and a diamond ring from P and took delivery of them against a building society cheque. The cheque turned out to be stolen and worthless. The question, arising on P's insurance policy, was whether P had lost the articles by theft. Parker and Bingham L.JJ. in the Court of Appeal Civil Division held that he had. Each of the judges, relying on *Lawrence* in the House of Lords, found this conclusion consistent with the hypothesis that property in the articles passed to D at the time of the delivery and purported payment.[61]

Obtaining ownership without possession

Suppose that D by deception induces P to agree to sell him goods and that   **2–91** the case is one in which the property in the goods passes (voidably) to D by virtue of the contract, although neither payment nor delivery yet takes place. D would thus obtain ownership by deception and commit an offence under section 15 by making the contract. According to Parker L.J. in *Dobson* v. *General Accident etc.*,[62] the making of the contract would also constitute an appropriation in such a case, because D would "by that act . . . [assume] the rights of an owner." The point is likely to remain theoretical in its application to the time of contracting, because of a tendency of the courts to find an intention that the property in specific goods is to pass to the buyer on payment rather than on the mere making of a contract of sale.[63] But it seems that if payment precedes delivery under a fraudulently induced sale, the buyer may steal the goods when he pays for them.

Obtaining possession only

If theft can be committed when the victim intends to part with his whole   **2–92** interest in the property in question (as *Lawrence*, at least in the Court of Appeal, and *Dobson* decide), it would seem remarkable if theft could not occur when D, intending to deprive P permanently of his property, tricks him into making a bailment of it. Yet that is what is held in two Court of Appeal cases.

In *Skipp*[64] D established the outward appearance of a haulage business. He secured instructions from P to collect three consignments of oranges and

---

[61] See *per* Parker L.J., *ibid.* at 280 (although, apparently, preferring the unorthodox view that property did not pass because it was intended to pass only in exchange for a valid cheque); *per* Bingham L.J. at 289 (although at the same time seeking to reconcile *Lawrence* and *Morris* by postulating that P "had not in truth consented to [D] becoming owner without giving a valid draft . . .").

[62] *Ibid.* at 280–281. Of the same opinion, Williams [1977] Crim.L.R. 127 at 136; [1981] Crim.L.R. 666 at 667 (noting a possible implication of *Kaur* v. *Chief Constable of Hampshire* (1981) 72 Cr.App.R. 359 to the contrary; but no deception was found in that case).

[63] See Sale of Goods Act 1979, ss.17 and 18, r. 1; *Lacis* v. *Cashmarts* [1969] 2 Q.B. 400, and other supermarket and cash-and-carry cases; *Dobson* v. *General Accident etc.* [1990] Q.B. 274.

[64] [1975] Crim.L.R. 114.

onions and to carry them from London to customers in Leicester. He loaded the goods on to his lorry at three different places in London and set off—but not for Leicester. He had intended all along to steal the goods. He was charged on one count of an indictment with theft of all the goods; and it was argued that the count was bad for duplicity as it concerned three appropriations at different times and places. The Court of Appeal (without referring to *Lawrence*) rejected this argument on the ground that, until all the loading was completed, and probably until D diverted from the route to Leicester, he had "not . . . got to the point of assuming the rights of the owner by doing something inconsistent with those rights." And in *Hircock*[65] a person who took a car on hire-purchase with the fraudulent intention from the outset of selling it as his own was held not to have stolen the car until he sold it. The result in each case was to uphold a theft conviction based on an act committed later than the obtaining by deception.[66]

2–93   If there was an appropriation in *Lawrence* when P was deceived into letting D take the extra £6, and in *Dobson* when D gave P the worthless cheque and took delivery of the watch and ring, it is difficult to see why there was not an appropriation in *Skipp* each time D collected a load of greengrocery or in *Hircock* when D received possession of the car. In each case delivery was obtained by deception and an offence under section 15 was committed at that time. Why should the offence of theft be postponed to a later stage?[67] Parker L.J., in *Dobson*,[68] attempted to distinguish *Skipp* by explaining it as a case of "much more than mere consent," of "express authority, indeed instruction to collect the goods." But the rogue in *Dobson* had express authority to take possession of the watch and ring; the instruction in *Skipp*, as in *Dobson*, was given only as a result of D's fraud; and no attempt is or, it seems, could be made to distinguish *Hircock*.

2–94   Under the old law, if D induced P by fraud to deliver property to him, he was regarded as "taking" the property "without the consent of the owner" so long as P intended to part with possession only. D was guilty of "larceny by a trick" if he intended to deprive P permanently. It is certain that the Committee assumed that what used to be larceny by a trick would be an offence under section 1 as well as under section 15; but, as has already been said, they anticipated that an obtaining of ownership by deception (formerly obtaining by false pretences) would be the section 15 offence only.[69] The outcome of *Skipp, Hircock* and *Dobson* is the reverse of what was intended: obtaining by false pretences becomes both theft and the section 15 offence; the old larceny by a trick becomes the section 15 offence only. This is very puzzling. It is firmly submitted that *Skipp* and *Hircock* are wrong as to the

---

[65] (1978) 67 Cr.App.R. 278. For more detailed criticism of this case, including demonstration that *Lawrence* was misread, see [1979] Crim.L.R. 292.

[66] Where the two offences occur at different times, though in respect of the same property, D may be convicted of both: *Hircock* (1978) 67 Cr.App.R. 278. But it is submitted that this should be avoided if possible, *e.g.* by not requiring a verdict on the count charging the later offence.

[67] The decisions were doubted by Gobbo J. in *Heddich* v. *Pike* (1981) 3 A.Crim.R. (Sup.Ct. of Victoria) in the light of the Court of Appeal and House of Lords decisions in *Lawrence*; see also *Baruday* [1984] V.R. 685.

[68] [1990] Q.B. 274 at 285. See also above, § 2–78.

[69] *Eighth Report*, paras. 38, 90.

time at which theft is committed when, with the intention of permanently depriving the victim, a bailment is obtained by fraud.[70]

Theft and obtaining by deception—the choice of charge

Where possession only is obtained by deception, *Skipp* and *Hircock* are   **2–95** for the time being unequivocal Court of Appeal authorities, however inconsistent with *Lawrence* and *Dobson* and the intention of Parliament, against a conviction of theft based on that obtaining. And it would be unwise to be dogmatic either about the scope of the decision in *Dobson* v. *General Accident etc.* (in which the two judgments pursued very different lines of reasoning) or about the exact meaning of *Lawrence* v. *Metropolitan Police Commissioner*, notwithstanding the recent rehabilitation of the main statements of the House of Lords in that case.[71] It is therefore clear that, whenever property has plainly been obtained by deception, it will be a prosecutor's course of prudence to proceed under section 15 rather than under section 1. Under section 15 it is immaterial whether it is ownership or possession that is obtained.

5. "WITH THE INTENTION OF PERMANENTLY DEPRIVING THE OTHER OF IT"

The basic rule

The Committee recommended that an intention to deprive P permanently   **2–96** of the property should be a necessary element in theft, as it was in larceny. They recognised that temporary deprivation can sometimes occasion great loss or hardship and that an intention to cause such deprivation "may involve dishonesty comparable with that involved in theft." But they considered that where there is an intention to return the property, the conduct is "essentially different from stealing" and that either the inclusion in theft of all dishonest borrowing or the creation of a general offence of temporary deprivation would be "a considerable extension of the criminal law [not] called for by any existing serious social evil."[72] Despite much controversy while the Bill was before Parliament, this view finally prevailed.[73]

So the general rule is that dishonest borrowing is not theft. If D takes P's property he is not normally guilty of stealing it if he intends in due course to return it or at least that P shall recover it. It is necessary to describe this as

---

[70] The following cases, for example, should be theft: (i) D induces P to put goods in his hands for sale, intending from the outset to sell the goods for his own profit and to pocket the proceeds; (ii) P delivers goods to D "on sale or return." When D receives them he intends neither to pay for them nor to return them.

[71] See above, § 2–73.

[72] *Eighth Report*, para. 56.

[73] For full argument of the contrary view, see Glanville Williams [1981] Crim.L.R. 129. In recent years the "borrowing" of films and cassettes to make pirate copies has afforded an example of a relevant "serious social evil"; see § 2–108, below.

"the general rule" because section 6 is at pains to provide expressly that one who intends a borrowing that is "equivalent to an outright taking" is to be regarded as intending to deprive permanently. Subject to this obscure provision, which is dealt with below, it is immaterial for how long D can be shown to have intended to enjoy possession of the property or for how long P is actually deprived of it. Immaterial, that is, as a matter of law. As a matter of common sense, of course, the longer the period is, the less plausible will be D's claim that he intended P to have the property back. But if that claim appeals to the court as a reasonable possibility, he will be entitled to an acquittal.

Some points of detail

2–97   *"With the intention . . ."* The intention of depriving P permanently must coincide with a dishonest appropriation. But this need not be D's first appropriation. He may take P's property intending at first merely to borrow it; he has "come by the property . . . without stealing it." If he later decides to keep it for good or to sell it, this is a "later assumption of a right to it by keeping or dealing with it as owner" and a fresh appropriation (s.3(1)). Theft occurs at this point.

Certain varieties of "conditional intention" are considered below, § 2–113.

2–98   *". . . of permanently depriving the other . . ."* The word "permanently" must be understood in the light of P's particular interest in the property. If P merely has temporary "possession or control" of the property, it nevertheless belongs to him for the purpose of his being a victim of theft (s.5(1)), and he can be "permanently" deprived by D's appropriation although he might have had to relinquish the property very shortly in any event.

2–99   *". . . of it."* It has long been understood, both in the law of larceny and under the present Act, that even if D means to return to P the indistinguishable equivalent of what he takes—the precise amount of cash[74] or an identical can of baked beans—he nevertheless has the necessary intention of permanently depriving P of the particular property appropriated. Whether he is guilty of theft depends on whether he appropriates that property dishonestly, a matter to which his intention to replace what he takes may be relevant.[75]

Belief in abandonment as excluding intention

2–100   Suppose that D sees in the street property which he wrongly believes (whether or not on reasonable grounds) to have been abandoned by its owner. He believes that the property does not "belong to" anyone. This

[74] *Velumyl* [1989] Crim.L.R. 299; *cf.* § 7–57, below (obtaining property by deception).
[75] See below, § 2–129.

belief by definition negatives any intention on D's part to deprive anyone of the property when he takes possession of it. There will therefore be no need, on a charge of theft from the owner, to consider the issue of dishonesty[76]; the absence of the required intention excludes the theft charged. Alternatively, D may find and take, on land occupied by P, property which he believes to have been abandoned there by its owner, O. Once again D, having that belief, does not intend to deprive O. His taking may, however, be adverse to an interest of P. If D nevertheless believes that P has no interest in the property, he might also claim, charged with theft from P, that he did not intend to deprive P of it. But it is probable that P, as occupier, had "control" within the meaning of section 5(1) and was a person to whom the property "belonged" for theft purposes.[77] D intentionally deprived P of that control. If that is right, it may strictly be more accurate in this case to understand D as denying dishonesty: he believed that he had in law the right to deprive P, or that P would have consented to the taking if he had known.[78]

A preface to section 6

Section 6 provides a partial definition of the phrase "with the intention of   **2–101** permanently depriving the other of it." That it is only a partial definition appears from the first words of the section, which show that it is concerned only with a case where a person appropriates property "without meaning the other permanently to lose the thing itself." The section identifies circumstances in which the appropriator is nevertheless to be regarded as having the intention of permanently depriving the other of the property.

The section was an unsatisfactory late amendment to the Bill.[79] It is badly drafted and employs language new to this branch of the law. For instance, a curious distinction is taken between "property" and "the thing itself"; yet as between subsections (1) and (2) the two phrases are used indifferently in precisely the same context: subsection (1) talks of D's treating "the thing" and subsection (2) of his treating "the property" as "his own to dispose of regardless of [P's] rights." In subsection (1) the phrases "having the intention" and "meaning" are both used, with no clear difference in meaning or intention. Subsection (1) ends with the obscure expression "equivalent to an outright taking or disposal." Rarely can a provision inserted for clarification have contributed more obscurity.

Limited function of the section

The draft Bill had no clause corresponding to section 6. The Committee   **2–102** described "cases where the offender intends to do something with the property which for practical purposes is equivalent to permanent deprivation" and thought that these cases would be treated as theft without need

[76] Very heavy weather was made of that issue in *Small* (1987) 86 Cr.App.R. 170, it would seem quite unnecessarily.
[77] See above, § 2–23.
[78] s.2(1)(a) and (b).
[79] For the illuminating, and remarkable, Parliamentary history of the section, see Spencer [1977] Crim.L.R. 653.

for special provision.[80] It was made clear in the House of Commons that the section was drafted largely with the same cases in mind. The Court of Appeal, in the leading case of *Lloyd*,[81] has declared a disposition to interpret the section "in such a way as to ensure that nothing is construed as an intention permanently to deprive which would not prior to the 1968 Act have been so construed."[82] In other cases the same court and the Judicial Committee of the Privy Council seem to have taken a somewhat less restrictive view of the section's potential.[83] But it is certainly the case, as the court in *Lloyd* confirmed, that *the section should be referred to in exceptional cases only*. It is important to emphasise this cautionary statement because of the impression of some students to the contrary and because of the strange uses to which the section has been put at first instance in some cases.[84]

Section 6(1)

2–103   "A person appropriating property belonging to another without meaning the other permanently to lose the thing itself is nevertheless to be regarded as having the intention of permanently depriving the other of it if his intention is to treat the thing as his own to dispose of regardless of the other's rights; and a borrowing or lending of it may amount to so treating it if, but only if, the borrowing or lending is for a period and in circumstances making it equivalent to an outright taking or disposal."

The first part of the subsection

2–104   The following situations are undoubtedly within the first part of the subsection:

(i) D takes P's chattel. His intention is to pretend that it is his own and to induce P to "buy" it. Thus P will not permanently "lose the thing itself." But D will be treating the chattel at his own to dispose of regardless of P's rights.

(ii) D takes an exhibit from an exhibition and holds it to ransom; he will return it only if the exhibitor fulfils some condition named by D. This is identical with situation (i) save that there is no deception.

(iii) D takes P's gold watch, intending to pawn it and to send the pawn ticket to P. He intends, that is to say, to treat the watch as his own to dispose of, although he hopes that P will recover the watch by redeeming it. (Even if D does not get as far as pawning the watch, his intention to do so is, of course, enough.)

2–105   Situations such as those in (i) and (ii) above (intended repurchase and intended ransom) were identified by the Court of Appeal in *Lloyd*[85] as aimed at by the first part of section 6(1). There seems no reason to doubt that

---

[80] *Eighth Report*, para. 58.
[81] [1985] Q.B. 829 at 836.
[82] The offence of larceny required an intention to deprive the victim permanently, but there was no statutory gloss on this requirement.
[83] See *Coffey* [1987] Crim.L.R. 498; *Bagshaw* [1988] Crim.L.R. 321; *Chan Man-sin* v. *R.* (1987) 86 Cr.App.R. 303.
[84] See *Warner* (1970) 55 Cr.App.R. 93; *Halstead* v. *Patel* (1972) 56 Cr.App.R. 334; *Cocks* (1976) 63 Cr.App.R. 79; *Harkindel Atwal* [1989] Crim.L.R. 293.
[85] [1985] Q.B. 829 at 836.

the court would regard situation (iii) as an analogous case. And it might be thought that an intention to keep P's property unless P will behave as D wishes might always be regarded in the same way as an intention to hold property to ransom; in effect, P must buy his property back. But the cases certainly do not go this far. In *Barnett and Reid*[86] the Court of Appeal thought that there might be rare circumstances in which taking property to hold as security for a supposed debt would not amount to treating it as one's own to dispose of regardless of the other's rights. And in *Coffey*[87] the court declined to treat as simply analogous to ransom the withholding of property until P should comply with D's wishes in another matter. The jury, it seemed to be said, might take the view that D's perception of the likelihood of P's complying was such that D's conduct was not "equivalent to an outright taking." But the requirement of equivalence to "an outright taking" is prescribed by section 6(1) only for a case of "borrowing"; and it is submitted that a taking of P's property to put pressure on him to do something is not a "borrowing."[88]

Although speaking restrictively of the first part of section 6(1), the court **2–106** in *Lloyd* did not directly cast doubt on the application of the subsection to some other situations illustrated by decisions of its own to which it referred:

(iv) P has written a cheque in favour of D but will deliver it only on performance of some act by D, *e.g.* the delivery of goods. D comes and takes the cheque without performing the act; he intends to pay the cheque into his bank for collection. The cheque, albeit cancelled and no longer having the character of a thing in action,[89] will in due course return to P (or at least will return to his bank and be available to him); but D's taking of it is with the intention of treating it as his own to dispose of regardless of P's rights.[90]

(v) D, an approved building contractor, is lawfully in possession of Inland Revenue vouchers to be used to claim exemption from deduction of tax upon payment of remuneration by the main contractors. D "sells" the vouchers to E so that E may claim such exemption. The vouchers, fraudulently completed by E, will in due course return to the Inland Revenue. D's appropriation by "selling" the vouchers is within section 6(1).[91]

The Judicial Committee of the Privy Council has made a further impor- **2–107** tant application of the subsection:

(vi) A person who issues a forged cheque on another's account intends thereby to "treat [the credit in the account] as his own to dispose of regardless of the [account-holder's] rights" and can therefore steal the credit although he knows that the right it represents will be unaffected by the forged instrument.[92]

---

[86] Unreported (C.A. Nos. 5818/C3/86; 5819/C3/86; July 21, 1987).
[87] [1987] Crim.L.R. 498.
[88] See below, § 2–110.
[89] This was the primary, but doubtful, basis of the decision in *Duru* (1973) 58 Cr.App.R. 151; for criticism, see § 2–14, above.
[90] Compare *Duru*, above (in which a cheque was obtained by deception and the prosecution was under s.15).
[91] *Downes* (1983) 77 Cr.App.R. 260; compare *Mulligan* [1990] S.T.C. 220.
[92] *Chan Man-sing* v. *Attorney-General of Hong Kong* (1987) 86 Cr.App.R. 303 (discussed below, § 2–150).

Borrowing

2–108   The second part of section 6(1) refers to cases of "borrowing" and "lend-ing." None of the situations (i) to (vi) above appears to be one of "borrow-ing"; it is thought that the word refers to a case where D assumes possession of property without deciding never to return it to P but, equally, without having in mind a use or dealing (such as sale, ransom, pledge) that would be inconsistent with a borrowing legitimately so called. Such a taking is theft "if, and only if, [it] is for a period and in circumstances making it equivalent to an outright taking."

The view of the Court of Appeal in *Lloyd* was that this part of the subsection:

> "is intended to make clear that a mere borrowing is never enough to constitute the necessary guilty mind unless the intention is to return the 'thing' in such a changed state that it can truly be said that all its goodness or virtue has gone."[93]

In *Lloyd* itself, films were removed from a cinema, each for a few hours only, to be copied on to master videotapes, so that many pirate copies of the film could be put on the market. This was not theft.[94] The films themselves, the physical property appropriated, did not lose their "virtue," however great the loss to the copyright owners and others.

2–109   The following case of "borrowing" is within the subsection:
(vii) D takes from P's ticket office a train ticket or a ticket giving access to a place. He cannot say this was not theft merely because he meant to surrender the ticket at the end of the journey or on entering the place and because thereby the ticket would return to P.

The following seems also to qualify:
(viii) D takes P's railway season ticket, intending to use it for as long as he may wish to do so, possibly for as long as it is valid. (But if he intends to keep the ticket for a limited time substantially shorter than the period for which the ticket is valid, the case would seem to be outside the section. The section's obscurities may be illustrated by asking what the effect will be of D's intending to return the ticket (say, a quarterly season ticket) a very short time before its expiry. At what point does a borrowing become "equivalent to an outright taking"?)

Borrowing and abandonment

2–110   D may take P's chattel, use it for a time and then abandon it. It will be

---

[93] [1985] Q.B. 829 at 836. This adopts a long-standing suggestion of Professor J. C. Smith; see now Smith, *Theft*, para. 138. The court's language is not entirely happy; its own example of the used ticket (see text below) shows that there need not always be a changed physical state. The notion of exhausted "virtue" can be overworked: see Professor Smith's comment on *Bagshaw* [1988] Crim.L.R. 321 at 322.
[94] See also *Warner* (1970) 55 Cr.App.R. 93, for a case of a mere indefinite borrowing which was not theft.

inadvisable for a court to treat such a case simply as one of "borrowing." If it does it will become enmeshed in the obscurities of section 6. The correct course, it is submitted, is to concentrate on the abandonment. If D leaves the chattel in such a place that he can virtually be regarded as returning it to P (*e.g.* he leaves a book with P's name in it in the office where P works), he will not be regarded as treating it as his own to dispose of. If, on the other hand, the facts of the abandonment show D to be indifferent whether P recovers the chattel or not, he can be regarded as, by abandoning it, "dealing with it as owner" (s.3(1)), having at that time the intention "to treat the thing as his own to dispose of." Even though D may have been content that P should recover the chattel, the case will be particularly strong if the circumstances of the abandonment show that he undoubtedly realised that P was extremely unlikely to do so.

Lending

Section 6(1) appears, finally, to contemplate the following kind of case: **2–111**
(ix) D is a bailee of P's chattel. He lends the chattel to E, telling E that he may keep and use it for as long as he likes. The circumstances, to D's knowledge, are such that the chattel may never be returned (*e.g.* E is going abroad) or that by the time it is returned its "virtue" may have gone (*e.g.* it is a ticket for a series of concerts and E may keep the ticket until the end of the series). In either situation there appears to be a "lending . . . for a period and in circumstances making it equivalent to an outright . . . disposal." D is not protected by his claim that he did not mean P permanently to lose "the thing itself."

Section 6(2)

One kind of case is specifically mentioned by section 6(2) as being within   **2–112**
section 6(1). Where D, "having possession or control (lawfully or not) of [P's property], parts with the property under a condition as to its return which he may not be able to perform, this . . . amounts to treating the property as his own to dispose of regardless of [P's] rights" if it is done for D's purposes and without P's authority.

An obvious case is that where D, a bailee of P's property, pledges the property with E as security for a loan by E to himself, intending to redeem it and to return it to P. There are two possible views of this situation. One is that D is guilty of theft only if he realises that he may be unable to redeem; the other is that the case must be within the subsection, as it can be asserted of every pledgor, life being full of uncertainties, that he *may* not be able to redeem his security. The former view is doctrinally the purer; the latter is more readily suggested by the terms of the poorly-drafted section.

"Conditional intention"

This phrase is a convenient heading under which to consider a number of   **2–113** states of mind in the description of which a conditional clause features as an important and possibly crucial element: "I shall steal from that pocket (or handbag or house) *if*, as I hope, there is anything attractive (or such as I seek) to be had in it"; "I shall keep this thing *if*, but only if, on examination it proves to suit my purpose"; "*if* this belongs to anyone, I shall deprive him of it." It will be seen that these intentions, and the conditions that qualify them, are of very different kinds. The fact is that the expression "conditional intention," which has had something of a vogue in this area of the criminal law, is a dangerous one—useful, perhaps, as a heading but not to be used in analysis unless its meaning in the context is made very plain.

Looking for something to steal

2–114   In *Easom*[95] D took up P's handbag where it lay near P in a cinema and looked into it to see whether there was anything worth stealing. There was not; so he replaced the bag, with its contents intact, where he had found it. It was held that his "conditional appropriation" of the bag and its contents did not suffice to establish theft of those things. He had formed no intention to deprive P permanently of the property named in the indictment.[96]

Easom came in due course to be seen[97] as the source of a doctrine that a "conditional intention to steal"—an intention, for example, to steal if there should prove to be anything worth stealing—was no intention to steal for the purpose of an offence requiring that ingredient. English law did indeed briefly flirt with such a doctrine, which for a time troubled the law of burglary and attempted theft before being renounced.[98] As to theft itself, what section 1(1) requires in terms is not an "intention to steal" but a more specific "intention of permanently depriving [P] of [the property appropriated]." It is productive of error to argue (as has been done) that what was conditional was not *Easom*'s appropriation but his intention. He had *no* intention to deprive P permanently either of the handbag or of the particular things he found in it. The attribution to *Easom* of a so-called "doctrine of conditional intention" is misconceived.

2–115   It was hinted in *Easom* itself that the appellant, who was plainly looking for something to steal, could have been convicted of attempted theft on a charge suitably framed.[99] Within a few years of *Easom* such a conviction became problematical for another reason—namely, a short-lived aberration of the law relating to "impossible attempts."[1] But impossibility of success has ceased to be a bar to conviction of attempt in such a case.[2]

[95] [1971] 2 Q.B. 315.
[96] ". . . and this was so notwithstanding the provisions of s.6(1) . . .": at 319.
[97] Koffman [1980] Crim.L.R. 463; but Parry [1981] Crim.L.R. 6, correctly demonstrates that *Easom* is not, as Koffman argues, inconsistent with other theft cases.
[98] As to burglary, see below, § 4–32; as to attempted theft, *Scudder* v. *Barrett* [1980] Q.B. 195n; *Bayley and Easterbrook* [1980] Crim.L.R. 503.
[99] [1971] 2 Q.B. at 321; and see cases cited in n. 98, above.
[1] *Haughton* v. *Smith* [1975] A.C. 476; *Partington* v. *Williams* (1975) 62 Cr.App.R. 220. (The difficulty was overlooked or ignored in *Bayley and Easterbrook*, above.)
[2] Criminal Attempts Act 1981, s.1(2); *Smith and Smith* [1986] Crim.L.R. 166 (and see *ibid.* at 167, comment on form of charge).

Keeping property for examination and for retention or return

If D is looking for money in P's handbag and finds only cosmetic parapher-   **2–116**
nalia, or if he sorts through a pile of mail looking for registered letters and
finds only unregistered ones,[3] he has no intention of permanently depriving
P, or the Post Office, of the particular things he examines. But if he finds
something that may on examination prove to conform to his requirements, it
is strongly arguable that he does steal it, or that on the particular facts he
may do so, when he keeps it for examination, even though he will return it to
its owner if it proves disappointing.[4]

The Supreme Court of Victoria has held such a case to be theft by virtue of
the first part of a provision identical to section 6(1): D intends "to treat the
thing as his own to dispose of regardless of [P's] rights."[5] An alternative view
would be that, for the time being, D's retention of the thing is only a
"borrowing" and that it is therefore necessary to ask whether, on the facts,
including D's own expectation as to the outcome of his trial of the thing, the
borrowing is "equivalent to an outright taking"—a question requiring a jury
judgment.[6] There is a problem, however, with either application of section
6(1). The subsection is expressed to apply only where D appropriates
property "without meaning [P] permanently to lose the thing itself," by
which the draftsman surely meant to indicate a case where D intends, or
supposes, or at least is content, that the thing will return to P. If that is right,
the typical case under consideration is outside the ambit of section 6(1):
when D takes the thing he has, for the time being, no such state of mind.

Is the case, then, one of theft without resort to section 6(1)? The answer   **2–117**
may be that it depends on the particular facts. D may best be understood as
having intended to keep the thing unless (unexpectedly) it should prove
unsuitable; and in this case he may properly be found to have formed a (so to
speak) defeasible intention to deprive P permanently of it. But if the facts
better suggest D's assumption that he will return the thing, but with the
reservation that he will keep it if (against the odds) it should prove suitable
to his purpose, it would be acceptable (save in one kind of case) to say that
theft was not (yet) committed. The excepted case is that in which it is known
that the thing did in fact answer D's requirements: it is proved that he
intended to keep the thing if it had certain qualities and that it had those
qualities. This perhaps establishes theft.

Realising that the property probably belongs to another

It has been argued that (assuming a finding of dishonesty) D should be   **2–118**

---

[3] See *Easom* [1971] 2 Q.B. 315 at 319.
[4] D's claim that he would have returned the thing in certain circumstances may stretch
credulity. But if that is his defence, as it was in *Sharp* v. *McCormick* (next note), the jury or
magistrates must be correctly advised as to its legal effect if they think it possibly true.
[5] *Sharp* v. *McCormick* [1986] V.R. 869. The court left open the question whether it would be
theft in the absence of the provision.
[6] Compare *Coffey* [1987] Crim.L.R. 498; above, § 2–105.

liable to conviction of theft if he acquires from E property belonging to P realising that E very likely has no title to it.[7] There is certainly an appropriation in such a case. The question is whether the intention of depriving the victim that is required by the definition of theft is satisfied by recklessness in respect of the deprivation or by nothing less than knowledge. What is in effect, though not in terms, suggested is that recklessness establishes a particular form of conditional intention: "If this is a deprivation of another, then it is one that I intend to commit."

This suggestion must probably be rejected.[8] It is, understandably, only for the case of strong suspicion, or realisation of a probability, that the conclusion of theft is suggested. Yet there is really no way of distinguishing between mild and strong suspicion that E has no title; in either case the conditional "intention" can be written in the same form. It seems, therefore, that D must know that he is "depriving" someone—though knowledge here may on general principles be taken to include the condition of "wilful blindness."[9]

6. "DISHONESTLY"

2–119 It may be assumed for the purpose of what now follows that D appropriates property belonging to P with the intention of permanently depriving him of it. Does he do so "dishonestly?" Some preliminary points may be made about this question. First, any question as to D's honesty must relate to the time of the appropriation. The Court of Appeal has several times had occasion to emphasise this point, notably in relation to the prosecution's difficult task of establishing theft of property to which section 5(3) applies.[10] Secondly, the question should be understood to relate to D's conduct considered as an appropriation—that is, as a dealing with property belonging to P—and not from some other point of view. In particular, the fact that D has a dishonest intention to default as P's debtor should not normally be relevant to a theft issue.[11] Thirdly, D will commonly need to ensure that the question of the honesty or otherwise of his conduct is a live issue, by giving evidence that he acted with one of the beliefs mentioned in section 2(1) or with some other state of mind that may cause the tribunal of fact to withhold a finding of dishonesty.[12] But, though D may have an evidential burden, the burden of proof on the issue remains always with the prosecution.[13]

The question is best stated in its negative form: When may D claim that he was *not* dishonest and therefore not guilty of theft. To this question section

---

[7] Spencer [1985] Crim.L.R. 92.
[8] As it is by Williams [1985] Crim.L.R. 432 at 438.
[9] Compare Draft Criminal Code Bill, cl. 18(a) (Law Com.No. 177, Vol. 1): "a person acts 'knowingly' with respect to a circumstance . . . when he avoids taking steps that might confirm his belief that it exists. . . ."
[10] *Hall* [1973] Q.B. 126; *Hayes* (1976) 64 Cr.App.R. 82; as to s.5(3), see above, § 2–30.
[11] s.5(4) may qualify this general rule, for it creates theft liability out of a decision not to pay one kind of debt.
[12] See below, § 2–128.
[13] *Falconer-Atlee* (1973) 58 Cr.App.R. 348, which illustrates the importance of a direction to the jury on a part of s.2(1) rendered relevant by the evidence.

2(1) provides a partial answer: D may claim on any of three grounds that as matter of law his appropriation was not dishonest.

Belief in a right to deprive

The appropriator who believes "that he has in law the right[14] to deprive" **2–120** of the property the person to whom it belongs is not guilty of theft, for his appropriation is not to be regarded as dishonest (s.2(1)(*a*)). Such a belief will protect him however mistaken or unreasonable it is, even if it is the result of self-induced intoxication,[15] and even if the claim he makes is of a kind completely unknown to the law.[16]

Unless D knows that the property in question is property belonging to **2–121** another (within the wide meaning given to that phrase by s.5), he cannot strictly be said to intend to deprive the other of the property. So where, for example, D takes P's umbrella from a stand, mistaking it for his own, or where D has got property by another's mistake and is under an obligation to restore it or its value to P, but D is unaware of the mistake and believes the property was intended for him, his taking in the former case and his retention of the property in the latter case[17] do not need to be defended by resort to section 2(1)(*a*); D does not intend to deprive P, let alone believe that he has a right to do so.[18]

Mistake of law

Occasionally section 2(1)(*a*) may be the ground of D's immunity when he **2–122** takes or retains property to which, because of a legal error, he makes a specific claim. For example, D, wrongly believing that ownership in certain goods has passed to him by virtue of a transaction, takes them from P's possession. The goods "belong to" P not only in the loose sense of the term, but as possessor under section 5(1). But D believes he has the right to deprive P.[19] D may have a similar belief where he has himself sold and delivered goods to P and repossesses them because of P's failure to pay the full price. Or D may find money whose owner he knows to be traceable, but appropriate the money because he believes "findings is keepings." In each of these cases section 2(1)(*a*) will protect D from liability for theft.

Claim to equivalent sum

Reliance on section 2(1)(*a*) will more often be required where D knew **2–123**

---

[14] Whether on behalf of himself or of another: s.2(1)(*a*).
[15] Compare *Jaggard* v. *Dickinson* [1981] Q.B. 527 (Criminal Damage Act 1971, s.5(2)).
[16] See Williams, *Criminal Law—The General Part* (2nd ed.), pp. 321–325; *Russell on Crime* (12th ed.), pp. 1023–1025.
[17] See s.5(4).
[18] See further, § 2–100, above (belief in abandonment).
[19] The summary jurisdiction of justices is not ousted by such an assertion of belief in title to personal property: *Eagling* v. *Wheatley* [1977] Crim.L.R. 165 (and see commentary at 166, pointing out that even if the case concerned real property, the justices would not be called upon to decide a question of title, but only a question as to D's state of mind, and their jurisdiction should be unaffected).

that the particular property (usually money) was P's, but alleges that he believed P owed him or a third person a sum equivalent in value to what he took. If with such a belief D removed the sum in question from the pocket of P's coat as it hung on a peg in their office, he will clearly not be guilty of theft. But it is important to notice that that belief would also suffice to acquit him if he chose some less acceptable and even, in other respects, seriously criminal method of debt-collecting. In *Robinson*,[20] D brandished a knife and used force to get from P money that he said P owed him. His conviction of theft was quashed because the jury had been directed that D could rely on section 2(1)(*a*) only if he believed that he was entitled to get his money in the way he did. This was a misdirection. Similarly, if D believes that she is legally entitled to £20 promised to her by P as a reward for sexual favours, she is not guilty of theft, whether she takes that sum by stealth or by force or extorts it by threatening to reveal P's indiscretions if he does not pay.[21]

Belief that the victim would consent

2–124   Section 2(1)(*b*) protects one who appropriates property in the belief that, if the person to whom it belongs "knew of the appropriation and the circumstances of it," that person would consent.[22] " 'The circumstances' are, of course, all the relevant circumstances"[23]; the hypothetical consent referred to would be "a true consent, honestly obtained."[24]

A typical case is that of the houswife who "borrows" a bag of sugar from a neighbour to whom she mistakenly attributes a spirit of local co-operation. She intends to deprive her neighbour permanently of the sugar she takes, though she may intend to offer later an equivalent quantity in return. So also with the man who borrows money from his colleague's wallet or his employer's till. He, like the housewife, if charged with theft, must succeed on the issue of dishonesty if he is to escape a conviction. Either of two familiar pleas may yield that success. The first is the section 2(1)(*b*) plea: "I thought P wouldn't mind." If this may be true it succeeds as a matter of law. The second is: "I intended to repay," which raises questions for the jury that are considered below.[25]

Belief that the owner cannot be discovered

2–125   If one appropriates property "in the belief that the person to whom [it] belongs cannot be discovered by taking reasonable steps," the appropriation is not to be regarded as dishonest—save in the case of the appropriator to whom the property came as a trustee or personal representative (s.2(1)(*c*)).

---

[20] [1977] Crim.L.R. 173; compare *Skivington* [1968] 1 Q.B. 166 (acquitted of robbery, of which larceny was, and theft now is, an essential ingredient, but convicted of offences against the person; might now also be convicted of blackmail).
[21] But in the latter case she might now be convicted of blackmail; see discussion of *Bernhard* [1938] 2 K.B. 264, below, § 13–33.
[22] "*A fortiori*, a person is not to be regarded as acting dishonestly if he appropriates another's property believing that with full knowledge of the circumstances that other person has in fact agreed to the appropriation." *Per* Viscount Dilhorne in *Lawrence* v. *Metropolitan Police Commissioner* [1972] A.C. 626 at 632.
[23] *Lawrence* [1971] 1 Q.B. 373, *per* Megaw L.J. at 377.
[24] *Attorney-General's Reference (No. 2 of 1982)* [1984] 2 Q.B. 624, *per* Kerr L.J. at 641.
[25] § 2–127.

The obvious example is the finder of lost property. Factors such as the place where the thing is found, its apparent value and the existence of any distinguishing marks or features will determine whether it seems worth while handing the thing to the police, advertising for the owner or taking other steps. For the purpose of the law of theft the finder may make his own assessment (i) of the likely outcome of the steps he might take, and (ii) (it is suggested[26]) of the reasonableness in the circumstances of his being required to take them. As to (i), the law seems strict in requiring a belief that the owner *cannot* be discovered rather than that he is unlikely to be. As to (ii), the law (if the suggestion here is correct) is both generous, in that liability for theft depends to this extent on the accused's own moral standard, and paradoxical, in that the less natural it is to him to put himself out for his neighbour, the less likely is his appropriation of his neighbour's goods to be dishonest.

Other cases besides those of finders fall within section 2(1)(*c*)—for instance, that of the person who gets property by another's mistake but does not know how by reasonable steps to identify or trace the person to whom he should make restoration.

A willingness to pay for the property

If D knows that P is unwilling to sell property to him, D cannot claim that **2–126** his appropriation of the property was necessarily honest just because he was prepared to pay for it or, indeed, because he actually paid P's asking price or a reasonable price for the property. A provision designed to exclude an argument to the contrary is contained in section 2(2).

Situations not within section 2(1): two questions for the jury

An appropriation of property is not to be regarded as dishonest if it is done **2–127** with any of the beliefs mentioned in section 2(1) and discussed above. A defence asserting any of those beliefs must, therefore, be left to the jury in terms of the relevant paragraph of section 2(1) (simply: is it possible that D acted with the asserted belief?); for if he may have had the belief he is entitled in law to an acquittal. The more general (*Ghosh*) direction next to be mentioned cannot strictly be adequate in such a case.[27]

In any other case in which the honesty or dishonesty of D's conduct is in question, its evaluation is, as the authorities stand, a matter for the tribunal of fact; what is "dishonest" is not a question of law. The leading case of *Ghosh*[28] requires that for a finding of dishonesty there should be affirmative answers to two questions:

   (1) Was what was done dishonest according to the ordinary standards of reasonable and honest people?

---

[26] *Contra*, Williams, *Textbook* (1st ed.), p. 664.
[27] *Pace* a mystifying dictum in *Kell* [1985] Crim.L.R. 239. In *Wootton and Peake* [1990] Crim.L.R. 201 the point was not firmly enough asserted; the court was influenced by *Woolven* (1983) 77 Cr.App.R. 231 (below, § 7–66), which, however, concerned an offence to which s.2 does not apply.
[28] [1982] Q.B. 1053. Trial judges have been advised to use the precise words of Lord Lane C.J. in this case when directing juries: *Ravenshad* [1990] Crim.L.R. 398.

(2) Must D have realised that what he was doing was dishonest according to those standards?

When is dishonesty a live issue?

2–128   A direction in terms of the *Ghosh* questions need not, and indeed should not, always be given. The cases make clear, in particular, that the second question need not be explicitly posed if there is no evidence to suggest that D believed that what he did was honest by ordinary people's standards.[29] But the Court of Appeal has tended to say that, if there is no such evidence, there is normally no need for "a *Ghosh* direction" at all—not simply no need to ask the second question. The reason is clear. A jury need hardly be asked as a matter of routine whether shoplifting, street mugging, a bank hold-up or obtaining property by deception is dishonest by prevailing social standards. If it is proved that D appropriated P's property with the intention of permanently depriving him of it, there would seem to be, at least in most cases, a clear prima facie case of theft. To render dishonesty a live issue there is need of further evidence, either bringing the case within section 2(1), or capable of inducing a reasonable jury to deny condemnation of the appropriation as dishonest, or capable of raising a doubt as to whether D knew that others would regard his conduct as dishonest.

Background to the Ghosh questions

2–129   *The first question.* The first of the *Ghosh* questions derives from the earlier Court of Appeal decision in *Feely*,[30] in which it was held that, the word "dishonestly" being "an ordinary word of the English language" which is "in common use," the jury do not need the help of the judge in its application.[31] They should simply decide whether an appropriation was dishonest by applying "the current standards of ordinary decent people."[32] For this purpose, of course, the jury may be taken to represent ordinary decent standards; they are in effect being invited, and may be expressly invited,[33] to apply their own standards.

In *Feely* itself D, the manager of a betting shop, took about £30 from his employers' safe. He left no IOU or other record of the transaction and did not tell his employers. His defence, when charged with theft, was that he would have repaid the money. The trial judge directed the jury that this

---

[29] *Roberts* (1987) 84 Cr.App.R. 117 (handling); *Price* (1989) 90 Cr.App.R. 409 (deception offences); *Squire* [1990] Crim.L.R. 341 (conspiracy to defraud); and see *Hagan* [1985] Crim.L.R. 598 (intent to defraud).

[30] [1973] Q.B. 530.

[31] *Ibid*. at 537–538; citing in support Lord Reid in *Brutus* v. *Cozens* [1973] A.C. 854 at 861: "The meaning of an ordinary word of the English language is not a question of law"—but for the "decline and fall" of this largely "ineffectual" dictum, see D. W. Elliott [1989] Crim.L.R. 323.

[32] In *Ghosh* "ordinary decent people" became "reasonable and honest people." Arlidge and Parry, *Fraud*, para. 1.24, are tempted by, but seem in the end to reject, the possibility that "honest" people are a narrower category than "ordinary" people. Surely the reference in *Ghosh* to "honest" people is hopelessly circular and must be a slip.

[33] See, for example, the direction in *Green and Greenstein* (1975) 61 Cr.App.R. 296 at 301, approved by the Court of Appeal; *McIvor* (1981) 74 Cr.App.R. 74 at 78.

commonplace defence was no defence in law. If D did not believe that his employers would have consented to his taking the money (and they had in fact prohibited the practice of borrowing from the till), he was guilty of theft even if he intended to repay, however soon, and had the means to do so. This was held to be a misdirection. Whether D had acted dishonestly was for the jury to say. D's conviction was quashed.

The second question. It is one thing to refer to the tribunal of fact the   **2–130** question whether the defendant's conduct was dishonest and therefore theft, rather than resolving the matter as a question of law. It would be quite another thing to refer the question to the defendant himself! Yet for a time it appeared that the courts were flirting even with this approach. There were statements in some judgments to the effect that if, at the time of his act, D may have believed that he was acting honestly, he would be entitled to an acquittal.[34] On this basis, a jury would seem to be required to prefer D's code of conduct to their own where the two appear to differ.

Perhaps these statements were merely badly expressed. On their face, however, they threatened rather serious consequences for the law of theft and other offences of dishonesty. A subsequent attempt by the Court of Appeal to clarify the law having proved unsuccessful,[35] the same court in *Ghosh* reasserted the authority of the principle in *Feely*, but (for a reason to be mentioned below[36]) added for the jury's consideration the second question, referring not to D's view of the honesty of his conduct but to his knowledge of the view that would be taken by "ordinary people."

Objections to the two questions[37]

The decisions in *Feely* and *Ghosh* have been regretted by most com-   **2–131** mentators. The objections to them include the following:

(i) *Feely*.[38] The *Feely* principle depends upon two related assumptions. One is that "dishonestly," because it is an "ordinary word," has an agreed range of meaning that the jury will identify without judicial help. But it is not true that all speakers of a language will necessarily share the same sense of the application or non-application of an "ordinary word" in a particular context. Even judges, a relatively homogeneous group of uniformly high

---

[34] See *Boggeln* v. *Williams* (1978) 67 Cr.App.R. 50 at 54; *Landy* (1981) 72 Cr.App.R. 237 at 247; and compare, before *Feely*, a dictum in *Gilks* (1972) 56 Cr.App.R. 734 at 738.

[35] *McIvor* (1981) 74 Cr.App.R. 74. (An additional problem deriving from *Landy*, above, and *McIvor* was an unsupportable discrepancy between conspiracy to defraud and theft in respect of the test for dishonesty. This discrepancy was eliminated by *Ghosh* [1982] Q.B. 1053.)

[36] § 2–133.

[37] See, more fully, [1985] Crim.L.R. 341.

[38] The most elaborate critiques of *Feely* are those of the Supreme Court of Victoria in *Salvo* [1980] V.R. 401, *Bonollo* [1981] V.R. 633, and *Brow, ibid.* 783. For academic comment, see Williams, *Textbook*, p. 725; Smith, *Theft*, para. 127; D. W. Elliott [1976] Crim.L.R. 707; Griew, *Dishonesty and the Jury* (Leicester U.P., 1974). The critics are themselves criticised, and the allocation of the dishonesty issue to the jury is vigorously defended, by Richard Tur in A. Phillips Griffiths (ed.), *Philosophy and Practice* (C.U.P., 1985), pp. 75–96.

linguistic competence, have been known to differ on the application of the epithet "dishonest" in a marginal case.[39] The other assumption is that there are shared community standards (the "standards of ordinary decent people"—that is, the jury[40]) for application in borderline as well as in clear cases. If this is not just another way of expressing the notion that people will agree upon the use of ordinary words, it can be nothing less than the assumption that "ordinary decent people," set to work by the word "dishonestly," will agree on the range of conduct that ought to be condemned as offences. To this there is the obvious objection that it ignores the great diversity of our very mixed society in terms of age, class, moral outlook and cultural background. The *Feely* question must tend, rather, to promote disagreement within individual juries and inconsistency of decision between different juries.

2–132 The above difficulties derive from a refusal to acknowledge that the dishonesty issue is one of law. The jury must, of course, find the facts: what did the defendant do? and with what possible intention, belief or other state of mind that is relevant within the law of the offence charged? It is the function of the law, it is submitted, to say whether so behaving, with such a state of mind, is dishonest and therefore an offence. This appears to have been the previous law.[41] In proposing the new form of the law, the Committee did casually refer to dishonesty as "something which laymen can easily recognise when they see it"[42]; but it is difficult to find warrant, either in the *Eighth Report* read as a whole or in a comparison of the form of the legislation with what it replaced, for the supposition that a revolution such as *Feely* effected was intended by the substitution of the word "dishonestly" for the word "fraudulently" which had occurred in the definition of larceny.[43]

2–133 (ii) *Ghosh*.[44] The question added by *Ghosh* (must D have realised that what he was doing was dishonest according to the ordinary standards being applied by the jury?[45]) is an even more dramatic innovation than the *Feely* question. It derives from a misapplication of the notion of a "state of mind." The Court of Appeal asserted that proof of dishonesty requires reference to D's state of mind. So, on any view, it undoubtedly does whenever there is any evidence suggesting that D's appropriation of P's property may not have been dishonest. For there must then be a finding as to whether he may have

---

[39] *Sinclair* v. *Neighbour* [1967] 2 Q.B. 279.
[40] There is a substantial literature on the dishonesty of "ordinary decent people"; see, *e.g.* J. Ditton, *Part-Time Crime*; S. Henry, *The Hidden Economy*. Are all jurors truly to apply their own standards?
[41] The relevant modern cases on larceny were *Williams* [1953] Q.B. 660; *Cockburn* (1967) 52 Cr.App.R. 134. For a valuable article just before the decision in *Feely*, see D. W. Elliott [1972] Crim.L.R. 625.
[42] *Eighth Report*, para. 39.
[43] See further [1985] Crim.L.R. 341 at 349. But see Glanville Williams (1985) 5 L.S. 183 at 188–189, seeming to reveal that the Committee did indeed expect that the jury might be left without guidance.
[44] See Smith, *Theft*, para. 128; Williams, *Textbook*, p. 728.
[45] Note: (a) the circularity of this question as part of a test for dishonesty; (b) the oddity of the question as satirised by J. R. Spencer [1982] C.L.J. 224: "What the jury thinks the defendant thought the jury would have thought."

acted with a belief or intention that might tend to negative dishonesty. May he (as he claims) have believed that he had a right to take the property or intended to repay the money taken? D's relevant state of mind once being found, however, the only question that should remain to be answered is whether section 2(1) applies or (if not) whether the jury's sense of ordinary standards makes D's conduct with that state of mind dishonest. This is a question, not as to what state of mind D had, but as to how his state of mind is to be characterised. Dishonesty is not itself a "state of mind" in the same sense that belief as to a fact or intention as to future action is a "state of mind."[46]

The Court of Appeal thought that the need to refer to D's "state of mind" entailed the asking of the second jury question as to D's understanding of what others would think dishonest. There is, with respect, a serious error in the court's reasoning at this point.[47] The error is clear to see when the court discusses the supposed case of a visitor from a country where public transport is free. He travels on a bus without paying. Does he do so dishonestly? The court says that "his conduct, judged objectively by what he has done, is dishonest." But this cannot be right. What the jury should judge by "ordinary standards" must be D's conduct as a whole—that is, his act in the context of the state of mind with which he did it.[48] In the case put, therefore, the jury will first have found that D believed (or may have believed) public transport to be free. Having so found, they can hardly declare his conduct dishonest. His state of mind has thus been taken into account in the only way necessary. The court, however, having mistakenly declared him dishonest when "judged objectively," has to introduce a further "subjective" element to rescue him. Hence the second question.

(iii) *Practical objection.* The Court of Appeal decisions on the dishonesty **2–134** issue must have an important practical bearing on the administration of the criminal law. A different approach to the issue might make clear that given conduct was dishonest as a matter of law, and such clarity would tend to determine cases without need for a trial. *Feely* and *Ghosh*, however, provide two bases upon which it may be worth a defendant's while to take his chance with a jury.[49] He may advance a "state of mind" which would before *Feely* have offered no defence at all. Or he may claim not to have realised that others would condemn his actions. Such claims must multiply and lengthen trials; and it must be in the interests of some defendants to introduce as much evidence as possible on the dishonesty issue in order to obfuscate it. The

---

[46] The phrase "state of mind" has caused trouble in this context before: see the 4th edition of this book at § 2–88a.
[47] [1982] Q.B. 1053 at 1063. The error is elaborately demonstrated by Kenneth Campbell [1984] C.L.J. 349.
[48] Physical acts are not in themselves honest or dishonest. The point is implicit in *Feely* itself; see, *e.g.* [1973] Q.B. 530 at 541.
[49] He is entitled to have the matter determined by the jury, however unreasonable an answer favourable to him would be: *D.P.P.* v. *Stonehouse* [1978] A.C. 55, for the general principle; and see *Clemo* (*Note*) [1973] R.T.R. 176; *Painter* [1983] Crim.L.R. 189. But an appeal based on an omission to leave the issue to the jury may fail on the ground that the jury could not but have found dishonesty: *e.g. Melwani* [1989] Crim.L.R. 565. An unreasonable acquittal by magistrates might be upset by the Divisional Court: *Bracegirdle* v. *Oxley* [1947] K.B. 349.

consequences in terms of expense and of increased difficulty for the jury, not to speak of the danger of unsatisfactory outcomes, are surely enough in themselves to raise serious doubts about the present state of the law.[50]

Dishonesty, laudable motive and necessity

2–135   A person charged with theft may claim that he acted with a laudable motive—perhaps in the interests of a moral or political crusade. But his own view of the justifiability of his conduct cannot secure an acquittal. Suppose, however, that he claims that his conviction was so passionately held that he believed "ordinary decent" members of society would regard his conduct as proper, even laudable. If this is treated as a claim to have been ignorant that the conduct was "dishonest" by ordinary standards, and if the jury think (as exceptionally they might) that the claim may be true, the second *Ghosh* question[51] produces an acquittal. This must be unacceptable; Robin Hood must be a thief even if he thinks that the whole of the right-thinking world is on his side.[52]

What if the jury themselves take the view that D's motive was morally praiseworthy, or that it so far justified his act that it ought not to be a crime? Good motive being in principle irrelevant, it ought not to be allowed in by permitting the limiting adverb "dishonestly" an unlimited function. It should be open to the court to say that a particular motive said to have inspired D's conduct cannot protect it from the label "dishonest." Even a claim to have acted from necessity (to save human life, perhaps) is not, it is thought, properly to be classified as a claim to have acted "honestly." If there is evidence that D was forced by "duress of circumstances" to appropriate P's property, he should be entitled to an acquittal of theft if he satisfies—but only if, and only because,[53] he satisfies—the conditions of the general defence now apparently recognised under that name.[54]

The solution, then, to the problems raised in both of the preceding paragraphs may be simply to say that matters of justification and excuse have nothing to do with the issue of dishonesty.

The dishonesty issue as one of law

2–136   Section 2(1) declares some appropriations to be not dishonest as a matter of law. Moreover, the judgment in *Feely*[55] itself suggests that there are limits

---

[50] Especially in fraud cases, to which equally the Court of Appeal decisions apply: *Ghosh* [1982] Q.B. 1053 at 1059 (deception offences; conspiracy to defraud); *Lockwood* [1986] Crim.L.R. 244 (fraudulent trading). See Fraud Trials Committee Report (H.M.S.O., 1986), paras. 3.4–3.8, 3.18 (calling for law reform consideration), and 8.16.
[51] Above, § 2–128.
[52] Smith, *Theft*, para. 128.
[53] This, of course, is without prejudice to D's possible, but distinct, claim that he believed that P would consent if he knew of the situation of necessity: see s.2(1)(*b*), above, § 2–124.
[54] See *Conway* [1989] Q.B. 290; *Martin* (1988) 88 Cr.App.R. 343. Contrast the view of the Law Commission in *Report on Defences of General Application* (Law Com. No. 83), para. 4.5, that "proof of dishonesty in theft may perhaps be negatived if, although the defendant knows an appropriation is without the owner's consent, he takes the property to avoid a greater evil, for example, to save life"; and, less tentatively, at para. 4.17: "Discussion of the defence [*sc.* of necessity] in the context of theft has now been settled by the terms of the Theft Act 1968."
[55] Above, § 2–129.

to the principle that in other cases it is a question for the tribunal of fact whether the conduct charged was dishonest. The case is put of a person acting in a way "to which no one would, or could reasonably, attach moral obloquy."[56] To hold the case to be theft, it is said, "would tend to bring the law into contempt." The point is generalised: "a taking to which no moral obloquy can reasonably attach is not within the concept of stealing . . . under the Theft Act 1968."[57] It appears to be proper, therefore, to instruct a jury that the meaning of the word "dishonestly" is limited at least to this extent as a matter of law. And a direction to acquit is surely contemplated in the case put.

The limiting function of the word "dishonestly" in offences under the **2–137** Theft Acts is not at present a matter of law except to the extent stated in the preceding paragraph. What is submitted here, however, is that the law should play a much more active role in identifying the scope of dishonesty offences. In the light of the case law, it is hardly open to the Court of Appeal to bring this about; but the House of Lords could do so. It might, for example, hold that the word "dishonestly" in the definition of an offence operates to exclude from the scope of the offence only cases of claim of right (as well as any, or any other, cases expressly excluded by statute)[58]; or only such cases and those involving no "moral obloquy." Another suggestion has been that in the case of theft "dishonestly" might be interpreted to mean "knowing that the appropriation will or may be detrimental to the interests of the owner in a significant practical way"[59]—a suggestion that could be modified to suit the needs of other offences. Alternatively (and preferably) this suggestion might be taken up by Parliament as a basis of remedial legislation.[60]

7. THEFT OF THINGS IN ACTION AND OTHER INTANGIBLE PROPERTY

Intangible property generally

Any kind of property can be the subject of theft. But the ways in which **2–138** different kinds of intangible property can be stolen are variously limited by the lack of available modes of appropriation (it is not possible to run away with a bank balance or physically to destroy a copyright) and, more seriously, by the difficulty of depriving of the property the person to whom it belongs. Nevertheless, anyone—such as a trustee, co-owner or agent for sale—who has the power to dispose of property can steal that property by a

---

[56] The case is "that of a manager of a shop who, having been told that under no circumstances was he to take money from the till for his own purposes, took 40p from it, having no small change himself, to pay for a taxi hired by his wife who had arrived at the shop saying that she only had a £5 note which the cabby could not change."
[57] [1973] Q.B. 530 at 539.
[58] This is the tendency of the Victorian decisions referred to at n. 38, above.
[59] Per McGarvie J. in *Bonollo* [1981] V.R. 633 at 656; Smith, *Theft*, para. 129.
[60] D. W. Elliott [1982] Crim.L.R. 395, suggesting that dishonesty is "a dispensable concept." For competing draft provisions, see *ibid.* at 409–410; and Williams (1985) 5 L.S. 183 at 189.

disposition intended to defeat the interests of others to whom the property belongs.[61] Moreover, both the *Morris* interpretation of the definition of appropriation as including an assumption of any of the rights of an owner,[62] and a statutory softening of the requirement of an intention of permanently depriving the victim of the property,[63] do something to facilitate the theft of intangibles. These points are illustrated in a separate discussion, below, of the theft of bank credits.[64]

2–139 Theft of certain kinds of property may be impossible in the absence of a power to dispose of the property or to control its disposition. The point may be illustrated by reference to trade marks, copyright and trade secrets (assuming, for the sake of discussion, the last to be a species of "property"[65]):

(i) *Trade marks.* The obvious case to be considered is the dishonest infringement of a trade mark, as by using the mark upon goods of the same description as that to which it applies. This may be an appropriation—an assumption of the rights of the owner in the trade mark. Yet there can hardly be said to be an intention to deprive the owner of the trade mark itself.[66] The infringement is therefore no theft.

(ii) *Copyright.* If D publishes copies of P's literary work without P's licence to do so, he may popularly be said to "steal" the benefit of P's skill and labour. He may also be said to appropriate P's copyright in the work by assuming one of P's exclusive rights, as copyright owner, in it.[67] Even so, he does not do so with the effect, or the intention, of depriving P of the copyright and so does not steal.[68]

(iii) *Trade secrets.* Even if trade secrets were "property," they would be difficult to steal. No doubt we may in a loose sense say that D "appropriates" P's secret if he dishonestly acquires the knowledge that P has a right to preserve to himself or makes use of the knowledge that P alone has the right to use. But D does not thereby *deprive* P of his knowledge: he deprives him only of an advantage attaching to it—its exclusiveness. On that analysis the thing appropriated is not the same as that of which P is deprived; but the basic definition of theft requires that it shall be ("appropriates property . . . with the intention of depriving [P] of it"). The conclusion must be that trade secrets cannot in general be stolen. But exceptional situations might be

---

[61] See above, § 2–25; *Attorney-General of Hong Kong* v. *Nai-keung* (1987) 86 Cr.App.R. 174.
[62] See above, § 2–65.
[63] s.6: see above, § 2–103.
[64] §§ 2–145, 2–150.
[65] Which they almost certainly are not: see above, § 2–19.
[66] D can hardly be said to intend "to treat the thing as his own *to dispose of*"; so s.6(1) should not affect this case; but *cf.* below, 2–150.
[67] Copyright, Designs and Patents Act 1988, ss.1(1), 2(1).
[68] He may be guilty of an offence under the Copyright, Designs and Patents Act 1988, s.107.

envisaged. For instance, D seduces from P's employment a chemist, Q, who alone knows a formula developed by Q for P; and D elicits from Q both the formula and the promise to keep it secret from P. This would satisfy the definition of theft, if secrets were property.[69]

Theft of bank credits[70]

A theft charge cannot be made out by proving that a company is so many   **2–140** millions of pounds worse off as the result of the depredations of, say, a dishonest director or accountant. It must be shown that, with the required intention, he appropriated particular property belonging to the company.[71] English law possesses no widely-defined general offence of fraud.[72] So, since large frauds within organisations almost inevitably involve the abuse of intangible assets such as bank accounts, the concept of the appropriation of such assets must be capable of flexible exploitation if the law of theft is to make an adequate contribution to the control of serious fraud. The topic now to be examined is plainly of the first importance.

Bank credits as "property belonging to another"

"Property." When a bank account is in credit, the account holder has   **2–141** "property" in the form of a thing in action—a claim available against the bank as his debtor.[73] If he has an enforceable overdraft arrangement with the bank, this too, it has been held, gives him "property" within the meaning of that word in the Theft Act so long as the overdraft facility has not been exhausted by drawings on the account.[74] At any time, however, when the account is in debit and no right to draw on it exists, the account holder has no relevant property capable of being stolen by abuse of the account.[75] It is plain that, when possible theft of a bank credit or overdraft facility is under consideration, careful examination of the banking relationship and of the history of the account in the relevant period may be necessary to establish whether there was property available to steal at the time of a suggested appropriation.[76]

D's account as property "belonging to another." Credit in an account may   **2–142** be capable of being stolen by an account holder himself if it is to be regarded as also "belonging to" another person by virtue of section 5. This will be the

---

[69] The oddity of acknowledging only such unlikely cases as theft is noted in *Stewart* v. *The Queen* (1988) 50 D.L.R. (4th) 1 at 14, as an argument against recognising confidential information as capable of being stolen.
[70] See further, [1986] Crim.L.R. 356.
[71] See above, § 2–20.
[72] See below, § 6–22.
[73] See above, § 2–11.
[74] *Kohn* (1979) 69 Cr.App.R. 395.
[75] *Ibid.* at 408. Nor can there be theft of a merely contingent liability: *Doole* [1985] Crim.L.R. 450.
[76] See [1986] Crim.L.R. at 359–360.

case if D and P have a joint account upon which D may draw only for the common purposes of himself and P[77]; if the account is one which D holds or controls as a trustee[78]; if the account, wholly or in part, represents property received by D which he is obliged to retain as a distinct fund and to apply only for the purposes of the persons from or on account of whom he received it[79]; or if the credit derives from an erroneous transfer of funds by P to D's account, or from a payment by D into his account of funds mistakenly paid to him by P.[80]

Appropriation of bank credits

2–143   *Some elementary background principles.* A legitimate dealing with a bank credit takes place when the bank pays cash or transfers funds on the instructions (or "mandate") of the account holder, or one acting with his authority, and debits the account accordingly. If an instruction given to the bank does not constitute a mandate upon which the bank is entitled to act by making a payment against the account, a debiting of the account on the strength of that instruction is nugatory: the bank will be obliged to restore the debit or (to put it another way) the bank continues to be its customer's debtor to the same extent as before.

A cheque issued by a bank's customer (the drawer) in favour of a third party (the payee) is an instruction by the drawer to the bank to pay to the payee (or subsequent holder) the amount for which the cheque is drawn. Payment of a crossed cheque must be to a bank; only if the cheque is uncrossed may payment be in cash. The drawing of a cheque in favour of a payee has no legal consequences until the cheque is delivered to the payee. When it is so delivered, the drawer becomes bound to honour the cheque if the bank fails to do so. But the issue of the cheque gives the payee no right against the drawer's bank; nothing in the transaction operates as an assignment to the payee of the debt to the drawer represented by the credit in his account.[81]

2–144   *Appropriation by authorised signatory.* In the seminal case of *Kohn*,[82] D was a company director who had authority to issue cheques for company purposes. He improperly issued cheques upon the company's account for his own purposes. The Court of Appeal upheld convictions of theft in respect, in the case of each cheque,[83] of the credit (or the overdraft facility) available to the company and appropriated by D. The court accepted the analysis of this kind of transaction offered in previous editions of this book—namely, that D

---

[77] Credit in the account "belongs to" P: s.5(1).
[78] Credit in the account "belongs to" the beneficiaries or to anyone having a right to enforce the trust: s.5(1)(2).
[79] Credit in the account "belongs to" those persons: s.5(3).
[80] For the application of s.5(4) to the case of credit got by mistake, see above, § 2–40.
[81] Bills of Exchange Act 1882, s.53(1).
[82] (1979) 69 Cr.App.R. 395.
[83] Except in one case, where the account was overdrawn beyond the agreed limit, so that there was no property to appropriate: see above, text at n. 75.

appropriates the debt owed by the bank, or part of it, by causing the company's credit balance to be diminished or at least taking the risk of such diminution. The case was said to be analogous to the theft of a chattel by destruction. This analysis, however, now appears not to be adequate, for two reasons. First, it does not commit itself to a view as to when the appropriation takes place—whether on the debiting of the account ("diminution") or on the issue of the cheque ("taking the risk of . . . diminution"). This question is discussed below.[84] Secondly, the analysis is inadequate for the case of an act giving the bank no right to debit the account.

Appropriation by act giving the bank no mandate. In *Chan Man-sin* v. *R.*[85]   **2–145**
the accountant of two companies, by using forged cheques, withdrew some millions of Hong Kong dollars from the bank accounts of the companies. His appeal to the Judicial Committee of the Privy Council against theft convictions[86] was based upon the undoubted fact that, as between the companies and their banks, the transactions were nullities; the banks could not sustain debits to the companies' accounts that were based on forgeries; there could be no "diminution" of the things in action said to have been stolen. The Judicial Committee nevertheless held that the appellant had appropriated the things in action: "[a]ny assumption of the rights of an owner amounts to an appropriation" (section 3(1)); this provision does not require the assumption of all the rights of an owner[87]; it was enough that the appellant had assumed the right of the companies as owners of the accounts to draw upon them. This reasoning[88] must be taken to have replaced that adopted in *Kohn*.

When and where does the theft occur? This question may be crucial in   **2–146**
relation to jurisdiction or extradition.
The Judicial Committee left open in *Chan Man-sin* the question whether theft is complete on the doing of the acts which will result in the debiting of the bank account or only when the account is actually debited.[89] Once it is decided, however, that the appropriation consists of D's assumption of the owner's right to deal with the account, the conclusion seems inevitable that theft is complete when he does the act that constitutes that assumption. The Divisional Court subsequently so held in *Governor of Pentonville Prison, ex p. Osman.*[90] It was alleged in that case that D, in Hong Kong, had transmitted a telex message conveying an instruction to a bank in the United States relating to an account held at that bank. The question (arising under the Fugitive Offenders Act 1967[91]) was whether the act of sending this message

[84] § 2–146.
[85] (1987) 86 Cr.App.R. 303.
[86] Under the Theft Ordinance (Hong Kong), identical in relevant respects to the 1968 Act.
[87] Applying the equivalent of s.3(1), as interpreted in *Morris* [1984] A.C. 320 (above, § 2–65).
[88] Applied by the Court of Appeal shortly before in *Wille* (1988) 86 Cr.App.R. 296.
[89] (1987) 86 Cr.App.R. 303 at 306. See also *Kohn* (1979) 69 Cr.App.R. 395 at 407 (*obiter*); *Doole* [1985] Crim.L.R. 450; *Navvabi* (1986) 83 Cr.App.R. 271 at 276.
[90] (1988) 90 Cr.App.R. 281 at 296–297.
[91] Repealed and replaced by the Extradition Act 1989.

could constitute a theft, committed in Hong Kong, of the credit in that account. It was held that it could.

A similar point (affecting jurisdiction) had arisen earlier in *Tomsett*.[92] In that case the Court of Appeal had rejected an argument that an agreement to send a telex instruction from England to New York in relation to funds temporarily on deposit there might found a conspiracy to steal in England because the funds in question were those of an English company. The court applied the principle that an appropriation, and therefore theft, of property prima facie occurs where the property is situated, and a debt is situated where the debtor is—in that case New York. But the court in *Osman* (consisting of two of the three judges who had decided *Tomsett*) did not regard *Tomsett* as binding on it on the question whether the typing of the telex message was itself an appropriation, for it had not been argued in the earlier case that it was.

2–147   Where D, for his own purposes, draws a cheque on P's account in favour of E (whether by forging P's signature or by abuse of his own status as authorised signatory), his theft of credit in the account appears to be complete when he delivers the cheque to E. If he draws a cheque in his own favour, language used in *Chan Man-sin*[93] seems to imply an understandable assumption that theft will occur at the earliest when he presents the cheque for payment or negotiates it to a third party.

2–148   *An act continuing until account debited?* The conclusion that theft of P's bank credit is complete when D assumes any right of an owner in it, as by delivering to a payee a cheque drawn upon it or sending to the bank an instruction relating to it, may exceptionally give rise to a serious practical problem. It could require an investigation of the state of the account at the moment when D delivered the cheque or sent the instruction. For if the account were then overdrawn (beyond any agreed limit), there will have been no relevant property belonging to P for D to steal. Yet it may be difficult or impossible to show at what time D's relevant act (*e.g.* the issue of a post-dated cheque) took place. This problem would not arise if the time of the theft were the time of the debiting of the account; for there need be no doubt about the state of the account at that time.[94] A possible solution, not excluded by the cases, is to treat D's act as continuing (as an appropriation or potential appropriation) until the account is debited. Whenever the account is first in credit up to that time, the act would take effect as an appropriation of the property then existing. On that view it would be sufficient, in order to prove that a theft has occurred, to show that the account was in credit at the time of the debiting if not before.

If theft of a bank credit can continue from the doing of the appropriative act in one country to the debiting of the account in another, the theft may be located in both countries, with important consequences for questions of jurisdiction and extradition.

[92] [1985] Crim.L.R. 369.
[93] (1987) 86 Cr.App.R. at 306.
[94] See *Navvabi* (1986) 83 Cr.App.R. 271 at 276.

The intention of permanently depriving P of the bank credit

D's act a mandate on which bank can act. Where D's dishonest act in   **2–149**
dealing with P's bank account is an effective mandate entitling the bank to
debit the account, so that it will result, in the ordinary course of events, in a
real diminution of the credit in the account (or of P's right to draw on the
account), there is no difficulty about asserting that D intends, to that extent,
to deprive P permanently of that credit (or right).[95]

D's act not a valid mandate. Where, however, D's act is not a mandate   **2–150**
upon which the bank is entitled to act, P's property—his right against the
bank—will in law be unaffected by the transaction. If D knows this, it may
safely be said that he does not intend P to lose his legal right; in the language
of section 6(1)), he does not "[mean P] to lose the thing itself." Even so, he
would, according to that provision, be regarded as intending to deprive P
permanently of his property if his intention were "to treat the thing as his
own to dispose of regardless of [P's] rights." Section 6(1) was invoked by the
Judicial Committee in *Chan Man-sin* v. *Attorney-General of Hong Kong*,[96] a
case of forged cheques, as the basis for summarily dismissing the argument
that the necessary intention cannot have been present. But the Board
justified reliance on the section by observing only that "the appellant was
purporting to *deal with* the companies' property without regard to their
rights."[97] This is no doubt so; but it is not clear how the appellant can be said
to have intended to treat "the thing itself" (P's strict legal right) as his own
"to dispose of". So the argument employed in *Chan Man-sin* may be inadequate. Still, it is submitted that it would be "[going] too far" to say that "unless
the debit to the account can be sustained against the customer there can . . .
be no theft."[98] When goods are stolen (otherwise than by an act that destroys
them) the owner is not deprived of his absolute interest in them but only of
their enjoyment. A bank credit, similarly, may be affected by an act that is
not a mandate to the bank. For so long as D's fraud remains undiscovered
the debit to the account that results from it will not be corrected and P will in
a practical sense be deprived of his asset. D may reasonably be presumed to
intend that his fraud should remain undetected, and therefore that the
account will be permanently debited. The doubtful case, turning on the
correctness of the application of section 6(1), must be that in which it
appears that D intended to reveal his fraud in due course or knew that it was
bound to be discovered.[99]

---

[95] Even if he intends to repay P an equivalent amount or to restore the debited sum to the
account: see above, § 2–99.

[96] (1987) 86 Cr.App.R. 303 at 306.

[97] Emphasis supplied.

[98] The language of the Court of Appeal in *Doole* [1985] Crim.L.R. 450 (transcript on LEXIS).
See Arlidge and Parry, *Fraud*, para. 3.05.

[99] When the fraud is discovered, the loser turns out to be the bank. But there is no theft from the
bank: *Navvabi* (1986) 83 Cr.App.R. 271; above, § 2–20. Other offences will commonly be
available: *e.g.* theft of cheque; forgery; false accounting; conspiracy to defraud (if two or
more are involved). The law of theft nevertheless needs amending to cater more clearly for
this kind of case.

8. INFORMATIONS AND INDICTMENTS

One offence per count or information

2–151   Rule 1(2) of the Indictment Rules 1971 provides:

"Where more than one offence is charged in an indictment, the statement
and particulars of each offence shall be set out in a separate paragraph
called a count."

Rule 12 of the Magistrates' Courts Rules 1981 provides that "a magistrates' court shall not proceed to the trial of an information that charges
more than one offence."[1]

Problems can arise in applying these rules where a person is alleged to
have stolen a number of things on different occasions, or at different times
and places on the same occasion; or where he is alleged to have stolen an
amount of money or a number of items during a certain period, but the time
or times at which he stole this or that amount or item cannot be demonstrated. It is clear that too narrow or technical a conception of an "offence"
for the purpose of the rules quoted above could have serious consequences
for the efficient prosecution of such cases. The courts have in fact avoided a
restrictive view. They have tended rather to facilitate prosecution and
conviction by the use of a number of concepts and devices.

One charge for a single "activity"

2–152   In *Wilson*,[2] an indictment for shoplifting contained two counts, among
others, each of which related to D's conduct in a different store. In one count
he was alleged to have stolen records and after-shave lotion from Boots; in
the other clothes of various kinds, electrical switches and a cassette tape
from Debenhams. The evidence showed that in each of these stores the
articles came from different "departments." The Court of Appeal applied a
principle recently stated in the Divisional Court in relation to informations,[3]
subsequently applied to indictments by the Court of Appeal,[4] and approved
in the House of Lords in these terms: "it will often be legitimate to bring a
single charge in respect of . . . one activity even though that activity may
involve more than one act."[5] The question whether the charge relates to one
offence or to more than one is to be determined "by applying common sense
and by deciding what is fair in the circumstances"[6]; it is "a question of fact

---

[1] This rule is of reduced importance since the House of Lords decided that a magistrates' court
may, if it is fair to do so, try two or more informations together without the consent of the
defendant: *Chief Constable of Norfolk* v. *Clayton* [1983] 2 A.C. 473.
[2] (1979) 69 Cr.App.R. 83.
[3] *Jemmison* v. *Priddle* [1972] 1 Q.B. 489, *per* Lord Widgery C.J. at 495; compare *Cullen* v.
Jardine [1985] Crim.L.R. 668.
[4] *Jones* (1974) 59 Cr.App.R. 120.
[5] *D.P.P.* v. *Merriman* [1973] A.C. 584, *per* Lord Morris of Borth-y-Gest at 593 (and see *per*
Lord Diplock at 607).
[6] *Ibid.*

and degree."[7] D's convictions on the two counts were upheld. Neither count, in the Court of Appeal's view, charged more than one offence, either on its face or in the light of the evidence. The decision may be felt to be a generous but realistic application of the notion of a single "activity."[8] In another case the court would even have been prepared if necessary to apply the "activity" test to sanction a single theft charge where a bogus haulage contractor loaded greengrocery in three different parts of London for carriage on the instructions of the same principal.[9]

One charge for a "continuous" offence

A number of cases decided before the Indictments Act 1915 concerned, respectively, mining operations conducted continuously over four years, involving the taking of coal belonging to many persons[10]; the cutting of eight trees with intent to steal them during a tree-felling operation carried out in a particular season[11]; the abstraction of gas from a main, by-passing the meter, day after day for several years[12]; and pilfering identified articles from an employer, the articles being found in the accused's possession on the day named in the indictment as that of the offence.[13] In each of these cases the course of conduct was held to constitute a "continuous taking." There is no reason to doubt that a correspondingly broad view would now be taken of similar facts, so as to permit the charging of a simple "continuous" offence. **2–153**

One charge for a "general deficiency"

A single count is convenient (indeed often unavoidable) in another familiar kind of case—namely, where a servant or agent, liable to account to his principal for money received or held for the principal, is found to have less of the principal's money in his hands than he should have, but where the dishonest appropriations causing the deficiency cannot be individually demonstrated. In such cases it was held under the Larceny Act 1916 that a count charging theft, embezzlement or fraudulent conversion of a general deficiency might be framed—that is, a count alleging that on a day between specified dates, D stole (etc.) £x (*i.e.* the total amount of the deficiency). A conviction on such a count was justified by evidence satisfying the jury that on some unknown day between the specified dates D did steal (etc.) some **2–154**

---

[7] (1979) 69 Cr.App.R. at 88. See also *Heaton* v. *Costello* [1984] Crim.L.R. 485 (switching price labels on one article and smuggling another through the check-out may be a single activity).
[8] The court found "not clear at all" the facts of *Ballysingh* (1953) 37 Cr.App.R. 28, where a count charging theft from (as the evidence showed) several "departments" of a store was regarded as defective. They appeared to contemplate that thefts from different departments of a large store like Harrods might not necessarily constitute a single activity (69 Cr.App.R. at 88). The size and layout of the stores in *Wilson* itself are not clear from the report.
[9] *Skipp* [1975] Crim.L.R. 114.
[10] *Bleasdale* (1848) 2 Car. & K. 765.
[11] *Shepherd* (1868) L.R. 1 C.C.R. 118.
[12] *Firth* (1869) L.R. 1 C.C.R. 173.
[13] *Henwood* (1870) 11 Cox 526.

part at least of the deficiency.[14] There can be no doubt that a similar count charging theft of a general deficiency is proper today.

Conviction based on defective indictment

2–155   A summary conviction obtained upon an information that is bad for duplicity must be quashed if challenged; the magistrates' court had no jurisdiction to try the information.[15] But on appeal against conviction on indictment it may be held that, although strictly the indictment was defective, no miscarriage of justice has occurred—the defendant not having been prejudiced in his defence by the form of the indictment[16] or his counsel having refrained from objection at the trial.[17] The proviso to section 2(1) of the Criminal Appeal Act 1968 may be applied and the appeal dismissed.

Theft of part or whole of a collection or quantity

2–156   On a charge of stealing several specific items there may be a conviction of stealing some of them if theft of them all is not proved.[18] The same principle should apply if what is charged is theft of an undifferentiated whole and theft of part only is proved. For theft of part of such a larger quantity is perfectly possible.[19] In *Gilks*,[20] for instance, P paid D £117.25 in cash when, as D realised, he should have paid £10.62. It was held that D was guilty of theft of £106.63.

If D is charged with stealing a part of a larger unit of property, he can be convicted as charged although it is proved that he stole the whole unit. Thus, in *Pilgram* v. *Rice-Smith*[21] D, a shop assistant, "sold" corned beef and bacon to her friend, at 83½p below the proper price. This was theft of all the meat, not merely, as the information alleged, of meat to the value of 83½p. It was held that that fact would not prevent a conviction on the information as laid.

9. ABSTRACTING OF ELECTRICITY; DISHONEST USE OF PUBLIC
TELECOMMUNICATION SYSTEM

2–157 The peculiar nature of electricity necessitates special provision for its dishonest use.[22] Section 13 provides:

---

[14] The modern cases were *Lawson* (1952) 36 Cr.App.R. 30; *Tomlin* [1954] 2 Q.B. 274; *Wilson* v. *Read* [1956] Crim.L.R. 418. See also *Balls* (1871) L.R. 1 C.C.R. 328. Compare *Cain* [1983] Crim.L.R. 802 (handling).
[15] See the terms of rule 12 (above, § 2–152).
[16] *Thompson* [1914] 2 K.B. 99.
[17] *Ballysingh* (1953) 37 Cr.App.R. 28.
[18] *Machent* v. *Quinn* [1970] 2 All E.R. 255.
[19] Smith, *Theft*, para. 113, citing *Tideswell* [1905] 2 K.B. 273.
[20] (1972) 56 Cr.App.R. 734. Compare *Levene* v. *Pearcey* [1976] Crim.L.R. 63 (below, § 7–03).
[21] (1977) 65 Cr.App.R. 142.
[22] Electricity is not "property" and cannot be stolen: *Low* v. *Blease* [1975] Crim.L.R. 513.

"A person who dishonestly uses without due authority, or dishonestly causes to be wasted or diverted, any electricity shall on conviction on indictment be liable to imprisonment for a term not exceeding five years."

The partial definition of "dishonestly" in section 2 is not made to apply for the purposes of this section (s.1(3)). So a person who believes that he has a legal right to use electricity, even without authority, or that the supplier or consumer concerned would consent if he knew of the use, is not on that account, *as a matter of law*, to be regarded as not dishonest (compare s.2(1)(*a*) and (*b*)). But it would be very unsatisfactory if a court or jury, although of the view that the defendant may have acted with such a belief, should nevertheless not acquit him in answer to the applicable question: was what he did dishonest by ordinary decent standards?[23]

Collins and Fox v. *Chief Constable of Merseyside*[24] concerned domestic use of electricity, unrecorded because the voltage link of the meter had been disconnected. It was said that dishonesty in such required knowledge of the non-recording and an intention that the consumption should not be paid for. This statement seems too generous to the defence. In theft, a person's appropriation of property "may be dishonest" notwithstanding that he is willing to pay for it (s.2(2)); and the prevailing approach to the dishonesty issue would make it a question for the jury whether particular use is not dishonest because it is intended to be paid for.[25]

A person who dishonestly uses a public telecommunication system with intent to avoid payment is guilty of an offence under section 48 of the British Telecommunications Act 1981.[26]

---

[23] *Ghosh* [1982] Q.B. 1053 (above, § 2–127); compare *Woolven* (1983) 77 Cr.App.R. 231 (below, § 7–66).
[24] [1988] Crim.L.R. 247.
[25] *Ghosh*, above.
[26] Replacing an offence (under the Post Office Act 1953) created by the Theft Act 1968, Sched. 2, Pt. I, para. 8.

Chapter 3

ROBBERY

1. DEFINITION

3–01   SECTION 8(2) creates two offences, both punishable on conviction on indictment with life imprisonment: robbery and assault with intent to rob. They are not triable summarily.[1]

Robbery is defined in section 8(1):

> "A person is guilty of robbery if he steals, and immediately before or at the time of doing so, and in order to do so, he uses force on any person or puts or seeks to put any person in fear of being then and there subjected to force."

Although this language (in the references to force and to putting in fear) contains pronounced echoes of the somewhat unclear and unsatisfactory offence that, together with certain aggravated offences, was latterly penalised by the Larceny Act 1916, it is not appropriate to resort to the old cases to elaborate the new definition; and the Court of Appeal, indeed, has firmly declined to flirt with "the old technicalities."[2]

2. THE DETAILS OF THE OFFENCE

"Steals"

3–02   A person is guilty of robbery only if he steals (or of an assault with intent to rob only if he intends to steal). So where D uses force or the threat of force in order to get from P property that he believes he is entitled to, he does not steal the property he obtains and the force or threat is not used in order to steal.[3] It is therefore a misdirection to instruct a jury on a charge of robbery that D can rely on a belief that he was entitled to deprive P of the property only if he also believed that he was entitled to get the property in the way he did.[4]

3–03   Where D has used force on P in order to steal from him but has failed to make himself master of P's property, it may be a nice question whether D

---

[1] Magistrates' Courts Act 1980, Sched. 1, para. 28(*a*).
[2] *Dawson* (1976) 64 Cr.App.R. 170.
[3] s.2(1)(*a*) (above, § 2–120).
[4] *Robinson* [1977] Crim.L.R. 173 (facts at § 2–123, above); compare *Skivington* [1968] 1 Q.B. 166. (He would need something like the latter belief to avoid a conviction of blackmail: s.21.)

has committed a robbery or only an assault with intent to rob. This depends on whether D's acts have amounted to an appropriation of any property or only to an attempted appropriation. This distinction has been discussed in the preceding chapter.[5] It was seen that the courts are not slow to find a complete appropriation. But in any case in which appropriation is at all doubtful it will be preferable to charge assault with intent to rob (if the assault can be proved) or attempted theft.[6]

"Uses force on" a person

The element of force in robbery, though expressed in simple language, involves questions that have called for judicial solution. They concern the meaning of "force" itself and the requirement that force be used "on [a] person."   **3–04**

"Force"

In *Dawson and James*[7] two men nudged P so that he lost his balance, and while he was off balance a third man stole his wallet. The Court of Appeal appears to have approved of the approach of the trial judge in leaving it to the jury to decide whether jostling having such an unbalancing effect amounted to the use of force. This was open to the objection that, the matter being one for uniform decision, the court should have held plainly and affirmatively on the question as a matter of law, which it certainly did not do. Subsequently, however, in *Clouden*,[8] the court interpreted *Dawson* as having so held. Perhaps what the court meant was that, as the court in *Dawson* regarded the conviction before it as not improper, it must be treated as having held that jostling causing P to lose his balance is "force." For if it is in one case, it must be in another. And presumably a jury should now be told so. If that is the position, the outcome is satisfactory.

"On [a] person"

Clouden also rather puzzlingly regarded *Dawson* as being an authority on a question with which it seems not to have been at all concerned. That is, the question whether force is used "on [a] person" within the meaning of section 8 when the force is used against property in order to detach the property from the person. The Committee said on this point: **3–05**

> "We should not regard mere snatching of property, such as a handbag, from an unresisting owner, as using force for the purpose of the definition, though it might be so if the owner resisted."[9]

[5] See § 2–69, discussing *Corcoran* v. *Anderton* (1980) 71 Cr.App.R. 104, a robbery case.
[6] For the possibility of a conviction of assault with intent to rob on an indictment for robbery, see above, § 1–16.
[7] (1976) 64 Cr.App.R. 170.
[8] [1987] Crim.L.R. 56; but this brief report does not reflect some aspects of the judgment (available on LEXIS) referred to in the text.
[9] *Eighth Report*, para. 65.

Just such a case was nevertheless held to be capable of being robbery in *Clouden*, where D approached P from behind and wrenched her handbag down and out of her grasp. *Dawson* was mysteriously said to "[make] it quite plain that . . . the distinctions which formerly undoubtedly existed[10] between force on the actual person and force on the property which in fact causes force on the person have all gone." Whether D was guilty of robbery had been properly left to the jury, who had simply been told the terms of the statutory definition.

This decision, whatever the manner in which it was achieved, certainly makes the law simpler than it was thought to be and renders academic any discussion based on the assumption that the deliberate drafting of the section gave effect to the Committee's intention.[11] Three comments may be made, however. First, this case in its turn presumably establishes that force on property "which in fact causes force on the person" is force "on [the] person." Once again the court was content with a direction that left the point to the jury; but once again it has no doubt decided a point of law. Secondly, it ought to be held that force is not used "on" P unless D realises that P may feel the effect of the force; for otherwise the very serious offence of robbery would be an offence of strict liability in respect of its distinguishing ingredient. Thirdly, and quite simply, it is respectfully thought that the decision in *Clouden* is wrong and that a simple handbag-snatching case ought to be treated as one of theft only and not of force "on [a] person."

"Puts or seeks to put . . . in fear"

3–06   It is sufficient if the thief "puts or seeks to put any person in fear of being then and there subjected to force."

Although a threat of future force will not suffice for robbery, one who obtains property by such a threat will normally be guilty both of theft and of blackmail, the essence of which is the making of an unwarranted demand with menaces.[12]

The putting in fear must be "in order to [steal]." So it seems that D must intend P to be put in fear and not merely do an act (to advance the theft) that in fact puts P in fear.

The words "or seeks to put . . . in fear" cover the case in which D intends to use the threat of force as a means of accomplishing his theft, but in which P remains either unconscious of the threat or unmoved by it. If there is no question but that D intended P to be fearful of the imminent use of force, there is no need for P to say, on D's trial, whether he was actually frightened—except as a matter possibly relevant to sentence.

"Any person"

3–07   There must of course be a victim of the theft (or, in the case of an assault

---

[10] That is, in the common law offence of robbery, as embodied in the Larceny Act 1916.
[11] See the 4th edition of this book, § 3–05.
[12] s.21. See Chap. 13.

with intent to rob, somebody who would be the victim of the theft proposed). But the victim of the use of force or of the putting or seeking to put in fear may be "any person"; he need not be the owner, possessor or custodian of the property (the person to whom the property "belongs"). D may use force on P, or put P in fear, in order to steal from P or from Q.

It follows that the force need not be used at the scene of the theft, so long as it is used immediately before or at the time of stealing and in order to do so. The Committee gives the example of force used on a signalman, and on no one else, in order to effect theft from a mail train.[13]

Immediately before or at the time of the stealing

The force, or the threat of force, must be used "immediately before or at **3–08** the time of" the stealing.

It was held in *Hale*[14] that a theft is not over and done with the very moment the thief lays hands on the property. Appropriation is a "continuous," not a momentary, act. Having already taken possession of a jewellery box in P's house, the accused men tied P up in order to ensure their escape; they thereby used force "at the time of" the theft and were guilty of robbery. It is in general, according to the Court of Appeal, a question for the jury whether the appropriation was finished before the force was used; but in *Hale* itself it was "a matter of common sense" that it was not. This decision goes far (happily, it is submitted) to undo the effect of the deliberate omission from section 8 of a reference to force, or the threat of force, used "immediately after" the stealing.[15]

Cases could arise in which it would be desirable to entertain a generous **3–09** conception of the period "immediately before" the stealing. Force might be used on a signalman or security guard some while before theft from a train or a warehouse actually takes place. It is thought that, if the force can realistically be regarded as an aspect of the physical accomplishment of the theft on the occasion of its occurrence, the court—or perhaps, in the light of *Hale*, the jury—will be justified in treating it as occurring "immediately before" the stealing.

"In order to" steal

The act of using force or of putting or seeking to put P in fear must be done **3–10** "in order to" steal. The mere fact that violence and theft occur as ingredients of the same transaction does not justify a conviction of robbery.[16] D may, for instance, attack P and steal from him a wallet that is shaken from his pocket by the violence. If the attack was not made for the purpose of theft, D cannot be convicted of robbery.[17]

[13] *Eighth Report*, para. 65.
[14] (1978) 68 Cr.App.R. 415.
[15] *Eighth Report*, para. 65. The words "or immediately after" appeared in the corresponding phrase in the old offence of robbery with violence: Larceny Act 1916, s.23(1)(*b*).
[16] See, *e.g. Shendley* [1970] Crim.L.R. 49; *Donaghy and Marshall* [1981] Crim.L.R. 644.
[17] On an indictment for robbery, D may be convicted of theft if force is not used, or not used at the appropriate time or in order to steal: see above, § 1–16.

In other respects the words "in order to do so" will be read fairly liberally as meaning not only "in order to accomplish the theft" but also "in order to do so more safely, more expeditiously," and so on. It will thus be robbery if force is used upon someone who might discover the theft and give the alarm.[18] So if D, immediately before or at the time of the theft, uses force on a jeweller at his home, to prevent him going to his shop where he would find D's confederates opening the safe, D and any confederates who are parties to this use of force will, it is submitted, be guilty of robbery if they succeed in stealing from the safe and of an assault with intent to rob if they do not.

Participation in robbery

3–11 Where two or more persons are together involved in a theft in which force or the threat of force is used, any of them, to be guilty of robbery, must himself either use or threaten force in order to steal or be a party to a use or threat of force, for that purpose, by a companion. It is not enough that, in stealing or being a party to theft, he takes advantage of force used for that purpose by another.[19] But one participant in theft may be a party to another's robbery if there was an express or tacit understanding that force might be used or threatened by that other or (perhaps) if, without such an understanding, he merely foresaw the use or threat of force by the other as a possible incident of the common enterprise of theft.[20]

---

[18] The point passed without comment in *Hale* (1978) 68 Cr.App.R. 415 (above, § 3–08).
[19] *Harris, The Times*, March 4, 1988.
[20] There is some uncertainty as to the precise general principle to be derived from the modern cases (all of which concern liability for murder): *Chan Wing-siu* v. *R.* [1985] A.C. 168; *Ward* (1985) 85 Cr.App.R. 71; *Slack* [1989] Q.B. 775; *Wakely and others* [1990] Crim.L.R. 119.

Chapter 4

BURGLARY AND AGGRAVATED BURGLARY

1. INTRODUCTION

SECTIONS 24 to 27 of the Larceny Act 1916, as amended by the Criminal **4–01**
Law Act 1967, provided a bewildering battery of offences involving breaking and entering, or entering or breaking out of, different kinds of buildings,
in which the accused intended to commit, committed or had before breaking
out committed an arrestable offence. Further, section 28 included an
offence of being found by night in any building with intent to commit an
arrestable offence therein. The scheme of offences was impossible to justify.
They applied variously to places of divine worship only, to dwelling-houses
only, or to a wide but not comprehensive range of buildings. Some could be
committed only at night, others at any time. The expressions "dwelling-
house," "breaks" and "enters" had highly technical meanings: guilt or
innocence of any particular offence, or of any offence at all, could turn on
circumstances of absolutely no moral significance.

For the provisions described above, the Theft Act substituted two
offences, one of which is merely an aggravated form of the other.

2. BURGLARY

Definition; mode of trial

Burglary is defined by section 9. It is committed by one who— **4–02**

  (i) enters any building or part of a building as a trespasser and with
      intent to commit therein[1] an offence of theft, inflicting grievous
      bodily harm, rape or unlawful damage (subss. (1)(*a*), (2)); or

  (ii) having entered any building as a trespasser, steals or attempts
       to steal anything therein or inflicts or attempts to inflict
       grievous bodily harm therein (subs. (1)(*b*)).

The section applies to an inhabited vehicle or vessel as it does to a building
(subs. (3)).

The maximum penalty for burglary is 14 years' imprisonment (s.9(4))[1a];
for aggravated burglary, considered below, it is life imprisonment (s.10(2)).

---

[1] This wording summarises the prevailing interpretation of the section's more elaborate
wording; but it is inaccurate in one minor respect: see the precise terms of s.9, and below,
§ 4–30.
[1a] Proposed to be reduced to ten years for burglary otherwise than in dwellings: see White
Paper, *Crime, Justice and Protecting the Public*, Cm. 965 (1990), para. 3.14.

93

4–03   Any (non-aggravated) burglary is triable either way *except* the following[2]:
(i) "burglary comprising the commission of, or an intention to commit, an offence which is triable only on indictment." The relevant offences triable only on indictment are rape (Sexual Offences Act 1956, s.1) and causing grievous bodily harm with intent (Offences against the Person Act 1861, s.18). So any burglary involving (a) entry with intent to rape, (b) entry with intent to inflict (and therefore cause) grievous bodily harm, or (c) entry and attempting to inflict (which must involve an intention[3] to cause) grievous bodily harm, is triable only on indictment. But burglary in the form of entering as a trespasser and actually committing an offence under section 20 of the Offences against the Person Act 1861—that is, maliciously inflicting grievous bodily harm—is triable either way, the section 20 offence being itself so triable.
(ii) "burglary in a dwelling if any person in the dwelling was subjected to violence or the threat of violence." Some other cases of "burglary in a dwelling," now triable either way, were originally triable only on indictment.[4] Their description included the phrase "building containing the dwelling," language which confirmed that where a "dwelling" is part of a larger building, burglarious entry into some other part of that building is not "burglary in a dwelling."[5]

Entry as a trespasser

4–04   Burglary depends upon entry as a trespasser and therefore in part upon the civil law of trespass to land. Trespass is a wrong committed against another's possession of land. A person enters premises as a trespasser if they are in the possession of another and he enters them without a right, by law or licence, to do so.

P's right to exclude D

4–05   A person's entry into a building or part of a building cannot be trespassory unless someone else has a possession that entitles him to exclude the entrant from that building or part. This platitude may be important when considering the liability for burglary of, for instance, D, the owner of a house, who enters the room of P in that house with intent to steal therein. If P has exclusive possession of the room—in which case he is probably a tenant—D requires P's permission to enter it (otherwise than for limited purposes for which the agreement between them may reserve to D a right of entry); and an entry without P's permission (otherwise than under such a reserved right) will be entry as a trespasser. On the other hand, P may occupy the room without having exclusive possession of it—for example, as a lodger, as where "[D] provides attendance or services which require [D] . . . to exercise

---

[2] Magistrates' Courts Act 1980, Sched. 1, para. 28(*b*), (*c*).
[3] Criminal Attempts Act 1981, s.1(1); as to the intention required, see *Pearman* (1984) 80 Cr.App.R. 259.
[4] s.29(2) (repealed).
[5] Smith, *The Law of Theft* (3rd ed.), para. 417.

unrestricted access to and use of the premises."[6] In such a case D's entry to steal P's property would not be burglary because it would not be trespassory.[7] The sometimes difficult distinction between tenant and lodger is not obviously a happy one in the law of burglary.

Trespass must be knowing or reckless

What if D wrongly believes that he is not trespassing? His belief may rest **4-06** on facts which, if true, would mean that he was not trespassing: for instance, he may enter a building by mistake, thinking that it is the one he has been invited to enter. Or his belief may be based upon a false view of the legal effect of the known facts: for instance, he may misunderstand the effect of a contract granting him a right of passage through a building. Neither kind of mistake will protect him from tort liability for trespass. In either case, then, D satisfies the literal terms of section 9(1): he "enters . . . as a trespasser." But for the purpose of criminal liability a person should be judged on the basis of the facts as he believed them to be, and this should include making allowances for a mistake as to rights under the civil law. This is another way of saying that a serious offence like burglary should be held to require *mens rea* in the fullest sense of the phrase; D should be liable for burglary only if he knowingly trespasses or is reckless as to whether he trespasses or not.

The Court of Appeal, accepting the view stated above, supplied the **4-07** required mental element in the remarkable case of *Collins*.[8] D stripped off his clothes and climbed to the window-sill of P's bedroom, intending to enter and to have intercourse with her, by force if necessary. P mistook him for her boyfriend. She beckoned or assisted him into the room and intercourse took place. The Court of Appeal quashed D's conviction of burglary, holding that:

> "there cannot be a conviction for entering premises 'as a trespasser' . . . unless the person entering does so knowing that he is a trespasser and nevertheless deliberately enters, or, at the very least, is reckless as to whether or not he is entering the premises of another without the other party's consent."[9]

D may not have satisfied this test, for it was not clear on the evidence "where exactly [D] was at the moment when, according to him, [P] manifested that she was welcoming him. . . . It was a crucial matter."[10] At the moment of

---

[6] *Per* Lord Templeman in *Street* v. *Mountford* [1985] A.C. 809 at 818.
[7] In *A.G. Securities* v. *Vaughan* [1988] 2 W.L.R. 689, four independent persons occupied a flat under separate agreements with the owner in circumstances making them all licensees rather than joint tenants. An unpermitted entry would not be a trespass as against such occupiers, though an entry by a stranger would be trespass as against the owner: see *per* Lord Bridge at 1207.
[8] [1973] Q.B. 100 ("about as extraordinary a case," according to Edmund Davies L.J., "as my brethren or I have ever heard either on the Bench or while at the Bar").
[9] *Ibid.* at 105.
[10] *Ibid.* at 103–104. The decisive point in the case was therefore "a narrow one, as narrow maybe as the window-sill" (p. 106).

entering the room he may have believed, ignorant of her mistake, that she was consenting to his entry.

4–08   Edmund Davies L.J., giving the judgment of the court in *Collins*, was probably using the word "reckless" in a restricted sense according to which D will be reckless as to whether he is entering premises without consent only if he realises that he may not have consent. This is suggested by the terms of his lordship's opinion in the later case of *Caldwell*,[11] in which he strongly dissented from the attribution of a wider meaning to the same word in another context. It is true that in *Collins* he hinted that a belief on D's part that P consented to his entry must be a reasonable one if it is to protect D from conviction of burglary.[12] But this is explained by the view his lordship then held of the weight of the authorities on the defence of mistake; see his dissenting speech in *D.P.P.* v. *Morgan*[13] three years later. By analogy with the decision in *Morgan*, D's belief that he has consent to enter is in fact inconsistent with recklessness on that issue (in the supposed *Collins* sense), whether that belief is reasonable or not.

But D's failure to realise that he is trespassing, or his belief that he is not, may be the result of intoxication. It seems that in such a case he probably does enter as a trespasser if the truth would be obvious to him were he sober.[14]

Right to enter granted by law

4–09   A person may be entitled to enter a building by virtue of a right granted by the law. A constable, for instance, does not trespass when he enters a building to execute a search warrant. But if, armed with a warrant, he enters the premises intending to steal therein and not to search, it is clear that he trespasses. It is otherwise if he enters to execute the warrant and after entry steals; for in such a case his entry can only be treated as trespassory by application of the doctrine of trespass *ab initio*, which does not apply to burglary.[15]

Licence to enter—whose licence?

4–10   To avoid trespass under the civil law, an entrant upon premises requires the licence of the occupier of the premises (the person with legal possession) or of someone acting with his authority. So where D enters P's house upon the invitation of Q, a member of P's household, D will nevertheless be a trespasser for the purposes of the law of tort if Q has no authority to permit

[11] [1982] A.C. 341.
[12] [1973] Q.B. 100 at 106.
[13] [1976] A.C. 182 at 230 *et seq*. The case concerned the analogous problem of mistake as to the victim's consent in rape.
[14] Compare *Caldwell* [1982] A.C. 341.
[15] *Collins* [1973] Q.B. 100 at 107.

D's entry. It was said in *Collins*[16] that such a result would be "unthinkable" in the criminal law. But would it be unthinkable? If D does not doubt Q's authority, he is innocent of burglary on another ground, established in *Collins* itself.[17] On the other hand, D may know or suspect that Q's pretended permission gives him no right to enter. Why then should it not be burglary if he enters with intent to steal (Q may, after all, be a party to that intent)? The context in *Collins* was a special one; Q was herself the intended victim of rape. Perhaps D needs the licence of the occupier (or of one acting with the occupier's authority) *or* of the intended victim of the ulterior offence.

Licence extending to part of building only

A licence to enter a building may extend to part of the building only. If so, **4–11** the licensee will trespass if he enters some other part not within the scope of the licence. To do so with intent to commit in that other part one of the offences specified in section 9(2), or to do so and then to steal or attempt to steal therein or inflict or attempt to inflict grievous bodily harm therein, will be burglary.

Entry "in excess of" permission to enter

A person may enter a building with intent to commit a relevant offence **4–12** (most commonly, to steal) but claim that he did not commit burglary because he had a licence to enter. This claim may be met by showing that, because of the purpose with which he entered, he entered not by licence but as a trespasser. That is to say, it may be shown that his entry was—and that he knew, or was reckless whether, it was—"in excess of" the permission he had to enter (as it was oddly expressed in the leading English case) or "for a purpose outside the scope of the permission" (to use the kind of language employed in an important Australian authority).

The English case is *Jones and Smith*,[18] in which the two appellants had entered the house of Smith's father (which Smith had a general licence to enter) for the purpose of stealing a television set. The Court of Appeal upheld their burglary convictions. The basis of the decision was that Smith's entry was "in excess of the permission that [had] been given to him." This expression appears to mean that the licence which Smith had to enter the house did not extend to an occasion on which he entered for the purpose of stealing. His father's general permission is read as subject to an unspoken limitation to this effect. Much more elaborate judgments than that in *Jones and Smith* were delivered in *Barker* v. *The Queen*[19] in the High Court of

[16] [1973] Q.B. 100 at 107.
[17] See above, § 4–07.
[18] (1976) 63 Cr.App.R. 47.
[19] (1983) 153 C.L.R. 338. P asked D to keep an eye on his house while he was away and told D how to gain access. D entered the house to steal furniture. This was burglary under section 76(1) of the Crimes Act 1958 (Vic.), as amended, which is in relevant respects in the same terms as section 9(1)(a) of the Theft Act.

Australia, of which account will have to be taken in any future consideration of the relationship between licence and unlawful purpose. Particularly challenging is the view of Brennan and Deane JJ. in that case that if a consent to enter premises is not limited, expressly or by necessary implication, by reference to the purposes for which entry may be effected, the fact that the entrant's purpose is in fact one of which the person giving consent would not have approved does not make that entry a trespassory one.[20]

Entering a shop to steal

4–13   The decision in *Jones and Smith* seems plainly to imply that one who enters a shop on a shoplifting expedition enters as a trespasser ("in excess of" the permission given to members of the public generally to enter the shop) and therefore commits burglary when he enters. The view of Brennan and Deane JJ. would not stand in the way of this result if the shopkeeper's licence to the public can be regarded as limited "by necessary implication" by reference to lawful purposes or at least to purposes which do not include theft from the shop. On that understanding *Jones and Smith* and the learned judges' view would in most cases lead to the same result. But the application of that view seems not to be so simple. For their Honours went on to illustrate it by saying that the ordinary invitation extended by a shopkeeper to the public, though no doubt limited to particular areas of the shop and to shopping hours, is not to be taken as limited by reference to purpose so as to exclude the would-be thief.[21] This, with respect, seems to narrow remarkably the notion of limiting a licence "by necessary implication"; and it makes application of the Brennan and Deane test difficult to predict with assurance. There is much to be said for a simple rule such as that suggested by counsel for the Crown in *Barker*,[22] namely, that anyone who enters premises in the possession of another with intent to steal therein enters as a trespasser. This is no doubt intended by *Jones and Smith*. If the thief masquerading as a shopper is not a burglar, the law of burglary may be thought to be too complicated.

Fraud to obtain entry

4–14   D may obtain permission to enter a building by pretending to be someone he is not or by falsely claiming to have a valid reason for entering. He may, for instance, claim to be the gas man come to read the meter. His entry is surely a trespass. A sufficient reason will be that the permission to enter, properly understood, does not extend to an entry made for D's secret nefarious purpose. One who obtains his licence to enter by fraud can hardly

---

[20] (1983) 153 C.L.R. at 357 *et seq*.
[21] *Ibid*. at 361–362. Nor were the other majority judges in *Barker* clear that an intending shoplifter was necessarily a burglar. And Mason J. (at 344) was not sure that *Jones and Smith* was a correct application of principle.
[22] Recorded by Brennan and Deane JJ., *ibid*. at 356.

be in a better position than one whose entry is "in excess of" a permission spontaneously given.

Objections to burglary liability of one exceeding licence

The foregoing paragraphs accept the correctness of the decision in *Jones*   **4–15**
and Smith,[23] if only for the sake of avoiding excessive complexity in the law of burglary. But the case has been vigorously criticised by Professor Williams.[24] His main objections appear to be these:

(i) That the decision is not well-founded in the tort authority relied on by the court.[25] This objection may be technically sound. The case in question was not concerned with entry for an unpermitted purpose. But this does not demonstrate that *Jones and Smith* is incorrect.[26]

(ii) That the decision takes inadequate account of the language of section 9, even to the point of rendering redundant the words "as a trespasser" in section 9(1)(*a*). For according to the decision an intent to commit a relevant ulterior offence suffices to make the entry trespassory; yet such an intent is itself an independent requirement under paragraph (*a*). It is respectfully suggested that this objection is not sound. If the intent is to commit an offence against someone other than the occupier, the entry will not necessarily be trespassory; the occupier may licence the entry, acquiescing in or being indifferent to the proposed offence. Moreover, the phrase "as a trespasser" excludes from burglary a person entitled to possession of the premises entered.[27] So it does have a function independent of the ulterior intent.

(iii) That the decision is inconsistent with the case of *Collins*.[28] Collins may   **4–16**
have believed that the girl was inviting him to enter the house. The jury's verdict nevertheless involves a finding that when he entered he intended to rape her if necessary. Entry with this intention (the argument runs) was surely entry "in excess of" the permission apparently given to him to enter. Yet his conviction was quashed. This implies that entry with a relevant criminal intention outside the terms of the licence granted does not negative that licence. Yet *Jones and Smith* holds that it does.

Two answers are available.[29] First, a distinction might be taken between an unqualified intention (that of Smith to steal) and a conditional one (that of Collins to have intercourse by force if necessary). Collins may fulfil his

---

[23] Above, § 4–12.
[24] Williams, *Textbook*, pp. 847–849. See also Pace [1985] Crim.L.R. 716.
[25] *Hillen and Pettigrew* v. *I.C.I. (Alkali) Ltd.* [1936] A.C. 65.
[26] The tort authorities are comprehensively reviewed in *Barker* v. *The Queen* (1983) 153 C.L.R. 338; above, § 4–12.
[27] As pointed out by Mason J. in *Barker*, above, at 347.
[28] [1973] Q.B. 100; above, § 4–07.
[29] Perhaps three. Because of P's apparent welcome, Collins may have abandoned even a conditional intention to rape by the time he entered: see Smith, *Theft*, para. 346; Williams and Weinberg. *Property Offences* (2nd ed.), pp. 303–304; compare Mason J. in *Barker* v. *The Queen* (1983) 153 C.L.R. 338 at 345. But Collins' conviction was quashed because he may not have entered as a trespasser, not because it was unsafe to conclude that he entered with intent to rape.

purpose without exceeding the licensor's purpose in admitting him; not so with Smith. This is a real distinction, but hardly a satisfying one. The second answer is simply that, for all that appears, the court in *Collins* did not advert to the effect upon the (supposed) licence of the ulterior intent. It may be *Collins* that is defective on this point.

4–17   (iv) That the decision is contrary to the purpose of the law of burglary. Burglary is aimed at the unwelcome intruder. It is not intended to deal with the entrant whose presence is expected, even welcome—such as the occupier's son (as in *Jones and Smith*), or his customer, guest or employee. The decision rests burglary on the entrant's state of mind, not on the "objective illegality" of his entry. This objection has considerable force. Burglary is a traditional category of crime protecting premises and their occupants against invasion, against entry that is "manifestly suspicious."[30] But the objection may be to the way in which section 9 was drafted, rather than to the way it has been interpreted in *Jones and Smith*.

Entry

Entry of part of the body

4–18   The question what amounts to an entry into a building for the purpose of section 9 arose in *Brown*,[31] in which D put part of his body through a shop window and stole goods from the shop. The Court of Appeal rejected a submission that a person does not "enter" a building unless his whole body is within the building. The court approved, in the context of the case, the trial judge's suggestion to the jury that "to put a hand, or an arm, or the upper part of your body through a broken shop window, is plainly an entry into that shop." But this was strictly speaking a suggestion only and not a firm direction. The Court of Appeal said that whether there has been an entry is a question of fact for the jury, apparently meaning that whether a proved intrusion amounted to an "entry" is a question for the jury's judgment. This is open to the familiar objection that it is capable of producing a different law of burglary for each of two identical cases. If D puts his forearm through a shop window and rummages around among goods, he should be guilty of burglary as a matter of law.

4–19   The court in *Brown* was attracted by the suggestion that a jury should be directed that what is required is "an effective entry" (though failure to use such terms in the instant case was by no means a misdirection). The notion of an "effective" entry was derived from a remark of Edmund Davies L.J. in *Collins*.[32] The learned Lord Justice had said that Collins could not properly be convicted unless he had made "an effective and substantial entry" before he was caused to believe that he was entering with consent. Too much has

---

[30] G. Fletcher, *Rethinking Criminal Law*, p. 128.
[31] [1985] Crim.L.R. 212.
[32] [1973] Q.B. 100 at 106.

been made of this unelaborated dictum in an extempore judgment; and the Court of Appeal has now happily made plain that the word "substantial" does not assist. The word "effective," with respect, is not much more helpful. It might be understood to suggest in one kind of case that it is necessary to be more or less completely in (was he "effectively" in?) and in another that it is enough if a slight degree of intrusion permits an attempt at the ulterior offence (was it "effective" to allow him to attempt theft?). The results in both cases may be sound; yet they will be achieved by giving different meanings to a word that does not appear in the statute.

Under the old law, the intrusion into the building of any part of the body, **4–20** however small, satisfied the requirement of an entry.[33] The court might in *Brown* have adopted the same simple rule. It did not do so; and its judgment is explicable only on the basis that the rule has not survived.[34] If that is right, we are left in need of further authority, preferably in firm terms that will make for uniformity of decision, to supplement our understanding of the range of cases in which a person "enters" a building although part of him remains outside. It might with advantage be clearly laid down that a person has "entered" a building (or part of a building) not only when he is entirely inside the building (or part) but also (i) when he has intruded so far into the building (or part) that he may be described more properly as inside it than as outside; or (ii) when his intrusion into the building (or part) suffices to permit him to attempt the intended offence (in a case under section 9(1)(a)) or to commit a relevant attempt (in a case under section 9(1)(b)).

Entry by an innocent agent

There is no decision on the question whether D "enters ... as a tres- **4–21** passer" within the meaning of section 9(1) when he does not himself phys- ically enter but trespasses through the instrumentality of an innocent agent (a child under 10, an adult without *mens rea*[35] or a well trained animal). It should be held that he is within the statutory wording in such a case. Burglary should be no exception to the general rule that crimes can be committed through innocent agents.[36]

Insertion of an instrument

There is a third category of problem cases on the meaning of entry. D may **4–22**

[33] *Davies* (1823) R. & R. 499.
[34] In *Watson* (1989) 89 Cr.App.R. 211 at 214, Lord Lane C.J. (*obiter*) seemed to assume that a burglary is committed "on [D's] foot crossing the threshold or windowsill."
[35] In *Paterson* [1976] 2 N.Z.L.R. 394, D asked E to fetch a television set from a flat which he described as his own; in fact the flat and the set were P's. E did as he was asked. D's conviction of burglary (depending on "breaking and entering") was upheld by the New Zealand Court of Appeal. Compare Hale, 1 *Pleas of the Crown*, pp. 555–556.
[36] Williams, *Criminal Law—General Part* (2nd ed.), pp. 349 *et seq.*; Draft Criminal Code Bill, cl. 26(1)(c), 3(a), in *A Criminal Code for England and Wales* (Law Com. No. 177), vol. 1. Authority under the Game Act 1831, s.30 ("commit any trespass by entering or being upon any land") is to the contrary effect: *Pratt* (1855) 4 E. & B. 860 at 864, 868; *Martin* [1911] 2 K.B. 90; but "he would be a bold lawyer who would argue from the Game Acts to any general principle of law": Williams, *op. cit.* p. 329.

insert an instrument into the building without any part of his own body intruding. Under the old law this was an entry if the instrument was inserted for the purpose of committing a relevant ulterior offence (*e.g.* theft or causing grievous bodily harm), but not if it was inserted merely to facilitate access to the premises. Such a distinction, slightly adapted, may continue to be serviceable. The insertion of an instrument simply as a means of access need not be regarded as an entry. D has not, by that insertion, made an "effective" entry in any sense of that adjective. His act seems to be described more convincingly as an attempt to enter the building than as an actual entry by him, and attempted burglary can be charged if nothing further occurs. On the other hand, when D inserts an instrument into the air-space of the building he certainly does trespass; the instrument can readily be regarded as an extension of his person,[37] and if by the instrument so inserted he is able to commit or attempt to commit one of the specified offences without intrusion of his own body, he has made as effective an entry as if he had inserted an arm with the same result. But should the hooked object, by which D proposed to steal, or the gun, with which he seeks to cause grievous bodily harm, enter only slightly and not far enough for the ulterior purpose to be attempted the case would again, it is submitted, be properly treated as attempted burglary.

Buildings and parts of buildings

4–23   "The imperfection of human language renders it not only difficult, but absolutely impossible, to define the word 'building' with any approach to accuracy. One may say of this or that structure, this or that is not a building; but no general definition can be given. . . ."[38]

The Act attempts no definition; nor need we. There must be a structure capable of being entered; it must presumably be a fairly permanent affair[39]; and further than this it is probably not safe to go. Difficulty will occur infrequently, but eventually the courts will no doubt have to decide whether a kiosk is a building; or a potting-shed; or a bandstand; and so on.[40] There is little point in trying to anticipate their decisions. Nor would it be wise to base any predictions upon decisions given on various structures under the numerous statutes in which the word "building" is used, for what is denoted by a word of this kind in a particular statute depends so much on the subject and purpose of the legislation.

The word "building" and the distinction taken by the Act between buildings and parts of buildings give rise to some tantalising problems.[41] In

---

[37] It is submitted that this consideration, if any be needed, is sufficient to distinguish the case of the hand-held instrument from that of the projected missile; compare Smith, *Theft*, para. 344.

[38] *Per* Byles J. in *Stevens* v. *Gourley* (1859) 7 C.B.(N.S.) 99 at 112.

[39] It is clear that a tent is not a building. The Committee were against giving tent-dwellers the protection of the law of burglary on the not very satisfying ground that "a tent seems too open a structure to be naturally regarded as the subject of burglary": *Eighth Report*, para. 78.

[40] Reported Crown Court decisions have concerned a large freezer container standing in a farmyard, without foundations (a "building": *B. and S.* v. *Leathley* [1979] Crim.L.R. 314); and a lorry trailer, supplied with mains electricity, used as a storehouse (not a "building": *Norfolk Constabulary* v. *Seekings and Gould* [1986] Crim.L.R. 167).

[41] For a valuable and ingenious discussion, see Smith, *Theft*, paras. 353–361.

considering the illustrations and explanations that follow, it must be remembered that burglary is committed if D intends to commit one of a number of offences either (a) in a *building* that he enters as a trespasser, or (b) in part of a building, that *part* being entered by him as a trespasser.

4-24

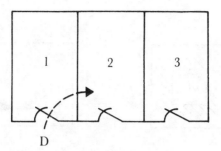

Premises 1, 2 and 3 are contiguous. If D enters 1, intending to pass from it into 2 or 3, there to steal, he is guilty of burglary if 1 and 2 or (as the case may be) 1, 2 and 3 constitute one "building."[42] This must depend on detailed facts as to structure and, perhaps, occupancy. A block of offices is surely one building. A row of terraced houses almost as surely is not; but it is possible to conceive of doubtful cases, such as that in which one large building has been converted into a row of residences with a common roof.

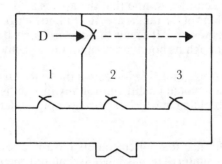

4-25

Here is a block of flats. D is lawfully in 1. He enters 2, intending to pass from it into 3 and to steal in 3. Assuming that the block of flats is one "building," do 2 and 3 constitute one "part," so that D enters that part as a trespasser with intent to steal therein? It is thought not.[43] In such a case, the relevant component portions of the building are clearly distinguishable; in other cases the meaning of "part" may seem less clear.

---

[42] He is also guilty of burglary if, when entering 1, he intends to do damage to 1 by damaging the wall between 1 and 2: Collins [1968] Crim.L.R. at 643–644. A similar point affects the next illustration.

[43] *Contra*, it seems, Smith, *Theft*, paras. 357–360, who argues that for the purpose of s.9 a building has only two parts: that where D may lawfully go, and the remainder. *Sed quaere?* The reading is desirable but strained.

4–26   (a)

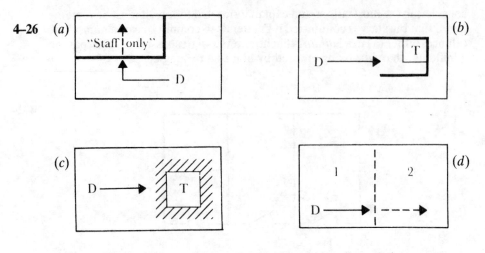

Each of these diagrams represents a floor of a shop. D is a customer, lawfully present in the shop.

(a) Here the prohibition imposed by the notice and the area to which it relates are clear. That area is a "part" of the building which D enters as a trespasser.

(b) A counter area is formed by three movable counters, with a till in one corner. D moves into the counter area in order to steal from the till. The jury are entitled to find that the area is a "part" of the building which members of the public are, to D's knowledge, impliedly prohibited from entering.[44] It seems that the area may be a "part" for this purpose although its boundaries cannot be exactly defined.

(c) There is "a single table" (with, say, a till on it) "in the middle of the store, which it would be difficult for any jury to find properly was a part of the building in which the licensor prohibited customers from moving."[45]

(d) D has the licence that all customers have in a shop to move from counter to counter. He has lawfully entered the shop and bought something from counter 1. He now moves to counter 2, intending to steal at it. If in doing so he is entering a different "part" of the shop, he may be guilty of burglary on the ground that his entry into that part with intent to steal is a trespassory entry.[46] But it does not seem likely that the courts will be hasty to divide buildings artificially into "parts" in the way that would be necessary to make a case of burglary out of the situation presented here.

[44] *Walkington* (1979) 68 Cr.App.R. 427.
[45] *Ibid.* at 434.
[46] See above §§ 4–12, 4–13.

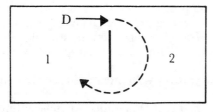

1 and 2 are distinct "parts" of a building. D is lawfully in 1 as a customer, guest, etc. He trespasses in 2 but commits no offence there. Later he comes back into 1, intending to steal therein. When he re-emerges into 1, does he enter that part as a trespasser? Applying the principle of *Jones and Smith*,[47] he probably does. Although he lawfully entered the *building* and has not yet left it, his re-entry into part 1 can be regarded as a distinct entry of a *part* of the building and as trespassory because of his intent to steal.

Inhabited vehicles and vessels

An inhabited vehicle or vessel, whether or not "the person having a habitation in it" is there at the time of the offence, is given the same protection as a building by section 9(3). Moreover, the law of burglary applies as between the parts of, *e.g.* an ocean liner as it does between the parts of a building.   **4-28**

Clearly a person ordinarily living in, or for the time being spending a holiday in, a caravan or a house-boat has a habitation in it; and the subsection does not cease to apply because he goes away for a few hours or days. It is not, however, so clear, for instance, whether during the winter a caravan left fully equipped on a caravan site for the purpose of occasional visits during the summer is an "inhabited vehicle" within the meaning of the subsection. It is tentatively suggested that it is not; that the phrases "inhabited" and "having a habitation in it" should be understood as referring to active or regular residential use in the period in which the alleged burglary occurs; and that in each case it must be a question of degree whether P currently has a habitation in the vehicle or vessel (whether it is *then* "inhabited"). It is easy to see the force of a contrary argument according to which, if the primary use of the vehicle or vessel is residential, one has a habitation in it so long as it is available (and equipped?) for use as an occasional home, no matter how long the gaps between visits. But this argument seems to give insufficient force to the word "inhabited." The language of the subsection is lamentably imprecise.

Nor is it clear to what use one must put a vehicle or vessel for it to be inhabited. Its mere casual use for sleep on an isolated occasion is presumably not enough. On the other hand, must it serve as a self-sufficient home? At

[47] (1976) 63 Cr.App.R. 47; above, § 4–12.

first sight one would suppose not; but if not, a vehicle fitted out for sleeping and for no other non-vehicular purpose might be "inhabited" and within the protection of the law of burglary when its tourist occupants are taking a meal elsewhere. There seems little need for such special protection.

Two modes of burglary: entry with intent; offence after entry

4–29   It must be proved *either* that D intended when he entered the building or part to commit one of the offences mentioned in section 9(2) (s.9(1)(*a*)), *or* that after entry he actually stole or inflicted grievous bodily harm on any person or attempted to do either (s.9(1)(*b*)). On the one hand, the only justification for the alternative provided by section 9(1)(*b*) is that it meets the case where the relevant guilty intention at the time of entry cannot be proved; there is no wider ground for making an offence more serious merely because it is committed by a trespasser. On the other hand, paragraphs (*a*) and (*b*) of section 9(1) are not mutually exclusive,[48] and in practice the existence of paragraph (*b*) enables the normal case of entry (with intent) plus theft to be charged as a single offence, instead of as two offences under paragraph (*a*) and section 1. Paradoxically, therefore, section 9(1)(*b*), justified by the exceptional (and probably bogus) defence, "I did not at the time of entering intend to steal; prove that I did," is used for the great majority of burglaries.[49]

4–30   It seems clear that, to satisfy section 9(1)(*a*), an offence of theft, inflicting grievous bodily harm or rape must be intended to be committed in the building that D enters as a trespasser or, as the case may be, in the very part that he enters as a trespasser, and not elsewhere against a person or property taken from the building or part[50]; and that the offence after entry required by section 9(1)(*b*) must be comitted in that building or part. Where D intends to do unlawful damage, the damage must be intended to the building he enters or to something therein, but here there is no limitation to the part trespassed in if D's presence in the building itself was lawful.[51]

The specified offences

4–31   Four offences are mentioned in section 9(2). The first two, and attempts to commit them, appear also, in substance, in section 9(1)(*b*). The four offences are those—

(i) *"of stealing anything in the building or part of a building in question"*

There can be no intent to steal unless the accused would be guilty of theft if

---

[48] *Taylor* [1979] Crim.L.R. 649.
[49] As to conviction under paragraph (*a*) on an indictment for an offence under paragraph (*b*), see above, § 1–17.
[50] Notwithstanding doubts expressed by White (1986) 150 J.P.N. 37, 56. It is thought also that the intention must relate to a thing or person in the building (or part) at the time of entry.
[51] See the precise terms of s.9(1)(*b*), (2).

the intended appropriation took place.[52] So, for example, his belief that he has a right to deprive of the property the person to whom it belongs will exclude burglary as it will exclude theft. Again, theft depends upon an appropriation of "property"; and as electricity is not "property," burglary is not committed by entering a building as a trespasser and abstracting electricity therein (or entering with intent to do so).[53]

A charge under section 9(1)(*a*), of entering a building or part of a building **4–32** as a trespasser "with intent to steal therein," without reference to particular property, is permissible.[54] On such a charge it is not necessary to prove either that D entered with intent to steal any specific thing,[55] or that anything, or anything such as he was seeking, was present in the building or part of a building in question.[56] "An intention to steal can exist even though, unknown to the accused, there is nothing to steal. . . ."[57] and even though his only intention is to steal anything that he may find worth stealing.[58] It follows that one who attempts to enter a building with such an intention can be convicted of attempted burglary.[59]

(ii) *"of inflicting on any person therein any grievous bodily harm"*

A distinction must be drawn between entry with intent to inflict harm and **4–33** the infliction of, or an attempt to inflict, harm after entry.

(a) *Entry with intent* (s.9(1)(*a*)). A person charged with entry with intent to commit an offence under this head must be proved to have intended the infliction of some harm which would be regarded by a jury as "grievous"— that is, "really serious bodily harm."[60]

(b) *Infliction of, or attempt to inflict, harm after entry* (s.9(1)(*b*)). A "specific intent" to inflict such harm is also plainly required for an attempt, after entry as a trespasser, to inflict grievous bodily harm.[61] But the Act is

---

[52] Nor, of course, an offence under s.9(1)(*b*) involving theft unless all the ingredients of theft are present; but failure to direct the jury about all those ingredients is not necessarily fatal to a conviction: *O'Sullivan and Lewis* [1989] Crim.L.R. 506 (doubtfully, but gratifyingly, distinguishing *McVey* [1988] Crim.L.R. 127).

[53] *Low* v. *Blease* [1975] Crim.L.R. 513.

[54] *Attorney-General's References (Nos. 1 and 2 of 1979)* [1980] Q.B. 180, approving the indictment in *Walkington* (1979) 68 Cr.App.R. 427.

[55] *Attorney-General's References*, above.

[56] *Walkington*, above; *Attorney-General's References*, above.

[57] *Per* Lord Scarman in *D.P.P.* v. *Nock* [1978] A.C. 979 at 1000; *Attorney-General's References*, above, at 194.

[58] These obvious propositions needed to be established because a doctrine to the contrary was in vogue, based on an unsatisfactory dictum in *Husseyn* (1977) 67 Cr.App.R. 131, on attempted theft. Some Crown Court rulings justified the impression that the law had for a time "taken leave of its senses": *per* Geoffrey Lane L.J. in *Walkington*, above.

[59] This was the specific point in the second of the *Attorney-General's References*, above.

[60] *Metharam* (1961) 45 Cr.App.R. 304 (on Offences against the Person Act 1861, s.18). For observations on what may provide evidence of such an intent, see *O'Neill and others*, *The Times*, October 17, 1986.

[61] Compare *Pearman* (1984) 80 Cr.App.R. 259 (on Criminal Attempts Act 1981, s.1(1)).

obscure as to the *mens rea*, if any, required for burglary committed by entering and actually inflicting grievous bodily harm. Section 9(1)(*b*), unlike paragraph (*a*), does not in terms require the commission of any "offence."[62] On a literal reading a trespasser could commit burglary by accident.[63] On principle, however, *mens rea* should be required. The offence to which paragraph (*b*) was undoubtedly intended to refer was that of maliciously inflicting grievous bodily harm under section 20 of the Offences against the Person Act 1961, which requires intention or ("subjective") recklessness as to the infliction of some, though not necessarily serious, bodily harm.[64] Thus: D trespasses in P's premises; P uses reasonable force to eject him; D resists P's force by a blow that D realises may cause a slight wound; the blow unexpectedly causes severe injury; D is guilty of burglary.

(iii) *"of raping any woman therein"*

4–34   Rape, as defined by section 1(1) of the Sexual Offences (Amendment) Act 1976, requires either knowledge that the woman is not consenting to the sexual intercourse involved or recklessness as to whether she is consenting or not. Attempted rape requires an intent to commit rape; and it was decided in *Khan*[64a] that that requirement is satisfied if D, intending to have intercourse with P, is reckless as to whether she consents. In the attempt context D's state of mind concerns P's *present* attitude (does she consent to what is now being attempted?). The intent to commit rape required for burglary is rather different; it is a state of mind about the (no doubt near) *future*. A case where, as he enters the building or bedroom as a trespasser, D has it in mind that he will have intercourse with P even if, when it comes to it, he should prove to be unsure whether she is consenting, can be imagined (with difficulty) but will surely not be encountered in practice. The rule in *Khan* is unlikely to have room for application. The nearest applicable rule is one of conditional intention: for a conviction of burglary it is sufficient if, on entry, D intends to have intercourse with P whether she consents or not.[65] If in the event she consents, or D believes that she does, no rape or attempted rape is committed, but liability for the burglary would strictly be unaffected.[66]

(iv) *"of doing unlawful damage to the building or anything therein"*

The question will be whether what D intended would have been an

---

[62] The drafting is the result of an inept amendment: see [1983] Crim.L.R. 386–387 (comment on *Jenkins*, next note).

[63] As apparently contemplated by the Court of Appeal in *Jenkins* (1983) 76 Cr.App.R. 313 at 318 (reversed on another ground [1984] A.C. 242).

[64] *Cunningham* [1957] 2 Q.B. 396; *Mowatt* [1968] 1 Q.B. 421; *W. (a minor)* v. *Dolbey* (1989) 88 Cr.App.R. 1 *Grimshaw* [1984] Crim.L.R. 108.

[64a] [1990] 1 W.L.R. 813.

[65] The contrary was not suggested in *Collins* [1973] 1 Q.B. 100, where the point was available for decision. (The point can, of course, be generalised: for instance, an intention, if P will not make a loan, to take his money willy-nilly will be sufficient intention to steal.)

[66] *Collins (Christopher)* [1976] Crim.L.R. 249. (This case has to be read in the light of *D.P.P.* v. *Humphrys* [1977] A.C. 1, on issue estoppel.)

offence under section 1 of the Criminal Damage Act 1971. Section 5 of that Act provides a special defence of "lawful excuse" and expressly preserves general defences.

3. AGGRAVATED BURGLARY

Definition

Burglary is the only offence under the Acts for which a higher maximum penalty is provided when the offence is committed in aggravating circumstances.

4–35

A person commits aggravated burglary if he "commits any burglary and at the time has with him any firearm or imitation firearm, any weapon of offence, or any explosive" (s.10(1)), and this offence is punishable on conviction on indictment with imprisonment for life (s.10(2)). It is not triable summarily.[67] The Committee regarded the offence as comparable with robbery, which also carries life imprisonment.[68]

The terms "firearm," "imitation firearm," "weapon of offence" and "explosive" are defined or partially defined in section 10(1).

Firearm

Apart from saying that " 'firearm' includes an airgun or air pistol," the Act does not define this term. It is extensively defined in the Firearms Act 1968 for purposes of that Act[69]; but that definition does not apply for purposes of the present section.[70] Where it is doubtful whether an article carried by a burglar was a firearm it will often fall within the section in any event as a "weapon of offence."

4–36

Imitation firearm

This means:

4–37

"anything which has the appearance of being a firearm, whether capable of being discharged or not."

The question is whether the thing that the burglar had with him had the appearance at that time of being a firearm. Two metal pipes, bound together with tape, one end being held by the burglar under his clothing or other material, may at that time have looked like a double-barrelled shotgun. It is a question for the jury.[71]

Weapon of offence

This means:

4–38

---

[67] Magistrates' Courts Act 1980, Sched. 1, para. 28(*a*).
[68] *Eighth Report*, para. 80.
[69] Firearms Act 1968, s.57(1), read with s.5(2).
[70] Compare *Seamark* v. *Prouse* (1980) 70 Cr.App.R. 236.
[71] *Morris and King* (1984) 79 Cr.App.R. 104 (decided under the Firearms Act 1968, s.18(1)).

"any article made or adapted for use for causing injury to or incapacitating a person, or intended by the person having it with him for such use."

This wording is borrowed almost verbatim from the definition of "offensive weapon" for the purpose of the Prevention of Crime Act 1953, which penalises the possession of an offensive weapon in a public place without lawful authority or reasonable excuse.[72] One addition to the 1953 definition, however, is the reference to incapacitation. It covers articles "such as cords for tying up, gags or pepper."[73]

There is an important distinction between two classes of articles referred to in the definition. If an article is "made or adapted for use for causing injury to or incapacitating a person"—if it is, as it is commonly put, offensive *per se*—the burglar who has it with him is guilty of aggravated burglary whether or not he intends it for such use. It need not be proved that he so intended.[74] But in the case of an article not offensive *per se* it must be proved that the burglar intended it for such use.[75]

"Made ... for use for causing injury ... or incapacitating"

4–39   An article is "made for use for causing injury" if it was originally made for such use.[76] The question is as to the purpose for which it was made, not that for which it may be used.[77] There are some articles of which the court will take judicial notice that they are made for the purpose of causing injury to a person, so that the matter does not have to be proved and the jury can be so directed. This was held in relation to flick-knives by the Court of Appeal in *Simpson*[78]; other articles judicially declared to be offensive *per se* have included coshes, knuckle-dusters, revolvers,[79] swordsticks,[80] bayonets and stilettoes.[81] Flick-knives are to be contrasted with sheath knives; it is not possible to declare of "every knife which may be in a sheath" that it is made for the purpose of causing injury to a person, and the question whether a particular sheath knife was so made is a question of fact for the jury to decide.[82]

---

[72] Prevention of Crime Act 1953, s.1(1); definition in s.1(4).
[73] *Eighth Report*, p. 128 (Notes on draft Bill).
[74] *Davis* v. *Alexander* (1970) 54 Cr.App.R. 398.
[75] *Petrie* (1961) 45 Cr.App.R. 72. In *Flynn* [1986] Crim.L.R. 239; *Rowe* [1990] Crim.L.R. 344, the question was left open whether it is enough that the jury agree on the article's having been an offensive weapon without agreeing either that it was "offensive *per se*" or that D intended it for a relevant use. A negative answer is proposed, surely correctly, by J.C. Smith [1988] Crim.L.R. 335 at 338.
[76] Compare *Hubbard* v. *Messenger* [1938] 1 K.B. 300 at 307 ("constructed or adapted for use for the conveyance of goods").
[77] *Simpson* (1983) 78 Cr.App.R. 115.
[78] (1983) 78 Cr.App.R. 115; approving the judgment of Griffiths L.J. in *Gibson* v. *Wales* (1982) 76 Cr.App.R. 60.
[79] All in *Petrie*, n. 75, above.
[80] *Davis* v. *Alexander*, above, n. 74; *Butler* [1988] Crim.L.R. 695.
[81] In *Simpson*, above, n. 77 at 791.
[82] *Williamson* (1977) 67 Cr.App.R. 35. The general statement in this case (at 38) that "in any case" it is a question for the jury to decide "whether the object . . . can properly be described as an offensive weapon" must now be read subject to *Simpson*, above.

"Adapted for use for causing injury . . . or incapacitating"

An article is "adapted for use for causing injury" if it has been altered so as **4–40** to be apt for such use.[83] Once again it seems to be a question of purpose; examples often given are "the bottle deliberately broken in order that the jagged edge may be inserted into the victim's face"[84] and the chair leg into the end of which nails have been inserted. It need not be proved that the defendant was a party to the alteration.

"Intended by the person having it with him for such use"

Many things, however, that are not "made or adapted" to injure or **4–41** incapacitate can be put to such use by one so minded: a razor, a kitchen knife,[85] a machete[86] or a rope, for instance. If such a thing is carried by a burglar as a potential weapon (a conditional intention is plainly enough), the aggravated offence is committed. The contemplated occasion for use of the weapon need not be the burglary itself.[87]

The judge should normally avoid reference in his direction to an intention to use the article to frighten or intimidate; but in a rare case the evidence may justify a finding that the intention was to injure by shock.[88]

D may commit burglary, having with him an article such as a crow-bar or a **4–42** torch—that is, an article not "offensive *per se.*" If he is surprised by the occupier and uses the article to cause the occupier injury, he will not necessarily be guilty of aggravated burglary. It is well established for the purpose of the corresponding definition in the Prevention of Crime Act 1953 that the intention to use the article to cause injury must be "formed before the actual occasion to use violence has arisen"[89] and not "*ad hoc.*"[90] The same principle should apply in the present context, and not simply because the Theft Act definition is identical in relevant respects. The mischief at which the Prevention of Crime Act is aimed is the carrying of weapons,[91] not their use. Similarly, it may be said, aggravated burglary consists, not in injuring or incapacitating a person in the building that is burgled, but in entering the building with a weapon available for that purpose (or at least,

---

[83] Compare *Hubbard* v. *Messenger*, above, and many other cases under the Road Traffic and Vehicles (Excise) Acts.
[84] *Simpson*, above, n. 77 at 117.
[85] *Stones* (1989) 89 Cr.App.R. 26.
[86] *Southwell* v. *Chadwick* (1987) 85 Cr.App.R. 235.
[87] *Stones*, above.
[88] *Rapier* (1979) 70 Cr.App.R. 17, purporting to apply *Edmonds* [1963] 2 Q.B. 142. The relevant dictum in *Edmonds* (at 151) suggests that an intention to frighten may be sufficient where "the frightening [is] . . . of a sort which is capable of producing injury through the operation of shock." But D's *intention* to injure through shock must be required, and not simply the fact that the frightening use of the article is "capable" of causing, or even likely to cause, such injury (see Criminal Justice Act 1967, s.8).
[89] *Ohlson* v. *Hylton* [1975] 1 W.L.R. 724; [1975] 2 All E.R. 490 (*per* Lord Widgery C.J. at 729 and 497 respectively).
[90] *Humphreys* [1977] Crim.L.R. 225.
[91] *Bates* v. *Bulman* (1978) 68 Cr.App.R. 21.

having entered as a trespasser, being armed with a weapon while in the building).

"Has with him"

4–43   It appears that, in order that a burglar may be said to have a firearm or weapon of offence "with him" within the meaning of section 10(1), there must be "a very close physical link" between him and the article and "a degree of immediate control" over it by him.[92] This test is surely satisfied (so that D is guilty of aggravated burglary as a principal offender) not only when D himself has custody of the article but also when, as he anticipates, it is carried into the building by a companion.[93]

The phrase "has with him" can properly mean only "knowingly has with him."[94] So a burglar who is ignorant that he has a firearm in his pocket is not guilty of the aggravated offence.[95] The point is more likely to arise when two or more persons commit burglary together and one of them has physical possession of an article within s.10(1). Then only such of them as know of the article can be guilty of aggravated burglary.[96] In one case, indeed, something more than knowledge of the article's presence is necessary. This is the case in which the article (not being a firearm, imitation firearm or explosive) is a "weapon of offence" only because D1 intends to use it for causing injury. For D2 then to be guilty of aggravated burglary he must know of D1's intention or have that intention himself.

"At the time has with him"

4–44   Whether a person is guilty of aggravated burglary depends on whether he has with him a weapon or other article within section 10 "at the time" he commits burglary.

Burglary contrary to section 9(1)(a) is committed at the time of entering a building or part of a building with intent to commit a relevant offence; D must therefore have the offending article with him when he enters if he is to be guilty of aggravated burglary. Burglary contrary to section 9(1)(b), on the other hand, is committed only when D steals (or commits another offence satisfying the paragraph) within the building or part that he entered as a trespasser; so that aggravated burglary depends on D's having the offending article with him at the time of the theft (or other offence). If by that time he has abandoned a weapon with which he entered he is guilty of simple burglary only.[97]

4–45   There remains the question whether one who enters a building without a weapon, arms himself with a heavy candlestick when inside and then steals

---

[92] *Kelt* (1977) 65 Cr.App.R. 74 at 78 (decided under the Firearms Act 1968, s.18(1)); *Murphy, Lillis and Burns* [1971] N.I. 193 (Firearms Act (Northern Ireland) 1968, s.18(1)); *Jones* (1987) 83 Cr.App.R. 259 ("is armed with": Customs and Excise Management Act 1979, s.86).
[93] So ruled in *Jones* [1979] C.L.Y 411 (Judge Solomon).
[94] Compare *Cugullère* (1961) 45 Cr.App.R. 108.
[95] One who has forgotten what he formerly knew is ignorant for this purpose: *Russell* (1985) 81 Cr.App.R. 315.
[96] Compare *Webley and Webley* [1967] Crim.L.R. 300.
[97] *Francis* [1982] Crim.L.R. 363.

can be convicted of aggravated burglary. On the face of it he can; he was armed when his burglary under section 9(1)(*b*) was committed. This natural reading of the section has been confirmed.[98]

---

[98] *O'Leary* (1986) 82 Cr.App.R. 341, rejecting an argument to the contrary rehearsed in previous editions of this book: see 5th ed., § 4–42.

Chapter 5

OFFENCES OF TAKING NOT AMOUNTING TO THEFT

5–01   EACH of the two offences to be considered in this chapter is designed to deal with a particular kind of mischief that is felt to require a special sanction by way of exception to the general rule that an unauthorised taking of property without an intention of permanently depriving of it the person to whom it belongs is not a criminal offence. As to the mischief constituted by the taking of motor vehicles and other conveyances and the need for an exceptional provision in relation to them there is no doubt. Section 12 in fact re-enacts, in an amended and extended form, an offence first created in 1930. The need for a special offence to deal with the removal of articles on display to the public is more controversial.

It will, of course, be understood that a person guilty of either of the offences about to be discussed may in fact be guilty of the full offence of theft. This is particularly likely in the case of an offence under section 11; most people who remove valuable articles from art galleries, museums and stately homes intend to deprive their owners permanently of them and can pretend to no right to do so. What sections 11 and 12 do is to provide for two classes of case: those (common enough in relation to conveyances) where there is in fact no intention of permanently depriving; and those in which that intention, though it may well have existed, cannot be proved.

A person charged on indictment with theft may be convicted of an offence under section 12(1) (normally, an offence of taking a conveyance other than a pedal cycle without lawful authority). But there is no corresponding provision for a conviction, on a charge of theft, of an offence under section 11. So where an article has been removed from a place within section 11 and there is any doubt about the offender's intention or any doubt about proving it, it will often be expedient to include in the indictment a count charging an offence under section 11.

1. REMOVAL OF AN ARTICLE FROM A PLACE OPEN TO THE PUBLIC

Introduction[1]

5–02   The clause that eventually became section 11 acquired the popular name "the Goya clause" while the Bill was before Parliament. This is because the need for the clause was suggested in particular by the notorious removal of Goya's portrait of the Duke of Wellington from the National Gallery. The portrait was returned after four years. Despite evidence that he had tried to make the Gallery buy the portrait back by paying a large sum to charity

---

[1] See *Eighth Report*, para. 57(ii).

(which was certainly evidence that at the time he took it he intended to deprive the Gallery permanently, and would now be evidence of the same intention for the purposes of theft[2]), the taker was acquitted of larceny of the portrait. There had been some other cases in recent years of the temporary removal of articles from public buildings—among them the removal of the Stone of Scone from Westminster Abbey. Art galleries, cathedrals and other places housing famous treasures are no doubt particularly vulnerable to temporary deprivation at the hands of eccentrics, exhibitionists and people with causes that can be brought to the public notice by removal of public property.

On balance, having considered arguments for and against the creation of a new offence, the Committee decided that there should be special provision for the protection of articles kept in places open to the public. But they included no such provision in the draft Bill, preferring to recommend the consideration of special legislation for the purpose. A first version of "the Goya clause" nevertheless appeared in the Bill presented to Parliament; and section 11 represents that clause in a much revised form.

The offence under section 11

Section 11 renders it an offence in certain circumstances to remove an **5–03** article from a place to which the public have access. The offence is punishable on conviction on indictment with imprisonment for five years (subs. (4)).

The section is drafted with a complexity disproportionate to the importance of the offence. The reader is referred to the text of the section of Appendix 1. What follows here is a statement of the conditions of the offence, with such commentary or explanation as seems to be required.

The offence under section 11 is committed if, and only if, the following conditions are satisfied[3]:

(i) There must be *a building to which the public have access*. **5–04**

We shall see (in (iv), below) that the section protects articles in the grounds of a building within the section as well as in the building itself. But the fact that the public has access to the grounds of a house in order to see its gardens and model railway is not enough to bring the section into operation if the public are not also admitted to the building itself for the purpose mentioned in (ii), below.

"It is immaterial . . . that the public's access to a building is limited to a particular period or particular occasion" (subs. (2)).

It may be that a "building" must have a roof. If so, an exhibition staged in the ruins of Tintern Abbey or Coventry Cathedral would not be protected.

(ii) The public must have access to the building *in order to view the* **5–05** *building or part of it, or a collection or part of a collection housed in it,*

---

[2] See above, § 2–104.
[3] All conditions, and qualifications of them, stated in the following account are justified by subs. (1), unless otherwise stated.

including a collection or part of a collection "got together for a temporary purpose."

A trial judge has ruled[4] that the question whether the public has access "in order to view" depends on the purpose of the occupier in giving access rather than on that for which people come in. This is no doubt true; but the principle can only be sensibly applied if the known motives of visitors are allowed to affect the description of the occupier's purposes. If a vicar knows (as surely he must) that many visitors to his church will come in just to look round, he must be construed, it is submitted, as giving access to the public "in order to view," although the primary reason for leaving the church door open is to enable people to enter for devotional purposes.

5–06   (iii) If the public have access to a building in order to view a collection rather than the building, the *collection* must be one *not "made or exhibited for the purpose of effecting sales or other commercial dealings."*

Where an artist's work is collected and put on show for sale, the application of the section to the collection may depend upon the nature of the building in which the collection is to be viewed. If the works are shown in a shop, there is little doubt that the collection must be regarded as made "for the purpose of effecting sales" even though an interested but impecunious public are welcome to view the collection with no idea of buying. On the other hand, if the collection is exhibited in a building which happens itself to be on show to the public or which contains some other collection which the public come to view and which is not excluded from the section by the motive of sale, the works exposed for sale fall within the section as it were parasitically. A familiar intermediate case is that of the educational institution which puts on a short-term exhibition of the work of a local artist. The public are invited to view the collection for their own pleasure; but the works are priced and the artist hopes to sell them as a result of the public's visits. From one point of view this is a collection "made or exhibited for the purpose of effecting sales"; and it may be safer to treat this contributory purpose as sufficient to prevent the section from applying.

5–07   (iv) There must be *a removal of the whole or part of an article from the building or its grounds.*

If the article is in the building the offence will be complete if it is removed from the building and, for example, hidden in the grounds. But a removal of an article from one part of the building to another or from one part of the grounds to another is not enough.

The word "grounds" is pleasantly untechnical. It could in an exceptional case cause difficulty. D is a gardener employed in the park of a great house to which the public have access, and he lives in a cottage within the park. He removes an article displayed outside the house and places it in the garden of his cottage, or in the cottage itself. Liability here is not as clear as it ought to be. It might not be improper to say that the gardener lives "in a cottage in the

---

[4] *Barr* [1978] Crim.L.R. 244 (vicar's evidence that his church was open only for devotional purposes and that the cross and ewer taken were displayed simply as aids to devotion; held, no case to answer).

grounds of the great house," and that the article has therefore not been removed from the grounds.

(v) The *article* removed must be one *displayed or kept for display to the public in the building* (or in the part of it that the public come to view) *or in its grounds*. **5–08**

The point, of course, is that the private belongings of the family who live in the great house, the overcoats and umbrellas of visitors to the museum, the bibles and hymn-books lying around the church, are not accorded special protection against unlawful "borrowing" merely because they happen to be within a building to which the section applies. It seems that an article is "displayed . . . to the public" only if the purpose, or one of the purposes, of its display is that it may be seen by those who are admitted to view the building or a collection housed in it—only if it is, in effect, "exhibited."[5]

An article within the protected class need not at the time of removal be actually on show. It is enough if it is "kept for display"; so an offence is committed by removing from a workshop within an art gallery an old master in the process of being cleaned but intended for exhibition in the gallery.

(vi) *The removal must in some cases be on a day when the public have access to the building* (subs. (2)), but in most cases the time of removal is immaterial. **5–09**

This condition as to the time of removal applies when the thing removed is not in the building or grounds as part of a collection intended for permanent exhibition to the public and is not on loan for exhibition with such a collection. The distinction intended is that between "a place, such as the National Gallery, which conducts a permanent exhibition . . ." and "a place such as a stately home which is open only occasionally to the public. . . ."[6] The purpose of making this distinction is to limit an anomaly. A servant or trespasser in an ordinary home not opened to the public view never commits an offence if he temporarily removes an article from it, however precious or priceless the article. By contrast, a servant or trespasser in a stately home sometimes open to the public may commit an offence if he takes something displayed to the public; yet his taking of the article may be quite unconnected with the fact that the public are granted access to the house—that is to say, it may not be an abuse of the privilege that that access constitutes, whereas the abuse of that privilege is the mischief intended to be penalised by the section. This anomaly is to some extent limited by providing, in effect, that if the thing removed is not on permanent exhibition it must be removed on a day when the public have access to it or there will be no offence.

In *Durkin*[7] D removed from an art gallery owned by a local authority a painting forming part of the authority's permanent collection. This painting, like other works in the collection, was not continuously on display; different parts of the collection were exhibited at different times. The painting nevertheless formed part of "a collection intended for permanent exhibition to the **5–10**

---

[5] *Barr*, above.
[6] H.C. Standing Committee H, June 25, 1968: Official Report, col. 56.
[7] [1973] Q.B. 786.

public" since the collection was intended to be permanently available for such exhibition, that intention being sufficiently manifested by the authority's settled practice of periodically displaying this and other pictures in the gallery. D was guilty of an offence under section 11(1), although he had taken the painting on a Sunday, when the gallery was closed.

5–11   (vii) The removal must be *without lawful authority*.

(viii) The remover must act *without the belief that he has lawful authority for the removal or that he would have it if the person entitled to give it knew of the removal and the circumstances of it* (subs. (3)).

This condition corresponds to the requirement of dishonesty in the offence of theft as that requirement is partially defined in section 2(1)(*a*) and (*b*).[8]

2. TAKING A CONVEYANCE WITHOUT AUTHORITY

Introduction

5–12   The unauthorised use of vehicles has long been a social mischief requiring penal sanctions. The conduct to be controlled may vary in gravity between a thoughtless adolescent joy-riding prank and the use of a handy car for a serious criminal purpose. At either extreme the temporary loss of the vehicle can seriously inconvenience its owner,[9] while the public are in danger from the uninsured use of the vehicle by an often reckless or immature driver. In many cases the police may rightly suspect the taking of a vehicle to be theft but be unable to prove the necessary intention of permanently depriving the owner. In such cases the provable wrong is better described as an unauthorised taking of the vehicle than as a theft of the petrol consumed by its use, which was all that could be charged before the taking of the vehicle was made an offence in itself.

The taking and driving away of a motor vehicle has been an offence since 1930. This offence, in an amended form, was extended by section 12 to all "conveyances." The main purpose of the extension was to provide for yachts, boats and pedal cycles.[10] Section 12 deals separately with conveyances other than pedal cycles and with pedal cycles alone.

Taking a conveyance other than a pedal cycle

5–13   Section 12(1) contains what may conveniently be called primary and secondary offences:

(i) The primary offence is that of taking a conveyance for one's own or another's use without having the consent of the owner or other lawful authority.

---

[8] Compare s.12(6), the remarks on which at § 5–31, below, apply equally to s.11(3).
[9] But this inconvenience does not itself justify a unique "theft of use" offence in the case of vehicles where there is none in the case of other property (*e.g.* industrial plant).
[10] *Eighth Report*, para. 83.

(ii) The secondary offence is committed by one who, knowing that a conveyance has been taken without authority, drives it or allows himself to be carried in or on it.

These offences were formerly triable either way but were converted by the Criminal Justice Act 1988, s.37(1), into summary offences,[11] punishable with a fine not exceeding level 5 on the standard scale or up to six months' imprisonment or both.[12] An attempt to commit an offence under section 12(1) is no longer an offence, for the Criminal Attempts Act 1981 applies only to attempts to commit indictable offences. But interference with a motor vehicle with the intention that an offence under section 12(1) shall be committed is an offence under section 9 of the 1981 Act (vehicle interference).

An offence under subsection (1) is an arrestable offence (as is an offence   **5–14** of conspiring to commit, or of inciting, aiding, abetting, counselling or procuring the commission of, an offence under the subsection).[13] The powers of arrest without warrant provided by the Police and Criminal Evidence Act 1984, s.24(4)–(7), therefore apply; and one who does an act with intent to impede the apprehension or prosecution of an offender may be convicted under section 4(1) of the Criminal Law Act 1967.[14] That offence is punishable with imprisonment for three years on conviction on indictment[15]—a fact possibly overlooked when the offences under section 12(1) were downgraded.

The ingredients of the offences under section 12(1) will be considered under four heads.

(1) *"Conveyance"*

Section 12(1) does not apply to pedal cycles (subs. (5)) or to any con-   **5–15** veyance constructed or adapted for use only under the control of a person not carried in or on it (subs. (7)(*a*)); but it applies to any other

> "conveyance constructed or adapted for the carriage of a person or persons whether by land, water or air . . .,"

and the word "drive" is to be construed accordingly (subs. (7)(*a*)). It is clear that any vehicle, vessel or aircraft which, as originally constructed or by

---

[11] But inclusion in an indictment of a count charging such an offence is possible in certain circumstances: Criminal Justice Act 1988, s.40(1), (3)(*b*). The offence is then tried as if it were an indictable offence; but the Crown Court may deal with the offender only as a magistrates' court could have done: *ibid.* s.40(2). A person charged on indictment with theft may be convicted of an offence under s.12(1) and, again, is liable to the same penalties as on summary conviction: subs. (4), as amended by the 1988 Act.

[12] An offence in respect of a motor vehicle attracts discretionary disqualification, obligatory endorsement of the offender's driving licence and eight penalty points: Road Traffic Offenders Act 1988, Sched. 2, Pt. II.

[13] Police and Criminal Evidence Act 1984, s.24(2)(*d*) and (3).

[14] By virtue of Criminal Law Act 1967, s.4(1A) (added by the Police and Criminal Evidence Act 1984, Sched. 6).

[15] *Ibid.* s.4(3)(*d*).

virtue of subsequent alteration,[16] makes physical provision for its "driver" to be carried in or on it is within the definition of "conveyance." If it were otherwise the section would not protect, for example, a goods van without a passenger seat.

A horse is not a "conveyance."[17] The section is "directed towards artefacts rather than towards animals."[18]

(2) *The prohibited conduct*

5–16   (i) The *primary offender* is he who "takes any conveyance for his own or another's use." The word "takes" will be satisfied by any movement intentionally[19] caused (*e.g.* by pushing, by lifting or by releasing a hand-brake). But some movement there must be. It appears that a "taking" for the purposes of the section has two ingredients: (a) an assumption of possession or control, and (b) movement. The Court of Appeal in *Bogacki*[20] said that before a person can be convicted of the primary offence it must be shown

> "that there was an unauthorised taking of possession or control of the [conveyance] by him adverse to the rights of the true owner or person otherwise entitled to such possession or control, coupled with some movement, however small ... of that [conveyance] following such unauthorised taking."

5–17   *"Taking" a conveyance already possessed.*[21] Several cases hold that a person may "take" a conveyance within the meaning of section 12(1) even though he already has possession of it as the owner's servant or bailee. This was first revealed in *Wibberley*,[22] decided under the Road Traffic Act 1960, s.217(1) (the predecessor of s.12). In that case D was employed to drive a truck. At the end of his day's work he should have returned it to one of his employer's yards. Instead he drove it to his home and, later that evening, used it for his own purposes. His conviction of taking and driving away was upheld. He was in no better position than if he had returned the truck to the yard and later taken it from there without consent.[23] A stronger case than this is *McKnight* v. *Davies*,[24] in which, again, D's duty was to return his lorry

---

[16] Compare *French* v. *Champkin* [1920] 1 K.B. 76; *Hubbard* v. *Messenger* [1938] 1 K.B. 300; *Taylor* v. *Mead* [1961] 1 W.L.R. 435; *Flower Freight Co. Ltd.* v. *Hammond* [1963] 1 Q.B. 275.
[17] *Neal* v. *Gribble* (1978) 68 Cr.App.R. 9.
[18] *Ibid.* at 11. See J. C. Smith at [1978] Crim.L.R. 501 on the failure of the law as drafted to deal with the mischief of riding animals without consent.
[19] *Blayney* v. *Knight* (1975) 60 Cr.App.R. 269 (movement caused by accidental pressure on accelerator; no "taking").
[20] [1973] Q.B. 832 at 837; see also *Marchant and McCallister* (1984) 80 Cr.App.R. 361 (where the full offence was plainly committed although the conviction was of attempt only).
[21] Glanville Williams and A. T. H. Smith (1984) 148 J.P.N. 115; Dine, *ibid.* 277.
[22] [1966] 2 Q.B. 214.
[23] *Ibid.* at 219. It seems that D's employer would not have complained if D had parked the truck outside his home until next morning.
[24] [1974] R.T.R. 4.

to his employer's depot when he had completed his round of deliveries. Instead he drove to a public house for a drink, drove around elsewhere for his own purposes, and parked the lorry for the night near his home. He returned it to the depot early the next morning. The Divisional Court held that an employed driver can be regarded as "taking" his vehicle

> "if in the course of his working day . . . he appropriates it to his own use in a manner which repudiates the rights of the true owner, and shows that he has assumed control of the vehicle for his own purposes."[25]

Applying such a test the court held that D "took the vehicle when he left the first public house."[26]

In so deciding *McKnight* v. *Davies*, the Divisional Court rejected the **5–18** pre-Act authority of *Mowe* v. *Perraton*[27] as being inconsistent with *Phipps and McGill*,[28] which the court preferred. The latter case was in one respect a stronger one still, for it involved not an employee, traditionally conceived as having mere custody of his employer's property,[29] but a person in possession as bailee. On condition that he would be back by 9.30 p.m., D borrowed P's car at Dagenham in order to drive to Victoria Station. He did not return that night, but drove the car next day to Hastings. His conviction was upheld. The direction to the jury, that "as from the time he decided not to return the car and drove it off on his own business . . ., if he did not have [P's] permission, he took it and drove it away," was "perfectly proper and accurate" and "supported by . . . *Wibberley*."[30]

The word "takes" is thus read as embracing the notion of entering upon an **5–19** unauthorised use other than that for which D has custody or possession. The reading is questionable on a number of grounds. First, its artificiality is at odds both with the principle of the strict construction of penal statutes and with the courts' own preference for the normal meanings of "ordinary words."[31] Secondly, it is not clear that the reading brings within the offence any mischief for which the section was intended to provide. Where a motor vehicle is concerned, the unauthorised use can often be prosecuted as an uninsured use; it is doubtful whether any other penal sanction is called for in a case where a conveyance has not been taken "without any reference to the owner."[32] Thirdly, there is an embarrassing discordance between the cases

---

[25] *Ibid.* at 8.
[26] *Ibid.* Thus the court avoided the unhappy conclusion that every driver who deviates from his route for the sake of a drink on his way back to base commits an offence under s.12 unless he thinks that his employer would consent if he knew. More generally: "Not every brief, unauthorised diversion from his proper route . . . in the course of his working day will necessarily involve a 'taking' of the vehicle for his own use" (p. 8).
[27] (1952) 35 Cr.App.R. 194. This case had been somewhat painfully distinguished in *Wibberley*, above.
[28] (1970) 54 Cr.App.R. 301.
[29] On this conception see Williams and Smith, *op. cit.*, n. 21, above, at 117.
[30] (1970) 54 Cr.App.R. at 304.
[31] "If the defendant initially gained possession with the consent of the owner how then can it be said that he *took* the vehicle without the owner's consent?": *Singh* v. *Rathour* [1988] 1 W.L.R. 422 at 428; [1988] 2 All E.R. 16 at 21 (May L.J., citing Hobhouse J. as trial judge).
[32] See *Peart* [1970] 2 Q.B. 672 at 675; compare *Whittaker* v. *Campbell* [1984] Q.B. 318 at 328.

on use beyond the consent given (penalised as "taking") and those on use sanctioned as a result of fraud (not penalised because not "without . . . consent"). The conflict, which will be demonstrated when the fraud cases are discussed,[33] should be resolved in favour of the latter.

5–20   *"For his own or another's use."*[34] The taking by D **must** be "for his own or another's use." In *Bow*[35] the Court of Appeal accepted a submission that this involves "that the conveyance should have been used as a conveyance, *i.e.* as a means of transport."[36] So if D, indulging his sense of humour, pushes P's car round a corner in order that P may think it has been stolen,[37] or releases its handbrake so that it runs away down a hill, the offence is not committed unless someone is in (or, presumably, on) it while it moves. But where, as in *Bow* itself,[38] D moves the conveyance "in a way which necessarily involves its use as a conveyance,"[39] it is immaterial that his motive in doing so is one to which that use is entirely subservient.

5–21   Notwithstanding the language of *Bow* quoted above, the Court of Appeal held in *Marchant and McCallister*[40] that the offence may be committed by taking control of, and moving, the conveyance (as by pushing it) with the intention that it shall be used as a conveyance later, although it is not so used at the time of the taking. In so deciding the court restored the authority of *Pearce*,[41] a decision which had seemed to be called into question by *Bow*. In *Pearce*, D took a dinghy, placed it on a trailer and towed it away. His conviction under section 12 was upheld. The case is understood in *Marchant and McCallister* as one in which D's purpose was to use the dinghy as a conveyance. The case of a boat "towed away to be used later" was certainly intended to be brought within the scope of this section by the removal of the words "and drives away" during the passage of the Bill.[42]

5–22   *Aiding and abetting.* Aiding and abetting this offence, like any other, requires full *mens rea*. D must be found to have been knowingly a party to the taking of the conveyance (that is, its removal from its original position). His mere voluntary presence when E takes the conveyance is not in itself participation in the taking; nor does his subsequently allowing himself to be carried in the conveyance necessarily establish that participation.[43] To be

---

[33] Below, § 5–28.
[34] This phrase is elaborately discussed by White [1980] Crim.L.R. 609.
[35] (1976) 64 Cr.App.R. 54. A gamekeeper used his Land Rover as an obstruction to prevent D, a suspected poacher, from making an escape. D sat in the driving seat of the vehicle and ran the vehicle downhill by releasing the handbrake. His only purpose was to remove the obstruction. Held, a taking "for his own use."
[36] (1976) 64 Cr.App.R. 54 at 57.
[37] *Stokes* [1982] R.T.R. 59.
[38] See n. 35, above.
[39] (1976) 64 Cr.App.R. 54 at 58. This description of D's conduct in *Bow* is questioned by J. C. Smith at [1977] Crim.L.R. 178.
[40] (1984) 80 Cr.App.R. 361.
[41] [1973] Crim.L.R. 321.
[42] H.L.Deb., vol. 291, col. 106.
[43] *C (a minor)* v. *Hume* [1979] Crim.L.R. 328 (where the secondary offence—see text following—could have been, but was not, charged).

guilty of aiding and abetting, D must, on general principles, either assist or encourage the taker in the commission of the offence.

(ii) The *secondary offender* is he who knows that the conveyance has been taken without authority and "drives it or allows himself to be carried in or on it." The secondary offence has three elements.

First, the conveyance must in fact have been taken without authority. There must be admissible evidence of this. D's confession that he was told of this primary offence by a person claiming to have committed it is not admissible for this purpose.[44]

5–23

Secondly, D must drive the conveyance or allow himself to be carried in or on it.

The word "drives" has been considered in many cases under the Road Traffic Acts, including cases under the present section's predecessors. Although the word has to be allowed a wide meaning, the alleged driver of a motor vehicle "must be in the driving seat, or in control of the steering wheel and . . . his activities are . . . not to be held to amount to driving unless they come within the ordinary meaning of that word."[45]

A motor vehicle can be driven without starting the engine,[46] but it cannot be driven by merely pushing it while controlling the steering wheel with one hand from the outside.[47] A person in command of the steering wheel and brakes of a vehicle on tow is driving it.[48] If there is any doubt as to whether a person drove a conveyance for the purpose of section 12(1) he can normally be charged with having allowed himself to be carried in or on it. The word "drive" has to be understood as referring to appropriate modes of controlling conveyances generally, and not just those in relation to which the word is normally used.[49]

A person does not "allow himself to be carried" in or on a conveyance merely by being present in or on it, even in anticipation of its being moved. There must be some actual movement.[50]

5–24

Thirdly, D must know that the conveyance has been taken without authority. The taking may in fact have amounted to theft; and D may know this or may simply know that it has been taken without authority. In either case he is within the section.[51] If he boards the conveyance without knowledge and learns the truth while being carried, he cannot presumably be guilty of the offence unless he remains on board after he has had a realistic

5–25

---

[44] *Francis* [1982] Crim.L.R. 694 (Judge Jolly); compare the proof of theft in a case of handling (below, §§ 14–07, 14–10).
[45] *MacDonagh* [1974] Q.B. 448 at 452, referring to *Roberts* [1965] 1 Q.B. 85 at 88. A merely accidental occurrence cannot be an act of driving: *Blayney* v. *Knight* (1975) 60 Cr.App.R. 269 (above, § 5–16).
[46] *Saycell* v. *Bool* [1948] 2 All E.R. 83; *Floyd* v. *Bush* [1953] 1 W.L.R. 242.
[47] *MacDonagh* [1974] Q.B. 448.
[48] *McQuaid* v. *Anderton* [1980] 3 All E.R. 540; *Caise* v. *Wright* [1981] R.T.R. 49.
[49] s.12(7)(*a*) (where the reference to "drive" is rather obscurely expressed, and can be read as also restricting the meaning of the word to "control by a person in or on the conveyance").
[50] *Miller* [1976] Crim.L.R. 147; *Diggin* (1980) 72 Cr.App.R. 204.
[51] *Tolley* v. *Giddings* [1964] 2 Q.B. 354.

opportunity of disembarking; he must, knowing the truth, "allow" himself to be carried.

(3) *The absence of consent or other lawful authority*

5–26   The taking must be without the consent of the owner of the conveyance or other lawful authority. In the case of a conveyance on hire or hire purchase, "owner" means the hirer (see subs. (7)(*b*)), and the fact that the taker does not have the consent of the legal owner is immaterial.[52] The reference to other lawful authority will cover such cases as the removal of a vehicle under statutory power by the police[53] or by a local authority.[54]

The consent required to exclude the offence is a consent actually given, not simply the consent that, as it may later transpire, the owner would have given had he been asked.[55]

5–27   *Consent obtained by fraud.* The use of fraud to obtain the owner's consent to the taking of a conveyance does not impair the effectiveness of that consent so as to found an offence under section 12. In *Whittaker* v. *Campbell*[56] D, who had no driving licence, obtained a van on hire from P by presenting to P the licence of one X and pretending to be X. The Divisional Court held that D did not take the van "without having the consent of [P]." The court declined to base this decision on the narrow ground that D and P did business face to face, so that P's mistake induced by the fraud was not as to the identity of the person he was dealing with but only as to one of his attributes (his holding a driving licence). No distinction, it seems, is to be drawn between mistakes as to fundamental and collateral matters respectively, or between mistakes preventing and those not preventing the formation of binding contracts. The mischief against which the section is directed does not require any such subtle inquiry. Where P has, in "commonsense terms," consented to part with the possession of his conveyance, but has done so as a result of D's fraud, the offence (if any) properly to be charged is one involving deception, which is the gravamen of D's conduct.[57] An earlier case in which fraud did not affect P's consent was *Peart*,[58] where P allowed D to borrow P's car, being induced to do so by D's lie about the nature of the journey he proposed to take. D committed no offence when he drove the car away; he did not take without consent.

5–28   The principle of these cases seems to collide with that of a group of cases (considered above[59]) which hold an offence under section 12 to be commit-

---

[52] *Tolhurst* v. *Woodhead* (1961) S.J. 16.
[53] See Road Traffic Regulation Act 1984, s.99, and regulations thereunder.
[54] See Refuse Disposal (Amenity) Act 1978, s.3.
[55] *Ambler* [1979] R.T.R. 217. A dictum of Woolf L.J. to the contrary in *Singh* v. *Rathour* [1988] 1 W.L.R. 422 at 430; [1988] 2 All E.R. 16 at 22, seems to be a slip.
[56] [1984] Q.B. 318.
[57] See especially [1984] Q.B. at 328–329, *per* Robert Goff L.J. Where a hiring is fraudulently induced there seems to be a plain offence of obtaining services by deception contrary to the Theft Act 1978, s.1. No deception offence is available, however, in a case of gratuitous borrowing such as *Peart* (text following).
[58] [1970] 2 Q.B. 672.
[59] §§ 5–18, 5–19.

ted when a person lawfully in possession of a conveyance enters upon a use which has not been authorised. The unsatisfactory state of the law appears most clearly when the cases of *Peart* and *Phipps and McGill*[60] are placed side by side. In *Peart* D's original journey was quite different from that which P had permitted, but the taking effected by driving off on this journey was held to be with P's consent. In *Phipps and McGill* D's original journey was the one authorised; but when he embarked on a further journey not authorised by P, he "took" the car without consent. It therefore appears that if one proposes to use another's vehicle for two purposes, one of which he might not consent to, it is safer to lie to him about both purposes than to be harmlessly truthful about the first and silent about the second. This can hardly be better law than sense.[61]

Taking obtained by force or duress. It seems that if the owner of a   **5–29**
conveyance is induced by force or duress to part with possession of it, his act may be regarded as one of submission rather than consent and an offence under section 12 can be found.[62]

(4) *Relevant states of mind; the relevance of intoxication*

The primary offence requires no "specific intent." In particular, it does   **5–30**
not require actual knowledge that the taking is without the owner's consent or other lawful authority. So conviction cannot be avoided by evidence that D was too drunk to form any intent or to know that he was taking without consent.[63] By contrast, knowledge that the conveyance has been taken without lawful authority is an express requirement of the secondary offence of driving or allowing oneself to be carried; and evidence of intoxication is clearly admissible in relation to this issue.

Section 12(6), on the other hand, provides equally for both offences a   **5–31**
limited form of "honesty" defence reminiscent of the law of theft[64]:

"A person does not commit an offence under this section by anything done in the belief that he has lawful authority to do it or that he would

---

[60] (1970) 54 Cr.App.R. 300.

[61] It is not suggested that any deception was in fact practised by the accused in *Phipps and McGill*. Note that in *Peart* "no issue was left to [the jury] as to whether . . . there could have been a fresh taking . . . of this particular van at some time after it was originally driven away" ([1970] 2 Q.B. 672 at 675); the conviction was quashed because of a misdirection on the only issue left to the jury, namely, whether there was at the outset an effective consent to the taking of the van. It seems to be suggested that on a direction canvassing "a fresh taking" a conviction might have been proper. But if there was evidence of only one journey, it is difficult to see at what point a new "taking" (without consent) could be identified; and even if D made, and all along intended to make, two distinct journeys, it would be highly artificial to regard a consent obtained by deception as applying only to the first.

[62] Compare *Hogdon* [1962] Crim.L.R. 563; *Whittaker* v. *Campbell* [1984] Q.B. 318 at 328 (without deciding the point).

[63] *MacPherson* [1973] R.T.R. 157. But White, *op. cit.* above, n. 34, argues that the phrase "for his own or another's use," correctly understood, renders the primary offence one of specific intent.

[64] See s.2(1)(*a*) and (*b*).

have the owner's consent if the owner knew of his doing it and the circumstances of it."

D, of course, can rely on this defence only if he adduces, or can point to, evidence tending to show that he held a positive belief within the subsection.[65] But if there is such evidence, the question will be whether the tribunal of fact is satisfied beyond reasonable doubt that D did not so believe; the persuasive burden rests on the prosecution.[66] And the question is simply as to D's belief, not as to whether D had lawful authority or whether the owner would have consented.[67]

It is submitted that D may rely on a belief within section 12(6) even if it is the result of self-induced intoxication. A close analogy exists in the form of authority on a provision to strikingly similar effect in the Criminal Damage Act.[68]

Taking a pedal cycle

5–32   It is a summary offence, punishable with a fine of £100,[69] to take a pedal cycle for one's own or another's use or to ride a pedal cycle knowing it to have been taken without such authority (s.12(5)). The exception for honesty provided by subsection (6) applies here also. The offences created by subsection (5) are not, of course, arrestable offences.

A difficulty may arise as to the correct classification of a motor-assisted pedal cycle. This was a motor vehicle for the purpose of the replaced offence of taking and driving away a motor vehicle, for which substantial penalties were provided. That offence could be committed by pedalling away such a cycle without using the motor[70]; but when the motor could not be used because of the absence of vital working parts, the vehicle was not a "motor vehicle" within the meaning of that phrase as defined in the Road Traffic Acts.[71] Perhaps a similar distinction can be drawn under section 12 as a means of identifying vehicles which at the relevant time are *mere* pedal cycles.

[65] *Gannon (Kevin)* (1987) 87 Cr.App.R. 254.
[66] *MacPherson*, above; *Gannon*, above. A failure to refer to this question on trial on indictment may, of course, be fatal to a conviction. But *Briggs* [1987] Crim.L.R. 708 is a surprising illustration: the Court of Appeal seemed to contemplate that the jury, though satisfied that D knew the motorcycle had been taken without lawful authority, might have thought that he possibly believed that he had lawful authority to drive it. The decision should be confined to its own facts.
[67] *Clotworthy* [1981] Crim.L.R. 501.
[68] *Jaggard* v. *Dickinson* [1981] Q.B. 527, decided on Criminal Damage Act 1971, s.5(2).
[69] Originally £50; thus, level 2 on the standard scale (Criminal Justice Act 1982, ss.37, 46), currently £100 (S.I. 1984, No. 447).
[70] *Floyd* v. *Bush* [1953] 1 W.L.R. 242.
[71] *Lawrence* v. *Howlett* [1952] 2 All E.R. 74.

Chapter 6

INTRODUCTION TO THE FRAUD OFFENCES

THE Theft Acts, by a variety of offences to be considered in Chapters 7 to **6–01**
11, make an important contribution to the armoury of the criminal law in its
fight against fraud. These offences require a general introduction, for two
reasons. First, an unassisted reader examining the relevant provisions, while
readily understanding each individually, would very likely be baffled as to
why they take the form they do. The first part of this chapter explains the
origins of the various provisions. Secondly, to study only the offences
considered in the following chapters would be to receive a misleading
impression of the range of important fraud offences. The second part of the
chapter refers briefly to the most significant of the other offences alongside
which the Theft Act offences stand. The chapter concludes with a brief
observation on the state of the law.

1. OFFENCES IN THE THEFT ACTS

The 1968 Act

In the *Eighth Report* the Committee canvassed arguments for and against **6–02**
some alternative schemes to provide for offences of deception.[1] Had the
scheme that the Committee favoured been accepted, there would have been
three main provisions. The first, to replace the old offence of obtaining by
false pretences,[2] would have dealt with obtaining property by deception; this
was accepted and is now embodied in section 15, which is the subject of
Chapter 7. The second would have been an improved and extended version
of the old offence of obtaining credit by fraud[3]; this was in itself uncontro-
versial. The third and highly controversial proposal was for a provision
making it an offence, dishonestly and with a view to gain, to induce a person
by deception to do or refrain from doing any act. This was included in the
Bill but foundered in the House of Lords. It was felt that it would effect too
wide and vague an extension of the criminal law. Instead, in place of the
second and third of the offences originally proposed, section 16 (obtaining
certain kinds of "pecuniary advantage" by deception) was hurriedly devised
to cover obtaining credit by deception together with so much of the rejected
general offence as was felt to be acceptable. The remnants of section 16,
after its partial repeal by the 1978 Act (as explained below), are examined in
Chapter 10. They deal with a variety of specialised transactions that ought
not to require individual mention in a well-drafted code.

[1] *Eighth Report*, paras. 97–100.
[2] Larceny Act 1916, s.32(1).
[3] Debtors Act 1869, s.13(1).

6–03   Sections 17, 19 and 20 contain modified versions, as recommended by the Committee, of some other pre-existing fraud offences. They are considered in Chapter 11. It would appear that the Committee desired to retain the substance of any offences in the replaced legislation that had anything distinctive to offer to the control of fraud.[4] The most important of these, undoubtedly, was falsification of accounts[5]—now re-enacted in modern guise, as false accounting, in section 17. Section 20(2) contains the only other offence meriting mention here. Procuring by deception the execution of a valuable security, which replaced a pre-existing offence of false pretences,[6] seems to have proved more useful to prosecutors than its predecessor was—arguably by courtesy in part of illegitimate interpretation.[7]

The 1978 Act

6–04   The most important case of the offence created by section 16 of the 1968 Act was that committed, under subsection $(2)(a)$, by one who by deception dishonestly obtained the reduction, or the total or partial evasion or deferment, of a debt or charge for which he made himself liable or was or might become liable. Happily it is no longer necessary to wrestle with the obscurities of this provision, to examine the difficult case law to which it gave rise or, in short, to understand in detail why it was said that the section had created "a judicial nightmare."[8] It was soon clear that section $16(2)(a)$ must be replaced. Proposals for amending legislation were made by the Committee in 1977 in their *Thirteenth Report* (with a draft Bill appended).[9] The outcome was the Theft Act 1978, which repealed section $16(2)(a)$ and created three new offences.

6–05   There are two ways of expressing simply what the Committee were seeking to achieve by clause 1 of their draft Bill. First, to use the language of the old law which had been replaced by section $16(2)(a)$, the aim was to penalise the obtaining of credit by deception—more precisely, the obtaining of credit in respect of the payment of money.[10] But the Committee were not in favour of employing the term "credit" in the drafting of the offence.[11] Secondly, the clause might be said to be aimed at the obtaining by deception "of services on which a monetary value is placed."[12] For an obtaining of credit in respect of a supply of property was already covered by section 15 of the 1968 Act, at least where an intention of permanently depriving P of the property existed; and what needed to be dealt with, to supplement section 15, was the use of deception to obtain on credit other valuable benefits such as a hiring of goods, the provision of labour or the grant of a licence—

---

[4] *Eighth Report*, paras. 102 *et seq.*
[5] Falsification of Accounts Act 1875, s.2.
[6] Larceny Act 1916, s.32(2).
[7] See below, §§ 11–14 to 11–17.
[8] *Per* Edmund Davies L.J. in *Royle* (1971) 56 Cr.App.R. 131.
[9] The Report was preceded by a Working Paper published in August 1974. An excellent account of the genesis of s.16 and of its history in the courts is provided in Appendix 2 to the Report.
[10] Working Paper, para. 25.
[11] *Thirteenth Report*, para. 8.
[12] *Ibid.* para. 9.

benefits that might collectively be called "services." But the Committee preferred not to employ the term "services" in the drafting of the offence.[13] Instead they offered in clause 1 an offence of dishonestly inducing another by deception to act on any person's promise of payment. This formula, attended by an adequate apparatus of definition, would have achieved the objects described above.

When the Bill was considered by the House of Lords, clause 1 was **6–06** criticised as too complex and a new clause was substituted, penalising the obtaining of services by deception. After the Bill had passed the Lords, the new clause was hurriedly referred to the Committee, who recommended instead the further version that was enacted as section 1 of the 1978 Act. The essential contribution of the Committee at this final stage was to provide a definition of "services" so as to ensure that the offence would be limited, as all along intended, to an obtaining of services "on which a monetary value is placed." On the other hand, the offence that emerged was so drafted as not to be limited to deception as to the prospect of payment; nor, indeed, need credit be involved at all. Moreover, section 1 does not (as the Lords amendment did) require the offender to have acted "with a view to gain or an intent to cause loss." The result is an offence not only of completely different design from that originally proposed, but also substantially wider in scope. It is examined in Chapter 8.

Section 2 (evading liability by deception) is considered in Chapter 9. **6–07** Whereas section 1, at least as originally drafted, was designed to control the deceptive obtaining of credit "at the outset of a transaction"[14] (that is, when liability to pay for services is originally incurred), section 2 is mainly concerned with the obtaining by deception of relief from some existing liability. But it also covers the obtaining by deception of an exemption from, or abatement of, liability to make a payment, which includes some cases of fraud committed before liability is incurred. Section 2 completed the task of replacing section 16(2)(*a*) of the 1968 Act.

The opportunity was taken at the same time to create, by section 3, a **6–08** general offence of making off without payment in a situation in which payment "on the spot" is expected. This deals with the mischief of "bilking," which was only partially, accidentally and artificially covered by sections 1, 15 and 16 of the 1968 Act.[15] The offence is examined in Chapter 12. Deception is not an ingredient of this offence.

2. OTHER OFFENCES

There follows a brief review of the more important fraud offences outside **6–09** the Theft Acts. The intention is to indicate, without treating in detail, the

---

[13] *Ibid*. para. 7.
[14] *Ibid*. para. 13.
[15] As explained below, §§ 12–03 to 12–05.

larger context in which the Theft Act offences require to be viewed, whether for the practical purpose of the selection of charges or as a basis for assessing the condition of this department of the criminal law.[16] The offences can conveniently be divided into four groups: general offences; offences involving companies; offences for the protection of investors; and fraud on the public revenue and social security fraud.

General offences

6–10   *Conspiracy to defraud.* The Criminal Law Act 1977 in principle limited conspiracy to agreements for the commission of crime.[17] The common law offence of conspiracy to defraud (which is not so limited) was nevertheless preserved, by section 5(2) of the 1977 Act, pending further consideration by the Law Commission of the steps that would need to be taken, to avoid unacceptable gaps in the criminal law, if it were abolished.[18] It now carries a maximum of 10 years' imprisonment.[19] Section 5(2) was amended in 1987 to ensure that an agreement to defraud that amounts also to a statutory conspiracy to commit an offence may be prosecuted either at common law or under the statute.[20] This laid to rest a notorious difficulty deriving from the unhappy original wording of the subsection.[21]

6–11   This is not the place for detailed consideration of conspiracy to defraud. It is sufficient to say that it is wide enough to embrace, not only agreements to commit many offences under the Theft Acts (including theft and most of the offences to be studied in the immediately following chapters), but also any other agreement to act dishonestly[22] to the prejudice[23] of the proprietary rights or economic interests of another or others.[24] So long, therefore, as two or more persons are involved, conspiracy to defraud substantially supplements the Theft Act offences. Deception need not be an intended means of effecting the fraud[25]; and the offence does not require an intention to obtain

---

[16] For a full exposition of the law as it stood in 1985, see Arlidge and Parry, *Fraud.*
[17] Criminal Law Act 1977, ss.1(1), 5(1).
[18] Law Commission Working Paper No. 56, *Conspiracy to Defraud* (1974); *Conspiracy and Criminal Law Reform*, Law Com. No. 76 (1976), paras. 1.14–1.16.
[19] Criminal Justice Act 1987, s.12(3). (This is the same maximum as for conspiracy to steal or to obtain property by deception.)
[20] *Ibid.* s.12(1)(2).
[21] *Ayres* [1984] A.C. 447; *Tonner* (1984) 80 Cr.App.R. 170; *Grant* (1986) 82 Cr.App.R. 324; *Cooke* [1986] A.C. 909; Criminal Law Revision Committee, *Eighteenth Report: Conspiracy to Defraud*, Cmnd. 9873 (1986); and see below, § 7–22, n. 39.
[22] *Landy* (1981) 72 Cr.App.R. 237. The requirement of dishonesty is governed by the principles in *Ghosh* [1982] Q.B. 1053 (see above, § 2–127).
[23] Including the risk of prejudice: *Sinclair* (1968) 52 Cr.App.R. 618; *Allsop* (1977) 64 Cr.App.R. 29; compare *Grantham* [1984] Q.B. 675.
[24] See, in particular, *Scott* v. *Metropolitan Police Commissioner* [1975] A.C. 819. In *Attorney General's Reference (No. 1 of 1982)* [1983] Q.B. 751 (agreement to sell whisky bearing counterfeits of a famous brand's labels) it was held that such defrauding must be the agreement's purpose (or "true object"); but Smith and Hogan, *Criminal Law* (6th ed.), pp. 271–273, show this to be questionable, particularly in the light of *Cooke* [1986] A.C. 809 (below, § 15–09), and suggest that it is enough that the conspirators recognise that the relevant loss or prejudice will be an inevitable consequence of their agreed conduct. The point is of reduced importance in the counterfeiting context since the addition (by the Copyright, Designs and Patents Act 1988, s.300) of s.58A to the Trade Marks Act 1938, creating an offence of applying or using a counterfeit trademark, with a maximum penalty of 10 years' imprisonment on conviction on indictment.
[25] *Scott* v. *Metropolitan Police Commissioner*, above.

any of the specific benefits with which the Theft Act offences are concerned (property belonging to another, services, the execution of a valuable security, a pecuniary advantage or the evasion of a liability).

Forgery is the offence committed by one who "makes a false instrument, **6–12** with the intention that he or another shall use it to induce somebody to accept it as genuine, and by reason of so accepting it to do or not to do some act to his own or another person's prejudice."[26] Another offence is that of using a false instrument, knowing or believing it to be false, with the intention of inducing somebody to accept it as genuine and thereby to act to his or another's prejudice.[27] The former offence is, of course, often preparatory to the commission of a Theft Act or other fraud offence that will occur when somebody is induced to act to his prejudice. Using a false instrument is commonly an attempt to commit such an offence. But "prejudice" is very widely defined,[28] and there is no requirement of dishonesty.[29] So forgery and using a false instrument somewhat extend the reach of the criminal law.[30]

Offences involving companies

Fraudulent trading. Section 458 of the Companies Act 1985 provides that **6–13** "[i]f any business of a company is carried on with intent to defraud creditors of the company or creditors of any other person, or for any fraudulent purpose," a person is guilty of an offence, carrying a maximum of seven years' imprisonment, if he is "knowingly a party to the carrying on of the business in that manner."[31] This offence was once capable of being prosecuted only in the course of the winding up of the company, because of the appearance of the offence in the same section as a provision providing for the civil liability of persons knowingly party to fraudulent trading that emerged "in the course of the winding up."[32] But the dependence of the offence upon a winding up was abandoned in 1961.[33] In consequence, the notion of carrying on the business of a company "for any fraudulent purpose" is now understood in its widest sense (and not, as it formerly was, as limited to frauds on existing creditors).[34] The offence is thus one of considerable utility. It can be used, for example, where it is desired to lay a single

[26] Forgery and Counterfeiting Act 1981, s.1. For making a copy of a false instrument, see *ibid.* s.2. For the meaning of "instrument" and "false," see *ibid.* ss.8 and 9(1).
[27] *Ibid.* s.3. For using a copy of a false instrument, see *ibid.* s.4.
[28] *Ibid.* s.10.
[29] *Horsey* v. *Hutchings, The Times*, November 8, 1984.
[30] See also the Computer Misuse Act 1990, s.2. This makes it an offence to cause a computer to perform any function with intent to secure unauthorised access to any program or data held in any computer (an offence under s.1), with the further intent to commit or facilitate an offence punishable with five years' imprisonment. The conduct so penalised may be conduct preparatory to fraud, or to forgery (of a "device on or in which information is recorded or stored by . . . electronic . . . means": see 1981 Act, s.8(1)(*d*)), or of false accounting in aid of, or to conceal, fraud (see below, § 11–01).
[31] Companies Act 1985, s.458, Sched. 24. In spite of the high maximum penalty on conviction on indictment, the offence is triable either way.
[32] Companies Act 1948, s.332(1) and (3); *D.P.P.* v. *Schildkamp* [1971] A.C. 1.
[33] Companies Act 1961, s.96.
[34] *Kemp* (1988) 87 Cr.App.R. 95.

fraud charge (rather than to rely on specific obtaining offences) against a person who, working alone but through his company, has conducted a sustained course of obtaining property or services by deception.[35]

6-14   *Other offences.* Numerous other offences capable of being committed specifically by companies or their officers (in addition to that under section 19 of the present Act), have, taken together, a great deal to contribute to the control of fraud.[36] Many involve the making of a misleading, false or deceptive statements or the falsification of accounts; others are directed at the misuse of company assets in fraud of the company itself, its shareholders or creditors.

Offences for the protection of investors

6-15   *Misleading statements, etc.* The protection of investors and others against deceptive inducements to risk their money is the special concern of important offences under section 47(1) of the Financial Services Act 1986 (investment generally)[37]; under section 133 of the same Act (contracts of insurance)[38]; and under section 35 of the Banking Act 1987 (the making of deposits).[39] These provisions, which carry maximum prison terms of seven years, are all drafted on the same model: they penalise the making of a statement, promise or forecast known to be misleading, false or deceptive, or the dishonest concealment of any material facts, or the reckless making (dishonestly or otherwise) of a statement, promise or forecast which is misleading, false or deceptive, for the purpose of inducing, or being reckless whether it may induce, another person to (in particular) enter into an investment contract or a contract of insurance or to make a deposit. A less serious offence, but one punishable with two years' imprisonment on conviction on indictment, is that (under section 70(1) of the Companies Act 1985) of authorising the issue of a company prospectus which includes an untrue statement.

6-16   *Creation of false market.* Section 47(2) of the Financial Services Act 1986 provides an offence (punishable with imprisonment for up to seven years) of creating a false or misleading impression as to the market in, or the price or value of, any investments (very broadly defined[40]) for the purpose (in effect) of inducing investment decisions based on that impression. Until the creation of this statutory offence such conduct could be prosecuted only as a conspiracy to defraud[41] and therefore only if two or more persons could be shown to be involved.

---

[35] "[P]rosecutors sometimes use this type of charge as a kind of one-man conspiracy to defraud": Arlidge and Parry, *Fraud*, para. 12.45.
[36] See, in particular, Companies Act 1985, ss.110(2), 114, 143(2), 151(3), 342(1)(2), 393, 450(1)(2); Insolvency Act 1986, ss.206–211 (and compare ss.353–359 for offences connected with bankruptcy). See also s.19 of the Theft Act 1968.
[37] Replacing s.13 of the Prevention of Fraud (Investments) Act 1958.
[38] Replacing s.73 of the Insurance Companies Act 1982.
[39] Replacing s.39(1) of the Banking Act 1979.
[40] By s.1(1) and Sched. 1, Pt. I.
[41] *Scott* v. *Brown, Doering, McNab & Co.* [1892] 2 Q.B. 724.

Insider dealing. Finally, mention should be made of the Company Secur-   **6–17**
ities (Insider Dealing) Act 1985, which contains provisions designed to
prevent the exploitation by "insiders" of "unpublished price sensitive information" relating to company securities.[42] The prohibition of such exploitation extends to those who have knowingly obtained such information from
insiders[43] and to public servants and those who have knowingly obtained
information from them.[44]

Frauds on the public revenue and social security fraud

Cheating at common law. The old common law offence of cheating was   **6–18**
abolished by the Theft Act 1968 "except as regards offences relating to the
public revenue."[45] According to modern decisions, the exception preserves
a broad offence of great utility, available to deal with any conduct intended
to defraud the revenue, whether consisting of positive act—as, for example,
the understating of income, profits or assets attracting tax, the overstating of
expenses or the claiming of fictitious allowances—or of omission.[46] There
are no maximum penalties for the offence, since it is punishable at common
law. But a person may be convicted of it although there exists a statutory
offence with limited penalties specially provided for such conduct as is
proved against him—as, for example, an offence specifically concerned with
failure to meet V.A.T. liability.[47]

Offences under revenue legislation. The most important statutory offences   **6–19**
relating to the public revenue occur under the Customs and Excise Management Act 1979,[48] the Value Added Tax Act 1983[49] and the Income and
Corporation Taxes Act 1988, s.561(10) and (11).[50]

[42] s.1(1)(2)(5). See also Companies Act 1985, s.323(1) (prohibition on directors dealing in share options).
[43] s.1(4)(6). Information received without being "acquired by purpose and effort" may be "obtained" for this purpose: *Attorney General's Reference (No. 1 of 1988)* (1989) 89 Cr.App.R. 60.
[44] s.2 (as amended by the Financial Services Act 1986, s.173).
[45] s.32(1)(a). The existence of the offence of cheating the revenue has been repeatedly confirmed in modern times, most recently in *Mulligan* [1990] S.T.C. 220.
[46] *Mavji* [1987] 1 W.L.R. 1388; [1987] 2 All E.R. 758 ("The common law offence of cheating does not require a false representation, either by words or conduct. Cheating can include any form of fraudulent conduct which results in diverting money from the revenue and in depriving the revenue of money to which it is entitled."); *Redford* (1988) 89 Cr.App.R. 1. The court's statement in *Mavji* refers only to conduct that results in actual disadvantage to the revenue. But the offence appears to embrace attempts to defraud the revenue as well as successful defrauding.
[47] Cases in last note.
[48] See in particular ss.50(2) (improper importation of goods: one variety of this offence involves an intent to defraud Her Majesty of chargeable duty), 167 (untrue declarations, etc.), 168 (counterfeiting documents, etc.), 170(1)(2) (fraudulent evasion of duty, etc.).
[49] s.39, as amended by the Finance Act 1985, s.12, Sched. 6. (One amendment made in 1985 was the raising of the maximum sentence of imprisonment from two to seven years, thus removing one ground for resort to the common law offence of cheating: see above, text at n. 47.) Compare the Car Tax Act 1983, s.1(4), Sched. 1, para. 8.
[50] These provisions are concerned with frauds involving the obtaining or misuse of certificates and vouchers required for exemption from the special deduction of tax (under s.559(4)) from payments made to sub-contractors in the construction industry ("the lump"). The offences are punishable on summary conviction with a fine not exceeding £5,000.

6–20   *Offences under the general law.* Fraud on the Inland Revenue is not, in general, the subject of offences under tax legislation, but is left to be dealt with under the general criminal law. Obvious available offences, apart from common law cheating, are a number under the Theft Acts (most obviously obtaining property by deception, evasion of liability by deception and false accounting) and the Forgery and Counterfeiting Act 1981. And the Perjury Act 1911 provides in section 5 an offence of knowingly and wilfully making (otherwise than on oath) a statement, false in a material particular, in a document (such as a tax return) required to be made by any public general Act of Parliament.

6–21   *Social security fraud* is the subject of a special offence under section 55(1) of the Social Security Act 1986. This renders liable to a fine not exceeding level 5 on the standard scale or to imprisonment for up to three months, or to both, a person who, "for the purpose of obtaining any benefit or payment under any of the benefit Acts, or for any other purpose connected with any of those Acts—(a) makes a statement or representation which he knows to be false; or (b) produces or furnishes, or knowingly causes or knowingly allows to be produced or furnished, any document or information which he knows to be false in a material particular." But the policy in relation to relatively small frauds is to avoid prosecution in favour of warning and the recovery of benefit wrongly obtained (commonly by deduction from future benefits).[51] Offences under the general criminal law, notably obtaining property by deception, are likely to be used for the more serious cases that require prosecution.

3. COMMENT

6–22   No one wanting to construct a rational, efficient law of criminal fraud would choose to start from the present position. The law sketched in the preceding parts of this chapter is in a very untidy and unsatisfactory condition. The various offences are not so framed and related to each other as to cover, in a clearly organised way and without doubt or strained interpretation, the range of fraudulent conduct with which the law should be able to deal. The only general offence available to catch wrongdoers who might slip through the mesh of other offences is conspiracy to defraud, which suffers from three vices: it requires two or more parties; it is a common law offence; and it may consist of an agreement to do something that is not an offence if done by one person (that is why it can catch those who might otherwise escape). Perhaps, indeed, the concept of criminal fraud needs to be as wide as it is in the conspiracy offence; but if so, a general offence committable by an individual is what is required. Such an offence has in fact been mooted by the Law Commission in an elaborate consultation paper concerned with the future of

---

[51] See comments of Lord Lane C.J. in *Stewart* [1987] 1 W.L.R. 559; [1987] 2 All E.R. 383.

conspiracy to defraud.[52] Whether or not this course were adopted, it is surely desirable that the pattern of fraud offences, including those to be studied in the following chapters, should be rationalised. Fraud is too important to be tackled with defective tools.

[52] Law Commission Working Paper No. 104, *Conspiracy to Defraud* (1987). The study of conspiracy to defraud is business left over from the Commission's earlier general work on the reform of conspiracy; see above, § 6–10.

Chapter 7

OBTAINING PROPERTY BY DECEPTION

1. THE OFFENCE

7–01 THE dishonest obtaining by deception of property belonging to another with the intention of permanently depriving the other of it is an offence punishable on conviction on indictment with up to 10 years' imprisonment (s.15(1)).

"For the purposes of this section a person is to be treated as obtaining property if he obtains ownership, possession or control of it . . ." (s.15(2)). "Property" and "belonging to another" have much the same large meanings as they have in the law of theft (s.34(1)). "Deception" is defined (s.15(4)) so as to include any deliberate or reckless deception as to a matter of fact or law, however effected. These definitions combine to produce a very wide offence.[1]

7–02 *Some irrelevant matters.* All the conditions of liability are stated in section 15(1). In a case of obtaining a social security benefit by deception it was argued that no offence could be proved in the absence of an adjudicator's decision that the defendant was not entitled to benefit. This remarkable argument, effectively making an administrative adjudication an ingredient of the offence, inevitably failed.[2] Nor, probably, is a person using deception to obtain a benefit saved by the fact that the truth he fails to declare would actually entitle him to benefit (though his knowledge or belief that he is legally so entitled may be relevant to whether he obtains the benefit dishonestly).[3]

Another matter that the Court of Appeal has had occasion to declare irrelevant is the tendency of the victim's trading policy, sought to be circumvented by the deception charged, to contravene European community law. The use of the criminal law is concerned with the dishonest deception charged, not with support for the victim's policy.[4]

---

[1] But the fact that the property obtained must have belonged to another seems strictly to have one serious limiting effect on the offence; see below, § 7–06. The offence is distinctly wider than that of obtaining by false pretences which it replaced: Larceny Act 1916, s.32(1). The main limitations of that offence were: that it applied only to the obtaining of any chattel, money or valuable security; that it applied only when ownership and not merely possession of property was obtained; and that the pretence had to be as to some present or past fact, not including the alleged offender's intentions as to the future.

[2] *Lally* [1989] Crim.L.R. 648.

[3] See below, § 7–66.

[4] *Dearlove and Drucker* (1988) 88 Cr.App.R. 279.

2. "OBTAINS PROPERTY BELONGING TO ANOTHER"

Property belonging to another

"Property"

The definition of "property" in section 4(1) is made to apply generally for   **7–03**
purposes of the Act by section 34(1), so that the offence under section 15 can
be committed in respect of any kind of property. There are no provisions, as
there are in the case of theft, limiting the circumstances in which land can be
the subject of the offence. Whatever can be transferred by one person to
another as property is in practice within section 15, for deception can induce
its transfer. So, for instance, a beneficial interest in property under a trust is,
it is submitted, itself property within the phrase "things in action and other
intangible property," and to induce the assignment of such an interest is
therefore to obtain property.

If D, by deception, induces P to pay him more money than he would have
paid but for the deception, there is an obtaining of property within the
section and D may be convicted even though the precise amount of the
excess cannot be specified.[5]

"Belonging to another"

The property obtained must be property "belonging to another."[6] The   **7–04**
wide definition of this phrase in section 5(1) is also made to apply here by
section 34(1). It is desirable to notice the force of this in conjunction with the
provision that "a person is to be treated as obtaining property if he obtains
ownership, possession or control of it" (s.15(2)). The result is that there is an
obtaining within section 15 if the effect of D's fraud is that he obtains
ownership, possession or control of any property which P owns, possesses or
controls or in which P has any proprietary right or interest.[7]

Of course, the normal case will be that in which D induces P to part with
property of which P is the owner. It will be enough if D obtains ownership
only or possession only. For instance, if D by deception induces P to agree to
sell him specific goods in a deliverable state so that, as prima facie occurs in
such a case,[8] the property in the goods passes to D on the making of the
contract, D is guilty even if he never acquires possession.[9] Conversely, D

---

[5] *Levene* v. *Pearcey* [1976] Crim.L.R. 63 (taxi driver telling passenger that normal route is blocked, using longer route and obtaining larger fare).
[6] A mistake in the information or indictment as to the person to whom the property belonged will be immaterial if the defendant nevertheless has enough information to know the nature of the charge; if the victim's identity is material, an error on the point can be cured by amendment: *Etim* v. *Hatfield* [1975] Crim.L.R. 234.
[7] With one immaterial exception: see s.5(1).
[8] Sale of Goods Act 1979, s.18, r. 1.
[9] By obtaining ownership, D puts himself in a position to pass ownership to a third person, who may buy in good faith and obtain a valid title as against P: Sale of Goods Act 1979, s.23; *Eighth Report*, para. 90.

may deceive P into lending or hiring goods to him, D's intention being to deprive P permanently of them, and here D is guilty although he does not acquire ownership.

7–05   Alternatively, D may himself be the owner and still commit the offence. Two obvious examples are the following:

(i) P contracts to sell goods to D, D using no deception to induce the contract. The circumstances are such that the property in the goods passes before delivery. P retains possession and is entitled to do so until D pays or tenders the price. D by deception induces P to part with possession (*e.g.* he gives P a cheque that he knows to be worthless).

(ii) D pledges goods with P. By deception he induces P to redeliver the goods to him.

Again, neither D nor the person deceived need be the owner. P may have possession or control of Q's goods. If D induces P to part with the goods, intending to deprive both P and Q of them, either P or Q can be named in the indictment as the person to whom the goods belong. It will no doubt be convenient to name P.

Newly created thing in action

7–06   The limitation of the offence to the obtaining of property belonging to the victim might be thought embarrassing in some cases. One such case is that in which, by deception and at the expense of P, D causes his bank account to be credited with a sum. D thus obtains a thing in action—he has a right enforceable against his bank.[10] But that right, which is the only "property" that he obtains, is plainly not something that has ever belonged to P. The point seems not to have been taken in Court of Appeal cases[11] in which D has presented for payment a cheque drawn by P that he has stolen from the payee,[12] or in which he has by fraud induced P bank to transfer funds to Q bank for the credit of his account with the latter.[13] In the former a conviction of theft of the cheque (or, on suitable facts, obtaining the cheque from the payee by deception) might suffice. In the latter the argument presented here, if correct, might mean that the rogue has committed no offence. This would be regrettable. But a rejection of the argument would seem to involve treating "obtains property belonging to another" as meaning, in cases like these, "obtains a thing in action equivalent in value to other property (not necessarily describable) belonging to P before the transaction induced by the deception." An obtaining so described ought no doubt to be within section 15; but it seems not to be within the section as drafted. Nor is an

---

[10] See § 2–141, above. Even if the credit merely goes to reduce D's overdraft, there is presumably for a fraction of time property that can be said to have been obtained by D.

[11] But it is understood to have been taken successfully before some trial judges.

[12] *Davies* (1981) 74 Cr.App.R. 94: cheque for £10,000, drawn by P1 in favour of P2, stolen from P2 and paid into D's bank; held, D obtained "the sum of £10,000" (but see above, § 2–11 at n. 33) "belonging to P1."

[13] *Thompson* (1984) 79 Cr.App.R. 191: D's account at P bank abroad inflated by D's fraud; credit transfer requested to D's account with E bank in England; charge, obtaining "£x the property of P bank"; conviction upheld.

obtaining by deception (*e.g.* by disguised multiple applications) of shares issued on flotation direct to the public. Such shares[14] are "things in action [or] other intangible property" existing for the first time as the property of the person to whom they are allotted.[15]

"Obtains"

For purposes of section 15:   7–07
(a) "a person is to be treated as obtaining property if he obtains ownership, possession or control of it." The flexibility that this gives to the offence has been illustrated above.
(b) " 'obtain' includes obtaining for another or enabling another to obtain or to retain." The following are examples:
(i) *Obtaining for another.* P has a lien on E's goods and D on E's behalf persuades P to give up possession to him (D) by promising to discharge E's debt. (Note that, as P is the only person whom D intends to deprive, he alone can be named as the person to whom the property belongs.)
(ii) *Enabling another to obtain.* In a similar situation, D prevails on P to deliver the property direct to E. In *Duru*,[16] D deceived P into making a loan to F, which P did by sending a cheque to F's solicitor, E. D had "enabled [E] to obtain" possession or control of the cheque; and it was irrelevant that E was not himself a party to the deception.
(iii) *Enabling another to retain.* E is in possession of P's goods. D deceives P into leaving them with E rather than claiming their return.
It is odd that enabling another to retain is obtaining within the section but that enabling oneself to retain is not. True, in most cases where D, by deception, and with the necessary intention, induces P to let him retain P's property, D will commit theft. But theft may not catch some cases—for instance, if D, P's bailee, induces P by deception to sell him the goods bailed and thus to leave them in his possession, it is possible that he will commit no appropriation until after the goods have ceased to belong to P.[17]

3. DECEPTION

Statutory definition

Section 15(4) provides a partial explanation of the term "deception":   7–08

"For purposes of this section 'deception' means any deception (whether deliberate or reckless) by words or conduct as to fact or as to law, including a deception as to the present intentions of the person using the deception or any other person."

The purpose of this provision is not to provide a definition in the full

---

[14] As opposed to relevant pieces of paper (letters of allotment, share certificates) transferred by the company.
[15] See also below, § 7–62, n. 31.
[16] (1973) 58 Cr.App.R. 151.
[17] See, however, above, § 2–91. See further, Smith, *Theft*, para. 201.

sense, but rather to make clear that the term "deception" used in this Act does not share some of the limitations of the term "false pretence" in the Larceny Act offence replaced by section 15.[18] In particular, it was not formerly an offence to obtain property by making a promise that the maker had no intention of keeping or by otherwise deliberately misrepresenting an intention. It was therefore thought desirable to single out fraudulent statements of intention for express reference. Section 15(4) is one of those provisions designed as important messages for the pre-Theft Act practitioner in particular.[19]

The parenthesis "whether deliberate or reckless" may conveniently be reserved to a discussion of the whole of the fault element of the offence.[20] The rest of the subsection requires extensive consideration at this point.

Deception requires a deceiver and a deceived

7–09   Towards the end of section 15(4) occurs the phrase "the person using the deception." This might suggest that deception is something employed (a lie or other tricking device) rather than something practised (a lie or trick having an effect upon a victim). But the Committee, in the course of justifying the choice of the word "deception" in place of the old phrase "false pretence," said that the new expression has:

> "the advantage of directing attention to the effect that the offender deliberately produced on the mind of the person deceived, whereas 'false pretence' makes one think of what exactly the offender did in order to deceive"[21];

and it is certainly true that there can be no deception without a deceived party. This part of the chapter—like section 15(4)—will be concerned only with the deceptive practice used by D; but it must not be forgotten that one element of a deception is P's being in some sense misled by that practice. In what sense he must be misled will be considered hereafter.

"Deceiving" a machine

7–10   It appears now[22] to be universally accepted that a deception offence cannot be committed by obtaining an advantage through misuse of a machine (whether a computer or a mechanical device) without the intervention of a deceived human being.[23] The terms of two of the deception offences seem to confirm this view. Sections 1 and 2 of the Theft Act 1978 (obtaining

---

[18] Obtaining any chattel, money or valuable security by any false pretence: Larceny Act 1916, s.32.
[19] Others are ss.3(1) and 4(1).
[20] See §§ 7–55, 7–56.
[21] *Eighth Report*, para. 87.
[22] The point was left open in *Davies* v. *Flackett* [1973] R.T.R. 8.
[23] There has been at least one ruling to this effect in the context of false V.A.T. returns (*Moritz*, 1961, unreported), with consequent amending legislation: Value Added Tax Act 1983, s.39(2C) (added by Finance Act 1985, s.12(5)).

services by deception; evasion of liability by deception) are both worded in a way which assumes the existence of a person who is not merely the victim of the offence but is also personally affected by the deception.[24] It would be odd if the offence of obtaining property, but not that of obtaining services, could be committed by feeding a false coin into a machine. The oddity would be compounded by the fact that where property is obtained, as from a vending machine, the transaction can perfectly aptly be prosecuted as theft.

The Law Commission has several times considered whether the need for a   **7–11**
human object of deception leaves a gap in the law of fraud that ought to be filled.[25] The tendency of its discussions so far seems to be that, although there is a case for law reform, the gap is only a small one, because the dishonest manipulation of machines almost always involves the commission of some other offence, often theft. But the gravamen of many transactions will be the actual dishonest obtaining of an advantage (otherwise than by theft) that a conviction of an offence such as forgery[26] or false accounting will only imperfectly reflect. Some reform of the law should certainly figure in any revision either of the Theft Acts or of the general law of fraud.

Deception by words or conduct

Section 15(4) explains that "deception" embraces "any deception . . . by   **7–12**
words or conduct." A conventional way of saying much the same thing is to say that one person may deceive another by either an express or an implied representation which is false; he represents something to be the case which is not. But it has been observed that some kinds of deception cannot properly, or at least without artificiality, be analysed as involving the making of representations.[27] Although this may be true, the conventional language remains useful. In every case of deception the victim will in some sense[28] be led to suppose that which is not; and in this chapter "that which is not" will be referred to as that which is "falsely represented" to be the case.

Adherence to this conventional usage in a general discussion does not imply that similar language is obligatory or even appropriate in the drafting of particular charges. What matters in charging is that the substance of the allegations should be clear to the defendant and to the court. It may or may not, depending on the type of case, be accurate and informative to assert that the defendant implied a particular false proposition (or "represented" something) by his conduct.

Deception as to fact or law

Law

The reference in section 15(4) to a deception "as to law" is included for the   **7–13**

---

[24] s.1(2): ". . . the other is induced to confer a benefit"; s.2(1)(*b*): ". . . induces the creditor . . . to wait for payment."
[25] Working Paper No. 56, *Conspiracy to Defraud* (1974), paras. 61–63; Working Paper No. 104, *Conspiracy to Defraud* (1987), paras. 4.9–4.14; *Computer Misuse* (Law Com. No. 186; Cm. 819: 1989), paras. 2.4–2.7.
[26] See Forgery and Counterfeiting Act 1981, ss.8(1)(*d*), 10(3)).
[27] Arlidge and Parry, *Fraud*, paras. 2.06 *et seq.*; Williams, *Textbook*, pp. 780–782.
[28] See below, §§ 7–41 to 7–45.

avoidance of doubt.[29] It was not settled whether a false statement as to a matter of law was a false pretence under the old law. There was no need for similar uncertainty under the present Act.

Fact and opinion; implied fact

7–14   A "deception . . . by words . . . as to fact" involves the making of an untrue statement as to some past or present fact; that the car being sold was first registered in a particular year; that the fire giving rise to an insurance claim destroyed the mink coat; and so on. Usually it is easy enough to identify a fact falsely asserted by the words used. But difficulties can occur where the defence is in a position to argue that the statement made was one of opinion rather than of fact; or where the prosecution need to argue that what was false was something implied by a true statement of fact or an apparent expression of opinion.

7–15   (i) *Fact and opinion.* In criminal law, as in civil law, liability does not normally derive from the giving of an unjustified or exaggerated opinion. A statement of opinion is not a statement of fact. A person seeking to make a sale is not penalised for over-praising his goods so long as he confines himself to statements as to value and quality. But he cannot with impunity assert that the goods have some attribute that is no mere matter of opinion and which it can be demonstrated that they do not have. The difference has been happily expressed as that "between saying that something is gold and saying that something is as good as gold."[30]

7–16   (ii) *Implied fact.* There may be deception "by words . . . as to fact" although no untrue fact is expressly stated. The assertion of one fact, for example, may be such as to imply the non-existence of some other fact which the maker of the assertion knows to exist and which might affect the mind of the person to whom the statement is made. For instance, a statement about the past fortunes of a business for sale may assert that the average turnover of the business during the past 10 years has been of a certain satisfactory order. This assertion may be literally true; but if the turnover has consistently decreased over the 10 years, so that the volume of business now being done is disastrously small, the concealment of this material fact should certainly involve potential liability for "deception . . . as to fact."[31] A neat example of an implied fact is provided by a case in which a car dealer turned back the odometer of a car and displayed a notice saying that the mileage

---

[29] *Eighth Report*, para. 101(ii).
[30] Smith and Hogan, *Criminal Law* (1st ed.), p. 410, comparing (*inter alia*) *Bryan* (1857) Dears. & B. 265 (opinion; but an unsatisfactory case) and *Ardley* (1871) L.R. 1 C.C.R. 301 (fact).
[31] Compare *Kylsant* [1932] 1 K.B. 442, decided on the wording of the Larceny Act 1861, s.84 ("statement . . . false in any material particular").

reading "may not be correct." He thereby falsely represented, as the indictment alleged, "that he had no reason to disbelieve" the reading.[32]

(iii) *Expression of opinion implying fact.* A statement that is, in form, one   **7-17**
of opinion may likewise imply some fact that can be shown to be untrue. To say that Mr. Smith is "a most desirable tenant" is to seem to assert at least that there are no facts known to the speaker that would justify the view that Mr. Smith does not deserve this description.[33] Similarly, the statement that the shares of a company would be a worthwhile investment is in form a value judgment; but it would surely be falsified by proof that the company was unable to pay its creditors and had no apparent means of achieving solvency. Another way of discovering a statement of fact in such cases is to say that D is asserting that he holds the opinion he expresses when in fact he does not hold that opinion at all. An indictment would accurately charge that D falsely represented that he "was of the opinion" or "believed" that such-and-such was the case.

Deception as to intention

The reference in section 15(4) to "a deception as to . . . present intentions"   **7-18**
makes clear that the doctrine of *Edgington* v. *Fitzmaurice*[34] operates in the criminal law as well as in the civil. D's statement that, for example, he intends to use for a particular purpose money that P is thereby induced to invest in D's enterprise is a deception if D does not then have that intention. The definition refers, of course, to "the present intentions of [D] *or any other person.*" So D's statement that E, or the limited company that D represents, intends to do something in the future is also within the definition, if E or the company has not that intention and D either knows this fact or does not believe his statement to be true.

Promises

The statement "I promise to do such-and-such" is in effect a statement of   **7-19**
intention; for after all a person may be taken to imply an intention to keep his promise. So with the enactment of the Theft Act 1968 it became an offence to obtain property by a false promise—that is, a promise which, at the time he makes it, the maker does not intend to keep.[35] Under the former

---

[32] *King* [1979] Crim.L.R. 122. *Banaster* (1978) 68 Cr.App.R. 272, illustrates the sometimes subtle distinction between what words mean and what they imply. A minicab driver told a passenger at London Airport that he was "an airport taxi." The jury, it was said, were rightly allowed to find that his words "implied" that it was "all official." The words no doubt *meant* that he had some official status. His conviction, which was upheld, was of obtaining the fare paid by the deception that it was "the correct fare" (meaning "authorised"?). The words he used seem not to have *meant* this; it is not even very plain that they *implied* it.
[33] Compare *Smith* v. *Land and House Property Corporation* (1884) 28 Ch.D. 7.
[34] (1885) 29 Ch.D. 459.
[35] For important observations as to statements of present intention, expectation or belief implied by the making of promises or forecasts, see cases decided under the Trade Descriptions Act 1968: *Sunair Holidays Ltd.* (1973) 57 Cr.App.R. 782; *British Airways Board* v. *Taylor* (1975) 62 Cr.App.R. 174.

law of obtaining by false pretences there were situations in which, although the essential wrongdoing was the making of a false promise, a conviction had to rest on the discovery of some pretence as to a fact other than intention. Thus, if D obtained money from P by promising to marry her, he could formerly be convicted of obtaining the money by false pretences only if he was not free to marry her and then only upon the ground that he had asserted that he was. He may now be convicted if, and because, he did not intend to marry P. But it is vital to stress that the criminal law has not become a vehicle for the enforcement of promises. What must be proved is that at the time of the obtaining D did not have the intention that his words or conduct could be taken to assert. It is neither necessary nor sufficient to prove that he later decided not to keep his promise (though the fact that he did not keep it may be evidence in favour of the conclusion that he never intended to do so).

Deception by conduct

Introduction

7-20   The scope of deception offences depends in part upon the readiness of courts to read into the behaviour of defendants the making of relevant representations. It also depends in part upon their readiness to conclude that the alleged victims of deception relied upon the representations in acting as they did. The present discussion concerns the former point: what statement of fact (if any) does D's conduct imply? The answer to this question is, of course, dependent to an extent upon the question whether P can be said to have relied upon such a statement; for a court will not think to read into D's conduct any statement upon which P cannot in some sense be said to have relied.[36] From the wealth of possible implications of D's conduct, therefore, the law selects certain implications only. But the discovery of *any* implication is an act of interpretation the validity of which cannot be demonstrated. In making such a discovery the court is in truth engaged upon an artificial exercise designed to ensure that the law of deception is given appropriate content. That law cannot be limited only to "deception by words." The question how much further it is to stretch is obviously one of policy. It is also one of plausibility. Any statement that a person is to be regarded as impliedly making in a given situation ought to be one that an honest person in that situation might be expected to confirm without question. And it ought to be one the truth of which may be supposed to be of significance to a person to whom it is treated as being addressed in the context of a transaction of the kind in question. It is thought that, so long as this requirement of plausibility is respected, it is proper for the law to use deception offences energetically in the control of dishonest activity.

Standard examples

7-21   The following are some standard examples of different kinds of fraud depending upon deception by conduct.

---

[36] As to reliance, see below, §§ 7–41 to 7–45.

(i) A person who sells property is normally taken to imply by his conduct that he has a right to do so. If he has not (and knows that he has not or does not believe that he has), he employs a deception which is likely to influence his buyer; for the buyer would be unlikely to buy if he knew that the seller had no title. If the buyer is so influenced, what he pays for the property is obtained by deception by conduct.[37]

(ii) The fraud perpetrated by one who wears a uniform to which he is not entitled has long been a classic of the textbooks because of the direction of Bolland B. in *Barnard* in 1837[38]:

> "If nothing had passed in words, I should have laid down that the fact of the prisoner's appearing in the cap and gown would have been pregnant evidence from which a jury should infer that he pretended he was a member of the university. . . ."

There is no reason why this popular illustration of an implied pretence should not survive as a simple example of deception by conduct.

(iii) A similar example is that of the fraud committed by establishing the   **7–22**
outward appearance of a genuine business or enterprise and thereby induc-
ing people to supply goods that will not be paid for, or to pay for non-existent goods, or to invest money in a worthless undertaking. Frauds of this kind are often large-scale operations in which several people are involved. They are commonly prosecuted as conspiracies—either to commit offences (as obtaining property by deception) or to defraud.[39]

(iv) A person who enters a restaurant and orders a meal impliedly repre-
sents that he intends to pay for the meal (and, in the ordinary case, that he intends to pay before leaving the restaurant).[40]

Cheques, cheque cards and credit cards

The representations involved in the use of cheques, cheque cards and   **7–23**
credit cards have been considered by the House of Lords in two cases.

[37] Compare *Edwards* [1978] Crim.L.R. 49 (squatter "letting" a room).
[38] (1837) 7 C. & P. 784.
[39] Conspiracy to defraud was preserved as an offence at common law by the Criminal Law Act 1977, s.5(2) (and is now punishable with a maximum of 10 years' imprisonment: Criminal Justice Act 1987, s.12(3)). Under s.5(2) in its original form, an agreement on a course of conduct amounting to or involving the commission of a substantive offence, even of fraud (such as obtaining property by deception), could be charged only under s.1 of the Criminal Law Act 1977 as a conspiracy to commit that offence, and not as a conspiracy to defraud (though if the agreement involved additional fraudulent conduct, not amounting to a sub-stantive offence, this aspect of the agreement could be charged as a conspiracy to defraud): *Ayres* [1984] A.C. 447 (as explained in *Cooke* [1986] A.C. 909). This inhibition continues to apply to agreements made before, and not subsisting on, July 20, 1987. But on that date s.12 of the Criminal Justice Act 1987 came into force, removing the inhibition (subs.(1)) and appropriately amending s.5(2) of the 1977 Act (subs. (2)). As to the choice of charge, see paras. 15–17 of the Code of Practice for Prosecutors made by the Director of Public Prosecutions under the Prosecution of Offences Act 1985, s.10.
[40] See *D.P.P.* v. *Ray* [1974] A.C. 370 (§ 7–33, below)—where there was no offence under s.15, because the intention not to pay was formed after the food had been consumed.

(i) *Cheques*. Professor Kenny long ago identified a number of representations as implied by "the familiar act of drawing a cheque."[41] (a) The first implied statement was "that the drawer has an account with [the] bank" upon which the cheque is drawn. There is no doubt that this statement is implied; and it is a convenient representation to allege where the drawer has no such account. (b) The second implied statement was "that [the drawer] has authority to draw on [the account] for [the] amount" for which the cheque is drawn. This implication, it has now been suggested, is incorrect. "A customer needs no authority from his banker to draw a cheque on him; it is the banker who needs authority from the customer to pay it on presentment."[42] It is in any case redundant, being, like the first statement, embraced by the third.[43] (c) In *Metropolitan Police Commissioner* v. *Charles*[44] the majority of their Lordships[45] accepted Kenny's third representation, namely:

"... that the present state of affairs is such that, in the ordinary course of events, the cheque will on its future presentment be duly honoured."[46]

Kenny went on to point out that the drawing of the cheque:

"does not imply any representation that the drawer now has money in this bank to the amount drawn for, inasmuch as he may well have authority to overdraw, or may intend to pay in (before the cheque can be presented) sufficient money to meet it"

—or, it may be added, may expect the account to be sufficiently fed by some other person. Indeed, the cheque may be considerably postdated; yet the same representation will be implied.[47] This does not mean that the drawer's act simply implies a representation as to the future, a prediction; this would not satisfy the requirement of a "deception ... as to fact."[48] Rather it implies a statement as to the existence of a "state of affairs" (to repeat Kenny's words) which includes the drawer's present intention or expectation. Nevertheless, it is certainly less pedantic to express it in Viscount Dilhorne's pithy terms: "a man who gives a cheque represents that it will be met on presentment."[49]

---

[41] *Outlines of Criminal Law*—see now 19th ed. (1966), p. 359. Kenny cited *Hazelton* (1874) L.R. 2 C.C.R. 134, and his analysis was adopted by the Court of Appeal in *Page* [1971] 2 Q.B. 330n.

[42] *Per* Lord Diplock in *Metropolitan Police Commissioner* v. *Charles* [1977] A.C. 177 at 182; see also *per* Viscount Dilhorne at 185.

[43] *Ibid.* at 190–191 (Lord Edmund-Davies).

[44] [1977] A.C. 177.

[45] Lord Diplock (at 182) restated the drawer's representation to be that "the cheque is one which the bank on which it is drawn is bound, by an existing contract with the drawer, to pay on presentment or, if not strictly bound to do so, could reasonably be expected to pay in the normal course of dealing."

[46] This was in fact Kenny's explanation of another statement by which he no doubt sought to express the same notion: "that the cheque, as drawn, is a valid order for the payment of that amount." But this can be read as referring to the future; so that the version quoted in the text, which is a representation as to existing fact, is now preferred: see *per* Robert Goff L.J. in *Gilmartin* [1983] Q.B. 953 at 960–961.

[47] *Gilmartin*, above.

[48] See *per* Robert Goff L.J. in *Gilmartin*, above, at 960.

[49] *Charles* [1977] A.C. 177 at 186. Compare *per* Lord Reid in *D.P.P.* v. *Turner* [1974] A.C. 357 at 367.

The transaction contemplated by Kenny is that where D uses a cheque to obtain property from the payee. When he demands cash from his own bank against his account he thereby represents that he believes the state of his account (no doubt including uncleared effects[50] and overdraft facilities) to be such that he is entitled to draw that amount. **7–24**

(ii) *Cheque cards and credit cards.* In *Charles* D obtained gambling chips at a club by giving 25 cheques for £30 each, supported by a cheque card. The use of the card in accordance with specified conditions created an undertaking by D's bank to honour the cheques. So the representation involved in giving the cheques was true; the cheques would undoubtedly be met, whatever the state of D's account. The House of Lords held, however, that when the drawer of a cheque presents a cheque card by way of guarantee, he represents to the payee that he has the bank's authority to use the card in relation to that cheque so as to create a contractual relationship between bank and payee. If the cheque is one which would not be met but for the use of the cheque card, he will lack that authority. The use of the card will then involve a misrepresentation. **7–25**

In *Lambie*[51] D selected goods in a shop and proposed to pay by Barclaycard. That is to say, she was using the card as a credit card. The shop had the usual agreement with D's bank that the bank would honour a voucher signed by the holder of a current card for a transaction within an agreed limit. D's transaction was within that limit. The shop manageress accepted this form of payment. The House of Lords held, applying its decision in *Charles*, that D had represented (falsely, on the facts) that she had authority to contract with the shop on the bank's behalf that the bank would honour the voucher signed by D.

A person dishonestly using a cheque card or credit card is guilty of an offence involving deception only if the payee is deceived by the cardholder's misrepresentation into accepting the cheque or voucher concerned. This aspect of deception is considered below.[52] The discussion may be anticipated by saying that convictions were confirmed in both *Charles*[53] and *Lambie*.[54]

The representations found in *Charles* and *Lambie* have attracted much criticism.[55] The gist of the criticism is that resort to the notion of the cheque card or credit card holder as agent of the issuer of the card is not necessary to explain the existence of a contract between the issuer and the payee or **7–26**

---

[50] In *Christou* [1971] Crim.L.R. 653, D paid in for the credit of his account cheques which were worthless, as he knew they were or might be. He then drew on the account before those cheques were presented. This was one indivisible deceptive practice.
[51] [1982] A.C. 449.
[52] §§ 7–41 *et seq.*
[53] What was obtained in *Charles* was a pecuniary advantage in the form of D's being "allowed to borrow by way of overdraft" (see below, §§ 7–53 and 10–12) and D was convicted accordingly under s.16(2)(*b*). He probably had not the intention of permanently depriving the club of the gambling chips, within the meaning of s.15 (though for an argument to the contrary, see J. C. Smith [1976] Crim.L.R. 330).
[54] The conviction in *Lambie* was under s.16(2)(*a*), since repealed. It might have been under s.15—and should have been: [1982] A.C. 449 at 456.
[55] Williams, *Textbook*, pp. 778–780; Bennion (1981) 131 New L.J. 1041 (on *Lambie*); Paulden (1981) 145 J.P.N. 708.

supplier; card-holders do not, on a true analysis, act as agents and a dishonest card-holder cannot properly be interpreted as asserting an authority which no card-holder has. Moreover, it is said, the payee or supplier with whom the card-holder deals is not interested in whether the latter has the bank's authority. He is interested only in whether the conditions that will entitle him to payment (by guarantee of a cheque or by payment against a voucher) are satisfied. This criticism asserts, in effect, that it is inept to identify a representation on which the representee cannot truly be said to rely.[56]

A strong case has undoubtedly been made that the language of agency in *Charles* and *Lambie* is inappropriate. The House of Lords might rather have said quite simply that the user of a cheque card or credit card impliedly represents that he is entitled as between himself and the bank to use the card for the transaction in question. This way of expressing the matter would, of course, still be open to the objection that such a representation is of no interest to the third party—a point that will be referred to again below.

Overcharging

7-27   A common mischief which may involve an offence under section 15 is that of serious overcharging for work done—as, for instance, domestic building repairs. An example was before the Court of Appeal in *Silverman*.[57] D was known to two elderly sisters because of work that he or his employers had done for their family over a long period. He charged them grossly excessive sums for work done on their property. He was held to have been rightly charged under section 15 with obtaining the sums by impliedly representing them to be "a fair and proper charge." The court interpreted the situation as being one of "mutual trust"—thus, it seems, referring to the trust likely to have been reposed in D by the sisters. The question was whether he had taken advantage of them "by representing as a fair charge that which he, but not [they], [knew] to be dishonestly excessive." He had; "his silence on any matter other than the sums to be charged was as eloquent as if he had said that he was going to make no more than a modest profit." Although liability on such facts may be supportable, its proper basis needs careful consideration if section 15 is not to be misused in cases of this kind. There is a world of difference between fraud (with which the section is concerned) and exploitation (with which it is not).

7-28   *What kind of representation?* The first question is: what is the substance of the deception? The suggested implied statement, "My charge is fair and proper" (or "My profit is only modest") looks like a statement of opinion rather than of fact, unless "fair and proper" can be understood as referring to an objective yardstick. The only yardstick available, it is submitted, is "the going rate for the job." To convert the alleged deception into a

---

[56] Compare above, § 7–20.
[57] (1987) 86 Cr.App.R. 213. The convictions in this case were quashed on a separate ground.

"deception . . . as to fact," conduct such as Silverman's must be interpreted as carrying some such implication as, "The price I am quoting or charging is within the range of prices likely to be quoted for the same services by other tradesmen (with similar overheads)."[58] This is a clumsy kind of implication to spell out in an information or indictment; but it is submitted that the defendant (and the tribunal of fact) should know that what is in substance alleged is that such an assertion was implied in the circumstances and that the victim paid the price in reliance upon it. It would be helpful, at any rate, if in a future case the phrase "fair and proper" could be explained, whether or not along the lines suggested here.

When is such a representation to be implied? Clearly such a representation **7–29** cannot be implied whenever a quotation for work is given or payment for work is demanded. The judgment in *Silverman*, which was concerned with rather special facts, does not go far to identify the circumstances that will justify the implication. It is submitted that it is helpful to refer in this context to the fact that deception, as explained in section 15(4), must be "deliberate or reckless." So D cannot be guilty of obtaining his price by deception unless he realises[59] that P may understand him to be implying the propriety (as above explained) of his price and may employ him, or pay him, on the strength of that understanding. But if D does so realise, it must become relatively easy to find a false representation (once granted that overcharging can ever found a conviction under section 15). D's knowledge of P's innocence and inexperience in relevant respects may be relevant; or his knowledge that P is likely to trust him on the strength of prior transactions or social connections (as in *Silverman* itself). Such knowledge may combine tellingly with the fact (no doubt a feature of most cases attracting the concern of prosecutors) that D has spontaneously approached P to propose the transaction and is not tendering in a competitive situation initiated by P.

Deception or extortion? The grosser the overcharging, the greater the **7–30** temptation may be to allege that a deception has occurred. But the more grossly excessive D's price is, the more hopelessly innocent and trusting P must be (and be thought to be) if he is to suppose D to be asserting the propriety of the price (and if D is to anticipate his reliance on such an assertion). Some people, indeed—as, apparently, the victims in *Sullivan*— are astonishingly gullible and a claim to have supposed that even an absurdly exorbitant price was a normal price may compel belief. But, paradoxically, the greater the price, the more critically considered must be the suggestion

---

[58] The alternative, "*I hold the opinion that* my price is reasonable" or "fair and proper" (which, like any statement about one's state of mind, is a statement of fact) means little until translated into a claim to hold an opinion about the price relative to the market; and once that translation is made, the simpler interpretation, "*It is the case that* . . ." seems permissible and preferable. (Silverman's victims thought that they were paying a "normal" or "standard" charge (86 Cr.App.R. at 215), not that Silverman was of that opinion.) A related interpretation, "Other tradesmen would think my price reasonable," recalls the likely meaning of "proper" in s.21(1)(*b*) (blackmail): see below, § 13–31.
[59] See below, §§ 7–55, 7–56.

that P was *deceived* into paying it. If deception is not the explanation, however, there must be some other. One possibility, where D announces the price of work already done, is that P feels under pressure to pay what D demands because the very demand for so excessive a sum carries a quality of menace. In a sufficiently clear case (and certainly where menaces are expressly used) the right charge may be blackmail rather than obtaining by deception.

Conduct to conceal facts

7–31   An interesting situation is presented by conduct of D which is intended to work a deception but of which, if the deception is to succeed, P must remain in ignorance. For instance, D may intercept a letter warning P of a fact that would be likely, if known to P, to make him refuse a proposed transaction, or D may hide physical evidence of the fact that P would otherwise see. It would appear to be open to a court to say that such conduct amounts to deception within section 15. A clearer case would be that where D conceals (as by filling in and painting over) a serious defect in goods, the goods then being examined by P. In this case the result of the work of concealment would be visible to P.[60]

Silence as conduct

7–32   In some situations D may be thought to have a moral duty (and may for other purposes have a legal duty) to reveal to P some fact which might affect P's mind in relation to a proposed transaction. Suppose that, after forming his intention that P shall be misled by his own ignorance, D does nothing active but pursues his dishonest purpose by maintaining silence. If a transaction then ensues in which D obtains property from P, the question may arise whether he has obtained that property by deception.[61]

Before considering particular examples of situations of this kind, the following general observations may be offered. First, the question for present purposes is not whether D had a duty to reveal facts but only whether he appeared to assert or deny them. But if D is not, according to the law of contract or of tort, under a duty to reveal a fact known to him, it is the more difficult to interpret his silence as a denial of that fact; and this consideration contributes to ensuring that the criminal law is not in practice more demanding than the civil. Secondly, there may in fact be no situation in which mere silence, mere inaction, alone can work a deception within the meaning of the Act. It may be necessary at least to find some other conduct of D in association with which his silence may be interpreted as making a representation.

---

[60] Compare under the Trade Descriptions Act 1968, *Cottee* v. *Douglas Seaton (Used Cars) Ltd.* [1972] 1 W.L.R. 1408 at 1417; [1972] 3 All E.R. 750 at 758, *per* Milmo J.
[61] See *Eighth Report*, para. 101(iv); Smith, *Theft* (4th ed.), paras. 170–172; Arlidge and Parry, *Fraud*, paras. 2.44 *et seq.*; A. T. H. Smith [1982] Crim.L.R. 721 at 729–731.

The main relevant authority under the Act is *D.P.P.* v. *Ray*.[62] D entered a   **7-33**
restaurant intending to pay for the meal he was to eat. The representation
implied by his conduct (that he intended to pay) was therefore true. After he
had eaten his meal he decided not to pay and sat at his table until the waiter
was out of the room. He then made his escape without paying. The House of
Lords held by a majority that he had obtained by deception the evasion of his
obligation to pay,[63] either because the initial representation made on entering and ordering the meal was "a continuing representation which remained
alive and operative" and had become false,[64] or because by remaining at the
table after forming his dishonest intention he continued to make from
moment to moment, but now falsely, the representation that he intended to
pay.[65] A corresponding case under section 15 would be provided by the diner
who forms his decision not to pay for his food between the time of ordering it
and the time of its being served.

*D.P.P.*v. *Ray* illustrates the situation where D makes an assertion to P   **7-34**
which is true when made but which becomes untrue before the relevant
obtaining. Three other situations may be briefly considered. The first is that
where D makes an assertion which he believes to be true but which is not.
Before he obtains any property from P, D learns that his assertion was false.
He does not correct it. He may probably be interpreted as now falsely
representing that he believes his original assertion to be true, or as continuing to make (but now falsely) that same assertion. The second situation is
that where P makes clear to D that he assumes some fact to be true which is
material to a negotiation between them. D knows the assumption is false
but, though he does not actively confirm it, he does nothing to disabuse P. It
is unlikely that a court would hold D's silence to be "conduct" within the
meaning of section 15(4). The third situation is even clearer. D simply
refrains from mentioning to P a fact, known to D, that might affect P's mind
in the transaction proposed between them. The fact that it will usually be
impossible to identify a clear statement to be inferred from D's silence
should suffice to exclude liability, quite apart from all other considerations,
including the consideration that no civil liability normally arises from simple
non-disclosure.

The falsity of the representation

The representation that D makes by words or conduct must be false if   **7-35**

---

[62] [1974] A.C. 370. See also *Nordeng* (1975) 62 Cr.App.R. 123, and commentary by J. C. Smith
[1976] Crim.L.R. 196.
[63] Contrary to s.16(2)(*a*), since repealed. The diner who makes off without payment will now be
prosecuted under the Theft Act 1978, s.3: see Chap. 12.
[64] *Per* Lord MacDermott (at 382).
[65] See *per* Lord Pearson at 391; and compare *per* Lord Morris of Borth-y-Gest at 385-386. (The
latter explanation may be necessary if the decision is to apply where the waiter allegedly
deceived is one who was not present until after the meal was served: see White (1986) 37
N.I.L.Q. 255 at 258.) Lords Reid and Hodson dissented. Lord Reid (at 379): "Deception, to
my mind, implies something positive. It is quite true that a man intending to deceive can build
up a situation in which his silence is as eloquent as an express statement. But what did the
accused do here to create such a situation? He merely sat still." Lord Hodson (at 389):
"Nothing he did after his change of mind can be characterised as conduct which would
indicate that he was then practising a deception."

there is to be a deception. It is not enough that he thinks he is telling a lie. If "quite accidentally and, strange as it may sound, dishonestly,"[66] he tells the truth, he cannot be convicted of an offence requiring deception. (He may, however, be convicted of an attempt, even if he obtains what he sets out to obtain.[67])

Falsity of representation as to law

7–36   When D is charged with an obtaining effected by a "deception as to law," it must be up to the judge to direct the jury as to the truth or falsity of the representation said to have been made. The representation may be an implied one, as where D is alleged to have obtained the price of property he had no right to sell. Whether he had such a right will usually turn on matters of pure fact. Exceptionally, however, where it depends upon the legal consequences of background events, those consequences are for the judge to declare.[68]

Multiple representations

7–37   It may be alleged that D induced P to act as he did by making a number of false statements. In such a case there may be a conviction only if the jury agree that D was so induced by at least one particular statement as to which they (or a sufficient majority[69]) are all satisfied. This is an application of the general proposition that:

> "where a number of matters are specified in [a] charge as together consti-
> tuting one ingredient in the offence, and any one of them is capable of
> doing so, then it is enough to establish the ingredient that any one of them
> is proved; but . . . any such matter must be proved to the satisfaction of the
> whole jury."

The general proposition and its particular application were laid down in *Brown*,[70] a case of fraudulently inducing an investment under the Prevention of Fraud (Investments) Act 1958, s.13(1).

7–38   The Court of Appeal in *Brown* sought to explain the earlier decision of *Agbim*,[71] which had been interpreted as requiring agreement only that P had

---

[66] *Deller* (1952) 36 Cr.App.R. 184, *per* Hilbery J. at 191.
[67] Criminal Attempts Act 1981, s.1(2)(3); *Shivpuri* [1987] A.C. 1.
[68] See, *e.g. Walker* (1983) 80 L.S.Gaz. 3238; [1984] Crim.L.R. 112 (above, § 1–25).
[69] Juries Act 1974, s.17. The same majority, of course, would need to be satisfied as to all other elements of the offence.
[70] (1983) 79 Cr.App.R. 115 at 119. As to the circumstances (controversially said to be "comparatively rare") in which a direction based on the *Brown* principle needs to be given, see *More* (1987) 86 Cr.App.R. 234 at 244 (the House of Lords, *ibid.* at 252, found it unnecessary to express an opinion on this point or on the correctness of *Brown*). For general consideration of the problem of "satisfying the jury," see J. C. Smith [1988] Crim.L.R. 335.
[71] [1979] Crim.L.R. 171—but more detail emerges in the judgment in *Brown*.

been induced by some false representation and not agreement that any particular representation had effected the inducement. *Agbim* was now said to be authority only for the proposition that the jury "need not be agreed as to the parts of the evidence which lead them to agree that the ingredients of the offence have been made out." One at least of the convictions in *Agbim* was on a count alleging the obtaining of a cheque[72] by the deception that a statement of expenses was correct. The several false items said to make that statement incorrect (fictitious heads of expenditure, exaggerated rates of expenditure, and so on) were not—in the language of *Brown*—"matters . . . specified in the charge." *Agbim*'s conviction was upheld although the jury had not been directed that they must agree upon a particular element of falsity; and the outcome appears to have been approved in *Brown*.[73] But it is submitted that it is unsatisfactory to describe different statements relied upon in a case like *Agbim* as "parts of the evidence" (about which jurors can take different views) merely because of the form of the charge. If D puts in one claim with 12 items, he is alleged to have obtained his payment by a single incorrect total claim; if he puts in 12 separate claims, the same payment might be described as induced by 12 false representations. Nothing should turn on the chance circumstance that the jury may be able to say in the former case, but not in the latter, that they are all agreed upon a "matter specified in the charge." Unless great care is taken they might (in an extreme case) convict, although every one of the impugned items of expenditure is accepted as correct by 11 of their number.

Proving a negative

Where the burden of proving the falsity of the representation involves **7–39** proving a negative, there is in common sense a limit to the quantity of evidence that the prosecution can be expected to adduce on the issue. If D has asserted that such-and-such is the case (*e.g.* the goods he sells cost eight times as much in the big shops), it is enough for the prosecution to speak of limited unsuccessful efforts to verify his assertion (seeking the goods at higher prices in a few shops). Reasonable efforts of that kind having been reported, it is not wrong for the judge to observe to the jury that the defence might be expected to give positive evidence, if it can be given, tending to support the representation.[74]

4. RELATION BETWEEN THE FALSE REPRESENTATION AND THE OBTAINING

The deception must precede the obtaining

This proposition should be too obvious to need stating. But it was the sole **7–40**

---

[72] Procuring the execution of a valuable security (s.20(2)).
[73] (1983) 79 Cr.App.R. at 118–119.
[74] *Mandry and Wooster* (1972) 58 Cr.App.R. 27, from which the illustrative facts in the text are taken.

reason required for the quashing of the conviction in *Collis-Smith*.[75] D had petrol put in the tank of his car at a petrol station. He then falsely stated that he was using the car for business purposes and that his firm would pay for the petrol. This was the substance of the deception charged and his appeal against conviction was rightly allowed; the petrol was not obtained by this deception.

The prosecution argued in *Collis-Smith* that after *possession* of property had been obtained D might by a deception then made obtain *ownership*, and that such a transaction would satisfy the section. This argument, it is submitted, was clearly correct in principle (though the court, seemingly anxious to protect criminal practitioners from "difficult points under the Sale of Goods Act," was not prepared to acknowledge this); but it was equally clearly inapplicable in the instant case, in which the property in the petrol must have passed on its being put into the tank.[76]

The effect of the representation on P[77]

Need P believe the representation?

7–41   "To deceive is, I apprehend, to induce a man to believe that a thing is true which is false." This well-known statement by Buckley J. in *Re London and Globe Finance Corporation*[78] was cited with approval in *D.P.P.* v. *Ray*.[79] It appears at first sight to state the obvious and to require no elaboration. Yet there is, on reflection, a good deal of uncertainty attaching to the notion of "believing that a thing is true"; and there has been no judicial consideration of what amounts to "believing" for this purpose.[80] It is submitted that, if indeed "believing" is an appropriate word in this context, it should not be understood only in the sense of firmly accepting the truth of the statement in question. The deception offences can hardly be limited to cases in which P is induced to hold a strong positive belief. P may be well aware that he does not know D, that there are rogues and liars abroad and that D may be one of them. He may act "on the strength" of D's assertion and in reliance upon it, but without in any positive sense either believing or disbelieving it. If D is lying, P is surely "deceived" for the purposes of section 15. It may in fact be

[75] [1971] Crim.L.R. 716.
[76] See above, § 2–47.
[77] For criticism of modern developments, see A. T. H. Smith [1982] Crim.L.R. 721.
[78] [1903] 1 Ch. 728 at 732.
[79] [1974] A.C. 370.
[80] The authorities on obtaining by false pretences largely avoided reference to any particular state of mind that the pretence must bring about. It was variously said that it must be proved that by his statement D "did so act on the mind of the prosecutor as that he did thereby obtain money, etc. . . . [and] if in fact the prosecutor was not . . . persuaded [by D's statement] . . . , the charge is not supported" (*Aspinall* (1876) 2 Q.B.D. 48 at 57, *per* Brett J.A.); that the offence was committed if "the property was parted with on the faith of the false pretence" (*Jones* (1884) 50 L.T. 726); that it must be shown that P was "influenced by the false pretence and would not have transferred [the goods] but for his reliance on it" (*Russell on Crime* (12th ed.), p. 1184; compare *Seagrave* (1910) 4 Cr.App.R. 156, as to reliance); that P must have been "induced by" the false statement to part with the property (*Smith* (1915) 11 Cr.App.R. 81). References to P's "believing" D's statement were rare; but see *Grail* (1944) 30 Cr.App.R. 81; *Sullivan* (1945) *ibid.* 132.

better to abandon the word "believe" and to say that to deceive is to induce a person to act in reliance upon a false representation.[81]

The test of whether P has been so induced is whether he would have acted   **7-42**
as he did if he had known that the representation made by D was false. This question (and not whether P believed D, or why P acted as he did) is therefore the question to which evidence should be directed. This appears from the decisions of the House of Lords in *Metropolitan Police Commissioner* v. *Charles*[82] and *Lambie*,[83] which have already been mentioned for another purpose.[84]

In *Charles* P accepted D's cheques because they were backed by a cheque card. He would not have done so if he had known that D had no authority to use the card. D's conviction under section 16 of obtaining a pecuniary advantage by deception[85] was upheld. It is quite clear from the evidence that P was at best agnostic on the question of D's right to use the cheque card. Their Lordships, in asserting that P "believed" that D was authorised to use it[86] must, on the facts, have been using "belief" to stand for ignorance of the truth plus reliance on the representation of authority; firm acceptance of the truth of that representation was not in question.[87] In *Lambie* the manageress was not asked in evidence whether she would have completed the transaction had she known that the customer was acting dishonestly *vis-à-vis* the bank, having no authority to use the credit card. But the House of Lords held that the manageress's answer "No" to that question could be assumed.[88] On that basis *Charles* was regarded as indistinguishable and the customer's conviction of a deception offence was confirmed.[89]

"Acting in reliance": need P be aware of the representation?

It is natural enough to describe a deceived person as "believing" the truth   **7-43**

---

[81] This paragraph was approved by the Court of Appeal in *Lambie* (1980) 71 Cr.App.R. 350 (reversed on another ground, [1982] A.C. 449).
[82] [1977] A.C. 177.
[83] [1982] A.C. 449.
[84] Above, § 7-25. See also below, § 7-44.
[85] For the pecuniary advantage, see below, §§ 7-53, 10-12.
[86] [1977] A.C. 177 at 183, 193.
[87] For analysis of the facts, see J. C. Smith at [1977] Crim.L.R. at 618-619.
[88] [1982] A.C. 449 at 460. It is assumed, that is to say, that she would not have been prepared to testify that, had she known the truth, she might have been willing to participate in a fraud on the credit card company. (But the reason cannot be—*pace* Lord Roskill—that an affirmative answer to the hypothetical question would have made her a party to the fraud.) See further, § 7-48, below.
[89] For elaborate criticism of *Charles* and *Lambie*, see J. C. Smith at [1977] Crim.L.R. 617-621 and at [1981] Crim.L.R. 713-717. The essential argument may perhaps be summarised thus: that the payee in a cheque card or credit card case (as witness the evidence in *Charles* and *Lambie*) has no interest in the state of the card-holder's account with his bank, for the very point of the card is to guarantee payment whatever the state of that account; that this is as much as to say that the payee has no interest in whether the user has authority to use the card; that a representation cannot be said to deceive one who is indifferent as to its truth; that the question whether the payee would have accepted payment by means of the card had he actually known of the lack of authority is improperly hypothetical; and that dishonest misuse of a cheque card or credit card in a transaction with a third party should not be held to be an offence of deception. See also A. T. H. Smith [1978] J.B.L. 129, especially at 135-136.

of what he is told; that is no doubt the standard effect of a successful lie. But positive belief is not required; so the typical victim may instead be described (as for convenience he is in this chapter) as acting, even agnostically, "in reliance on" what he is told. Yet even this language—or any expression suggesting that D's representation must have some effect on P's mind—is not perfectly appropriate for many cases. Although the victim of a deception by words will be exactly aware of the representation made by D, this is not necessarily the case with deception by conduct. There must be many cases in which the relevant implication of D's conduct (that which a court will recognise[90] and a well-drawn indictment will allege) is not present to P's mind at all.

7–44   For example, presumably it rarely occurs to a British Rail passenger that the steward serving him in the buffet car may be engaged on a fraud on his employers, selling his own food rather than theirs, intending to keep the purchase price and defraud his employers of the profit they should make. But cases on this kind of fraud make clear that if, knowing the truth, the customer would not buy the steward's food, the price he pays in ignorance of the truth is obtained from him by deception.[91] Such a victim is deceived although, almost inevitably, the relevant implication of the deceiver's conduct ("This is British Rail's food") never crosses his mind. This seems to confirm that, so far as concerns the relationship between D's conduct and P's act, the sufficient questions are: Did D's conduct imply a particular statement? And did P act in response to D's conduct in a way in which he would not have acted if he had known the contrary of the statement? References in this chapter to P's "relying" on what is implied by D's conduct must be understood in this sense.

7–45   Take by way of another example the case of a competition in which only one entry is permitted from each competitor. D puts in two entries in different names. The judge considers one of D's entries and awards it a prize. It seems plain that D has obtained consideration of the entry, and perhaps[92] a prize, by deception even though it did not occur to the judge that the entry might be one of two or more entries submitted by the competitor, still less that its submission implied that it was a unique entry. This example is stimulated by the surprising reason reported for the failure of a prosecution for the obtaining by deception of an allotment of shares by disguised multiple applications: "the prosecution could not prove that the shares were issued in the belief that this was the only application."[93] It is submitted that the prosecution were expected to prove too much.

[90] See above, § 7–20.
[91] Especially *Doukas* (1977) 66 Cr.App.R. 228; *Cooke* [1986] A.C. 909. The cases concern the offence of going equipped to cheat (s.25) and are discussed below, § 15–10.
[92] Acknowledging a possible argument about causation.
[93] *Best, The Times*, October 6, 1987. The obtaining charge having failed, there was a conviction of attempt. *Sed quaere?* Was the defendant proved to have intended to induce the "belief" that he failed to induce?

P's knowledge of falsity or indifference to truth

If D makes a false statement of fact to P, intending thereby to induce P to   **7–46**
lend him money or sell him property, and P knows that the statement is false
but nevertheless lends the money or sells the property, D is not, despite
himself, guilty of obtaining by deception. He may, however, be convicted of
an attempt.[94]

Another possibility is that P is misled by D's statement but is indifferent to
the matter about which the statement is made and therefore transfers
property without reliance on it; he would act in the same way even if he knew
the truth. Here again, though D may have committed an attempt, he has not
committed an offence under section 15.

On the other hand, if D's representation is a factor operating on P's mind
as an inducement to part with his property, the offence is complete. It is
irrelevant that other factors also operated on his mind.[95]

Evidence of effective representation

To prove that P was induced to part with his property by the particular   **7–47**
false representation charged, the prosecution are normally obliged to
adduce P's evidence to this effect. There are two points here.

(a) First, it is *necessary to charge and prove the representation that operated
on P* as the relative inducement. This was not done in *Laverty*.[96] D, having
acquired a stolen car, registration number JPA 945C, put different number
plates on it—DUV 111C. He sold the car to P. He was charged with
obtaining the price from P by the false representation that the car "was the
original motor car DUV 111C." There was no evidence that P bought the car
in reliance upon the representation that it was the car for which that
registration number was originally issued. Nor could it safely be inferred
that he would not have bought the car if he had known that its number had
been changed. His evidence was that he bought it because he thought that P
was its owner. The representation charged should have been that D was
entitled to sell. D's conviction was quashed.

(b) Secondly, it is *normally necessary for P to give evidence of the induce-*   **7–48**
ment.[97] The obtaining by the deception charged must, after all, be proved
beyond reasonable doubt. P's reliance on the particular representation may,
however, be a matter of irresistible inference from other proved facts; and if
that is so and P's evidence on the point "is not and cannot reasonably be
expected to be available," that reliance may be found as a fact.[98] P should
nevertheless be produced as a witness unless his absence can be explained.[99]

[94] Compare *Hensler* (1870) Cox C.C. 570; *Edwards* [1978] Crim.L.R. 49.
[95] Compare, *e.g. Lince* (1873) 12 Cox C.C. 451.
[96] (1970) 54 Cr.App.R. 495.
[97] *Laverty* (1970) 54 Cr.App.R. 495.
[98] *Lambie* [1982] A.C. 449 at 460–461; applying *Sullivan* (1945) 30 Cr.App.R. 132; and see
Tirado (1974) 59 Cr.App.R. 80; *Etim* v. *Hatfield* [1975] Crim.L.R. 234. For criticism of
D.P.P. v. *Ray* [1974] A.C. 370 (above, § 7–33) on this point, see J. C. Smith, *Theft*,
para. 163.
[99] *Tirado*, above (P not able to be brought to this country). In *Etim* v. *Hatfield*, above, post
office counter clerks were understandably not called to give evidence about particular giro
cheque transactions, which presumably they would not recollect.

The conviction in *Lambie* depended, as has been seen,[1] on the confidence of the House of Lords that the manageress, had she been asked, would have said that she would not have accepted Ms Lambie's credit card voucher if she had known that Ms Lambie lacked authority to use the card. But the case can hardly establish an irrebuttable presumption that one who is aware that his customer no longer has a right to use his credit card or cheque card will refuse to accept payment involving its use.[2] The point arises, of course, in a hypothetical way. In practice P will not have known the truth; he will justifiably have regarded the card as guaranteeing payment whatever the position as between D and his bank.[3] But it may not be impossible to persuade P to admit that, *had* he known the truth, he *might* have been unscrupulous and still accepted that mode of payment. He ought therefore to be available for cross-examination.

The effect of intervening events and transactions

7–49   A common purpose of deception is to induce the victim to enter into a contract under which (perhaps after a considerable lapse of time) he will transfer property or pay money to the deceiver or a third person. If the property or money is obtained *by* the deception, it is immaterial that a contract has intervened between the deception and the transfer or payment. A striking instance occurred in the old case of *Martin*.[4] D by false pretences induced P to contract to build him a vehicle. P built the vehicle and delivered it to D although in the meantime D had countermanded the order. A conviction of obtaining the vehicle by false pretences was upheld, the jury having been entitled to find that the pretence was a continuing one.

7–50   It was said in the modern case of *King and Stockwell*[5] that "the question in each case is: was the deception an operative cause of the obtaining of the property?"; and that this question is "to be answered as a question of fact by the jury applying their common sense."[6] In that case the defendants posed as representatives of a known firm of tree surgeons and persuaded the victim that trees in her garden urgently needed removing, work which they would do for £470. She agreed. The fraud was uncovered before any money was paid. It was held that there was ample evidence to justify convictions of attempting to obtain money by deception—that is, money that would have been paid over "as a result of the lies."[7] The upholding of these convictions was plainly correct. But language such as that in which the court framed the crucial question of fact appears to be unsuitable for the lay tribunal; and it can surely be avoided.

7–51   It is true that such language runs through the cases. In *Clucas*,[8] for example, the Court of Criminal Appeal held that one who induces a book-maker to accept a large bet on a horse by falsely pretending that he is a

---

[1] Above, § 7–42.
[2] Compare *Cooke* [1986] A.C. 909 at 921: would British Rail passengers necessarily refuse to buy from staff engaged in a restaurant car fiddle?
[3] See n. 89, above.
[4] (1867) L.R 1 C.C.R. 56.
[5] [1987] Q.B. 547.
[6] *Ibid*. at 533.
[7] *Ibid*. at 534.
[8] [1949] 2 K.B. 226.

commission agent acting on behalf of a number of persons does not by the pretence obtain the sums paid when the horse wins; it is the backing of the winning horse which is "the effective cause" of the payment.[9] In *Button*,[10] by contrast, D, an able runner, obtained a big handicap in a race by pretending to be E, a runner with a poor record. D won the race and claimed the prize. He was guilty of attempting to obtain the prize by false pretences. Matthew J. described the original pretence as "not too remote."[11]

It is thought that the appropriate result can be achieved without asking the   **7–52** jury to classify the deception as an "operative" cause, or as a "remote" cause, of the obtaining, or the deception or any other antecedent as its "effective" cause. It is submitted that the only question of fact is whether P, *at the time when he made the payment or transferred the property*, was induced (that is, influenced in part at least) by D's earlier false statement to do so.[12] If that is right, the abstract language of causation can be avoided. Cases like *Clucas* suggest that a deception can be too remote a cause as a matter of law. But this may mean no more than that the judge should direct an acquittal if no reasonable jury could answer the question of fact in the affirmative.

Deception of P, obtaining from Q

D may deceive P and thereby obtain property from Q or a pecuniary   **7–53** advantage at Q's expense. If there is "a causal connection"[13] between the deception and the obtaining D may be convicted under section 15 or section 16 as may be appropriate. The phrase "causal connection" is rather vague and the scope of the principle may at some time need to be more closely determined. The following are examples of the operation of the principle:

(a) *Property obtained.* An insurance agent by deception induces P to insure with Q company and may be convicted of thereby obtaining commission from the company in respect of the policy.[14]

(b) *Pecuniary advantage.* D wrongfully uses a cheque card to induce P to accept his cheque. D's bank is thereby obliged to honour the cheque so that his bank account is to that extent overdrawn. D may be convicted of obtaining by deception the pecuniary advantage of being "allowed to borrow by way of overdraft" (s.16(1) and (2)(*b*)).[15]

---

[9] See also *Lewis* (1922), unreported, referred to in *Russell on Crime* (12th ed.), p. 1186n. A schoolteacher obtained an appointment by misrepresenting her qualifications. She was acquitted of obtaining her salary by this pretence, "on the ground that she was paid because of services she rendered, and not because of the falsehood." *Lewis* and *Clucas* combine to explain the provision of s.16(2)(*c*), below, § 10–14. In *King and Stockwell* (see text above) the court plainly entertained some doubt about the correctness of *Lewis*.
[10] [1900] 2 Q.B. 597.
[11] *Ibid.* at 600.
[12] It was suggested in earlier editions of this book that there is another question: whether D was still making his deceptive statement, expressly or impliedly, at the time of the obtaining. But it is now thought that there is no such positive additional requirement as, in effect, a "continuing" deception (compare *Martin* (1867) L.R. 1 C.C.R. 56 at 60: "there must be a continuing pretence"), which is in this context an unnecessary fiction.
[13] *Kovacs* (1973) 58 Cr.App.R. 412 at 416; approved in *Metropolitan Police Commissioner* v. *Charles* [1977] A.C. 177; *Clarkson* [1987] V.R. 962 at 980 (Supreme Court of Victoria).
[14] *Clegg* [1977] C.L.Y. 619 (Judge Beaumont).
[15] Cases cited at n. 13, above. Also *Smith* v. *Koumourou* [1979] R.T.R. 355. And see *Beck* (1984) 80 Cr.App.R. 355 (procuring execution of valuable security); below, § 11–16.

5. THE MENTAL ELEMENT

7-54 There are three strands in the mental element of the offence under section 15. D cannot be convicted of the offence unless it is proved:

    (i) that his deception was "deliberate or reckless";
    (ii) that he obtained the property "with the intention of permanently depriving [P] of it"; and
    (iii) that he obtained the property "dishonestly."

"Deliberate or reckless" deception[16]

7-55 "Deception" means "any deception (whether deliberate or reckless) . . ." (s.15(4)). "Deception" is, as it were, a two-sided word; it involves both the making of a deceptive statement and the effect of that statement upon the person to whom it is made. Conformably with the nature of the word they qualify, the words "deliberate" and "reckless" also do double duty. There are two senses, that is to say, in which D may deliberately or recklessly deceive P. He may know or be reckless as to the falsity of the statement; and he may make the statement intending to deceive P or reckless whether P is deceived. There is no doubt that both of these senses of the compressed expression "deception (whether deliberate or reckless)" must be satisfied. On the other hand it would seem that recklessness in both of the relevant respects will suffice. So D is guilty of deception if (a) by words or conduct he makes to P a statement which is false, and (b) he is at least reckless as to its falsity, and (c) he is at least reckless as to its misleading P and (d) it does mislead P. But he is not guilty of deception if, though he makes a false statement, he genuinely believes that P will not be misled by it—if, for instance, he believes that P knows it to be untrue.

7-56 A question arises as to the meaning of "reckless." The House of Lords has held that in some other modern criminal statutes the word includes failing to advert to a risk that ought to be obvious—in effect a case of gross negligence.[17] It can be argued that the word has the same meaning in section 15 and that the present offence is committed by one who makes a statement that he crassly fails to recognise may be false and who dishonestly obtains property as a result. This is in fact an unlikely case. One who dishonestly *obtains* by deception (as section 15 requires) is almost bound to have *deceived* dishonestly; he will have realised that his statement might be false and might mislead. The House of Lords decisions mentioned above did not specifically refer to offences of dishonesty or to existing authority requiring more than mere negligence for reckless deception.[18] It is submitted that

---

[16] See *Eighth Report*, para. 101(i).
[17] *Caldwell* [1982] A.C. 341 (Criminal Damage Act 1971, s.1); *Lawrence* [1982] A.C. 510 (reckless driving: Road Traffic Act 1972, s.2; now R.T.A. 1988, s.2).
[18] *Staines* (1974) 60 Cr.App.R. 160; *Royle* (1971) 56 Cr.App.R. 131; and see *Waterfall* [1970] 1 Q.B. 148, where the point is expressed to relate to the requirement of dishonesty rather than to that of deception.

deception requires at least indifference to the truth of the representation.[19] This would keep the criminal offence in line with House of Lords authority on the tort of deceit.[20]

"With the intention of permanently depriving the other of it"

The effect of this phrase is that, as in the case of theft, there will be no offence if D intends by his deception to obtain the property from P only temporarily. D may deceive P into lending him a chattel or letting it to him on hire. If he intends to return it when the period of the loan or hiring is over, he commits no offence under section 15. It is necessary, however, to distinguish carefully between a loan of money and a loan of other property. When D, pretending to be down on his luck, persuades P to lend him £10 in cash, he intends to deprive P permanently of the particular notes and coins handed to him; and, so far as this aspect of the mental element of the offence is concerned, his conduct is within the section although he may intend to repay his debt.[21] And where by deception D obtains a loan from P by cheque, he intends to deprive P permanently of the cheque, for once it is paid it ceases to be in its substance the thing that it was before.[22]

7–57

D has the necessary intention for the purpose of section 15 if he intends to deprive P entirely of whatever interest P has in the property. As has been seen,[23] P need only have possession or control of the property or any proprietary right or interest in it, in order to be the victim of this offence. So, for example, if P has a lien on D's goods, and D by deception induces P to deliver the goods to him, intending to defeat the lien, the offence is committed. Similarly, D may trick P into parting with possession of property which P is entitled to possess for a short while only, and this will be an offence under section 15 even if D intends to return the property to its owner (for whom, indeed, he may have practised the fraud).

7–58

Application of section 6 for section 15 purposes

It will be remembered that the expression "with the intention of permanently depriving the other of it" is partially defined for the purpose of theft by section 6.[24] By section 15(3) that section is made to apply also for purposes of section 15 "with the necessary adaptation of the reference to

7–59

---

[19] Compare *Large* v. *Mainprize* [1989] Crim.L.R. 213 (on "recklessly furnishing false information").

[20] *Derry* v. *Peek* (1889) 14 App.Cas 337. Common law fraud is committed by one who makes a false statement "(1) knowingly, or (2) without belief in its truth, or (3) recklessly, careless whether it be true or false": *per* Lord Herschell at 374. Lord Herschell observed that "(3)" is really only an instance of "(2)".

[21] The point is illustrated in *Halstead* v. *Patel* (1972) 56 Cr.App.R. 334. For comment on this distinction between fungibles and non-fungibles, see Williams and Weinberg, *Property Offences* (2nd ed.), p. 166. In England and Wales, unlike Victoria, its effect is mitigated by the existence of the offence of obtaining services (*e.g.* the hiring of a chattel) by deception.

[22] *Duru* (1973) 58 Cr.App.R. 151.

[23] Above, §§ 7–04, 7–05.

[24] See above, §§ 2–103 *et seq*.

appropriating." Section 6 is therefore to be read for purposes of section 15 as though for the word "appropriating" in section 6(1) there were substituted the words "obtaining by deception." There are obviously some difficulties involved in applying a section that is sufficiently obscure in its primary context to another offence for which it is, in a number of places, even less happily worded.

7–60   (a) Cases in which D obtains *ownership* of P's property by deception "without meaning [P] permanently to lose the thing itself," yet intending "to treat the thing as his own to dispose of regardless of [P's] rights," must be rare indeed.[25] We may construct one, admittedly unlikely, case by way of example. D is hard up. By deception he induces P to sell him a valuable article at a very low price. He merely wants to raise money on the article. He pawns it for a large sum and sends the pawn ticket to P with an apologetic letter.[26]

(b) It is easier to imagine cases in which section 6 might be relevant where D by deception obtains *possession* but not ownership of the property in question. Suppose that D dishonestly deceives P into giving him possession (not by way of loan) of some property other than land.[27] The effect of section 6 is that if, though he does not mean P permanently to lose the thing itself, D intends to treat it as his own to dispose of[28] regardless of P's rights, the mental element of the present offence, as of theft, is satisfied. The reader is invited to consider the three situations suggested in § 2–104 and to suppose that possession in each situation is obtained by deception. In each case D will on the altered facts have committed an offence under section 15.

7–61   (c) D may induce P by deception to lend him property. If he intends to return it, but only when it is "in such a changed state that all its goodness or virtue has gone,"[29] his borrowing is "equivalent to an outright taking" and he may be said to be treating it as his own to dispose of regardless of P's rights. His intention so to treat it is regarded as an intention of permanently depriving P of it.

(d) If D obtains property by deception, intending to lend it to E for a period and in circumstances making the lending equivalent to an outright disposal, he will be regarded as intending to deprive P permanently (s.6(1)). So also if he obtains the property intending for his own purposes to part with it under a condition as to its return which he may not be able to perform (s.6(2)). It must be doubtful whether such cases, though provided for by the terms of section 6 as applied to section 15, ever actually arise.

7–62   (e) In some of the situations dealt with above, D may be guilty both of obtaining property by deception and of theft. But this is not possible if the property is land: you cannot by the same transaction obtain land by decep-

---

[25] In *Duru*, above, the Court of Appeal would if necessary have held s.6(1) to be relevant.
[26] Compare situation (iii) in § 2–104.
[27] As to land, see (e), below.
[28] But not simply to use, however dishonestly and to P's disadvantage: *pace* Judge Fricker Q.C. in *Harkinder Atwal* [1989] Crim.L.R. 293 (obtaining credit and charge cards); compare comment at 294.
[29] *Lloyd* [1985] Q.B. 829 at 836; above, § 2–108.

tion and also steal it.[30] It is clear, however, that an offence under section 15 can be committed by a deception which obtains an existing interest in land (by the assignment of a lease, for example). But suppose that D by deception induces P to grant him a lease. In this case what D "obtains" must be the land, by obtaining possession of it (s.15(2)); it is the land which is "property belonging to [P]."[31] The question that might arise is whether a fraudulent lessee can ever be described as intending to deprive a lessor permanently of the land the subject of the demise. What, in particular, if D obtains a very long lease? Leaving aside section 6 for the moment, is there any point short of the assignment of P's whole interest at which the quality of temporariness ceases and that of permanence takes over? If D obtains a lease for 99 years or more it is certainly tempting to say that he intends to deprive P permanently of the land. It cannot be confidently predicted that the courts would yield to this temptation without the aid of section 6: it is sufficient here to hint at the possibility of their doing so. But suppose that P's age and the length of the lease permit D a plausible claim that he did not intend to permanently deprive P personally (let alone his successors in title) of the land. Does D nevertheless intend, within the meaning of section 6(1), to treat the land as his own to dispose of regardless of P's rights? It would not seem so, unless the taking of the lease can be treated as "a borrowing . . . for a period and in circumstances making [the borrowing] equivalent to an outright taking." In *Chan Wai Lam* v. *The Queen*,[32] where deception induced a government grant of a sub-lease expiring (in 1997) three days before expiry of the head lease, the Court of Appeal of Hong Kong considered questions raised in this paragraph and concluded, no doubt correctly, that an offence under the local equivalent of section 15 could be committed only where D intends to deprive P of the whole of his interest.

Nor does the Act cater in clear terms for the case—surely not a fanciful one—of the person who by deception obtains a tenancy or short lease, intending, when his contractual right is determined by notice or effluxion of time, to claim security of tenure under relevant legislation.

"Dishonestly"

Dishonesty and recklessness

The word "dishonestly" in section 15(1) contributes, it is thought, to   **7–63** limiting "reckless" deception to cases in which D is indifferent to the truth of his representation and not merely negligent in making it. This has been discussed above.[33]

---

[30] See s.4(2), which limits the circumstances in which land can be stolen, but which does not apply to s.15 (s.1(3)).

[31] The leasehold interest carved out of P's estate in the land does not exist before it is created by the lease and it never belongs to P. It cannot itself, therefore, be said to be the subject-matter of an offence. Compare *Chan Wai Lam* [1981] Crim.L.R. 497.

[32] Above.

[33] § 7–56. Dishonesty and deception are, in fact, separate issues; but they are quite commonly confused or telescoped in the cases. Examples may be found in *Waterfall* [1970] 1 Q.B. 148 (see (1970) 33 M.L.R. 217); *Potger* (1970) 55 Cr.App.R. 42; *Halstead* v. *Patel* (1972) 56 Cr.App.R. 334; *Green and Greenstein* (1975) 61 Cr.App.R. 296; *Lewis* (1975) 62 Cr.App.R. 206; *Ravenshad* [1990] Crim.L.R. 398.

Questions for the jury

7-64   The word "dishonestly" qualifies the phrase "obtains property"; it is the obtaining that must be dishonest. Guilt depends upon affirmative answers to the two *Ghosh*[34] questions:

> (i) was what D did dishonest according to the ordinary standards of reasonable and honest people? and
> (ii) must D have realised that it was dishonest according to those standards?

These are matters for decision by the jury; but they need not be troubled with question (ii) unless there is some evidence to suggest that D believed that what he did was honest by ordinary people's standards.[35]

7-65   This double test for dishonesty has been fully discussed in the chapter on theft.[36] General explanation and comment need not be repeated here; but it is of interest to note that in relation to deception offences the *Ghosh* test contradicts earlier Court of Appeal and Divisional Court authorities without explicitly overruling them. For it had been held that as a matter of law it could be no defence that one had intended to repay a loan obtained by deception[37] or a sum of money obtained across a post office counter by a cheque drawn on an empty giro account.[38] These authorities were silently overturned when the leading theft case of *Feely*[39] was applied[40] to deception offences.[41] That application was not perhaps quite inevitable, for, except in cases where D believes he has a legal right to the thing obtained, it might have been possible to hold that D's deception itself supplies a sufficient

---

[34] [1982] Q.B. 1053. (The case concerned offences under ss.15 and 20(2).)
[35] See above, § 2–128.
[36] Above, §§ 2–127 *et seq*.
[37] *McCall* (1970) 55 Cr.App.R. 175.
[38] *Halstead* v. *Patel* (1972) 56 Cr.App.R. 334. In *Potger* (1970) 55 Cr.App.R. 42, the Court of Appeal had said that the word "dishonestly" had a "wider ambit" than the phrase "intent to defraud" used in the old law of false pretences. This suggested that a number of situations which under that law were cases of intent to defraud were now as a matter of law to be classified as cases of dishonesty: see especially *Naylor* (1865) L.R. 1 C.C.R. 41; *Carpenter* (1911) 22 Cox C.C. 618; and, as to conspiracy to defraud, *Allsop* (1976) 64 Cr.App.R. 29.
[39] [1973] Q.B. 530 (the source of question (i) in the text above).
[40] By *Green and Greenstein* (1975) 61 Cr.App.R. 296; and then, with the gloss of question (ii), by *Ghosh* itself. In the former case D applied for shares being issued to the public. He knew that the issue would be oversubscribed and that shares would be allotted to applicants in proportion to the size of their applications. Cheques had to be sent with applications; an applicant allotted less shares than he applied for would be sent a "return" cheque for the change with the letter of allotment. D applied for very large amounts of shares, sending cheques which could not possibly be met on first presentation without the help of the proceeds of the issuing houses' own return cheques (which he knew could be speedily cleared). Granted that D obtained the letters of allotment by deception, the question was whether this method of conducting a "stagging" operation (applying for an allotment of shares or stock in order to sell immediately at a profit—an operation not in itself illegal) was "dishonest." This was the first prosecution to test the question. The question was held to be for the jury to decide, a remarkable allocation of law-making power to the jury. Speculation is justified as to the kind of precedent the jury's decision constituted: D. W. Elliott [1976] Crim.L.R. 707 at 715. The jury convicted.
[41] The point was confirmed, specifically in respect of *McCall* (above, n. 37), in *Melwani* [1989] Crim.L.R. 565.

element of dishonesty.[42] But it is hardly surprising that the principle that the jury should apply their own understanding of the meaning of the word "dishonestly" was regarded as valid in all contexts if valid in one.

Belief in legal entitlement

There is no provision (corresponding to s.2(1)(*a*) in relation to theft) **7–66** declaring that a person does not obtain property dishonestly if he believes that he is entitled in law to obtain it. Nor are the jury to be directed to that effect. The expectation appears to be that, with the benefit of an ordinary *Ghosh* direction, the jury will achieve the right result.[43] If the right result is inevitably an acquittal, it is surely preferable that the jury be told so; their function should merely be to say whether he may have believed as he claims. If the right result is not inevitably an acquittal, there is a strange inconsistency between theft and other offences: although (by virtue of s.2(1)(*a*)) I am innocent of theft if by no matter what unlawful force I induce P to give me what I wrongly think I have a claim to,[44] I may (depending on the view of the jury) be guilty under section 15 if by lying I induce him to do the same.[45] It is submitted that there should be no question of a conviction if D by deception obtains property in any of the following cases:

(a) D believes that the property belongs to him and that P is not entitled to retain it.
(b) D believes that the property belongs to E, for whom he is obtaining it, and that P is not entitled to detain it from E.
(c) D believes, or it is the case, that P owes D or E money; and he believes that the obtaining of the property in question from P is a proper way of enforcing his or E's claim against the defaulting debtor.[46]

6. JURISDICTION

The place of the obtaining

A court in England and Wales will be competent to try an offence under **7–67** section 15 only if it was committed within the jurisdiction; and that depends on the property's having been obtained here.[47] This principle has been

---

[42] Compare, at least as to "deliberate" deception, *Potger* (1970) 55 Cr.App.R. 42; *Ghosh* [1982] Q.B. 1053 at 1060, where Lord Lane C.J. is tempted by the point but does not pursue it; *Cooke* [1986] A.C. 909, *per* Lord Mackay at 934.
[43] *Woolven* (1983) 77 Cr.App.R. 231.
[44] See above, § 2–123.
[45] This unbecoming distinction does not exist in Victoria: *Salvo* [1989] V.R. 401.
[46] Compare *Williams* (1836) 7 C. & P. 354; Williams, *Criminal Law—The General Part* (2nd ed.), pp. 330–331.
[47] *Harden* [1963] 1 Q.B. 8; *Tirado* (1974) 59 Cr.App.R. 80 (notwithstanding doubts expressed by Lord Diplock in *Treacy* v. *D.P.P.* [1971] A.C. 537 at 563); *D.P.P.* v. *Stonehouse* [1978] A.C. 55, *per* Viscount Dilhorne at 74; compare *Ellis* [1899] 1 Q.B. 230; *Governor of Pentonville Prison, ex p. Khubchandani* (1980) 71 Cr.App.R. 241; *Thompson* (1984) 79 Cr.App.R. 191.

severely criticised; modern jurisdictional rules should "render fraudsters liable to prosecution here in every case where either their activities or the consequences of those activities are connected with England and Wales."[48] Admirable proposals to this end have not yet been implemented.[49]

The operation of the present law may be illustrated by supposing a transfer of property between a victim (P) and a rogue (D) of whom only one is in England and Wales at all material times.

(i) D in England, P abroad

7–68   If D, communicating from England with P who is abroad, deceives P into sending him property that in due course arrives in this country, D will usually "obtain" that property here and not abroad and will thus commit an offence here. The property may, however, be obtained abroad in an exceptional case. This occurred in *Harden*[50] (decided under the Larceny Act 1916, s.32), where D, in England, wrote to a finance company in Jersey, offering to sell goods for letting on hire-purchase to D's customers. D wrote. "This offer may be accepted ... within one month ... by sending your cheque for the net amount." It was held that D thus agreed that the posting of the cheque in Jersey should be equivalent to receipt by him. He therefore obtained the cheque in Jersey and could not be convicted of obtaining it by false pretences in England. This is unsatisfactory; it is curious, to say the least, if by a careful choice of wording D can determine where he commits his crime and thus his amenability to justice.

The Court of Appeal, in *Tirado*,[51] has made it clear that the principle in *Harden* will not be extended. It depends upon a finding that D agreed to accept posting as delivery to himself. In *Tirado* the jury did not so find. D ran an employment agency in Oxford. He obtained bankers' drafts from Morocco, sent on behalf of people for whom he falsely claimed to have jobs in England. He had requested his fee with the client's application form, to be sent through a Moroccan bank or by post. He was held properly convicted of obtaining the drafts in England. One view of what he had written was that he was merely indicating ways of sending the fees that his clients might adopt.[52]

(ii) D abroad, P in England

7–69   In the converse case, where ownership in property that the victim dispatches from England passes at the time and place of dispatch, D will have committed an offence within the jurisdiction and can be convicted here if he becomes amenable to process. If ownership does not pass at that time but

---

[48] *Jurisdiction over Offences of Fraud and Dishonesty with a Foreign Element* (Law Com. No. 180), para. 2.7.
[49] Fraud, etc. (Jurisdiction) Bill, appended to Law Com. No. 180 (last note).
[50] [1963] 1 Q.B. 8.
[51] (1974) 59 Cr.App.R. 80.
[52] *Ibid.* at 87.

only when D receives the property abroad, it seems that the English courts will have no jurisdiction.[53]

Attempts

(i) D in England, P abroad

If D in England writes to P abroad in an unsuccessful bid to obtain property by deception, his liability for attempt to commit an offence under section 15 depends on whether there would be jurisdiction to try him for the complete offence if he were successful. For the offence of attempt requires an act done with intent to commit an offence which, if it were completed, would be triable in England and Wales.[54] So (applying the principle stated above) there will be an offence if, but only if, the attempt was to bring about an obtaining in this country.[55]   **7–70**

(ii) D abroad, P in England

In *Baxter*,[56] D in Northern Ireland posted a letter to football pool promoters in England making a false claim to a prize. The promoters were suspicious and no prize was paid. D was held to have committed within the jurisdiction an attempt to obtain property by deception by means of a letter transmitted to England and intended to produce an obtaining from a victim within the jurisdiction. The same principle, though applied more subtly on the facts, justified D's conviction of attempt in *D.P.P.* v. *Stonehouse*.[57] In that case D was a famous public figure. He insured his life in England in favour of his wife. He then staged the appearance of his death by drowning in Florida and disappeared. The news of his supposed death naturally reached his wife and the insurers, as he intended. The case differs from *Baxter* in that no claim was actually made; but D's false representation was communicated in England so that it could be used by his innocent wife to obtain the assured sum. D was held properly convicted in England of attempting to obtain (that is, to enable his wife to obtain: s.15(2)) property by deception. The English courts had jurisdiction because "acts constituting an attempt to commit a crime under English law [were] done abroad and intended effects [were] felt in England."[58]   **7–71**

7. LIABILITY OF COMPANY OFFICERS, ETC.

Any director, manager, secretary or other similar officer of a body corporate, or any person who was purporting to act in any such capacity, may be   **7–72**

---

[53] See cases cited in note 47, above.
[54] Criminal Attempts Act 1981, s.1(1)(4).
[55] *Governor of Pentonville Prison, ex p. Naghdi* [1990] 1 All E.R. 257.
[56] [1972] Q.B. 1.
[57] [1978] A.C. 55.
[58] *Ibid.* at 92.

proved to have consented to or connived at an offence under section 15 committed by the body corporate. If so, such a person is also guilty of the offence (s.18(1)).[59]

An officer of a company who actively encourages or participates in the offence will be liable on ordinary principles independently of this provision. Indeed, depending on his status and function in the company, it may be his acts and states of mind which render the company itself guilty of the offence together with him.

Section 18 therefore strikes at the officer who is not guilty as an ordinary principal or accessory party to the offence. It assumes, that is to say, that the company has committed the offence by the conduct of some other officer or officers, but treats as fully liable the officer who inactively acquiesced in what was done. The section therefore involves a striking example of criminal liability for omission.[60]

Connivance on the part of a company officer seems to consist in (i) knowing that the offence in question is being or will be committed, or at least realising that this may be the case, and (ii) intentionally failing to take steps that he might take to prevent the offence.[61] It is difficult to believe that in practice consent can involve anything less, for consent can hardly be manifested except by active participation or encouragement (for which the section is not needed) or by deliberate passivity.

---

[59] As to bodies corporate managed by their members, see s.18(2).
[60] There are numerous precedents for this kind of liability.
[61] See *Codification of the Criminal Law* (Law Com. No. 143), para. 11.18; Draft Criminal Code Bill, cl. 31(1)(*a*) in *A Criminal Code for England and Wales* (Law Com. No. 177), Vol. 1.

Chapter 8

OBTAINING SERVICES BY DECEPTION

1. THE OFFENCE

SECTION 1(1) of the Theft Act 1978 provides: "A person who by any **8–01**
deception dishonestly obtains services from another" is guilty of an offence.
The offence carries the following penalties: on conviction on indictment, up
to five years' imprisonment (s.4(2)); on summary conviction, up to six
months' imprisonment and/or a fine not exceeding, for the time being,
£2,000 (s.4(3); Criminal Penalties, etc. Increase Order 1984 (S.I. 1984,
No. 447)).

The background to the creation of this offence has been described in
Chapter 6.[1]

Liability of company officers, etc.

Section 18 of the 1968 Act applies in relation to the offence as it does in **8–02**
relation to section 15 of the 1968 Act (1978 Act, s.5(1)).[2]

2. "BY ANY DECEPTION DISHONESTLY OBTAINS"

"By any deception"

The word "deception" has the same meaning here as in section 15 of the **8–03**
1968 Act—namely, the meaning stated in section 15(4) of that Act (1978
Act, s.5(2)). The discussion of the word in that context may therefore be
referred to.[3] So may the discussion, in connection with the section 15
offence, of the necessary relationship between the false representation and
the relevant obtaining.[4]

It should be noted that the present offence may be committed by means of
any deception. The Committee's original draft clause limited their proposed
offence to deception "going to the prospect of payment being duly made."
But under section 1 as eventually enacted "services" may be obtained by
deception as to any matter, which may or may not be concerned with the
question of payment.

"Dishonestly"

The obtaining of services must be achieved "dishonestly." There is no **8–04**

---

[1] See especially §§ 6–05, 6–06.
[2] s.18 is discussed at § 7–72.
[3] §§ 7–08 to 7–39, and §§ 7–55, 7–56.
[4] §§ 7–40 to 7–53.

need to repeat here what has already been said of the same element in the offence of obtaining property by deception under section 15 of the 1968 Act.[5]

3. "OBTAINS SERVICES FROM ANOTHER"

"Services"

8–05   "It is an obtaining of services where the other is induced to confer a benefit by doing some act, or causing or permitting some act to be done, on the understanding that the benefit has been or will be paid for" (subs. (2)).

It was important that the notion of "services" should be broadly understood; hence the explanation in terms simply of the conferring of a benefit by the doing of any act or by causing or permitting any act to be done. But purely gratuitous services (such as lending a lawn-mower or "lending a hand") ought to be excluded; hence the need for a benefit conferred "on the understanding that [it] has been or will be paid for."

It seems clear that "services" is established by the definition as a term of art and that anything falling within the definition ought to be treated as "services" for the purposes of the offence, even something not generally thought of as "services" or "a service." But the Court of Appeal has not consistently understood the legislative technique of the section in this way, as will appear below.[6]

"Confer a benefit"

8–06   There are two competing approaches to the reference to P's being induced to "confer a benefit." According to the first approach, which is probably most generally favoured, the reference imports a limiting requirement into the section. It is understood to mean that there are some acts beneficial to D (or to a third party) and some non-beneficial, and that an offence is committed only if deception is used to include the doing, causing or permitting of an act of the former class.[7] It is thought that this approach is erroneous. It renders the offence too vague at its outer edge and promises the introduction of an unsatisfactory and unnecessary issue into prosecutions under the section. The alternative approach may be introduced by observing on the difficulty that would have attended the drafting of the end of section 1(2) if some such notion as that of conferring a benefit had not been employed earlier in the subsection. Some word or short phrase was apparently needed to stand for the thing that "has been or will be paid for." It is thought that "to

---

[5] §§ 7–63 to 7–66.
[6] § 8–08.
[7] See J. R. Spencer [1979] Crim.L.R. 24 at 27 ("To some extent as yet uncertain . . . the use of the word 'benefit' cuts down the extreme wideness of the phrases which follow it."); Smith, *Theft*, paras. 230–234 (suggesting the exclusion from the class of benefits of some criminal and some unlawful acts).

confer a benefit by [doing, etc.]" is simply a drafting device that makes the phrase "the benefit" available for this purpose. The device need not be understood as modifying the sense of the subsection. Precisely because someone is understood to be prepared to pay for an act or a permission to do an act, the doing or causing of that act or the giving of that permission is perfectly sensibly described as the conferring of a benefit on him.[8] Who else is to be the judge of the matter? If it were not a benefit to him he would not pay for it.

"Doing some act, or causing or permitting some act to be done"

P may perform, or cause his employee to perform, some professional **8–07** service, for example, or some work such as driving, building or repairing. Or he may give permission to D (or to E, for whom D uses the deception) to do some act (*e.g.* permission to use equipment, as when D hires a car[9] or the use of a computer, or an amenity such as a tennis court). Many benefits will involve P in both the doing or causing of acts and the giving of permission (*e.g.* the provision of hotel accommodation).

Loans; savings accounts

One who makes a loan which will have to be repaid with interest seems to **8–08** confer a benefit upon the borrower by doing an act on the understanding that the benefit will be paid for. There seems to be no reason, therefore, why the obtaining of a loan by deception should not amount to an offence under section 1. Yet in *Halai*[10] the Court of Appeal held that "a mortgage advance cannot be described as a service"; obtaining such an advance by deception was not caught by section 1. This decision is puzzling and regrettable. The hint of an explanation is given in the observation that a mortgage advance is "a lending of money," so that obtaining an advance by deception "can properly be charged under section 15 of the 1968 Act, if the facts support it." But the explanation is inadequate. First, there is no reason why the transaction should not amount to an offence under both sections. Secondly, there are some loans that may not, on a proper analysis, involve the obtaining of any "property" that can be described as having formerly "belonged to" the lender; so that section 15 of the 1968 Act may not be available.[11]

The court in *Halai* was on firmer ground in holding that a building society's act in opening a savings account for an investor was not "services" because it was not an act that would be paid for. The further reason, that the opening of a building society or bank account when the customer pays money in is not in ordinary parlance the conferring of a benefit on the customer, is, with respect, questionable. It is, in ordinary parlance, a benefit to have a bank account; in any case, it is doubtful, as argued above, whether

---

[8] Compare the convenient use of the same language in the *Thirteenth Report*, para. 9.
[9] Or takes goods on hire-purchase: *Widdowson* [1986] Crim.L.R. 233.
[10] [1983] Crim.L.R. 624.
[11] See above, § 7–06.

the reference to the conferring of a benefit need be regarded as a limiting factor in the section[12]; and the fact that the act in question would not normally be called a service should be irrelevant.[13]

Agreements; omissions

8–09   An offence under section 1 is not committed merely by inducing P's agreement to confer a benefit. He must actually confer a benefit by doing, or causing or permitting to be done, an act that has been or is to be paid for. It is submitted that this is not P's act of agreement but some act that he will do, or cause or permit to be done, in performance of the agreement. Partial performance should be enough where P abandons performance after discovering the deception or where D, perhaps anticipating detection, disappears and thus frustrates further performance. If detection occurs before anything is done under the agreement, the inducing of the agreement may, of course, depending on the circumstances, be enough to constitute an attempt.

It seems clear that neither P's forbearance to act (as by not enforcing a debt or realising a security) nor his causing an omission (as by instructing his employee not to retake possession of hired goods from D) is "doing some act" within the meaning of section 1(2).

Obtaining services for another

8–10   Section 1(2) does not specify that the act be one that is done for, or permitted to be done by, the person using the deception. So D may commit an offence under section 1 by obtaining services for E.

"On the understanding that the benefit has been or will be paid for"

8–11   The reference to an "understanding" as to payment is a novel one. The meaning of this word should rarely cause difficulty. The alleged deception will normally relate to the question of payment and will induce P's "understanding" about the matter; and this will suffice. In an exceptional case, however, where the alleged deception relates to something other than payment, P's understanding that the benefit will be paid for ought surely to be a well-founded understanding. It should be necessary to prove a transaction on the strength of which a reasonable observer would share P's understanding.

8–12   The section is no doubt mainly directed to deception relating to payment or the prospect of payment. Consideration of such deception may, indeed, have influenced the wording of subsection (2). But the subsection does not

---

[12] § 8–06.
[13] Above, § 8–05.

provide, as it might easily have done, that P's "understanding that the benefit has been or will be paid for" must itself be induced by deception, or even, for that matter, that the understanding must be false. Notwithstanding the way in which the final words of subsection (2) were introduced in Parliament,[14] those words do nothing to limit the range of relevant deceptions. They simply restrict the benefits that are to be regarded as "services" to benefits for which payment is required. It seems, therefore, that there will be an obtaining of services by deception even where P does an act that D will in fact pay for, being induced to do the act by the deception, for example, that he is dealing with somebody other than D (where it is known that he is unwilling to deal with D) or that D was first-comer among a number of persons seeking the benefit.[15]

Transactions contrary to law or unenforceable

It does not matter that the transaction is one in respect of which the victim **8–13** of the deception could not in any case enforce payment. A man may be convicted under the section if he obtains the services of a prostitute without intending to pay her; or if he similarly obtains services which it is positively a criminal offence for his victim to provide.

The wording of the section seems, however, to exclude gaming and wagering contracts. If D bets with a bookmaker on credit, he may perhaps be said to induce the bookmaker to confer a benefit on him by doing an act—namely, by recording the bet. But even if this is so, the act is done on the understanding, not that the benefit "will" be paid for, but only that it "will in a certain event" be paid for. Such a case is, however, within section 16(2)(c) of the 1968 Act.[16]

No view to gain or intent to cause loss is necessary

If D's deception need not concern the fact or prospect of payment, it is **8–14** remarkable that he is not required to act with a view to gain or an intent to cause loss. As it is, if the above analysis of subsection (2) is correct, the offence may be committed by a person who pays or will pay the proper price for the services he will obtain. A 17-year-old who misrepresents his age in order to gain admission to a cinema showing a film with an "18" classification appears to commit the offence, so long as his conduct is regarded as dishonest.[17]

---

[14] Mr. Brynmor John explained that the words "are there to cover two possibilities: ... the giving of a dud cheque ... [and] the deception which persuades the victim that he has already been paid" (Standing Committee D, June 27, 1978: Official Report, cols. 4–5).

[15] Compare Parry (1978) 128 New L.J. 663. (The equivalent point may be made, of course, about the offence of obtaining property by deception.)

[16] Below, § 10–14.

[17] Compare Parry, *loc. cit.*, n. 15, above. For an attempted justification of the omission of any reference to gain or loss, see H.L.Deb., Vol. 394, col. 1647: the omitted phrase produces "inconsistent results when applied to services." The examples given do not, with respect, explain the difficulty.

Chapter 9

EVASION OF LIABILITY BY DECEPTION

1. THE OFFENCE[1]

9–01   SECTION 2 of the Theft Act 1978 penalises a range of conduct previously covered or intended to be covered by section 16(2)(*a*) of the 1968 Act. (The background to the 1978 Act has been described in the first part of Chapter 6.) Section 2 deals with deception that secures the remission of an existing liability, or induces an existing creditor to wait for payment or to forgo payment, or obtains exemption from or abatement of a liability. The offence created by the section attracts the same penalties as the offence under section 1: on conviction on indictment, up to five years' imprisonment (s.4(2)); on summary conviction, up to six months' imprisonment and/or a fine not exceeding, for the time being, £2,000 (s.4(3); Criminal Penalties, etc. Increase Order (S.I. 1984, No. 447)).

Liability of company officers, etc.

9–02   Section 18 of the 1968 Act applies in relation to this offence as it does in relation to section 15 of the 1968 Act (1978 Act, s.5(1)).[2]

2. "BY ANY DECEPTION"; "DISHONESTLY"

"By any deception"

9–03   The word "deception" has the same meaning here as in section 15 of the 1968 Act—namely, the meaning stated in section 15(4) of that Act (1978 Act, s.5(2)). The discussion of the word in that conext may therefore be referred to.[3] So may the discussion, in connection with the section 15 offence, of the necessary relationship between the false representation and its relevant effect.[4]

"Dishonestly"

9–04   A person charged with an offence under this section must be proved to have acted "dishonestly." Reference may be made to the discussion of this word in the context of section 15 of the 1968 Act.[5]

---

[1] For criticism see J. R. Spencer [1979] Crim.L.R. 24 at 34–35.
[2] s.18 is discussed at § 7–72.
[3] §§ 7–08 to 7–39, and §§ 7–55, 7–56.
[4] §§ 7–40 to 7–53.
[5] §§ 7–63 to 7–66.

(i) As under section 15, so here, the word "dishonestly" contributes to limiting "reckless" deception to cases in which D is indifferent to the truth of his statement and not merely negligent in making it.[6] Only if he does not believe in the truth of his representation is that representation "dishonest."[7]

(ii) Under section 15 the word "dishonestly" qualifies "obtains," so that the obtaining of property must be dishonest. Here it qualifies "secures," "induces" or "obtains" (s.2(1)(*a*)(*b*) and (*c*) respectively) with the like effect. It is possible, therefore, though cases must be rare, that a deceptive evasion of liability otherwise falling within section 2 may not be an offence because D believes that he (or, as the case may be, E, for whose benefit he acts) is legally entitled to the advantage secured or is legally entitled to use the advantage as a means of enforcing a right against P.[8]

(iii) Under section 15 there is, of course, the need for an intention to deprive P of the property obtained by the deception. The present section does not in terms require an intention to secure whatever relevant advantage derives from the deception, but "dishonestly" performs the corresponding function. D does not by deception dishonestly induce P to wait for payment, for example, unless his object in using the deception is that P shall be so induced.[9]

3. "LIABILITY TO MAKE A PAYMENT"

Each part of section 2(1) refers to some existing or prospective "liability to make a payment." Such liability may have a contractual, quasi-contractual or delictual origin. It may arise in equity, as under a trust. Or it may exist as a matter of public rather than private law. The Committee gave as an example of the application of section 2(1)(*c*) the case of a ratepayer who makes a false statement in order to obtain an abatement of his liability to pay rates.[10]   **9–05**

"Liability" means "legally enforceable liability"

The section is concerned only with "legally enforceable liability" (subs. (2)). So, for example, no offence under the section can be committed against a bookmaker or other party to a gaming transaction, against a prostitute, or against a person conducting an unlicensed consumer credit business in respect of a regulated agreement unenforceable by virtue of the Consumer Credit Act 1974, s.40(1). A minor cannot commit the offence in respect of his "liability" under a contract unenforceable against him because made by him when a minor.   **9–06**

There is a partial inconsistency between sections 1 and 2. D may induce P by deception to perform a service for an abated price. If the contract for the service is illegal or *contra bonos mores*, D cannot be convicted under section 2(1)(*c*) but is liable to conviction under section 1.

---

[6] See above § 7–56.
[7] *Waterfall* [1970] 1 Q.B. 148; *Royle* (1971) 56 Cr.App.R. 131.
[8] Compare above, § 7–66.
[9] Compare *Locker* [1971] 2 Q.B. 321 (decided under s.16 of the 1968 Act).
[10] *Thirteenth Report*, para. 15; for further examples, see Appendix 2 to that Report, para. 7.

9–07   A liability is presumably not "legally enforceable" (although it may possibly be enforceable by lawful means other than action) if action to enforce it is statute-barred, or if it arises under a contract of guarantee unenforceable by action for want of a note or memorandum of it signed by or on behalf of the guarantor.

Liability for wrongful act or omission

9–08   P may claim to have a right to compensation from D in respect of an alleged tort or other "wrongful act or omission." So long as D has not "accepted" liability and P has not "established" it, no deception used by D to induce P to abandon his claim or reduce his demand can found an offence under the section (subs.(2)). Once D has accepted liability, however, it seems that he may commit an offence by some deception affecting the determination of quantum.[11] It is not clear whether liability may be "accepted" for this purpose even though its admission occurs in negotiations that are properly described as being "without prejudice." It is thought that it may be. The test, it is submitted, should be whether it is clear, from a statement made by D or on his behalf, that liability is not in dispute.

Meaning of "existing liability"

9–09   The "existing liability" required by section 2(1)(*a*) and (*b*) must, it is suggested, be an actual and not merely a potential or contingent liability (*debitum in praesenti*), though payment may be due only in the future (*solvendum in futuro*). The fact that liability to pay under an existing contract may be conditional upon performance by the other party should not prevent the liability's being "existing" for this purpose. If P has agreed to deliver goods next week against D's promise to pay within the month, D, it is submitted, has an "existing liability." But an insurer or a surety would seem to have only a potential and not an "existing" liability until the occurrence of the insured risk or the default of the primary obligee. The distinction suggested here is not entirely satisfactory, but the rather informal language of the section prompts the manufacture of some artificial dividing line.

4. SECURING REMISSION OF EXISTING LIABILITY

Section 2(1)(a)

9–10   A person commits an offence under section 2(1) who

"... by any deception—

  (*a*) dishonestly secures the remission of the whole or part of any existing liability to make a payment, whether his own liability or another's. ..."

This is the case of the debtor who persuades his creditor by a lying hard-luck

---

[11] Compare *Thirteenth Report*, para. 16.

story to let him off the debt altogether; or that of the purchaser of goods or services who, some time after the bargain is concluded (so that there is an "existing liability"), falsely claims to belong to an association to whose members the supplier customarily gives a discount, with the result that a percentage is knocked off the bill. It is equally an offence if D induces P to remit E's liability rather than some liability of his own.

What mainly distinguishes paragraph (*a*) of section 2(1) from paragraph (*b*) is that under paragraph (*a*) the creditor intends an extinction (in whole or in part) of the debtor's liability, whereas under (*b*)[12] he intends only a deferment of payment. It must be immaterial that the creditor's agreement to the extinction is not binding on him, because it was obtained by fraud, and that the debtor whose fraud is uncovered may in the result, like the paragraph (*b*) offender, gain temporary relief only.[13]

Meaning of "remission"

A "remission" of liability seems to require knowledge on the creditor's **9–11** part of what is being remitted. It is submitted that the following case is not within section 2(1)(*a*). D hires a car from P. The sum that D must pay at the end of the hiring depends in part on the extent to which he has used the car. Before returning the car to P, D tampers with the odometer so that its reading is lower than it should be. P therefore charges a smaller sum than is actually due. This, it is submitted, is not a "remission" of liability. (It may be an "abatement" of liability within the meaning of section 2(1)(*c*).)

It is further submitted that "remission" of liability also requires knowledge that the liability exists. So where P is persuaded that D has already paid him, he does not "remit" D's liability.[14] (He is induced to "forgo payment" within the meaning of paragraph (*b*).)

It has been held that a person who pays a debt by using a stolen credit card secures the remission of his liability and is guilty of an offence under paragraph (*a*).[15] The creditor certainly regards the use of the card as effectively discharging the debtor's liability; but the decision comes close to treating the acceptance of a form of payment as the "remission" of liability to pay and somewhat stretches the language of the paragraph.

5. INDUCING CREDITOR TO WAIT FOR OR FORGO PAYMENT

Section 2(1)(b)

A person commits an offence under section 2(1) who   **9–12**

---

[12] If the words "or to forgo payment" at the end of para. (*b*) are ignored. See below, § 9–15.
[13] Compare A. T. H. Smith [1971] Crim.L.R. 259 at 262–263. J. C. Smith argues that a "remission" requires an agreement effective in law to destroy the debt, at least in part (as in the case of a composition by D with his creditors): Smith, *Theft*, paras. 240–243; but it does not seem credible that s.2(1)(*a*) should be as narrow as this view would make it.
[14] Smith, *Theft*, para. 243, agrees. *Contra*, G. Syrota [1978] Current Law Statutes Annotated, and (1979) 42 M.L.R. 301 at 304–306; and it must be acknowledged that the Committee seem to have intended "remission" to be understood in a wider, but surely inadmissible, sense: *Thirteenth Report*, para. 16.
[15] *Jackson* [1983] Crim.L.R. 617.

"... by any deception—...

> (*b*) with intent to make permanent default in whole or in part on any existing liability to make a payment, or with intent to let another do so, dishonestly induces the creditor or any person claiming payment on behalf of the creditor to wait for payment (whether or not the due date for payment is deferred) or to forgo payment. ...."

There are two different cases here. In either of them D may himself be the debtor, or he may be acting (not necessarily with E's authority) to enable E to escape liability. The ensuing discussion will assume that D is the debtor.

Inducing creditor to wait for payment

9–13   This is a controversial case. The stalling debtor is not in general guilty of a criminal offence, and there is a strong argument that his use of deception should not be distinguished from, say, keeping deliberately out of the creditor's way. At the other extreme it is contended that one who deceives his creditor into waiting for payment should be guilty of an offence even if he intends to pay at some time. The present provision is a compromise between these views. Deceiving the creditor into waiting for a payment is an offence only if the debtor intends never to pay. This solution effectively brings paragraph (*b*) into line with paragraphs (*a*) and (*c*): remission, exemption or abatement will inevitably be secured by one who intends to avoid payment altogether. It does not follow that the solution is a virtuous one.[16]

9–14   The requirement that P be induced by deception to wait for payment does not seem to imply that P need have any alternative. Suppose that D has decided not to pay P. He puts P off most easily by pretending that he is short of ready funds. P says: "Oh, very well; but you must pay next week." This acquiescence means that what P would do if D simply refused to pay him is never put to the test. Probably he could not avoid waiting for payment (though he might promptly resort to litigation and would no doubt refuse credit for further transactions).

P may be induced by deception to wait for payment even if the fact is that D could not in any case pay now. This kind of situation was familiar from the case law on section 16(2)(*a*). D owes P money. He induces P to accept a cheque. P is thereby "induced to wait for payment," as is expressly provided by section 2(3). D knows that there is no prospect of the cheque's being met. He has induced P to take the cheque by deception.[17] If he intends to make permanent default and is dishonest, he is guilty of the offence—even, it seems, if he has no present means of paying cash.[18]

D may give his creditor a cheque in accordance with credit terms agreed between them. Even if the cheque is known by D to be worthless, it seems that in such a case the creditor is not induced by deception to take the cheque in payment or, therefore, to wait for payment (despite the terms of s.2(3)).[19]

[16] See Professor Glanville Williams' powerful Note of Reservation to the *Thirteenth Report* (para. 5 at p. 20); J. R. Spencer, *loc. cit.*, n. 1, above, at 34.
[17] See above, § 7–23.
[18] *D.P.P.* v. *Turner* [1974] A.C. 357.
[19] *Andrews and Hedges* [1981] Crim.L.R. 106 (Mr. Recorder Sherrard Q.C.).

Inducing creditor to forgo payment

The Committee did not explain the difference between remitting liability   **9–15**
(paragraph (*a*)) and forgoing payment. A parliamentary request for an
explanation received an unconvincing reply.[20] It has already been suggested[21] that a "remission" of liability requires an intention to extinguish a
liability of the existence of which the creditor is aware. If this is correct,
"remission" does not cover two types of case:

(i) P is induced to give up a claim to payment by being induced to accept
that D has no liability. D pretends, for example, that he has paid already[22];
or that he has a set-off; or that the goods P sent did not arrive or were
worthless.

(ii) P is induced to abandon any hope of payment. He does not agree to the
extinction of liability; but he goes further than merely agreeing to wait for
payment, for in the circumstances as represented to him he expects never to
see it—he writes off the debt.

Both types of case must be taken to be covered by the phrase "induces [P]
. . . to forgo payment," though the language is not ideal.

6. OBTAINING EXEMPTION FROM OR ABATEMENT OF LIABILITY

Section 2(1)(c)

A person commits an offence under section 2(1) who   **9–16**

". . . by any deception—. . .

   (*c*) dishonestly obtains any exemption from or abatement of liability to
      make a payment;"

and for this purpose he "obtains" any such exemption or abatement if he
obtains it for another or enables another to obtain it (subs.(4)).

Unlike paragraphs (*a*) and (*b*), this paragraph does not require an "existing liability."[23]

"Exemption"

An "exemption" most obviously occurs where a creditor or potential   **9–17**
creditor grants that a liability that would ordinarily arise shall not arise in the
circumstances represented by D to exist—as where D obtains a service free
by representing that he belongs to class of persons (*e.g.* P's employees)

---

[20] See H.L.Deb., Vol. 389, col. 265. The example of "remission" given on behalf of the
Government is an example of "forgoing" according to the distinction suggested in the text,
and not one of "remission." But it would be one of "remission" according to the Committee:
see n. 14, above.
[21] Above, § 8–11.
[22] As in *Holt and Lee* (1981) 73 Cr.App.R. 96.
[23] *Firth* [1990] Crim.L.R. 326.

whom P does not charge. But the decisions to be mentioned in the following paragraphs allow the word a wider scope; they extend it to cases where (i) the creditor makes no charge because he is not aware of a liability rather than because he grants an "exemption" in the usual sense of that word, or (ii) the creditor thinks that the relevant liability has already been discharged.

9–18   In *Firth*[24] a consultant did not tell a hospital that patients whom he referred for treatment were private patients. There was held to be a deception constituted by this "omission," as a result of which the patients were treated without charge under the National Health Service. But the act of referring the patients to the N.H.S. hospital, nothing being said about their status, seems to be positive conduct implying that they are N.H.S. patients. So far as the hospital knows, no liability arises. Any stretching of the notion of "exemption" that is involved in upholding the consultant's convictions under paragraph (*c*) can be interpreted as filling what would otherwise be a gap in the legislation. The consultant obtains a "benefit" that ought to be paid for, without, however, "an understanding that the benefit ... will be paid for"; and such a benefit is not "services" within section 1.

9–19   In *Silbartie*[25] D, at a London Underground interchange station, waved at a ticket inspector a season ticket that did not cover the whole of either part of a journey that he was taking on two lines. This attempt to persuade the inspector that he had a ticket covering his journey was held to be an attempt to obtain exemption from the balance of his liability. The inclination to uphold D's conviction is understandable; but here the notion of "exemption" is surely stretched too far. One does not "exempt" another from a liability that one thinks has been discharged.

"Abatement"

9–20   Other examples of the offence occur where D by deception obtains a service at a reduced rate; or where by a false statement he procures a lower assessment to tax than would otherwise have been made on him (or on his principal). It could be objected that D's fraud does not, strictly speaking, affect his liability to pay but only affects the other party's demand.[26] This objection would destroy paragraph (*c*) almost entirely. It is submitted that the words of the section cannot be understood in their strictest sense.[27]

"Abatement" is not limited to an arrangement at the outset of a transaction. It will cover a case where D persuades P that his existing liability is smaller than P would otherwise have thought; indeed, a false return of income for tax purposes might be such a case. Paragraph (*c*) therefore overlaps paragraph (*b*) (as to forgoing payment). It also overlaps section 1, for many cases of obtaining an abatement of liability by deception will involve an obtaining of services by deception.

[24] Above.
[25] [1983] Crim.L.R. 470. Para. (*b*) would have been an apter home for this case: see text at n. 22, above.
[26] See Smith, *Theft*, para. 246.
[27] See *Thirteenth Report*, para. 15.

7. RELATIONSHIP BETWEEN THE PARAGRAPHS OF SECTION 2(1)

It is one thing to acknowledge that there is a degree of overlap between the **9–21** paragraphs of section 2(1), as the Court of Appeal has indeed contemplated more than once.[28] It would be quite another thing to conclude that the paragraphs may be "simply different ways of describing the same end result"—a view which presented itself to Lawton L.J. in *Holt and Lee*[29] as at least a possibility. His Lordship went so far as to state that "the differences between the offences relate principally to the different situations in which the debtor–creditor relationship arises." There is surely no warrant for this view. The section mainly concerns existing liability and events which can affect it. One and the same debt might be the subject of a remission by the creditor, a decision by the creditor to wait for payment or to forgo payment, an abatement (a reduction in the amount required by the creditor) or, on the court's own interpretation, an exemption. Such events, though they overlap, are on the whole distinct; indeed, there must be a strong presumption that Parliament intended every part of the subsection to makes its own contribution to the control of the mischiefs with which the 1978 Act was concerned. So the dicta in *Holt and Lee* ought not to carry weight. Moreover, prosecutors and courts might be a little more critical of the precise choice of charge than they have sometimes been.

---

[28] *Silbartie* [1983] Crim.L.R. 470; *Jackson* [1983] Crim.L.R. 617.
[29] (1981) 73 Cr.App.R. 96.

Chapter 10

OBTAINING A PECUNIARY ADVANTAGE BY DECEPTION

1. THE OFFENCE

10–01   SECTION 16(1) of the 1968 Act provides:

"A person who by any deception dishonestly obtains for himself or another any pecuniary advantage shall on conviction on indictment be liable to imprisonment for a term not exceeding five years."

Section 16(2) sets out "[t]he cases in which a pecuniary advantage within the meaning of this section is to be regarded as obtained for a person." Those "cases" were originally three in number; but the first, prescribed by the notorious section 16(2)(*a*), was despatched to a welcome oblivion by the Theft Act 1978, as explained above in the first part of Chapter 6.[1] All that remains is the limited group of cases specified in section 16(2)(*b*) and (*c*), which are examined below.

"Pecuniary advantage"

10–02   It was rightly said in *D.P.P.* v. *Turner* that "we do not have to consider what is meant by pecuniary advantage"[2]—plainly because, by telling us in what case "a pecuniary advantage ... is to be regarded as obtained," subsection (2) establishes its whole meaning for the purpose of the section.[3] Yet, to deal with the argument (in a case under subs. (2)(*a*)) that a person with no means could gain no pecuniary advantage by evading a debt, Lord Reid further held that the phrase "is to be regarded as obtained" also means "is to be deemed to have been obtained even if in fact there was none"[4] (that is, no pecuniary advantage). This involves treating the phrase "pecuniary advantage" in the section as having both *only* a technical meaning (*i.e.* the meaning, and only the meaning, allowed by subs. (2), read as a definition) and *also* a "natural" meaning (*i.e.* what you would look for by way of pecuniary advantage if subs. (2), read as a deeming provision, did not render this unnecessary)! This is a small miracle of syntax.

Liability of company officers, etc.

10–03   Section 18 applies to offences under section 16. Reference may be made to the text of section 18 in Appendix 1 or to the discussion at § 7–72, above.

---

[1] § 6–04.
[2] [1974] A.C. 357 at 364.
[3] *Waites* [1982] Crim.L.R. 369.
[4] [1974] A.C. 357 at 365.

2. "BY ANY DECEPTION"; "DISHONESTLY"

"By ... deception ... obtains for himself or another"

(i) "*Deception*." Section 16(3) provides that for the purposes of the section "deception" has the same meaning as it has in section 15. It is therefore sufficient to refer to the definition of "deception" in section 15(4) and to the discussion of that definition in the treatment of the offence of obtaining property by deception.[5]

10–04

(ii) "*Obtains*." The obtaining of the pecuniary advantage must be a consequence of the deception; once again reference may be made to the discussion of the corresponding point in relation to the offence under section 15.[6]

(iii) "*For himself or another*." The result of the words "for another" is that D may commit the offence by, for example, obtaining by deception for E the granting of an overdraft facility by E's bank (subs.(2)(*b*)) or an opportunity for E to earn remuneration in employment (subs. (2)(*c*)).

"Dishonestly"

A person charged with an offence under section 16 must be proved to have acted "dishonestly." Reference may be made to the discussions of this word in the context of section 15[7] and of the Theft Act 1978, s.2.[8]

10–05

3. OVERDRAFTS, INSURANCE POLICIES AND ANNUITY CONTRACTS

Section 16(2)(b)

A pecuniary advantage is to be regarded as obtained for a person

10–06

"where—. . . (*b*) he is allowed to borrow by way of overdraft, or to take out any policy of insurance or annuity contract,[9] or obtains an improvement of the terms on which he is allowed to do so . . ." (s.16(2)(*b*)).

"Is allowed to borrow by way of overdraft"

Borrowing by way of overdraft

A person borrows "by way of overdraft" by drawing upon a bank account

10–07

---

[5] See above, §§ 7–08 to 7–39, and §§ 7–55, 7–56.
[6] Above, §§ 7–40 to 7–53.
[7] Above, §§ 7–63 to 7–66.
[8] Above, § 9–04.
[9] Even a policy or contract void because of the mistake induced by the deception: *Alexander* [1981] Crim.L.R. 183.

that is not in credit[10] when the drawing is effective—that is, when the account is debited. He thus borrows from the bank, becoming its debtor to the extent of the overdrawing. The transaction is to be distinguished from a bank loan, which is typically made by the bank's crediting the customer's account with the amount of the loan and correspondingly debiting a separate loan account.[11] The wording of section 16(2)(b) is very specific and ought to be strictly construed as referring to the former kind of transaction only.

10–08   Take, for example, the following case of "documentary advances." Under a facility agreed with P (a bank), D discounts with P bills of exchange drawn on E for 90 per cent. of their value, the discounted sum being credited to D's current account and the full value of the bills being debited to a "discount account." The "advance" with interest will be repaid when the bills are paid on maturity; but if the bills are not paid the current account will be debited with their full value. In fact D by deception induces P to discount further bills, the discounted value of which keeps his account apparently in balance. In spite of a confident dictum to the contrary,[12] it is submitted that the deception cannot found liability under section 16. No borrowing "by way of overdraft" results from such deception. As a result of the deception the current account is credited, not debited. The "advance" against the fresh bills is debited to the discount account, which is not an account to be drawn upon. Nor, by the same token, is the overall facility—allowing D to discount bills for "advances" up to a stated limit—an overdraft facility.

10–09   Section 16(2)(b) no doubt specifies a borrowing by way of overdraft because such a borrowing will not normally involve the obtaining by D of property[13]; he merely becomes P's debtor. Other modes of borrowing, however, will commonly involve the transfer of property—either money or documents creating rights to money.[14] When such a transfer occurs as a result of deception, an offence under section 15 is committed. Yet it must be noticed that if a loan is effected by the crediting of a bank account there is, for section 15 purposes, the apparent difficulty that what the borrower obtains (a thing in action) has never belonged to the lender.[15] The borrower would seem, however, to obtain services within the meaning of section 1 of the Theft Act 1978; the making of the loan is the conferring of a benefit that will be paid for in the form of interest. But the puzzling case of *Halai*[16] denies this, as has been seen in Chapter 8.

Being "allowed to borrow by way of overdraft"

10–10   An obvious case within section 16(2)(b) is that where by deception D

---

[10] Or not in credit to the extent of the drawing.
[11] See Ellinger, *Modern Banking Law*, pp. 475–476.
[12] *Golechha* (1989) 90 Cr.App.R. 241 at 249. No offence under s.16 was charged. Nor any under s.2 of the Theft Act 1978, which the Court of Appeal also thought apt. The reference is presumably to inducing P to wait for payment (s.2(1)(b)); but this needs an "intent to make permanent default." For the issue with which the court was concerned, see below, § 11–06.
[13] *Pace* Judge Paul Clarke in *Watkins* [1976] 1 All E.R. 578 at 579.
[14] If the latter, s.20(2) is also available.
[15] See above, § 7–06.
[16] [1983] Crim.L.R. 624; above, § 8–08.

induces his bank manager to sanction an overdrawing (or further overdrawing) of his account. A trial judge has ruled that the offence is complete when the overdraft facility is granted.[17] This ruling is supported, as the judge observed, by the phrase beginning "or obtains an improvement," which also points to the time when the arrangement is made. The same is true of the reference to the taking out of an insurance policy or an annuity contract.

Paragraph (*b*) seems not to cover the case where D by deception induces **10–11** his bank not to call in an existing overdraft. The case is within section 2(1)(*b*) of the Theft Act 1978, but only if D acts "with intent to make permanent default."

Misuse of cheque card. It seems to have been accepted without argument **10–12** in the leading case of *Metropolitan Police Commissioner* v. *Charles*[18] that D, a bank's customer with a cheque card and an overdrawn account, obtains a pecuniary advantage when, having no right to overdraw further, he uses the card to guarantee a cheque drawn on the account. The bank has to honour the cheque and D's overdraft increases. Argument in *Charles* concentrated on the deception (of the payee) and its effect in obtaining the advantage.[19] Strangely, a plausible objection to conviction was neither advanced in argument nor faced by the House of Lords: that, although D does "borrow" by way of overdraft, it is hardly convincing to describe him as "allowed to borrow"; for the bank is merely unwillingly obliged to honour its guarantee and may actually (as in *Charles*) have prohibited further drawing against the account. The Court of Appeal has subsequently rationalised the decision in *Charles* thus: by using the guaranteed cheque D impliedly requests the advance by way of overdraft[20]; and the bank, however constrained by its guarantee to the payee, meets the cheques voluntarily (by "an act of will"); it thus "reluctantly agrees" to the request and "allows" the borrowing.[21] The somewhat desperate character of this explanation suffices to cast doubt on the application of section 16(2)(*b*) where the deception is not practised on the bank itself.

Place of offence

The pecuniary advantage of being allowed to borrow by way of overdraft **10–13** is obtained where the account is held; so a deception abroad that obtains an overdrawing in England founds an offence within the jurisdiction.[22]

---

[17] *Watkins* [1976] 1 All E.R. 578.
[18] [1977] A.C. 1; approving *Kovacs* (1974) 58 Cr.App.R. 412.
[19] See above, §§ 7–25 and 7–42.
[20] Compare *Cuthbert* v. *Robarts Lubbock & Co.* [1909] 2 Ch. 226 at 233.
[21] *Bevan* (1986) 84 Cr.App.R. 143. See also *Waites* [1982] Crim.L.R. 369; by issuing the card the bank gives D the "power" to borrow. But this "allowing" is not obtained by the deception (of the payee) in question.
[22] *Bevan*, above.

4. OPPORTUNITY TO EARN REMUNERATION OR TO WIN MONEY BY BETTING

Section 16(2)(c)

10–14   A pecuniary advantage is to be regarded as obtained for a person

> "where—... (c) he is given the opportunity to earn remuneration or greater remuneration in an office or employment, or to win money by betting" (s.16(2)(c))

There is no doubt why this paragraph is included. A person was understood to be not guilty of an offence of obtaining money by false pretences under the old law (1) if he obtained employment by deception (as by falsely claiming certain qualifications) and then drew his salary; the salary was regarded as paid because of the work done and not because of the deception[23]; or (2) if by a false pretence he induced a bookmaker to accept a bet on a race and then collected the winnings when his horse won.[24] Paragraph (c) ensures that in each case D will commit an offence, if not in obtaining the remuneration or winnings, at least in obtaining the opportunity to do so; it will, of course, be irrelevant whether D is actually paid.

It may be felt that the wording of paragraph (c) sticks over-closely to the particular cases that revealed the mischief to be remedied. The paragraph certainly has an oddly narrow and selective appearance. This point may be pursued by reference to each of the kinds of case for which paragraph (c) provides.

"The opportunity to earn remuneration . . . in an office or employment"

10–15   The phrase "in an office or employment"markedly limits the scope of this provision. The word "office" has surely to be understood in a relatively narrow sense.[25] One who is appointed to a directorship or to a public position that is rewarded with pay will earn remuneration "in an office." But a person to whom a brewery grants the tenancy of a public house will not hold "an office." Nor will he be in the "employment" of the brewery.[26] "Employment" may in fact be limited to the relationship that used to be called that of master and servant. Although it is tempting to regard (for example) a freelance author as "employed" by publishers to write a book, or a solicitor as "employed" by his client to perform professional services, neither of them, it would seem, earns his remuneration "in" an employment. The independent contractor may not be within the reach of the paragraph. If he is not, the defect is the result of drafting with a particular case in mind.

---

[23] *Lewis* (1922) unreported: see above, § 7–51, n. 9.
[24] *Clucas* [1949] 2 K.B. 226: see above, § 7–51.
[25] Compare *Edwards* v. *Clinch* [1982] A.C. 845 (decided on the Income and Corporation Taxes Act 1970, s.181(1)), especially the opinion of Lord Bridge.
[26] *McNiff* [1986] Crim.L.R. 57. Nor is his power as tenant to apply for a justices' licence (an "office" leading to "remuneration"?) an opportunity to earn remuneration: *ibid.*

There appears to be no proper ground for distinguishing the office-holder or employee from the independent contractor. The words "in an office or employment" might surely have been omitted.

"The opportunity to win money by betting"

The opportunity to win money by betting is distinguished in the case law **10–16** from the opportunity to win a prize by competing in a contest. The fraudulent punter was not guilty of obtaining his winnings by false pretences[27]; but the runner fraudulently procuring an excessive handicap was guilty of that offence if he obtained the prize.[28] But even if the distinction between the two cases subsists for the purpose of section 15, it does not follow that they should be distinguished for the purpose of the present section. Perhaps the explanation for the exclusion of the dishonest runner from paragraph (c) lies in the fact that to have included him would have meant creating a different unjustifiable distinction—namely, that between the runner who competes for a money prize and the runner who competes for something other than money. Section 16 is concerned with pecuniary advantages and paragraph (c) is drafted accordingly.

[27] See above, § 10–14 at n. 24.
[28] *Button* [1900] 2 Q.B. 597; see above, § 7–51.

Chapter 11

OTHER FRAUD OFFENCES

1. FALSE ACCOUNTING

Introduction

11–01 SECTION 17 creates two offences—in short, the falsifying of accounts and the use of false or deceptive accounts. Both offences are punishable on conviction on indictment with seven years' imprisonment. The section supplements both the law of theft and deception and the law of forgery and using false instruments.

If D fraudulently doctors a cash-book or destroys copy invoices and other sales records, he may not obtain or intend to obtain any property thereby. His conduct may rather be designed to cover up offences already committed. But the particular crime concealed by the false accounting may be hard or impossible to identify; or, though it may be clear, for instance, that D has systematically "milked" an enterprise of which he is a member or an employee, it may not be possible to frame an indictment for theft or to rely solely on a charge of theft.[1] For such reasons as these the criminal law is provided with a weapon which strikes at the falsification of the accounts rather than at the dishonest gain that those accounts assist or conceal.

Again, the destruction or falsification of a document or record under section 17(1)(*a*) may in truth be merely an act of *preparation* for a criminal purpose yet to be accomplished; or the use of a deceptive account under paragraph (*b*) may be an *attempt* to commit some other offence, very likely one of the offences discussed in the preceding four chapters. In this respect offences under section 17 are akin to forgery and using a false instrument, which they considerably overlap. The fabrication or use of false documentation is regarded as a sufficient commitment to the criminal purpose to have the status of a distinct substantive offence. Within the narrow accounting field, section 17 covers conduct not caught by the Forgery and Counterfeiting Act 1981 and is an important ally of that essentially preventive statute.

Falsifying accounts (s.17(1)(a))

11–02 A person commits an offence under section 17(1)(*a*) if, dishonestly and

---

[1] Where it is clear that over a period D has stolen money amounting in total to not less than a certain sum, he can be convicted on an indictment charging the theft of that amount between specified dates: see above, § 2–154. But the property stolen must be accurately alleged and proved: compare *O'Driscoll* [1968] 1 Q.B. 839; commentary at [1967] Crim.L.R. 303. This will not always be possible. It may not be possible, for instance, to prove whether D stole the goods in the shop he managed or money from the till. For observations on the use of "twin" counts charging theft and false accounting, see *Eden* (1971) 55 Cr.App.R. 193.

with a view to gain for himself or another or with intent to cause loss to another, he destroys, defaces, conceals or falsifies any account or any record or document made or required for any accounting purpose.[1a]

It was held in *Attorney General's Reference (No. 1 of* 1980)[2] that a document may be "required" for an accounting purpose if its recipient will in certain events use it for such a purpose although the maker (who is charged with falsifying it) makes it solely for a non-accounting purpose. The case concerned false statements in a personal loan proposal form addressed by a would-be borrower to a finance company. If the proposal were accepted, the company would use the form for an accounting purpose. But ought not the maker at least to know of the intended use? The decision does not require such knowledge. Moreover, a reading of the section which extends it to the making of false statements about such matters as personal and financial circumstances is surprising. The maker will no doubt have a view to gain or an intent to cause loss by the making of such statements, but not by the use of the document as an accounting document, which is surely what the section contemplates.

"Falsifying"

Section 17(2) provides that a person is to be treated as falsifying an **11–03** account or other document if he

(i) makes or concurs in making in it an entry which is or may be misleading, false or deceptive in a material particular, or
(ii) omits or concurs in omitting a material particular from it.[3]

In *Edwards* v. *Toombs*[4] a turnstile operator at Tottenham Hotspur's ground omitted to record on the turnstile meter the passage of paying spectators into the ground. This was a "falsifying" of a "record" within the meaning of subsection (1)(*a*). The argument that the record was not "an account or other document" within the meaning of subsection (2), which alone expressly refers to the omission of particulars as a mode of falsification, was rejected as misconceived.[5] It was held that subsection (2) does not provide a definition but is merely a deeming provision, so that if there was a conflict between subsection (1)(*a*) and subsection (2) the latter could be ignored.

[1a] In *Governor of Pentonville Prison, ex p. Osman* (1990) 90 Cr.App.R. 281 at 299, the Divisional Court thought it impossible to lay down a general rule as to where false accounting is committed if a document is falsified in one place and to be used for an accounting purpose in another.

[2] (1980) 72 Cr.App.R. 60.

[3] It seems that a particular omitted from a document is not a material particular if there was no duty to enter it in the document: see, *e.g. Keatley* [1980] Crim.L.R. 505 (public house manager; no duty to enter in employer's books details of transactions conducted on his own account in breach of his contract of employment: Judge Mendl).

[4] [1983] Crim.L.R. 43. See also *Levitz, The Times*, June 1, 1989, for the view that wiring a "meter mute" to a telephone, causing calls not to be metered, would be false accounting.

[5] The argument was based on a passage in earlier editions of this book (4th ed., § 10–02), suggesting a possible *casus omissus* in the section. The passage was rejected by the court and is not repeated.

Another liberal reading of the section was employed to sustain convictions in *Shama*.[6] A British Telecom operator did not record international calls made through him by his grandmother. He failed to fill in forms (or "charge tickets") in a pile of forms provided for the purpose. He was held to have falsified documents required for an accounting purpose—namely, the forms (any in the pile) that he *ought* to have used. This is a robust decision. The ill-drafted section appears on its face to refer only to the omission of particulars from identifiable documents and to leave untouched the more thoroughgoing default of not creating a document at all in the case of an accounting system that happens to use separate documents for individual transactions rather than a composite document for transactions of a class. The Court of Appeal found itself able to read the section in a way that avoided that absurdity.

"Dishonestly"

11–04   Little need here be said about the requirement of dishonesty, which is discussed above in relation to other offences.[7] The falsification may be dishonest although it does not conceal a separate dishonest transaction, as where D makes a false entry in an account in order to conceal a muddle and to put off the evil day of having to sort out the muddle and make good the resulting loss.[8]

"With a view to gain or an intent to cause loss"

11–05   The requirement of a view to gain or an intent to cause loss is to be understood in the light of the definitions of "gain" and "loss" in section 34(2)(*a*). Gain and loss "in money or other property" are alone relevant, but the intended gain or loss may be only temporary. So D may, for example, falsify an account in order to facilitate an intended unlawful borrowing from the funds of his employers; and he may be guilty of the offence although he intends to replace what he takes.

11–06   *"With a view to gain."* " 'Gain' includes a gain by keeping what one has, as well as a gain by getting what one has not" (s.34(2)(*a*)(i)).
In *Golechha*[9] D discounted trade bills with P (a bank). The question arose whether a falsification practised with a view solely to inducing P to forbear from enforcing its rights under the bills would be a falsification "with a view to gain." It was held not; P's forbearance to enforce D's indebtedness is not a gain "in money or other property" to D. "Property" is defined in section 4(1) to include things in action; but "the [thing] in action represented by the debt

---

[6] [1990] 1 W.L.R. 661; [1990] 2 All E.R. 602.
[7] See especially, §§ 2–127 *et seq.*, 7–63 *et seq.*, 9–04.
[8] *Eden* (1971) 55 Cr.App.R. 193.
[9] (1989) 90 Cr.App.R. 241; above, § 10–08.

is owned by the creditor." D neither obtains nor retains from P's forbearance anything "on which he can draw or which he can convert into cash or goods."

The full implications of this decision are not clear. On the one hand, the court expressly forbore to pass judgment on the trial judge's interpretation of section 17, which appears in effect to have treated an intention to make an indirect gain as "a view to gain."[10] It is thought that that interpretation is correct. If, for example, D falsifies the accounts of the department he manages so as to show inflated profits, his object being to avoid dismissal from his job, it is thought that he is guilty of falsifying the accounts "with a view to" obtaining his continued salary.[11] *Golechha* does not plainly undermine this submission. On the other hand, the quite general proposition in that case that a debtor has no "view to gain" when he intends to induce a forbearance to sue in his creditor seems to rule out as "a view to gain" an intention to gain indirectly by "keeping what one has" as the result of not having to satisfy a (judgment) debt. Perhaps this implication was not intended.

"With intent to cause loss." " 'Loss' includes a loss by not getting what one **11–07** might get, as well as a loss by parting with what one has" (s.34(2)(*a*)(ii)). So (subject to a similar uncertainty about the implications of *Golechha*) an intention to induce a creditor not to sue may be "an intent to cause loss," for by not suing the creditor will not get what he might get (at least in a case where the debtor has assets against which a judgment might be enforced).

Use of misleading, false or deceptive accounts (s.17(1)(b))

Section 17(1)(*b*) strikes at the production or use of an account, or of a **11–08** record or document made or required for an accounting purpose, which, to the knowledge of the producer or user, is or may be misleading, false or deceptive in a material particular. Such production or use in furnishing information for any purpose is an offence if committed with the same *mens rea* as that required under section 17(1)(*a*), just discussed. The material particular need not be directly connected with the accounting purpose for which the document is made or required; it is sufficient if the document is misleading, false or deceptive in a particular that is material for the purpose for which it is being produced or used—that is, the purpose for which information is being furnished.[12]

This offence is similar to those of uttering a forged document under the Forgery Act 1913, s.6 (now repealed) and using a false instrument under the Forgery and Counterfeiting Act 1981, s.3. A person "uttered" a forged document when he "used" it.[13] The forgery authorities on "uses" may accordingly be relevant for the interpretation of the phrase "makes use of" in the present paragraph.[14]

[10] *Ibid.* at 247–248.
[11] Compare *Wines* (1953) 37 Cr.App.R. 197 (falsification "with intent to defraud" under the Falsification of Accounts Act 1875); and, in another context, *Eighth Report*, para. 96.
[12] *Mallett* (1978) 67 Cr.App.R. 239.
[13] Forgery Act 1913, s.6(2).
[14] See in particular *Harris* [1966] 1 Q.B. 184 ("use" by posting a copy).

A document may offend section 17(1)(*b*) notwithstanding that every statement or entry in it is individually true. It may omit facts material to the purpose for which the information is furnished, so as to be effectively false or so that it may mislead those who will rely upon it.[15] If D knows of or suspects the omission and knows that because of it the document may be misleading in some material respect, he is as guilty as if the document contained a positive lie.

Liability of company officers, etc.

11–09   Section 18 applies to offences under section 17. The reader may refer to the text of section 18 in Appendix 1 or to the discussion at § 7–72, above.

2. FALSE STATEMENTS BY COMPANY DIRECTORS, ETC.

11–10   If a company director, intending to deceive members or creditors of the company about its affairs, is party to the publication of a written statement or account which to his knowledge is or may be misleading, false or deceptive in a material particular, he is guilty of an offence carrying seven years' imprisonment on conviction on indictment. Section 19, which so provides, applies in fact to all officers of bodies corporate or of unincorporated associations and to all persons purporting to act as such.

3. SUPPRESSION OF DOCUMENTS, PROCURING EXECUTION OF VALUABLE SECURITIES

11–11   Section 20 preserves, with certain amendments desirable to achieve conformity with other provisions in this part of the Act, offences formerly found in the Larceny Acts of 1861 and 1916. These offences are best regarded as supplementary to offences already considered, as will be indicated in the descriptions of them which follow. The reader is referred to the text of the Act in Appendix 1 for the full terms of the section. The offences created by it are punishable on conviction on indictment with imprisonment for seven years.

Suppression, etc., of certain documents

11–12   Section 20(1) concerns the destruction, defacement or concealment of certain classes of document—namely:

  (i) any "valuable security"; this phrase is defined in very wide terms by subsection (3)[16];
  (ii) any will or other testamentary document;
  (iii) any original document of or belonging to, or filed or deposited in, any court of justice or any government department.

The *mens rea* of the offence is the same as that required for an offence of

---

[15] Compare *Kylsant* [1932] 1 K.B. 442; *Birshirgian* (1936) 25 Cr.App.R. 176.
[16] See below, § 11–14.

falsifying accounts under section 17(1)(*a*), and the discussion in that context need not be repeated. Indeed the two offences have very much in common. The destruction or concealment of a deed or a will, like that of an accounting document, may be a mere act of preparation with a view to the eventual accomplishment of a fraudulent purpose. The main value of section 20(1)[17] is to provide a sanction against the preparatory act where the essence of the matter is a fraudulent purpose in contemplation rather than, for instance, the offence of criminal damage that may also be involved.[18]

Procuring execution of a valuable security

Section 20(2) renders it an offence, dishonestly and with a view to gain or   **11–13**
with intent to cause loss, by any deception to procure the execution of a valuable security.

"Deception" has the same meaning in this context as in the offence of obtaining property by deception (subs.(3)).[19] The procuring must be *by* the deception; the discussion of the relation between a false representation and the obtaining of property required for an offence under section 15 applies here with necessary modifications.[20] The *mens rea* of the offence is the same as that required under section 17(1)(*a*); reference may be made to the earlier discussion.[21]

"Valuable security"

"Valuable security" is defined by subsection (3) to mean: **11–14**

"any document creating, transferring, surrendering or releasing any right to, in or over property, or authorising the payment of money or delivery of any property, or evidencing the creation, transfer, surrender or release of any such right, or the payment of money or delivery of any property, or the satisfaction of any obligation."

It was held in *Benstead*[22] that this definition embraces an irrevocable letter of credit (notwithstanding that the liability created by such a document is conditional upon acts to be performed by the seller). The document creates a thing in action in favour of the beneficiary and therefore a "right . . . in . . . property." But it has been objected that this phrase should be understood to refer only to rights in existing property and not to property created by the document itself; for otherwise all written contracts, since they create things in action, would appear to be valuable securities, which can hardly be intended.[23]

---

[17] If it has any value in practice. It is doubtful whether there were any modern prosecutions under the corresponding repealed provisions: see *Eighth Report*, para. 106.
[18] See *ibid.*
[19] See above, §§ 7–08 *et seq.*
[20] See above, §§ 7–40 *et seq.* In *Beck* (1984) 80 Cr.App.R. 355, it was accepted that the deception of one person might procure the execution of a valuable security by another; compare above, § 7–53.
[21] Above, §§ 11–04 to 11–07.
[22] (1982) 75 Cr.App.R. 276.
[23] J. C. Smith [1982] Crim.L.R. 457.

In *Beck*[24] it appears to have been accepted without argument that a travellers' cheque form, never issued by the bank for which it had been printed but simply forged by D, was a "valuable security." But this is very doubtful; it is not clear how such a forgery comes within the statutory definition. In the same case D was also convicted under section 20(2) in respect of his use of a stolen credit card. It is not quite plain whether the thing conceived to be a "valuable security" was the card itself or the voucher D signed when he used it. The accuracy of either conception needed demonstrating, but this point also passed without argument.

"Execution"

11–15   The word "execution" is a shorthand expression for an extensive range of acts spelt out in section 20(2) itself, which may be consulted in Appendix 1. They include "the making, acceptance, indorsement, alteration, cancellation or destruction" of a valuable security (in whole or in part). These are all words peculiarly apt to describe acts in connection with bills of exchange and other negotiable instruments. The need to make a criminal offence of the fraudulent obtaining of a drawee's acceptance of a bill drawn upon him was revealed by a case in 1857[25]; and the gap in the law was remedied by legislation[26] soon replaced by section 90 of the Larceny Act 1861. That section (subsequently the Larceny Act 1916, s.32(2)) made it an offence to fraudulently cause or induce a person to "execute, make, accept, endorse, or destroy" a valuable security. The present Act has added some items to that list. It seems quite plain from the history, and from the very particular list in which the term occurs, that "acceptance" has here its technical meaning in the law relating to bills of exchange. That is, it refers to the drawee's act of writing on the bill, and signing, his assent to the order of the drawer.[27]

11–16   This interpretation was not apparently considered in the surprising case of *Beck*.[28] D had travellers' cheques which had been stolen in transit between the printers and the bank by which they were to be issued. He forged the cheques and cashed them abroad. The deceived foreign payers presented the cheques to the bank in England, and the bank felt obliged, though it was not in the circumstances legally bound, to honour them. It was held that D had procured the "acceptance" of the cheques within the jurisdiction. Although, it was said, the cheques had first been "accepted" within the meaning of section 20(2) when their monetary value was paid by a person by whom they were "accepted as genuine," they were "accepted" a second time when payment on them was made by the bank. This final act was within the jurisdiction. (A similar analysis was applied to the payment by Diners Club Ltd. (in England) of bills incurred abroad by D, when he used a stolen club card, forging the name of the authorised holder.)

[24] (1984) 80 Cr.App.R. 355; below, § 11–16.
[25] *Danger* (1857) 7 Cox C.C. 303; cited by Stephen, *Digest of the Criminal Law* (9th ed.),
[26] 21 & 22 Vict. c. 47.
[27] Bills of Exchange Act 1882, s.17.
[28] (1984) 80 Cr.App.R. 355.

The Court of Appeal has subsequently been persuaded, on the strength of **11–17** the historical argument summarised above, that the word "acceptance" in section 20(2) has only its technical meaning in the Bills of Exchange Act.[29] But the court has for the time being loyally maintained the authority of the *Beck* decision to the effect that payment of an instrument is an "execution" of it,[30] treating "execute" as meaning "give effect to or carry out the terms of the document."[31] In the most recent case, however, the court, while constrained by the precedents, "acknowledg[ed] the attraction and force of the argument" that a valuable security "is 'executed,' properly speaking, only by the maker."[31] This is clearly what "execute" meant in the precursors of section 20(2), when, as mentioned above, the word figured merely as the first in the list of technical expressions. The drafting technique now used is to make the word stand for them all; but this can hardly have been intended to change its meaning.

"Execution" (s.20(2) provides) includes the signing of a paper in order **11–18** that it may be made or converted into, or used or dealt with as, a valuable security. The purpose referred to by the words "in order that" may be that of D alone and not that of the person deceived into signing; indeed, a typical deception which the subsection certainly covers is a deception as to the very nature of the document being signed.[32] Nor, according to old authority, need the "valuable security" into which the document is intended to be converted be one which will in fact be valid if put to use.[33]

"Procuring" execution

The word "procure" was said in *Beck*[34] to be a word which "a jury can be **11–19** relied on safely to understand." They will understand it, it seems, to mean "to cause or to bring about." D, who uses forged travellers' cheques and a stolen credit card, thereby "procures" the payments that the bank and the credit card company will eventually make (whether or not as a matter of strict legal obligation) to those deceived by D. Notwithstanding the invocation of the jury as interpreters of "a word in common usage," this seems to be a judicial interpretation. It rejects the well-known definition of the word by Lord Widger C.J. (in the context of secondary liability) as involving purpose.[35]

---

[29] *Nanayakkara* (1986) 84 Cr.App.R. 125: stolen U.S. Treasury social security orders delivered to a bank, to be cleared before crediting of the amounts to an account with the bank, were not "accepted" by the bank within the meaning of s.20(2).
[30] *Nanayakkara*, above, at 131 (agreeing, *obiter*, that "[i]n *Beck* there was clearly an execution"); *Kassim* [1988] Crim.L.R. 372 (payment of cheques; *Beck* and *Nanayakkara* followed).
[31] *Kassim*, above.
[32] Compare *Graham* (1913) 8 Cr.App.R. 149.
[33] *Graham*, above.
[34] (1984) 80 Cr.App.R. 355 (above, § 11–16) at 360.
[35] *Attorney General's Reference (No. 1 of 1975)* [1975] Q.B. 773 at 779: "To procure means to produce by endeavour. You procure a thing by setting out to see that it happens and taking the appropriate steps to produce that happening."

Effects of section 20(2)

11–20   Section 20(2) supplements other offences in two ways.

(i) First, it strikes at conduct analogous to obtaining property or services, or evading liability, by deception. The aim of a fraud within section 20(2) will commonly be the imposition of some liability upon the victim or a third person[36] (as when D procures P's signature to a deed, a cheque or a guarantee) or the extinction of some liability of D or a third person (as when D by deception induces P to cancel a bill of exchange of which he is the holder). Such a fraud may or may not involve another offence under the Acts. Where it does not section 20(2) enlarges the range of the Acts.

(ii) Secondly, the ultimate aim of one who by deception procures the execution of a valuable security may in fact be the obtaining of property or of some other advantage by use of the security. Section 20(2) therefore makes a separate substantive offence out of conduct which may be merely preparatory to commission of one of the offences discussed in earlier chapters.

11–21   Such, at any rate, were the effects of section 20(2) until recently. The doubtful decision in *Beck* (referred to several times above) significantly enlarges the functions of the offence. That case holds that a person "executes" an instrument when he accepts that he must pay in response to it and does so. If D obtains P's payment on an instrument by deception, he in any case commits an offence under section 15. But if (as in *Beck*) D's deception is practised on O, who pays D, and O in his turn obtains payment from P, D has surely not "obtained" P's payment by "enabling" O to obtain it within the meaning of section 15(2).[37] *Beck* holds, however, that D has "procured" P's payment. So where (again as in *Beck*) D's acts and O's payment occur abroad and only P's payment to O occurs in England, D has nevertheless committed an offence within the jurisdiction. This is a very surprising outcome. No doubt it might be argued that on these facts D has defrauded P within the jurisdiction. But that would not in itself involve an offence in the absence of a conspiracy.

---

[36] Compare *Thornton* [1964] 2 Q.B. 176 at 182.
[37] "Obtain" includes "enabling another to obtain."

Chapter 12

MAKING OFF WITHOUT PAYMENT

1. THE OFFENCE. POWER OF ARREST

AN offence is committed by "a person who, knowing that payment on the   **12–01**
spot for any goods supplied or service done is required or expected from
him, dishonestly makes off without having paid as required or expected and
with intent to avoid payment of the amount due" (Theft Act 1978, s.3(1)).
The offence is punishable on conviction on indictment with up to two years'
imprisonment (s.4(2)(*b*)), and on summary conviction with up to six
months' imprisonment and/or a fine not exceeding, for the time being,
£2,000 (s.4(3); Criminal Penalties, etc. Increase Order 1984 (S.I. 1984
No. 447)).

The change in the law effected by section 3

Criminal law sanctions are not generally provided against the dishonest   **12–02**
debtor. Section 3 makes an exception for one who, by physically removing
himself from the scene at which his obligation arises, may effectively put
himself beyond his creditor's grasp. The mischief is commonly termed
"bilking." Only certain examples of it were formerly subject to control.
Section 3 provides a comprehensive sanction. The following paragraphs
explain the change in the law effected by the section.

(i) *Theft or no theft.* If D dishonestly makes off without paying for goods   **12–03**
supplied to him, he is not guilty of theft if the property in the goods has
already passed to him and the supplier has ceased to have possession or
control of them.[1] The present section, therefore, apart from extending the
law, avoids nice questions of civil law even in a case where it may in fact be
possible to prove theft.

(ii) *Original or supervening dishonesty.* When D runs out of a restaurant   **12–04**
without paying for his meal, conviction under section 15 of the 1968 Act
requires proof that his intention not to pay was formed before he obtained
the food, so that it may be found that he obtained it by deception as to his
intention to pay.[2] Exactly the same point applies under section 1 of the 1978
Act, as to obtaining services by deception. Under the present section there is

---

[1] See above § 2–47. It is assumed that D has not got the goods by the supplier's mistake in
circumstances bringing the case within s.5(4) of the 1968 Act (above, § 2–38). No one, in any
case, wants to rely on s.5(4) if something simpler will do.
[2] See above, § 7–18.

197

no need to prove that a prior deception induced the supply of goods or the rendering of the service.

12–05   (iii) *Making off achieved by deception or otherwise.* Where prior deception cannot be proved (and property in the goods, if any, has passed) D may still be guilty under section 2 of the Theft Act 1978 of evading his liability to pay if by deception he induces his creditor to wait for payment. The corresponding offence before 1978 was that under section 16(2)(*a*) of the Theft Act 1968 (now repealed) of obtaining the evasion of a debt by deception (as a form of "pecuniary advantage"). As a result of the decision of the House of Lords in *D.P.P.* v. *Ray*,[3] D might be convicted of this offence if, having decided to make off from a restaurant, garage forecourt or barber's shop without paying, he waited until P (a person aware of his transaction) had turned his back and then fled. P was to be treated as relevantly deceived and D's evasion as being effected by the deception. It is doubtful whether *D.P.P.* v. *Ray* can be adapted to the 1978 evasion offence; but even if it can, the extensive notion of deception upon which it rests and the distinction between the situations it would catch and those it would not are equally disreputable. There should be an offence in all of these situations or in none. Section 3 provides an offence in all of them.

Power of arrest

12–06   Unlike the offences created by sections 1 and 2 of the 1978 Act, which carry a maximum penalty of five years' imprisonment, this offence is not an arrestable offence within the meaning of the Police and Criminal Evidence Act 1984, s.24(1). A special power of arrest without warrant is therefore provided in respect of anyone who is or, with reasonable cause, is suspected to be, committing or attempting to commit the offence (s.3(4)). This is a so-called "citizen's arrest" power; the waiter, hotel receptionist or petrol pump attendant may arrest the customer who is "making off" or attempting to do so. The arrest must be made, however, while the offender is still "making off"; there is no power to arrest a person who is, or who is suspected of being, "guilty of the offence"[4] but who is no longer (suspected to be) "committing" it.[5] The problem of determining when the "making off" ends can therefore arise. It is not one that can be resolved by a general formula.[6]

2. THE DETAILS OF THE OFFENCE

There must be some "goods supplied" or "service done"

Goods supplied

12–07   The section is particularly designed to cover the kind of sale transaction

---

[3] [1974] A.C. 370; above, § 7–33.
[4] Compare Police and Criminal Evidence Act 1984, s.24(5) and (6).
[5] As in *Drameh* [1983] Crim.L.R. 322: arrest at home half an hour after making off from taxi—unlawful (Judge Pickering).
[6] Compare "the course of the stealing" in s.22(1) of the 1968 Act.

under which property in the goods inevitably passes before payment is expected—the transfer of petrol from pump to fuel tank, for example, or the service of a meal to a diner who will pay after eating. But it will also apply to a delivery of goods in anticipation of the passing of property. A common case is that of the wrapping and pricing of goods at a supermarket food counter, the goods being handed to the customer to be paid for at the cashier's desk. It is submitted that these goods are "supplied" at the food counter although they are not yet "sold"; so that if the customer dishonestly leaves without paying, he commits the present offence, which is thus an alternative to a charge of theft. This does not mean that the standard case of shoplifting is necessarily an offence under section 3; goods simply exposed for sale are not, it is thought, "goods supplied."[7]

"Goods" has the meaning stated in section 34(2)(*b*) of the 1968 Act (s.5(2)).

Service done

The definition of "an obtaining of services" by section 1(2) is not matched   **12–08**
by a definition of "service done" in section 3(1). Nor is the shift from "services" to "[a] service" explained. It is submitted, however, that "service done" should be liberally interpreted, as "obtains services" is broadly defined. For example, permitting a person to use a tennis court in a public park or a rowing boat on a private lake should be regarded as the doing of a service, even though nothing is done apart from the giving of permission to use the amenity. But something in the way of permission (if only a permission to be inferred from deliberate inaction) appears to be necessary. The section does not cover a making off from a cinema or dance hall that has been clandestinely entered through a back door or window. An amenity thus involuntarily provided is not a "service done."[8]

"Service done" must cover the letting of goods on hire (which is, however, more obviously a supply of goods[9]), as it will also cover the letting of a room in a guest house or hotel.

Transactions contrary to law or unenforceable

Making off without having paid is no offence if the supply of goods or the   **12–09**
doing of the service was contrary to law or if the service done is such that payment is not legally enforceable (s.3(3)).

The contract under which the goods are supplied or the service done may itself be "contrary to law."[10] Thus, it may be an offence to supply the goods in question (*e.g.* a flick knife) or to do the service; or to conduct the sale in a particular manner (*e.g.* in contravention of the Mock Auctions Act 1961); or to supply the goods to the particular customer served (*e.g.* intoxicating liquor to a minor).

---

[7] *Contra*, as to self-service shops, Smith, *Theft*, para. 251.
[8] See *Thirteenth Report*, para. 21.
[9] Compare *Cahaine* v. *Croydon L.B.C.*, *The Times*, March 20, 1985 (Trade Descriptions Act 1968, s.1).
[10] See this heading in Treitel, *An Outline of the Law of Contract* (4th ed.), pp. 152 *et seq.*

12–10   The supply of goods or the doing of the service may be "contrary to law" because of some breach of the law committed in carrying out the transaction.[11] All depends upon the correct construction of the statutory provision that is contravened: is it intended to affect the contract in performance of which the contravention occurs, or does it merely impose penalties for the contravention?[12] A new jurisprudence on this difficult question could well arise from the present section. It will merely be observed here, by way of example: (a) that the lack of a necessary licence—*e.g.* a street trader's or hackney carriage driver's licence—will very probably take the transaction outside section 3; (b) that a serious breach of the Motor Vehicles (Construction and Use) Regulations may render the doing of a service "contrary to law"[13]; but (c) that it can hardly be intended that a relatively trivial breach of the same Regulations should render a taxi-driver's contract with his passenger "contrary to law" so that he cannot in theory sue for his fares or in practice arrest the passenger for an offence under section 3.[14]

12–11   Services for which payment is not legally enforceable include, most obviously, services under contracts void by statute (*e.g.* gaming contracts) or as being contrary to public policy (*e.g.* the services of a prostitute or other "immoral" services).

D must know that "payment on the spot is required or expected"

12–12   The word "payment" here seems to refer to any transaction that would discharge the debtor's obligation. The establishment that welcomes cardholders[15] and the restaurant that accepts luncheon vouchers are plainly protected by the section although they do not expect cash.

Payment "on the spot" is payment "then and there"—that is, before leaving the place at which the goods are on that occasion supplied or the service is on that occasion done. It also includes "payment at the time of collecting goods on which work has been done or in respect of which service has been provided" (s.3(2)). It does not matter that the car has been repaired on an earlier day or that the clothes have been dry-cleaned off the premises from which they are being collected.

The transactions covered by the section are mainly of an informal type, and the language of the section is correspondingly informal at this point. The terms governing payment will rarely be express; if they are, payment on the spot may be expressly "required." The obligation to pay on the spot will much more often derive from common usage; such payment will be "expected" as a matter of common understanding.

The debtor must know of the requirement or expectation. If he thinks that he enjoys credit terms, he cannot be guilty of the offence, however dishonest

---

[11] The topic is not suitable for full treatment here. See Chitty, *Law of Contracts* (25th ed.), Chap. 16, especially at paras. 1143 *et seq.*
[12] *St. John Shipping Corporation* v. *Joseph Rank Ltd.* [1957] 1 Q.B. 267.
[13] As in *Ashmore, Benson, Pease & Co. Ltd.* v. *A. V. Dawson Ltd.* [1973] 1 W.L.R. 828 (overloading lorry).
[14] Compare *St. John Shipping Corporation* v. *Joseph Rank Ltd.*, above, at 281.
[15] For payment by credit card as discharge of the customer's obligation, see *Re Charge Card Services Ltd.* [1989] Ch. 497.

he may be. If, conversely, he has in fact been served on credit terms, but believes that payment on the spot is required or expected, again he cannot commit the offence; for one cannot "know" what is not the case.[16]

"Makes off"

The words "makes off" do not stand alone—the making off must be dishonest. This being so, the words can be applied "in their ordinary natural meaning." A person "makes off" when, quite simply, he departs from the spot where payment ought to be made.[17] (If he is stopped before he passes that spot, so that he does not achieve such a departure, he may be guilty of an attempt to commit the offence.[18]) No particular mode of departure is required, such as stealth or haste. The departure may occur with the knowledge and assistance of the creditor or his staff, as where a cool customer calls for his hat and coat, requests that a cab be summoned for him and sends his compliments to the chef.   **12–13**

It has been argued that the mischief struck at by the section is "leaving in a way that makes it difficult for the debtor to be traced."[19] But if the implication of this view is that no-one can "make off" if his identity and address are perfectly well known to the creditor, it produces a very strange reading of the section. Moreover, it is doubtful whether it hits the whole of the mischief. Some typical creditors in whose interests the offence was created depend entirely on payment then and there, their debts being far too small to warrant pursuing.

Deception to achieve departure

There has been controversy as to whether a person can be said to "make off" where by deception he induces the creditor to consent to his departure. It is thought that he can.[20] It is, of course, agreed that "the creditor's consent to the fetching by a person of the means of payment is not to be treated as consent to his departure"[21] (P the taxi-driver waits while D will—so he pretends—"just pop indoors to find the fare"). The problem is with other kinds of deception. Does D "make off" when he gives counterfeit coin to the flower-seller in pretended payment or misleads the restaurateur into believing that he has paid the waiter? The preferable solution, it is thought, is to say that he does, following the Court of Appeal in the view that "makes off" simply means "departs." Discrimination between cases can then turn on whether D has departed "without having paid as required or expected."   **12–14**

[16] Strictly, he may be guilty of an attempt.
[17] *Brooks and Brooks* (1982) 76 Cr.App.R. 66.
[18] *McDavitt* [1981] Crim.L.R. 843 (Mr. Recorder M. Mann Q.C.); approved in *Brooks and Brooks*, above.
[19] J. R. Spencer [1983] Crim.L.R. 573.
[20] Smith, *Theft*, para. 250, in general agrees (though he is wrongly credited with the opposite opinion in *Brooks and Brooks*, above, at 68). But he yields to the persuasion of J. R. Spencer, *loc. cit.* above, to the extent of accepting that one "who leaves a worthless cheque with his true name and address" does not "make off" because, being traceable, he is outside the mischief of the offence.
[21] Bennion [1983] Crim.L.R. 205, elaborating his argument at [1980] Crim.L.R. 670 in favour of a narrow interpretation of "makes off."

"Without having paid as required or expected"

12–15   It is suggested that a person "makes off without having paid as required or expected" if he leaves without doing what he ought to do to discharge his obligation. One who leaves foreign coins in the newsvendor's tray or gives forged banknotes for his petrol does not "pay." Giving stolen money is a different case, however; the innocent creditor acquires a good title to stolen currency that is passed to him, so that the debtor's obligation is discharged.

Some difficulty is caused, however, by the case of one who gives in purported payment a cheque that he realises will not be met on presentment. One view of this case is that it involves no "making off"[22]; but that view has been criticised above. Assuming now that there is a "making off," it would seem odd to describe as "payment" the giving of a worthless cheque. On the other hand, it is precisely for such a case that section 2(3) is at pains to provide, for purposes of section 2(1)(b), that the creditor who is given a cheque is not to be treated as being paid but as being induced to wait for payment.[23] The silence of section 3 on this point may possibly imply that the contrary is intended for purposes of that section; and it has indeed been argued that one who gives a cheque that is sure to bounce nevertheless "pays" by making a conditional payment.[24] It was at one time widely thought that section 3 did not require an intention to avoid payment permanently. If this were true, the section might have been employed in a deception case in which section 2(1)(b) would not be available for want of an "intent to make permanent default." Now that the contrary has been held,[25] the point discussed above ought to be academic; there will be no advantage in charging under section 3 and no room for argument if section 2 is used, as surely it should be. In case section 3 should be used, however, it is suggested that common sense provides the preferable solution: one who leaves a worthless cheque does not "pay."

"With intent to avoid payment of the amount due"

There must be an "amount due"

12–16   The supply of goods or doing of a service must obviously be such as to give rise to a payment obligation. If the supplier has earned no money (perhaps because of breach of contract or because he has not completed performance of his own obligations), there is no "amount due." If the supplier's breach of contract or failure to complete performance discharges the customer from obligation under the supply contract, the customer commits no offence if he departs.[26] It is otherwise, however, if it is the customer who, by his very departure, prevents completion of the supply. In such a case the supplier becomes entitled to the value of his performance so far.[27] If the customer's

---

[22] Bennion and Spencer, *loc. cit.* above; *Hammond* [1982] Crim.L.R. 611 (Judge Morrison).
[23] See above, § 9–14.
[24] Syrota [1980] Crim.L.R. 413.
[25] See below, § 12–17.
[26] In *Troughton* v. *Metropolitan Police* [1987] Crim.L.R. 138, a conviction was quashed on the basis of such an interpretation of the facts.
[27] *Planché* v. *Coburn* (1831) 8 Bing. 14.

making off is with intent to avoid payment even of that amount, he ought to be guilty of the offence. This has to be secured by treating the amount as "due" because the very act of making off makes it so. The slight paradox is supportable.

D must intend never to pay

It was for a time a widely held view that the phrase "intent to avoid **12–17** payment," read in its context and in the light of the contrast with section 2(1)(*b*), clearly meant an intention to avoid the on-the-spot payment known to be required, and that an intention never to pay was not necessary. The contrary, however, was held by the House of Lords in *Allen*.[28] D left the hotel where he had been staying, without paying his bill. It was held that his defence, that he had been prevented from paying the bill by temporary financial difficulties but expected to be able to do so from the proceeds of certain business ventures, should have been left to the jury. The arguments which prevailed with the House of Lords[29] were: (1) that the phrase "with intent to avoid payment" would add nothing to the other ingredients of the offence if it merely meant "with intent to avoid payment on the spot," for anyone leaving dishonestly without paying must have that intent; and (2) that there were other and preferable ways of drafting section 3(1) if that was the meaning to be conveyed.

The decision concludes the point and it would not be justifiable to devote **12–18** much space to an attempt to counter these arguments. Suffice it to observe: (1) that the first doubtfully assumes that every phrase in a statutory provision must have an entirely independent function, a proposition that an eminent draftsman has contradicted, by chance referring to this very provision as an example of the "technique of overlap"[30]; and (2) that it would equally have been easy to insert the word "permanently," as in some other provisions, if that was what was meant.

What is more important is the outcome; section 3 turns out not to do the whole of the job that it ought to do. In the case of sellers and suppliers of services who undertake very small transactions on the basis of immediate payment, the mischief to be controlled is the very act of making off; and, as Lord Hailsham suggested,[31] there may well now be a case for the creation of a summary offence of making off with intent to avoid the on-the-spot payment required. In the meantime the decision in *Allen* threatens an increase in the number of contested cases as bilkers run bogus, but possibly just plausible, defences of "I was going to go back and pay later."

Where D believes that nothing is due

D may think that payment has already been made, by himself or a **12–19**

---

[28] [1985] A.C. 1029.
[29] They were those of Boreham J. for the Court of Appeal: see *ibid.* at 1034.
[30] Bennion, *Statute Law* (2nd ed.), p. 176.
[31] [1985] A.C. 1029 at 1035.

companion. In this case, not knowing there is an "amount due," he cannot be said to intend to avoid payment of it.

A similar defence may be made by a customer who pays or tenders less than the sum charged on the ground that the sum is excessive. He may claim that the price (not notified or negotiated in advance) is unreasonable; or that defects in the goods or service reduce what he is legally obliged to pay. His contention in either case is that what he pays or tenders is the whole "amount due" and that his making off is not, therefore, with intent to avoid payment of that amount.

Defences such as those just discussed equally, of course, deny dishonesty.

"Dishonestly"

12–20   The general principle[32] is that it is for the jury or the magistrates as judges of fact to say whether the accused's conduct was "dishonest" within the meaning of that word as "an ordinary word of the English language," applying for this purpose "the current standards of ordinary decent people."[33] If it was, a further question arises (if, at least, there is evidence capable of raising a doubt about it[34]): must the defendant have realised that what he did was dishonest according to those standards?[35]

---

[32] See above, § 2–127.
[33] *Feely* [1973] Q.B. 530.
[34] See § 2–128.
[35] *Ghosh* [1982] Q.B. 1053.

Chapter 13

BLACKMAIL

1. INTRODUCTION

BEFORE the passing of the Act the term "blackmail" was not a term of art   **13–01**
in English law. The word had been used by lawyers as a convenient way of
referring to a number of offences contained in the Larceny Act 1916,
ss.29–31, where, however, the word did not appear. By laymen it was
understood to mean the obtaining of some advantage by the use of improper
threats, especially threats to make use of information discreditable to the
victim. The layman's use of the word was naturally looser than the lawyer's;
but layman and lawyer were not far apart in their understanding of what
amounted to blackmail, and they both regarded the kinds of conduct they
had characteristically in mind as among the most serious criminal or moral
offences.[1]

The complex statutory provisions replaced by section 21 of the present   **13–02**
Act have been aptly described as "an ill-assorted collection of legislative
bric-à-brac which the draftsman of the 1916 Act put together with scissors
and paste."[2] There was a considerable number of offences, carrying widely
different maximum penalties. These offences, by their own terms and still
more by virtue of their interpretation at the hands of the courts, overlapped
to a perplexing and unsatisfactory degree. The overlap was, if anything,
rendered more serious by the fact that the most important of the provisions
were so drafted as to involve fundamentally different approaches to one of
the central problems of this part of the law. The problem, shortly expressed,
is this: from what point of view, in considering the lawful or unlawful
character of a demand with menaces, is the propriety of or justification for
the relevant conduct to be judged? Should the fact that what D demands is
rightly due to him be relevant? If it should, should it be relevant that, though
what D demands is not something to which he has a valid claim, yet he thinks
it is? If blackmail can be committed even by demanding something to which

---

[1] The worst cases of extortion, or attempt to extort, by threats to commit legal wrongs (and *a
fortiori* threats to commit serious crimes) are uncontroversially bad offences. But a substantial literature is devoted to puzzled attempts to resolve the alleged "paradox of blackmail." The offence typically embraces cases in which D threatens to do what he is legally, and
perhaps morally, entitled to do (even, in some cases, what he ought to do, such as report a
crime) if P does not do what he (D) is perfectly at liberty to request (and may be entitled to
demand). The paradox was neatly stated by Williams [1954] Crim.L.R. at 163: "two things
that taken separately are moral and legal whites together make a legal black." Several
theories are reviewed, and his own offered, by Lindgren (1984) 84 Col. Law Rev. 670. For
elaborate discussion from a liberal perspective, with implications for the narrowing of the
offence, see Joel Feinberg, *Harmless Wrongdoing* (*The Moral Limits of the Criminal Law*,
vol. 4), pp. 238–276.
[2] Hogan [1966] Crim.L.R. 474.

D is (or believes he is) entitled, by what criterion is the propriety of his using a particular threat to support his demand properly to be judged—by his own subjective opinion, or by an objective standard, whether represented by the terms of a statute or by the opinion of a court or jury? To these questions the Larceny Act, as interpreted, afforded no clear or consistent answers.

13-03   Questions of the kind mentioned in the preceding paragraph may be plausibly answered in a number of different ways. The Act provides a unified and tolerably coherent solution. In order to achieve this solution and a general simplification of the law, the Committee largely dispensed with the language of the repealed provisions. The only words of importance preserved from the Larceny Act are the words "demand" and "menaces," which reflect the language of the Larceny Act 1916, ss.29(1)(i) and 30. Apart from the use of these two words, the offence created by section 21 of the Theft Act 1968 was new in form and in approach, as well as in name. It proceeded from the necessity that the Committee felt "to go back to first principles and to consider as a matter of policy what kind of conduct should amount to blackmail."[3]

The problem of policy was answered thus. Any demand with menaces should, prima facie, be condemned, and it should be caught by the Act if its purpose is a property gain or loss. But honesty should win exemption; the Act does not strike at the conscientious mind. One should be entitled to plead, in effect: "I thought my demand was justified and my pressure acceptable"; such language comes as close as the subject-matter allows to the notion of honesty. This solution inevitably proved controversial.[4]

2. DEFINITION OF BLACKMAIL. GENERAL OBSERVATIONS

The statutory definition

13-04   There are three ingredients of the crime of blackmail:
(i) D must make a "demand with menaces."
(ii) The demand with menaces must be "unwarranted"; and it will be unwarranted unless D makes it "in the belief—(a) that he has reasonable grounds for making the demand; and (b) that the use of the menaces is a proper means of reinforcing the demand."
(iii) D must make the demand "with a view to gain for himself or another or with intent to cause loss to another."

The crime is thus defined in section 21(1). Some slight assistance in the interpretation of "demand" and "menaces" is afforded by subsection (2). Subsection (3) provides a maximum penalty of fourteen years' imprisonment on conviction on indictment. Blackmail is not triable summarily.[5]

---

[3] *Eighth Report*, para. 115.
[4] For the controversy, see *Eighth Report*, paras. 108 *et seq.*: McKenna [1966] Crim.L.R. 467; Hogan, *ibid.* at 474; H.L.Deb., Vol. 289, cols. 212 and 230 (debate on Second Reading of the Bill); *ibid.* Vol. 290, col. 524 (clause considered in Committee); *ibid.* Vol. 291 (clause considered on Report); H.C.Deb., Vol. 763, col. 1435 (debate in Second Reading Committee); and consideration of clause in Standing Committee H, June 25 and 27, 1968: Official Report, cols. 77 and 81.
[5] Magistrates' Courts Act 1980, Sched. 1, para. 28(a).

General observations

The ingredients of the offence require to be separately considered. First, **13–05**
however, some general observations may be helpful.

Only rarely is the application of section 21 likely to cause difficulty, or its
policy to give rise to possible concern. Most of the cases for which provision
is required and for which the section will in practice be used can readily be
seen to fall within its terms. D threatens to publish discreditable details
about P's private life unless P pays him for silence; a corrupt policeman
threatens to lay a fictitious charge against P but suggests that the charge may
be avoided by a suitable payment; a thug offers his "protection" to a club or
café proprietor while two or three large demi-thugs lounge in the doorway; a
shop proprietor is told that a bomb has been hidden on his premises and will
be allowed to go off unless he hands over a stated amount in cash: in cases
like these the fact that a crucial issue in the offence of blackmail is cast in
subjective terms will have a splendid irrelevance. The worst cases that ought
to be blackmail are clearly blackmail.

Even if what D threatens is something that may lawfully be done (or that
he thinks may be lawfully done), this is never by itself enough to protect him
if his threat to do it is a means of reinforcing a demand. D is perfectly
entitled, as a matter of law, to tell P's wife of P's adultery, and there may be
circumstances in which he may regard it as the morally correct thing to do.
Further, he may properly warn P that he proposes to tell P's wife of the
adultery. What he cannot do is to invoke these liberties as a sufficient ground
for using them as a means of extortion.

Only when D claims that what he demands is in some way his due does the **13–06**
subjective test adopted in the section begin to affect the matter. Only when
D can plausibly say something like: "I thought the sum I named was properly
due to me," *and* "I thought my threat was a proper way of getting it"—only
then can his demand with menaces escape the condemnation of the section.
Very occasionally a person of low moral standards, holding or claiming to
hold unusually liberal views as to the means which it is permissible to use to
obtain what seems to be his due, may escape a conviction that he would have
suffered had an objective criterion been embodied in the section.[6] There is a
converse possibility—that a person of unusually high moral standards and
veracity on oath may suffer a conviction merely because he has failed to live
up to his own standards and has made a demand with menaces not "war-
ranted" by his own understanding of what is proper! But this is surely an
academic rather than a real-life possibility.

A more important limitation of the scope of blackmail than the use of the **13–07**
subjective test of propriety is the requirement that D's demand be made with
a view to gain or with intent to cause loss. Gain and loss mean only "gain or
loss in money or other property" (s.34(2)(*a*)). So it is not blackmail (though
it may be some other offence) to demand, with whatever supporting threats,
the custody of a child, the victim's sexual favours, a release from lawful

[6] But see § 13–31, below.

custody or the withdrawal of evidence proposed to be given in support of a prosecution. Differing views may be held as to the propriety of excluding all such demands from the offence. The point is stressed here because it is one that it is desirable to have in mind throughout a consideration of the other aspects of blackmail.

3. THE MAKING OF A DEMAND WITH MENACES

The demand

13–08   It must be clear from the circumstances that D is demanding something (some act or omission) from P. But it is not necessary that he should actually use language such as invariably carries the force of a demand. "It is not necessary that the language should be explicit," observed Lord Reading C.J. in *Studer*[7]; "it may be in language only a request." He might have added, with the facts of that case in mind, that it may on its face be only a suggestion made for P's benefit. D told P that £250 was the sum he would need from P in order that he might induce a detective to withdraw an otherwise inevitable charge against P; but D was guilty of demanding money with menaces, for the detective and the alleged charge were both fictitious. D was menacing P with talk of a supposed peril and demanding £250 as the price of its evasion. The case was but a subtle and unusual version of the more familiar transaction of which *Collister and Warhurst*[8] is an example. There police officers threatened to bring a bogus charge against P but made it clear that he could avoid the charge by a payment. Although their demand was not express, it was implicit in their words and conduct,[9] and they too were guilty of demanding money with menaces.

13–09   Words, in fact, are not necessary at all, so long as D's conduct conveys a demand. If D holds a gun at the head of P's sleeping child and points at a safe of which P alone knows the combination, D's conduct is as eloquent as words could be and there is a strong prima facie case of blackmail. (If the gun were pointed at P himself or at his waking child, so that P or the child were put in fear, the natural offence to charge would be assault with intent to rob. There is a clear overlap between that offence and blackmail.)

The act or omission demanded

13–10   Section 21(2) expressly provides that "the nature of the act or omission

---

[7] (1915) 11 Cr.App.R. 307; see also *Robinson* (1796) 2 Leach 749.
[8] (1955) 39 Cr.App.R. 100.
[9] The threat was to arrest P on a charge of importuning. One of the accused said to P: "This is going to look very bad for you." A meeting was arranged for the following day, and it was made clear to P that a report on his alleged conduct would be typed but would be used only if P failed to keep the appointment. When he met the accused the next day, P was asked if he had brought anything with him. Pilcher J.'s direction to the jury (39 Cr.App.R. 100 at 102), approved on appeal (*ibid.* at 105), remains of value on the meaning of a demand: it was enough if the jury were satisfied "that, although there was no express demand . . ., the demeanour of the accused and the circumstances of the case were such that an ordinary reasonable man would understand that a demand . . . was being made upon him. . . ."

demanded is immaterial." This provision was included in the draft Bill "in order to avoid any argument that, because the offence depends on the demand being made with a view to gain or with intent to cause loss, the thing demanded must be property."[10]

Some examples of demands for different kinds of act and omission will be given in the last part of this chapter.[11]

The making of the demand

Section 21 requires only that a demand with menaces be made, not, of   **13–11** course, that it be complied with. But equally, if the demand is complied with the offence is nonetheless committed.

A question which may occasionally arise and which on one set of facts has reached the House of Lords is whether the full act of making a demand with menaces involves the effective communication of the demand to P. A letter sent to P may miscarry; a message may remain undelivered; P may not hear D's words or observe his gestures. The question is whether the posting of the letter, the entrusting of the message, the speaking of the words or the making of the gestures, amounts to the making of the demand which it is D's purpose to convey.

Posting of a letter

In *Treacy* v. *D.P.P.*[12] the House of Lords, by a majority, held that a   **13–12** demand conveyed by a letter is made when the letter is posted, so that where the letter is addressed to a victim abroad, its being posted in England completes an offence of blackmail within the jurisdiction. Lord Hodson's opinion to this effect (in which Lord Guest concurred) depended mainly on the consideration that the act of posting would formerly have constituted a complete offence under the Larceny Act 1916, s.29(1)(i).[13] That offence, however, was one of "uttering" a letter or writing demanding property with menaces; and "uttering" was an old technical expression that embraced a wide range of actions in relation to documents, including posting. Lord Diplock applied what he conceived to be the linguistic sense of "ordinary literate men and women": a man in ordinary conversation, he thought, would say "I have made a demand" as soon as he had posted a letter containing a demand.[14]

Lords Reid and Morris of Borth-y-Gest dissented. Their linguistic sense was not, apparently, what Lord Diplock would have supposed. Each gave a number of examples of factual situations illustrating the proposition that "[a] demand is not made until it is communicated."[15] This proposition would seem to be true at least of the case of a message entrusted by D to E for

---

[10] *Eighth Report*, p. 131 (notes on draft Bill).
[11] Below, § 13–37.
[12] [1971] A.C. 537; discussed by Pace (1971) 121 New L.J. 242.
[13] [1971] A.C. 537 at 557–558.
[14] *Ibid.* at 565. See also *Austin* v. *The Queen* (1989) 166 C.L.R. 669 at 674–675.
[15] [1971] A.C. 537 at 556, *per* Lord Morris of Borth-y-Gest.

delivery to P, whether the message is oral or in writing. The effect of *Treacy* may be to make a special rule for the case where E is the Post Office, although the majority did not expressly rely on any peculiarity of the post as a means of transmission.

Ineffective utterances

13–13   The case of an oral utterance which fails to communicate a demand requires separate consideration. If the words are incapable of being heard by any victim, it is submitted that no demand is made.[16] But if D shouts "Your money or your life!" at P, D probably does, as a matter of language, "make a demand with menaces" even if P is stone deaf. In any event, it would be unsatisfactory to have one rule for words which P does not hear and another for words which he does not understand, and it seems clear that if P does hear the words but does not understand their demanding or threatening implications, D has made a demand with menaces so long as an ordinary person in P's position would have understood what D was intending to convey.[17]

Letter posted abroad

13–14   In *Treacy* v. *D.P.P.*[18] "it appears that all their Lordships were disposed to hold that had it been a case of a demand dispatched abroad which had arrived in England, there would have been jurisdiction here to try the offence. . . ."[19] There are two ways of achieving this result consistently with the actual decision in *Treacy*. The method preferred by Lord Diplock avoids the substantive question of when and where the demand is made. In his view, there being in section 21 no "geographical limitation on where the described conduct of the offender takes place or where its consequences take effect," the offender may be convicted in England if either the conduct or the consequences occur there.[20] The second method involves holding that a demand conveyed by post continues to be "made" until the letter reaches its addressee. Thus the demand would be "made" within the jurisdiction although it originates abroad. This possibility was left open by the Court of Appeal and by Lord Hodson.[21] It is supported by a combination of the Court of Appeal's reference to "the inchoate nature of [blackmail] and its similarity to an attempt"[22] and the decision of the same court in *Baxter*[23] that

---

[16] Edwards (1952) 15 M.L.R. at 346, puts the case of the loudspeaker, concealed in P's house, that fails to function when D seeks by means of it to convey a demand to P; surely a mere attempt. (But if the words are heard by an unintended victim and affect him as a demand with menaces, the offence will be complete.)

[17] See to the same effect John Stephenson J. in *Treacy* in the Court of Appeal: [1971] A.C. 537 at 543.

[18] [1971] A.C. 537.

[19] *Baxter* [1972] 1 Q.B. 1 at 13, *per* Sachs L.J.

[20] [1971] A.C. 537 at 559–564.

[21] *Ibid.* at 543 and 558 respectively.

[22] *Ibid.* at 545.

[23] [1972] 1 Q.B. 1 (above, § 7–71). In this case convictions in England of attempts to obtain property by deception by means of letters posted in Northern Ireland and received in Liverpool were upheld.

attempt is itself an offence that continues from the time when it is first committed until the time when it fails.

Attempted blackmail

If a blackmailing demand is "made" as soon as it is spoken or dispatched beyond recall, the possibility of a case of attempted blackmail is limited to fanciful situations such as those where D is affected by a stammer or interrupted in the act of posting.[24] In fact there is some authority for the proposition that there cannot be an attempt to demand,[25] blackmail being itself "in substance an attempt to obtain money."[26] Whether this proposition is wholly justified (fanciful situations apart) will depend upon the way in which some of the questions discussed above are worked out in a developing case law.   **13–15**

The menaces

Under the Larceny Act 1916, ss.29(1)(i)[27] and 30,[28] the word "menace" was given a wide meaning. In the leading case of *Thorne* v. *Motor Trade Association*,[29] Lord Wright said: **13–16**

> "I think the word 'menace' is to be liberally construed and not as limited to threats of violence but as including threats of any action detrimental to or unpleasant to the person addressed. It may also include a warning that in certain events such action is intended."

There is no doubt that the word is intended to have a wide meaning in section 21 also. The possible varieties of menace are innumerable. Apart from threats of physical violence (to P or to some other person), of prosecution or of the revelation of criminal conduct or sexual misbehaviour (whether real or pretended), all of which have already been referred to in this chapter, we may add a few examples suggested by important cases under the old law: a threat to publish attacks on a company calculated to lower the value of its shares[30]; a threat to reveal that P has not honoured a debt[31]; a threat to place P on a trade association's "stop list" unless he pays a fine imposed by the association for breach of its rules[32]; a threat not to give evidence in an action.[33] These are but illustrations thrown up by the chances of earlier litigation.

[24] And see n. 16, above.
[25] *Moran* (1952) 36 Cr.App.R. 10 at 12 (criticised by Edwards (1952) 15 M.L.R. at 346; by Smith [1961] Crim.L.R. at 445; and by Williams, *Criminal Law—General Part* (2nd ed.), p. 615, n. 9, instancing the case of the letter that does not arrive); *Treacy* in the Court of Appeal: [1971] A.C. 537 at 554; and in the House of Lords, *per* Lord Hodson, *ibid.* at 558 (the proposition is "correct as a general rule").
[26] [1971] A.C. 537 at 545, *per* John Stephenson J.; and see text above, at n. 22.
[27] The offence was that of uttering a letter or writing "demanding of any person with menaces, and without any reasonable or probable cause, any property or valuable thing."
[28] The offence was committed by one who "with menaces or by force demands of any person anything capable of being stolen with intent to steal the same."
[29] [1937] A.C. 797 at 817.
[30] *Boyle and Merchant* [1914] 2 K.B. 339.
[31] *Norreys* v. *Zeffert* [1939] 2 All E.R. 187.
[32] *Thorne* v. *Motor Trade Association* [1937] A.C. 797.
[33] *Clear* [1968] 1 Q.B. 670.

Trivial threats and common sense

13–17   Although menaces may take many forms, not every trivial threat will satisfy the section. The Committee in fact chose the word "menaces" in preference to "threats" because they regarded the former word as the stronger of the two.[34] "Give me £50 or I shall tickle you with this feather" is not on the face of it a threat strong enough for blackmail even if P is known to be ticklish.[35] In one case[36] a student had offered shopkeepers, for a modest contribution to charity, copies of a poster guaranteeing protection from rag activities that might inconvenience them. The jury were directed that as a matter of common sense no "menaces" were involved.

No "definition" needed in straightforward cases

13–18   It is indeed in most cases a matter of common sense whether proved conduct amounted to the use of "menaces." "It is an ordinary word of which the meaning will be clear to any jury," so that only rarely will a judge need to embark on anything in the way of a "definition."[37] The kind of elaboration that may be necessary in an exceptional case is calculated merely to confuse the jury in a straightforward case—typically one in which there is no evidence that the victim was anything other than (in the language favoured by the courts) "an ordinary person of normal stability and courage"[38] or that his response to the defendant's conduct differed from the response to be expected of such a person. In the straightforward case, definition (or, more accurately, explanation) is best avoided.

Some cases requiring special direction

13–19   In *Garwood*,[39] a case of physical threats, the Court of Appeal identified two kinds of situation about which the jury may need a special direction. The first is that in which "the threats might affect the mind of an ordinary person of normal stability [so as to accede unwillingly to the demand[40]] but did not

---

[34] *Eighth Report*, para. 123. This view was "notwithstanding the wide meaning given to 'menaces' in *Thorne's* case" (above, at n. 29).

[35] Contrast the case put below, § 13–21.

[36] *Harry* [1974] Crim.L.R. 32.

[37] *Garwood* (1987) 85 Cr.App.R. 85; *Lawrence and Pomroy* (1971) 57 Cr.App.R. 64.

[38] The phrase originated in *Clear* [1968] 1 Q.B. 670 (see n. 40, below), before which the courts tended to refer to persons of "ordinarily firm mind": *Tomlinson* [1895] Q.B. 706; *Boyle and Merchant* [1914] 3 K.B. 339. The jury in *Garwood*, above, were understandably mystified by "normal stability," but seem to have settled for regarding it as duplicating "normal courage"; they thought the victim in their case to be "probably rather timid, *i.e.* not normally stable (whatever that is)": note to trial judge, quoted (1987) 85 Cr.App.R. at 87.

[39] (1987) 85 Cr.App.R. 85 at 88. The headnote to this report derives from the case a complex form of direction that would cater at once for the two different situations identified by the court. It is hardly possible to conceive of a case in which the whole of this direction would be appropriate.

[40] It seems desirable for the sake of clarity to supply these words from a passage in the pre-Theft Act case of *Clear* [1968] 1 Q.B. 670, at 679, that the trial judge in *Garwood* had quoted to the jury and the Court of Appeal plainly had in mind. In *Clear* the court had referred to "threats and conduct of such a nature and extent that the mind of an ordinary person of normal stability and courage might be influenced or made apprehensive so as to accede unwillingly to the demand. . . ."

affect the person actually addressed." If these are the facts that the jury may find, they should be told that that would be a case of "menaces," even though the menaces had no effect. The other exceptional situation is "where the threats in fact affected the mind of the victim, although they would not have affected the mind of a person of normal stability." On these facts there would be a case of "menaces" if, but only if, the defendant "was aware of the likely effect of his actions upon the victim"; so the jury would have to be told that they could convict only if they were satisfied of this further fact.

"Menaces": a suggested general principle

It is important not to read the valuable judgment in *Garwood* as though it lays down general principles exactly applying to all kinds of blackmail. In the context of physical threats it is reasonable, when concerned with the relevance of the victim's response, to refer to a standard of "normal stability and courage" (abbreviated in *Garwood* to "normal stability"). That language is less appropriate, however, in other kinds of cases. Some threats are clearly "menaces" although "stability and courage" hardly describes the qualities relevant to resisting them. An example is a threat to prosecute for a serious offence. Of course the jury can hardly ever require special assistance on the word "menaces" in such a case. More important is the case of the extortionate demand made of a person who is specially vulnerable to pressure, not because of temperament but by reason, for example, of past misdeeds, social position or medical condition. If in any such case a direction on "menaces" is necessary, the language used in *Garwood* seems at least to need adaptation. But that case would also be misleading if it were thought to imply either that a threat must have "in fact affected the mind" of a specially vulnerable person or that the person using the threat need not know of the vulnerability. **13–20**

The judgment in *Garwood* is of general importance in deprecating unnecessary direction on a word which ought to give no difficulty in most cases. But it does not preclude search for a general principle to which resort may be made in deciding in other kinds of cases whether the jury need help to protect them from error. It is suggested that the following propositions are justified: (a) a threat may amount to "menaces" within the meaning of section 21 if, on all the facts known to D, including the nature and circumstances of P, it is a threat that might be capable of reducing P's ability to resist the demand; and (b) if D knows nothing special about P, P may for this purpose be taken to be a person neither by nature nor by reason of circumstances unusually susceptible to pressure from such a threat. Applying proposition (a), if P were known to be dangerously allergic to feathers, a threat to tickle him with one, made to reinforce a demand for money, should after all be "menaces" whatever his response. **13–21**

The source of the threatened evil

To be guilty of blackmail D must make or be party to the making of a **13–22** demand with menaces; but "it is . . . immaterial whether the menaces relate to action to be taken by the person making the demand" (s.21(2)). An example of a menace relating to action to be taken by another has already been seen in the case of *Studer*[41] (though in that case the circumstances were extreme in that both the threatened action and the person who would take it were fictitious).

4. THE DEMAND WITH MENACES MUST BE "UNWARRANTED"

13–23 It is as well to set out the relevant part of section 21(1) again. Blackmail depends upon the making of an *unwarranted* demand with menaces;

> "and for this purpose a demand with menaces is unwarranted unless the person making it does so in the belief—
> (*a*) that he has reasonable grounds for making the demand; and
> (*b*) that the use of the menaces is a proper means of reinforcing the demand."

Burden of proof and evidential burden

13–24 The passage quoted above from section 2(1) is merely a part of the definition of blackmail. It has nothing to say about the incidence of the burden of proof in relation to any ingredient of the offence. The section says that a demand with menaces is unwarranted unless D has certain beliefs when he makes the demand. It does not say that he shall be presumed not to have had those beliefs unless he affirmatively proves that he did. The unwarranted nature of the demand is one of the ingredients of the crime of blackmail—an ingredient in respect of which, as with any other, the prosecution bear the burden of proof. The jury, in order to convict, must be satisfied that D did not hold the relevant beliefs.[42] This does not mean that it will always be necessary for the prosecution to take special steps for the purpose of satisfying the jury on the issue. The prosecution need not negative the existence of a belief of which there is no evidence. The effect of the section is to place on D an evidential burden. Unless he introduces evidence, worthy of consideration, to the effect that he held the beliefs required by the section, the jury will be bound to find that the demand with menaces was unwarranted. Accordingly no direction to the jury on the topic will be required.[43]

13–25 This, at any rate, is the position in most cases; it is not certain that it is the position in all. There may occasionally be a case in which, having heard the

---

[41] Above, § 13–08. Compare *Smith* (1850) 1 Den. 510.
[42] Yet see the *Eighth Report*, para. 121, where the Committee consider whether, under the new law, persons in the position of accused persons in two cases decided under the Larceny Act "would *establish*" the beliefs required by s.21. (Italics supplied.) It is assumed that the word "establish" (and similar language in the same passage) was used *per incuriam*.
[43] *Lawrence and Pomroy* (1971) 57 Cr.App.R. 64; *Harvey* (1980) 72 Cr.App.R. 139 at 142 (no "live issue").

prosecution evidence, the jury are of the opinion not only that D *did* have reasonable grounds for making the demand (this may well be undisputed), but also that the use of the menaces *was* a proper means of reinforcing the demand. Strictly speaking, the jury's view of the justice of the demand and the propriety of the menaces is irrelevant under the section. Yet if the jury take a view favourable to the accused on both matters, are they not entitled to suppose that he took the same view himself when he made the demand?[44]

Belief in reasonable grounds for making the demand

D's belief that he has reasonable grounds for making the demand may be justified on any view. If P owes him money or ought to pay him compensation for a tort, it is reasonable for D to demand payment of the debt or of a reasonable sum by way of compensation, and D's belief that he had reasonable grounds for making his demand follows almost automatically from the fact that such grounds existed.   **13–26**

Difficulty arises only when D did not in fact have reasonable grounds for making his demand (or cannot give credible evidence to the effect that he did) or when there is room for doubt as to whether he had such grounds.

Grounds of different kinds

The section draws no distinction between the different kinds of grounds that D may believe to exist for the making of his demand. He may believe, wrongly as a matter of *fact*, that what he demands is due (he believes P owes him money, but P has in fact paid him). He may believe, but be wrong in his *opinion*, that a certain sum constitutes reasonable compensation for P's tort (actual or supposed). He may believe, wrongly as a matter of *law*, that P is bound to pay him a certain sum. He may believe, but be, in the opinion of others, wrong in his *moral judgment*,[45] that he is entitled to demand the act or omission that he demands of P. Any of these types of belief, if genuinely held, will be within the section.   **13–27**

D's view of the precise demand made

To escape liability D must have believed that he had reasonable grounds   **13–28**

[44] Even so, once a demand with menaces has been proved (and assuming evidence of a view to gain or an intent to cause loss), a submission that the accused has no case to answer may not ever be technically correct, because of the way in which s.21(1) is worded. But the jury might at the end of the prosecution case be invited to stop the case if they take a view of D's conduct strongly favourable to him.

[45] Contrast s.2(1)(*a*), under which, for the purposes of theft, an appropriation of property is not to be regarded as dishonest if D believes that he has *in law* the right to deprive P of the property. A moral "claim of right," even if it would not be an answer to a charge of theft, will provide a partial answer to a charge of blackmail. So, for instance, D may claim that he thought himself morally entitled to demand a rise in wages, without alleging that he had any contractual right to a rise. And a lady in the position of the defendant in *Bernhard* [1938] 2 K.B. 264 (referred to in the text, below) would not be reduced, as she was under the Larceny Act 1916, s.30, to claiming that as a result of an error of law she thought she had an enforceable claim against P for money promised to her for a past immoral consideration; she would now say that she thought she was morally justified in pressing her claim.

for making the particular demand that he made. If the sum demanded is disproportionate to the claim asserted or to the interest that D is seeking to protect, the likelihood that D believes himself entitled to make the demand naturally diminishes. The point may be illustrated by reference to a question litigated under the old law. The question was whether it was lawful for a trade association to demand from one of its members or from some other person the payment of a fine for a breach of the association's rules, the demand being supported by a threat to place the member or other person on the association's "stop list" if he did not pay the fine. Under the Larceny Act 1916, s.29(1)(i), the legality of such a demand depended on whether it was made with "reasonable . . . cause." It was ultimately held that it was so made if the sum demanded was a reasonable sum having regard to the legitimate business interests of the association.[46] The test was purely objective. Under section 21 the question becomes whether D himself (perhaps the secretary of the association) believes the sum is a reasonable sum to demand, or at least believes that the association's decision to impose the fine renders it lawful and reasonable for him to demand it on behalf of the association (for this would be quite consistent with his personally considering that the sum is too great).

Unreasonable belief

13–29   There is no requirement that D's belief be reasonable. In holding the belief that he holds, D may reveal himself as eccentric or unusually stupid or grossly careless or deficient in moral sense; but this will be quite irrelevant. The test applied to determine whether the demand with menaces is "unwarranted" is entirely subjective.

The unreasonableness of D's alleged belief goes only to its credibility. His suggestion that he acted under a particular belief may strain credulity too far. The jury may take the view that no one could have believed that the law was as D asserts he believed it to be. They may consider that D's demand for compensation was so plainly extortionate that D cannot have believed he was entitled to so large a sum. In these cases D will be convicted because of the jury's utter disbelief and not because of their disapproval. That at least is the theory upon which a conviction of blackmail should rest. In practice, of course, the jury's own standards are likely to be important in conditioning their willingness to give credence to D's evidence; and in that sense their disapproval is not completely irrelevant.

Belief in the propriety of using the menaces

13–30   It will commonly be much harder for D to allege with any plausibility that he believed the use of the menaces to be a proper means of reinforcing his demand than it will be to allege a belief in reasonable grounds for making the demand. "I thought that P owed me money" or "I thought the sum I demanded was reasonable compensation" will often enough be convincing

---

[46] *Thorne* v. *Motor Trade Association* [1937] A.C. 797.

statements. But D's evidence obviously becomes less attractive at the point where he has to add: "and I thought it proper to seek to make P pay by threatening to reveal that as a solicitor he had misappropriated his client's money."

The prevailing view (and that of the jury) may be that a threat to expose P's fraud, or to bring criminal proceedings, or to announce to the world that he defaults on his debts of honour, is not a proper means of reinforcing a demand—even where what is demanded is due or believed to be due. But the general view is irrelevant—except to the extent that it provides a standard whereby to judge whether D himself may genuinely have believed the use of menaces to be "proper." The question of D's own belief must be left to the jury.[47] In assessing the genuineness of D's alleged belief, both the nature of the demand and the precise threat used must of course be taken into account. "A threat to do some harm disproportionate to the amount of a disputed claim would be strong evidence of the absence of any belief in the propriety of the threat."[48]

Meaning of "proper"

There has as yet been little in the way of authoritative elucidation of the   **13–31**
word "proper" in this context. The Committee suggested that the word "directs the mind to a consideration of what is morally and socially acceptable."[49] With this in mind it has been argued that whether D believed his use of the menaces to be "proper" requires reference to his understanding of "the standards of English society generally." Did he believe that it was "morally and socially acceptable" by those standards?[50] According to this test the question would be, not whether D took an indulgent view of his own conduct (the argument assumes that he always would), but whether he thought that other people would do so. He might genuinely think that they would; he might, in the jury's view, be wrong; and in such a case, but only in such a case, the subjective character of the offence would operate in his favour.

The suggested test is attractive. It seems, however, to need an amendment. D can hardly be intended to have to rely on a belief that *all* respectable people would find his conduct acceptable. That would not cater for the case that should most obviously be catered for, where the matter is close to the moral borderline. It is in such a case that, although the prosecution is a credible one, D may most plausibly claim that he thought his use of menaces "proper." He should be protected against a conviction of blackmail by a belief that a significant body of respectable opinion would not disapprove. The test need not postulate, or require D to conceive of, a single prevailing standard or a uniform body of general opinion.

[47] *Harvey* (1980) 72 Cr.App.R. 139.
[48] *Eighth Report*, para. 121.
[49] *Ibid.* para. 123.
[50] Smith, *Theft*, paras. 332–337; see also Law Commission Working Paper No. 61, *Offences relating to the Administration of Justice*, para. 82. Compare the second limb of the test for dishonesty in *Ghosh* [1982] Q.B. 1053 (above, § 2–127).

217

13–32   A somewhat similar criticism has been offered of a generalisation in
Harvey,[51] the only relevant appellate decision so far. The case was one of
dishonour among villains. P had promised the appellants a large quantity of
cannabis and they had paid their share of the price. No cannabis was
forthcoming. The appellants kidnapped P's wife and child and threatened to
commit serious criminal offences (murder, rape or maiming) against them if
P did not restore what he had been paid. The Court of Appeal understandably took the view that no jury could have accepted that the appellants
might have believed in the propriety of their menaces. The generalisation
offered by the court was that no act known by D to be unlawful can be
believed by him to be "proper" (even though he may himself hold it to be
"justified"). This statement goes some way towards vindicating the test
discussed above. But it has been criticised as, in effect, factually untrue in its
application to some less heinous varieties of unlawfulness than threats to kill
and rape.[52] It must be agreed that there are some unlawful threats which the
person making them may in special circumstances believe to be "morally and
socially acceptable" (at least to some), let alone find acceptable to himself.
So the reference in *Harvey* to what is known to be unlawful seems to need
cautious interpretation in the light of the facts of the case.

Illustrations from pre-Act cases

13–33   The Committee, to test the likely operation of the section, took the
situations in the famous cases of *Bernhard*[53] and *Dymond*.[54] In the former
case a Hungarian lady demanded money that had been promised to her in
consideration of her past services as P's mistress. She threatened that if he
did not pay her she would expose him to his wife, and to the public by means
of a newspaper advertisement. In *Dymond*, D claimed payment (of an
unspecified amount) from P for an alleged indecent assault upon her. Her
threats were that P would "gett summons" and that she would "let the town
knowed all about your going on." The Committee anticipated that under the
new law "Dymond probably (assuming the facts were as the defence wished
to prove[55]) and Bernhard certainly, would easily establish[55] that they
believed that they had reasonable grounds for making the demand."[56] This
would clearly be to achieve the easier half of their tasks. Each would now
have to allege further that she believed her threats were a proper means of
reinforcing her demand for payment. Each, in her righteous indignation,
may conceivably have believed so; but she would find it a harder matter to
give satisfactory evidence on this point than on the other.

---

[51] (1980) 72 Cr.App.R. 139. In the only other reported case (*Lambert* [1972] Crim.L.R. 422)
the jury were told that D's guilt or innocence depended upon "his own opinion as to whether
he was acting rightly or wrongly." Such a direction can produce a striking acquittal, as the
case itself suggests. D told P, whom he suspected of having an affair with his wife, that £250
would buy D's rights to the wife; if P would not pay, D would tell P's wife and employer of his
suspicions. D was acquitted of blackmail.
[52] Williams, *Textbook*, p. 837.
[53] [1938] 2 K.B. 264.
[54] [1920] 2 K.B. 260.
[55] But see above at n. 42, as to the propriety of this language.
[56] *Eighth Report*, para. 121.

Whether D will succeed on this issue may depend in part on such matters   **13–34**
as his standard of education, his intelligence and his social environment.
Miss Dymond's illiteracy and Mrs. Bernhard's foreign extraction might be
material to support the suggestion that they did not have an accurate sense of
what was "proper." Conversely, if D is in business in the City, he may find it
hard to assert a belief in the propriety of threatening to publish among P's
social circle the fact that P had not paid a trading debt. He, though not Miss
Dymond, would know that such a thing is not "done," and he would
probably himself believe that a threat to do it is an improper way of seeking
to recover the debt.

5. A VIEW TO GAIN OR AN INTENT TO CAUSE LOSS

"With a view to gain . . . or with intent to cause loss"

A demand with menaces is not blackmail unless made with a view to gain   **13–35**
for oneself or another or with intent to cause loss to another. This language
has been considered in the context of offences under section 17, and the
reader is referred to that discussion.[57] It has already been observed[58] that the
requirement of a view to gain or an intent to cause loss constitutes an
important limitation on the scope of blackmail. Gain and loss "in money or
other property" are the only aims of D's demand relevant to his guilt under
section 21.

"Gain or loss in money or other property"

Although " 'gain' and 'loss' are to be construed as extending only to gain   **13–36**
or loss[59] in money or other property" (s.34(2)(a)), both words are given
artificially wide meanings. By section 34(2)(a)(i), " 'gain' includes a gain by
keeping what one has, as well as a gain by getting what one has not." By
sub-paragraph (ii), " 'loss' includes a loss by not getting what one might get,
as well as a loss by parting with what one has."

A person may have a view to gain property even if he will at the same time
gain another's services in the supply of that property; and the "property"
may take the form of a drug to be supplied directly into his body. In
Bevans,[60] D demanded an injection of morphine at the point of a gun and
was rightly convicted of blackmail.

Blackmail therefore covers much more than simply demands for the   **13–37**
transfer of money or other property. The following demands seem all to be
among those capable of being blackmail:

(i) A demand that P pay a debt that he owes D. A payment of money (or a
transfer of other property) to D is no less a "gain" to him because he is

[57] Above, §§ 11–05 to 11–07.
[58] Above, § 13–07.
[59] "Whether temporary or permanent."
[60] (1987) 87 Cr.App.R. 64.

entitled to it.[61] This view accords with the intention of those who framed the Act.[62] The gravamen of the offence of blackmail is the use of menaces, not conceived by D to be "proper," to reinforce a demand; and "the nature of the act or omission demanded is immaterial" (s.21(2)). Even a just demand should not be *so* supported.[63]

(ii) A demand that P give D a job, in which D will earn a salary. D has a view to gain.[64]

(iii) A demand that P permit D to take indecent photographs of her, D's purpose being to sell prints of the photographs. Here too D has a view to gain.

(iv) A demand that P abandon a claim to property that he is making against D. If D's aim is to keep particular property, he has a view to gain for himself, as well as an intent to cause loss to P by P's not getting that property. But it seems that particular property must be identifiable as that which D will preserve and which P will not get. P's mere forbearance to sue to enforce a financial obligation will not involve a "gain" to D or (presumably) a "loss" to P.[65]

(v) A demand by D that P deceive Q into abandoning a claim to specific property against E. The section does not require the intended loss to be a loss to the person of whom the demand is made; and a view to gain "for another" is sufficient.

(vi) A demand that P destroy letters written by D to P. P will suffer "a loss by parting with what [he] has."[66]

[61] *Contra*, Hogan [1968] Crim.L.R. 474 at 476 (but before amendment of the definitions of "gain" to include "getting what one has not").
[62] *Eighth Report*, para. 119.
[63] The point appears to have passed *sub silentio* in *Lawrence and Pomroy* (1971) 57 Cr.App.R. 64; it has been the subject of an express Crown Court ruling in *Parkes* [1973] Crim.L.R. 358 (Judge Dean Q.C.). Unusual facts were before the court in *Helal* (1980) 2 Cr.App.R. (S.) 381, in connection with sentence: executrix's demand for property belonging to testator. (The harassment of contract debtors by, *inter alia*, demands accompanied by alarming threats may be prosecuted summarily under the Administration of Justice Act 1970, s.40.)
[64] Compare, in a very different context, the reference, at § 11–06, above, to *Wines* (1953) 37 Cr.App.R. 197. But a demand that P appoint D to an honorary office will not be blackmail.
[65] See *Golechha* (1989) 90 Cr.App.R. 241, above, § 11–06.
[66] Compare *Eighth Report*, para. 117.

Chapter 14

HANDLING

1. DEFINITION

SECTION 22(1) defines the offence of handling stolen goods:

"A person handles stolen goods if (otherwise than in the course of the stealing) knowing or believing them to be stolen goods he dishonestly receives the goods, or dishonestly undertakes or assists in their retention, removal, disposal or realisation by or for the benefit of another person, or if he arranges to do so."

Section 22(2) provides a maximum penalty of imprisonment for 14 years on conviction on indictment.

The word "handling" is a term of art. The offence may be committed without physically touching the stolen goods; and one may physically handle them, even with guilty knowledge, without committing the offence. Under the Larceny Act 1916, s.33, the corresponding offence was limited to the "receiving" of goods. The offence was extended by the Criminal Law Act 1967, s.4(7), so as to be almost as wide as the present offence. The word "handling" was introduced by the Theft Act merely as the name of the offence; it ought not to be regarded as having any other significance.[1]

2. STOLEN GOODS

There must be stolen goods

Section 22(1) begins: "A person handles stolen goods if . . ." and goes on to describe a variety of acts that may be done in relation to "them." The offence therefore depends upon the existence of "stolen goods" at the time of an act of handling. One example of the offence occurs when a person "believing them to be stolen goods . . . dishonestly receives the goods" or does one of a number of acts in relation to them. This wording does not render guilty of handling a person who deals with goods which he wrongly believes to be stolen at the time of his act.[2] (But he may be guilty of attempted handling.[3]) Another variety of handling is that committed by one

---

[1] It does not (*pace Smythe* (1980) 72 Cr.App.R. 8 at 13) represent a "new concept" or lend itself to interpretation. For a powerful critique of the handling provisions, see I. D. Elliott (1977) 26 I.C.L.Q. 110 at 135–144.

[2] *Haughton* v. *Smith* [1975] A.C. 476.

[3] Criminal Attempts Act 1981, s.1(1) (2) (3) (in this respect reversing *Haughton* v. *Smith*); see *Shivpuri* [1987] A.C. 1 (House of Lords; declaring to have been wrong the decision of the House to the contrary in *Anderson* v. *Ryan* [1985] A.C. 560).

who arranges to receive stolen goods or, for instance, to dispose of them. For this purpose the goods must be stolen before the arrangement is made.[4] (But an arrangement relating to goods to be stolen in the future may constitute a conspiracy to handle stolen goods[5]; and one person may be guilty of inciting another to commit handling although there are no relevant goods at the time of the incitement.[6])

"Stolen"

14–03 Section 2(4) gives an extended meaning to the word "stolen." Its effect is that, for the purpose (among others) of the offence of handling, goods are to be regarded as stolen, not only if they have been the subject of theft as defined in section 1, but also if they have been obtained by blackmail or by deception (that is, by an offence under section 15).[7] Moreover, references in the relevant provisions of the Act to stolen goods include the proceeds of dealings with such goods by a thief or handler, as is mentioned immediately below. Throughout this chapter, therefore, as in those provisions, the words "steal," "stolen," "theft" and "thief" are all to be understood in correspondingly wide senses.

The theft need not have occurred in England and Wales, nor since the commencement of the Act. It is sufficient if (a) the goods were appropriated or obtained anywhere and at any time by a transaction satisfying the definition of theft in section 1, of obtaining property by deception in section 15 or of blackmail in section 21 *and* (b) that transaction was an offence when it was committed in the country where it was committed.[8]

"Goods" and their proceeds

14–04 "[Goods] ... includes money and every other description of property except land, and includes things severed from the land by stealing" (s.34(2)(*b*)). Handling can therefore be committed in respect of everything except land.

There is a complicated provision (s.24(2)) to secure that the taint of the theft may apply to the proceeds of stolen goods and that the offence of handling shall extend to proceeds so tainted as to the original goods. The reader is referred to the text of this provision in Appendix 1. The following are some illustrations of its effect.[9]

14–05 (a) A steals goods. (i) He sells them for £1,000 in *cash*. The goods and the cash are now both "stolen goods." (ii) B receives part of the £1,000 knowing

---

[4] *Park* (1988) 87 Cr.App.R. 164.
[5] *Ibid.* at 173.
[6] Compare *McDonagh* (1963) 47 Cr.App.R. 37.
[7] See, *e.g. Dabek* [1973] Crim.L.R. 527 (goods obtained on credit by deception as to matters relevant to the giving of credit: "stolen" goods).
[8] s.24(1)(4). It would seem that the prosecution must prove as a fact the relevant matters of foreign law in order to show that the theft was an offence thereunder: compare *Naguib* [1917] 1 K.B. 359 as to the proof of foreign marriages in bigamy cases. Questions as to foreign law are nevertheless for the judge to decide: Administration of Justice Act 1920, s.15; *Hammer* [1923] 2 K.B. 786 (both apparently overlooked in *Ditta and others* [1988] Crim.L.R. 42).
[9] See also n. 60, below. In *Solomon* v. *Metropolitan Police Commissioner* [1982] Crim.L.R. 606, Milmo J. invoked s.24(2) in dismissing a thief's civil claim in relation to the proceeds of her theft.

that it represents stolen goods. He is guilty of handling. (iii) With the rest of the £1,000 A buys a *car*. This too is "stolen." C, knowing the truth, undertakes to dispose of the car for A. He is guilty of handling. So is D, who buys the car, if he has guilty knowledge, for the car "at [one] time represented the stolen goods in the hands of the thief" (s.24(2)(*a*)).

(b) A steals £1,000 in £10 notes. (i) A owes B £500 and pays him with £500 of the stolen money. B knows it is stolen and is therefore a handler. If B buys *goods* with the £500, these goods are "stolen," as will be money he receives on a resale of those goods. (ii) A pays the remaining £500 to C for services rendered. C does not know the money is stolen and is therefore not a handler. C buys *goods* with his £500. Those goods are not "stolen," for they do not represent "stolen goods in the hands of a handler" (s.24(2)(*b*)).

(c) A by deception obtains a cheque for £1,000 from his employer. Being **14–06** so obtained, the cheque is "stolen." (i) A pays the cheque into his bank account. The *bank balance* (as a thing in action and therefore "goods" within the meaning of section 34(2)(*b*))[10] may be goods representing the cheque in the hands of A as being the proceeds of his disposal or realisation of them; if so, it is "stolen."[11] (ii) A draws *£300 cash* from the account and pays it to B. B may thus receive "stolen goods." There is no difficulty about this if the bank account has been fed only by stolen cheques or consisted only of the proceeds of stolen goods.[12] But in the case of an account fed by both "stolen" and "honest" money, the prosecution must be able to prove, by reference to the history of the account, that the cash was capable of representing stolen goods. This may perhaps be possible even if honest money in the account could alone cover the withdrawal; but it would need to be shown that A intended to withdraw stolen rather than honest money.[13] (iii) A gives C a *cheque for £300* drawn on the account. C may cash this cheque or the cheque may be collected for the credit of his bank account. If so the discussion in (ii) above applies to the cash or to the resulting debt owed to C by his bank as it applies to the cash considered in (ii). But it is not clear that it applies to the cheque itself. To be "stolen" the cheque must "represent . . . [the original cheque] in the hands of [A] as being the proceeds of [a] disposal or realisation . . . of . . . [the bank balance] representing [the original cheque]": s.24(2)(*a*). But the cheque now drawn by A is surely not the *proceeds* of such a disposal or realisation but rather the means of effecting one.[14]

Proof that the goods are stolen

On a charge of handling, then, the prosecution must prove that the goods **14–07** were stolen within the above extended sense of the word. Sometimes they

---

[10] *Attorney-General's Reference* (*No. 4 of 1979*) (1980) 71 Cr.App.R. 341 at 348. The bank balance must be a *credit* balance for this analysis to be sound.
[11] Unless the victim of the theft has ceased, because of a mixing of funds, to have a right to restitution: see the discussion by J. C. Smith at [1981] Crim.L.R. 52, and *Theft*, para. 405, referring to s.24(3) (below § 14–15).
[12] *Attorney-General's Reference*, above, at 348.
[13] *Ibid.* at 349. B's intention to receive stolen money or his belief that it was stolen is no evidence as to its stolen character: *ibid.*; see below, § 14–07.
[14] But see the court's tentative view on the point: *ibid.*

will be able to show clearly how the goods were stolen and by whom. Sometimes the fact that they were stolen will be established by the evidence of the person to whom they belong as to the manner in which they were lost,[15] though without necessarily identifying the thief. Exceptionally, the fact that they are stolen may be the proper inference from evidence that establishes the identity neither of the victim nor of the thief. In particular, the circumstances in which the alleged handler acquired the goods (at a gross undervalue, for example, in a place where such goods are not normally sold) may be fairly capable of only one interpretation as to their history.[16] The court may know of those circumstances from the reported statements of the accused himself, which are of course admissible against him.[17] But his account of what he was told about the goods is mere hearsay and inadmissible even against him.[18] Nor, it has been held, is his own belief or conclusion that they were stolen admissible to prove that they were—even if his conclusion seems "fair and safe to rely upon."[19]

14–08   Yet it has been said that "whether a belief has any evidential value must depend upon the facts of the case"[20]; and on the strength of this dictum it is still perhaps open to argument in a suitable case that D's own experience in the relevant trade renders his opinion effectively that of an expert and admissible on that account as evidence of the character of the goods.[21] Some authorities,[22] moreover, have been said to suggest that a defendant's bare informal admission (not expressed to be based on hearsay) that the goods were stolen is admissible as the basis of a possible inference that they were, unless he explains in evidence that his admission merely reflected what he had been told (or, presumably, what he surmised).[23] But there seems to be no ground for treating "It is stolen"[24] as prima facie meaning "I saw it stolen" rather than "I was told it was stolen" or "I concluded or assumed so"—quite the contrary; and, if there is not, the suggested rule simply creates an obligation to give evidence out of a remark no doubt left incautiously incomplete because of its maker's ignorance of the hearsay rule.[25]

[15] As to evidence by statutory declaration in proceedings for handling goods stolen in the course of transmission, see s.27(4).

[16] *Sbarra* (1918) 13 Cr.App.R. 118 (by a side door during the night); and cases in next note.

[17] *Overington* [1978] Crim.L.R. 692; *Hulbert* (1979) 69 Cr.App.R. 243 (clothing in quantity bought for low prices in pubs); *McDonald* (1980) 70 Cr.App.R. 288 (television set bought for £90 from unidentified man in betting shop); *Korniak* (1983) 76 Cr.App.R. 145 (jewellery bought for £100 from stranger originally asking £2,000).

[18] *Hulbert*, above; and see *Marshall* [1977] Crim.L.R. 106.

[19] *Hulbert*, above (the words quoted are from p. 247); *Overington*, above; *Attorney-General's Reference (No. 4 of 1979)* (1980) 71 Cr.App.R. 341; *De Acetis, The Times*, January 22, 1982; and see Crown Court rulings in *Porter* [1976] Crim.L.R. 58; *Hack* [1978] Crim.L.R. 359. Cases in which the stolen character of goods has been inferred from D's conduct (*e.g.* hiding them, as in *Young* v. *Spiers* (1952) 36 Cr.App.R. 200) must now be treated with caution to the extent that such conduct may reflect hearsay or D's belief: A. T. H. Smith [1977] Crim.L.R. 517 at 521–523; but the seminal case of *Fuschillo* [1940] 2 All E.R. 489 is perhaps unaffected in this respect.

[20] *McDonald*, above, *per* Lawton L.J. at 290.

[21] See *Stone* (1979) 129 New L.J. 1018 at 1019, citing *Gibbons* [1971] V.R. 79; and compare, as to the identity of drugs, *Chatwood* (1979) 79 Cr.App.R. 39.

[22] *Korniak*, above; *Gibbons*, above.

[23] Ashworth and Pattenden (1986) L.Q.R. 292 at 306.

[24] Or (in *Korniak*, above), "You'll just have to do me for receiving stolen property."

[25] This objection should not be taken to imply any attachment to the application of the hearsay rule in this context.

An inference of theft should not be too lightly drawn from circumstances **14–09** of suspicion. The unknown "thief" may have believed he had a right to the goods[26]; furtive behaviour and false explanations may conceal some other sinister truth than that the goods were stolen. Or it may be that the goods were indeed stolen, but by the accused himself; in which case a conviction of handling would only rarely be proper.[27]

Acquittal or conviction of another person for theft

For the purposes of a prosecution under section 22, the fact that the goods **14–10** were stolen has to be proved against D, the alleged handler, not against the thief.

An *acquittal* of C, the alleged thief, is not necessarily inconsistent with D's conviction of handling.[28] On a trial together of C and D, there may be evidence admissible against D (most obviously, a statement of his own about the theft) that is not admissible against C. If C is tried first and acquitted, a later prosecution of D may succeed because evidence of the theft is available that was not available on the earlier trial. More strikingly, the same evidence that failed to persuade C's jury that C stole the goods might satisfy D's jury of that fact. C's acquittal is not admissible in D's favour.

By contrast, the fact of C's prior *conviction*[29] for the theft of the goods is admissible as evidence against D that C stole the goods, the latter fact being relevant to an issue in the proceedings against D.[30] C is to be taken to have committed the offence—and hence, the goods are to be taken to have been stolen—unless the contrary is proved.[31] If it is established that C's conviction relates to the goods that D is charged with handling[32] and D wishes to dispute that they were stolen, he "will have to prove on a balance of probabilities . . . that [C's] conviction was wrong."[33]

When goods cease to be stolen goods

Section 24(3) refers (rather clumsily) to events after which goods, **14–11** although they may be proved to have been stolen, shall not "be regarded as having continued to be stolen goods." If such an event occurs before D's alleged act, that act is not an offence of handling. There are two categories of case.

[26] See above, § 2–120. In *Farrell* [1975] 2 N.Z.L.R. 753, the supposed thief had been acquitted of theft on the ground of insanity; in *Walters* v. *Lunt* (1951) 35 Cr.App.R. 94, he was under the age of criminal responsibility.
[27] See below, §§ 14–44 to 14–48.
[28] *Close* [1977] Crim.L.R. 107, depends upon this proposition but is a very puzzling application of it on the facts.
[29] "by or before any court in the United Kingdom or by a Service court outside the United Kingdom."
[30] Police and Criminal Evidence Act 1984 s.74(1).
[31] *Ibid.* s.74(2).
[32] As to evidence to identify the facts upon which C's conviction was based, see *ibid.* s.75.
[33] Criminal Law Revision Committee, 11th Report, *Evidence (General)* (Cmnd. 4991), para. 219(i); for discussion of authorities on the corresponding provisions of the Civil Evidence Act 1968, s.11, see Phipson, *Evidence* (13th ed.), p. 661.

Restoration of goods to victim or to other lawful possession or custody

14–12   The first is that in which, before the handling, the goods "have been restored to the person from whom they were stolen or to other lawful possession or custody."

Restoration to the person from whom the goods were stolen may be taken to mean a return to his possession or to that of his agent. An act by or on behalf of the victim of the theft falling short of a deliberate exercise of control over the goods will not suffice to amount to a restoration of them. So, for example, cartons of cigarettes stolen from a company by an employee and placed by him in the company's lorry were not "restored" to the company by the acts of the company's security officer in initialling the cartons for the purpose of identification and of police officers in following the lorry to where the cigarettes were sold by the thief to D; they were still "stolen" when D bought them.[34]

The phrase "the person from whom they were stolen" is somewhat casual, since property may be stolen from a variety of persons having disparate interests in it.[35] Whether the phrase refers to the person, if any, specified as the victim in the indictment or to any person who might have been so specified is rendered less important than it might have been[36] by the additional reference to other lawful possession or custody.

14–13   Goods are "restored" to lawful possession or custody, notwithstanding the inappropriateness of the verb, if they are "taken by a police officer in the course of his duty and reduced into possession by him."[37] The principle that such restoration will deprive the goods of their "stolen" status can therefore embarrass police operations. For instance, police officers seize goods in the hands of the thief. The thief then co-operates with them to trap D, an intending receiver. D receives the goods from the thief and is promptly arrested. If it can be proved that D's arrangement to receive the goods was made after the goods were stolen[38] and before they came into the hands of the police, D can be convicted of handling on an indictment carefully drafted. But if no arrangement occurring in that period can be proved, there can be no conviction of handling, because the goods were not "stolen" when they were received.[39]

14–14   In some cases, however, it is less clear whether the goods have been restored to lawful possession. In *Attorney-General's Reference (No. 1 of 1974)*[40] a police constable found in an unattended car packages of clothing

---

[34] *Greater London Metropolitan Police Commissioner* v. *Streeter* (1980) 71 Cr.App.R. 113; contrast *Villensky* [1892] 2 Q.B. 597.

[35] s.1(1) read with s.5; s.15(1) read with s.5(1).

[36] See *Schmidt* (1866) L.R. 1 C.C.R. 15; *Villensky* [1892] 2 Q.B. 597. As to naming the victim in the indictment, see below, § 14–58.

[37] *Attorney-General's Reference (No. 1 of 1974)* [1974] Q.B. 744 at 750; *Alexander and Keeley* [1981] V.R. 277. (It is doubtful whether the word "custody" adds much in the present context. In *Attorney-General's Reference* the words "possession," "custody" and "control" were used interchangeably by Lord Widgery C.J. (at 753).)

[38] See above, § 14–02, at n. 4.

[39] But there may be a conviction of attempted handling or of conspiracy to handle: compare § 14–02, above.

[40] [1974] Q.B. 744.

that he suspected were stolen (as they indeed proved to be). He removed the rotor arm from the car to immobilise it, and kept watch. When D appeared and tried to start the car, the constable questioned him. He gave an implausible explanation and was arrested. The trial judge directed D's acquittal on a charge of handling, ruling that the goods were no longer "stolen" when D came to the car. On a reference under the Criminal Justice Act 1972, s.36, however, the Court of Appeal's opinion was that whether the constable had taken possession of the goods "depended primarily on [his] intentions." Had he made up his mind to "reduce them into his possession or control, take charge of them so that they could not be removed and so that he would have the disposal of them"? Or did he act as he did simply to ensure that he would be able to question the driver about the goods when he appeared, having meanwhile an open mind as to whether the goods were to be seized? This was an issue that should have been left for the jury's determination.[41]

Cessation of right to restitution

Secondly, the goods will cease to be stolen when the person from whom **14–15** they were stolen "and any other person claiming through him have . . . ceased as regards those goods to have any right to restitution in respect of the theft." For instance, the owner of goods which have been obtained from him by deception may, on discovering the fraud, affirm the transaction in question and so lose all title to the goods; a third party may have acquired a good title to the goods by virtue of some exception to the rule *nemo dat quod non habet*; or, exceptionally, the owner's title may have been extinguished by the expiration of six years following a conversion not "related to the theft."[42]

3. WHAT CONDUCT AMOUNTS TO HANDLING

Assuming that D has the necessary *mens rea*, he will be guilty of handling if **14–16** ("otherwise than in the course of the stealing"[43]) he:

(a) receives stolen goods; or
(b) arranges to receive stolen goods; or
(c) undertakes or assists in the retention, removal, disposal or realisation of stolen goods by or for the benefit of another person; or
(d) arranges to act as in (c).

It is worth repeating that goods dealt with as in (a) or (c) must in fact be stolen and that an arrangement within (b) or (d) must relate to goods already stolen.[44]

---

[41] *Ibid.* at 753–754. In the light of the Court of Appeal's opinion, some pre-Act cases on the present topic are now of little, if any, authority; especially *King* [1938] 2 All E.R. 662.
[42] Limitation Act 1980, ss.2, 3(2), 4.
[43] But for the thief as potential handler, see below, §§ 14–44 to 14–48.
[44] See above, § 14–02.

(a) Receiving

14–17   Before 1968 the corresponding offence under the old law was limited to receiving and was called by that name. Receiving involved nothing less than the acquisition of exclusive control of the property or of joint possession with the thief or another receiver.[45] Handling is now a much wider offence, but presumably the meaning of receiving itself remains as before.[46] If D examines goods in the thief's presence while negotiating with him, he does not thereby handle them in the technical sense. On the other hand, if, for example, the thief leaves the goods with D by way of loan or on approval, D handles when he knowingly accepts the possession so given to him; *a fortiori* if he acquires possession of the goods by gift or purchase.

14–18   The question whether a person who finds stolen goods and takes possession of them can be said to "receive" them has arisen in two unreported Court of Appeal cases. In one the court apparently assumed that he could[47]; in the other it held that he could not.[48] The latter opinion is preferable. The word "receive" seems to imply an act of transfer by another to the receiver. One who finds goods whose owner might be discovered by taking reasonable steps steals those goods if he dishonestly decides to keep them. His realisation that they are already stolen goods, apart from tending to confirm his dishonesty in not reporting his finding to the police, is irrelevant to the occurrence of this further theft.[49]

14–19   It is not necessary in every case for the judge to direct the jury in detail about the meaning of "possession"; but an explanation of the word, suitable to the context of the case, will be called for where the question whether D acquired possession of the stolen goods (either alone or jointly with the thief) is crucial.[50] It may be crucial, for example, where D and the thief are found together with the goods[51] or where the goods are found on premises occupied by D. In the latter case, in order to prove a receiving by D it must be shown either that the goods came on his premises "at his invitation or by arrangement" (their acceptance by his employee, acting without authority or instructions to take them, will not suffice) or that after they came on the premises he "became aware of them and exercised some control over them."[52]

(b) Arranging to receive

14–20   If D negotiates with C, a thief, for the purchase of the stolen goods, D is

[45] *Hobson* v. *Impett* (1957) 41 Cr.App.R. 138; *Frost and Hale* (1964) 48 Cr.App.R. 284. D's control may, of course, be exercised through someone acting with his authority, or through a bailee at will (from whom he may physically recover the property on demand): relevant authorities were reviewed in *Cottrell* [1983] V.R. 143.
[46] See *Smythe* (1980) 72 Cr.App.R. 8.
[47] *Kelly*, November 19, 1984 (C.A. No. 5624/B1/83).
[48] *Haider*, March 22, 1985 (transcript on LEXIS).
[49] See below, § 14–49: most handlers also commit new thefts by handling.
[50] *Apostoli and Apostoli*, 1984, Court of Appeal (unreported: transcript on LEXIS); compare *Comerford* (1964) 49 Cr.App.R. 77.
[51] As, for example, in *Seiga* (1961) 45 Cr.App.R. 26.
[52] *Cavendish* (1961) 45 Cr.App.R. 374.

not on this account guilty of handling. What is required is at least an arrangement to receive the goods. The conclusion of a bargain between C and D will normally involve at least an arrangement by D to receive the goods and therefore a complete offence. There must be an arrangement by D to acquire possession on his own account. Consequently, if D, when he buys from C, arranges for C to deliver the goods direct to E, a sub-purchaser, D presumably does not "arrange to receive" the goods, though it appears that he assists in their realisation by C.[53]

Making an offer to buy from the thief, with a view to taking delivery if the offer is accepted, is an attempt to handle (an attempt to arrange to receive).

(c) Undertaking or assisting in retention, removal, disposal or realisation

Once he has accomplished his theft the thief faces major problems for   **14-21** which he may need all manner of facilities. The goods may need to be stored. They may have to be carried to a place of safety or to a purchaser. Gold and silver articles may require melting down. Stolen cars require new number plates and registration documents and the execution of skilled work to conceal their identity. Contact must be made with "fences" and negotiations conducted. Anyone who assists in or undertakes any of these or similar operations for the thief or for another handler is guilty of handling if he knows or believes the goods to be stolen and acts dishonestly. The net is flung very wide.

"Undertakes or assists . . . by or for the benefit of another person"

The act undertaken or assisted must be "by or for the benefit of another   **14-22** person." This vital phrase qualifies each of the four nouns, "retention," "removal," "disposal" and "realisation."[54] The whole phrase is often recited, without attention to its meaning, even when part of it cannot apply. The House of Lords clarified the provision in the leading case of *Bloxham*.[55] What the handler "undertakes" must be an activity *for the benefit of* another person; and what he "assists in" must be an activity undertaken *by* another person. Moreover, an activity is not "for the benefit of" another just because it happens to benefit him, but only if it is undertaken for his benefit. So, in particular, a seller does not sell goods "for the benefit of" his purchaser. It seems also that a person who makes a gift of stolen goods does not in doing so undertake their disposal "for the benefit of" the donee, although only the donee will benefit from the transaction. The House of Lords effectively treats the notion of an act undertaken "for the benefit of another person" as that of an act done on behalf of another person; it is an act that the other might do himself. "[An] act of purchase" (or the receipt of a gift) "could not

---

[53] See § 14–27, below.
[54] *Sloggett* [1972] 1 Q.B. 430.
[55] *Bloxham* [1983] 1 A.C. 109. The House adopted the reading proposed by J. R. Spencer [1982] Crim.L.R. 682, in an article severely criticising the decision of the Court of Appeal in the same case ((1981) 72 Cr.App.R. 323) and anticipating all the arguments employed by the House.

sensibly be described as a disposal or realisation of the stolen goods *by* [the purchaser]" (or the donee).[56] This reading satisfactorily fulfils, without going beyond, the legislator's purpose in providing the badly-drafted second limb of the offence.

Retention

14–23   It has been held that the meaning of "retain" is a matter of law. The word means "keep possession of, not lose, continue to have."[57]

One who stores stolen goods as a bailee obviously undertakes their retention for the benefit of the bailor. Where D knows that stolen goods are on his premises, mere failure to reveal them to police officers who are searching for them may be evidence that he has permitted the goods to remain on his premises and is thereby assisting in (or perhaps more accurately, undertaking) their retention, but it cannot itself amount to so assisting. To hold otherwise would be to encroach on the principle that one is not bound to answer police questions.[58]

The activity of "retention" of goods continues over time. It may begin innocent and continue guilty. One who discovers that property he is holding for another is stolen property must therefore be active to disburden himself of it. In *Pitchley*[59] D received money from his son and paid it into his own post office savings account on his son's behalf. According to him he realised only afterwards that the money was stolen. It was held that even on that basis he was rightly convicted of handling, for after learning the truth he made no withdrawal from the account and had been (as the court doubtfully expressed it) "assisting in the retention of the money."[60]

14–24   A number of decisions have clarified the position of a person in the household or employment of a thief or handler who keeps stolen goods in the home or at the workplace. Merely "[being] willing for the goods to be kept and used in the house and thinking that it [is] nice to have them there, although they [are] stolen goods" does not constitute assisting in their retention[61]; nor does actively using them as a member of the family or an employee.[62] What is required is the doing of something, intentionally and

---

[56] [1983] 1 A.C. at 114.
[57] *Pitchley* (1972) 57 Cr.App.R. 30.
[58] *Brown* [1970] Q.B. 105.
[59] (1972) 57 Cr.App.R. 30. (The headnote is misleading as to the facts.)
[60] It should surely have been, if anything, "undertaking the retention of a thing in action," namely a debt owed to D by the bank. The argument would be that that debt was the proceeds of a realisation of the stolen money: see s.24(2). In fact it is highly doubtful whether the wording of s.24(2) was satisfied in *Pitchley*. At first sight the thing in action may appear to "represent ... the stolen goods in the hands of a *handler* ..." (s.24(2)(*b*)). But for this purpose the thing must be "the proceeds of [a] realisation of ... the stolen goods handled by him." At the time of the realisation, however, D did not know the money was stolen and therefore the goods realised were not "goods *handled* by him." It is thought that the conviction should have been quashed. There is a tendency even among lawyers to think of credit at the bank as being "money" for the purposes of the Act; in *Pitchley* itself there are many references to "money in the savings book" (*sic*). But "money at the bank" is a loose expression. See above, § 2–11.
[61] *Kanwar* (1982) 75 Cr.App.R. 87.
[62] *Sanders* (1982) 75 Cr.App.R. 84; *Thornhill*, May 15, 1981 (unreported: referred to in *Sanders* and in *Kanwar*, above).

dishonestly, for the purpose of enabling the goods to be retained, such as concealing them or telling lies (not necessarily successful lies) to the police to prevent their being found.[63]

Removal

This word obviously covers anyone carrying or transporting stolen goods **14–25** for another's benefit or assisting therein. An illustration may conveniently be given here of the fact that D's act need not be done solely for the benefit of another. D may, for example, help C to carry C's stolen goods into D's shop, there to negotiate. In doing so D assists in the removal of the goods by C for C's benefit; the fact that he also acts for his own purposes does not affect his liability for handling.

Disposal

This word seems apt to cover a wide range of acts, including destruction, **14–26** dumping, transformation by heat or by chemical means and distribution by way of gift. This opinion is offered in the teeth of the weighty view of Professor Williams, who regards "disposal" as referring only to an "alienation" of the goods.[64] With respect, it is not clear that its meaning is so limited. One who melts down gold objects for the benefit of a thief or handler performs an act quite as significant as that of the person who then transports the metal to the point of sale. From the inclusion of retention and removal in the list of offending activities it seems that the offence was intended to cover virtually all those who lend assistance in dealing with stolen property.

A person does not "assist in" the thief's disposal of stolen goods just because the disposal benefits him; assisting requires an act of helping or encouraging.[65]

Realisation

Realisation of goods occurs when they are exchanged for money or **14–27** anything else of value.[66] Realisation for the benefit of another occurs when an agent sells on behalf of a principal. A person selling on his own behalf does not "undertake" the sale "for" the benefit of the purchaser, even though the latter may derive a benefit from the transaction. So where D bought stolen goods without knowing they were stolen (and thus did not handle them by receiving) and later, having learnt that they were stolen, sold

---

[63] *Kanwar*, above.
[64] Williams, *Textbook*, p. 867.
[65] *Coleman* [1986] Crim.L.R. 56; compare above, § 14–24.
[66] In *Tamm* [1973] Crim.L.R. 115, Judge David Q.C. ruled that D assisted in the realisation of goods by C if, having the power and duty to prevent payment to C for the goods, he permitted the payment to be made.

them to E, this realisation of the goods was not a handling under the second part of section 22(1).[67]

Where C (perhaps the thief) sells stolen goods, D who buys from him may perhaps be described as assisting in C's realisation of them (though it would normally be more appropriate to charge him with receiving or, if delivery has not occurred, with arranging to receive them). In one case the Court of Appeal regarded the buyer's conduct as accurately described by an indictment alleging that he undertook the realisation of the goods[68]; but the House of Lords has since rejected the suggestion that a purchase of goods may be a realisation by the purchaser.[69]

(d) Arranging to act as in (c)

14–28   If D merely arranges to do or assist in doing any of the kinds of things referred to under the preceding head he will be guilty of the complete offence of handling. The Act is indeed remarkable, here as in theft, in the extent to which it treats as major substantive offences transactions of a preliminary or accessory character. It would be as well to bear this in mind in interpreting the word "arranges." Very little formality and precision need attend an arrangement—nothing in the nature of a contract or solemn promise. But there should be an element of finality.

To illustrate the problem and the kind of approach suggested, we may take the case of D who says that he is prepared to lend a hand in carrying some parcels from C's house to a lorry outside. It is suggested that—(i) if a time is fixed, there is an arrangement, however casually made; (ii) if all that occurs is D's expression of willingness in principle, there is no arrangement within the section; (iii) in any intermediate case the court should be most wary of finding an arrangementt. Whether D has arranged to assist depends as a matter of degree on the details of the case. If, for instance, all is finally settled except the time of the operation, which C will communicate to D, it would not be improper to say that D has arranged to assist.

It may be noted that, the act of arranging being the complete offence, it will be mere mitigation that D in the end decided not to lend his assistance.

4. THE MENTAL ELEMENT

Knowledge or belief

14–29   Handling is committed by one who knows or believes that the goods are stolen. Only knowledge or belief on the part of the person charged will satisfy the requirements of the section; it is not sufficient that any reasonable person would have realised that the goods were stolen.[70] What is required, of

[67] *Bloxham* [1983] 1 A.C. 109. The result (as observed *ibid.* at 114) is consistent with s.3(2)—a bona fide purchaser of property cannot steal it by anything done after learning that he has acquired no title by his purchase. But see below, § 14–35.
[68] *Deakin* (1972) 56 Cr.App.R. 841.
[69] *Bloxham*, above, at 114.
[70] *Atwal* v. *Massey* (1971) 56 Cr.App.R. 6; *Stagg* [1978] Crim.L.R. 227; *Bellenie* [1980] Crim.L.R. 437.

course, is knowledge of or belief in *facts* which result in the goods having as a matter of law a stolen character. D may know or believe that the goods have been acquired in some way amounting to an offence of theft or obtaining by deception or by blackmail; but he may not know in just what kind of circumstances they were acquired, or he may positively believe in facts which, if true, would indeed result in the goods being stolen, but which are not the true facts. He will still be guilty: there is no need for him to identify the class of "theft" concerned.

Nor need D know the nature of the goods with which he is dealing. It is enough if he knows or believes, for instance, that the goods in the unopened suitcase he is looking after are stolen goods.[71]

Meaning of "knowing" and "believing"

D may know that goods are stolen from having witnessed the theft. Apart **14–30** from that obvious case, he "may be said to know," explained the Court of Appeal in the leading case of *Hall*,[72] ". . . when he is told by someone with first-hand knowledge," such as the thief himself. Belief, on the other hand,

"may be said to be the state of mind of a person who says to himself: 'I cannot say I know for certain that these goods are stolen, but there can be no other reasonable conclusion in the light of all the circumstances, in the light of all that I have heard and seen.' "

A person with such a state of mind "believes" although (misusing language) he also says to himself: "Despite all that I have seen and all that I have heard, I refuse to believe what my brain tells me is obvious." Mere suspicion, however ("I suspect that these goods are stolen, but it may be on the other hand that they are not") is not within the words "knowing or believing."[73] This applies even to very strong suspicion.[74] Moreover, believing that the goods are probably stolen or that it is more likely than not that they are is not "believing [them] to be stolen" within the meaning of the section.[75]

The Court of Appeal had at one time insisted that a trial judge should not **14–31** interpret the word "believing" for the jury.[76] In *Hall*, however, the court seemed quietly to abandon that position, expressing the opinion that a jury "should be directed along [the] lines" of its explanation of the word in that case. But other divisions of the court have since held that this direction is not necessary in every case.[77] The main concern appears to be that suspicion

[71] *McCullum* (1973) 57 Cr.App.R. 645.
[72] (1985) 81 Cr.App.R. 260 at 264.
[73] *Ibid.* Similarly, as to suspicion, *Grainge* (1973) 59 Cr.App.R. 3; *Griffiths* (1974) 60 Cr.App.R. 14; *Smith (Albert)* (1976) 64 Cr.App.R. 217; *Grainge* [1984] Crim.L.R. 493.
[74] *Pethick* [1980] Crim.L.R. 242; *Moys* (1984) 79 Cr.App.R. 72. A different view is suggested by *Bellenie* [1980] Crim.L.R. 437, where it was said that suspicion is not enough unless it amounts to belief.
[75] *Reader* (1977) 66 Cr.App.R. 33.
[76] *Smith (Albert)*, above; *Ismail* [1977] Crim.L.R. 557; *Reader*, above.
[77] *Harris* (1986) 84 Cr.App.R. 75; *Toor* (1986) 85 Cr.App.R. 116.

should not be treated as belief, so that "where much reference is made to suspicion, a judge [may well] think it prudent, if not necessary," to give a *Hall* direction.[78] The view that such a direction is not routinely required suggests that the court is not similarly concerned that the jury might without guidance treat belief that goods are probably stolen as belief that they are.

14–32   The Court of Appeal's interpretation of "believing" is not an inevitable one. A person may also properly be said to "believe" something if he feels that it is so likely to be true that he is prepared to act upon the assumption that it is, even if he is not confident enough to say that the evidence compels that conclusion. One who receives goods with such a strong impression that they are probably stolen is acting with a recklessness that might reasonably be brought within the offence of handling,[79] without, it is thought, improperly inhibiting dealings with goods of unknown provenance.[80] And if this view is unacceptable, consider the case where the receiver, strongly suspecting that the goods are stolen, but preferring not actually to "know" that they are,"[81] deliberately refrains from an inquiry that he might make to allay or confirm his suspicion. Such "wilful blindness" has been recognised as turning strong suspicion into "knowledge of the second degree"[82] for the purpose of some statutory requirements of knowledge. The case should be regarded as one of "knowing or believing" in the present context.[83]

"Inferring" knowledge or belief

14–33   The cases before *Hall*[84] in fact contain many references to a person's "deliberately closing his eyes to the circumstances" or "shutting his eyes to the obvious." The leading theme is that a jury may infer D's knowledge or belief that the goods were stolen from the fact that, suspecting as much, he "deliberately closed his eyes to the circumstances"; but that it is a misdirection to advise them that, on such facts, they must as a matter of law find such knowledge or belief.[85] This, with respect, is obscure. It treats "wilful blindness" as something from which a state of mind can be inferred. But the jury have, *ex hypothesi*, already found a state of mind: "suspecting as much"—which is not enough. They are now to be invited to go on to find another: "knowledge or belief." It is not clear why the defendant is to be credited with two states of mind, one which does not suffice and one which does. There seems to be no reason why wilful blindness should be regarded

---

[78] *Toor*, above, at 120.
[79] See J. R. Spencer [1985] Crim.L.R. 92 and 440.
[80] See Glanville Williams [1985] Crim.L.R. 432, replying to Spencer, above.
[81] Apparently there are those who find dealing in stolen goods acceptable, and believe it to be less dangerous, if the origin of the goods, though well understood, is not made explicit ("stolen," "nicked"); and those who suppose that whatever is not spelt out in words is not known. See S. Henry, *The Hidden Economy*, pp. 56–57.
[82] See *per* Devlin J. in *Roper* v. *Taylor's Central Garage* [1951] 2 T.L.R. 284.
[83] For a proposal to include "wilful blindness" in a Criminal Code concept of "knowledge," see Draft Criminal Code Bill, cl. 18(a), in *A Criminal Code for England and Wales* (Law Com. No. 177), Vol. 1.
[84] Above, n. 72.
[85] See especially *Griffiths* (1974) 60 Cr.App.R. 14; *Moys* (1984) 79 Cr.App.R. 72.

only as evidence of knowing or believing. The principle, as suggested above, should rather be that "suspecting as much," coupled with a deliberate avoidance of knowledge, *is* "knowing or believing" within the meaning of section 22.

Time of knowledge or belief[86]

In a case of *receiving* the offence is not committed unless D knows or believes at the time he receives the goods that they are stolen.[87] And the same must be true of an *arranging* to receive or to do any of the other acts listed in the section; the guilty knowledge or belief must exist at the time of the arranging. But there is no reason why it should exist when D begins *assisting* in, or *undertaking*, one of those acts; to continue the assistance or the operation involved in the undertaking[88] after learning or divining the truth must surely be an offence. This will be no less the case where the undertaking, itself originally innocent, follows upon an innocent receiving. D receives the goods and then begins to deal with them for the benefit of another; he handles them when he continues to deal with them after learning that they are stolen.[89]   **14–34**

If D is a bona fide purchaser of goods, no subsequent dealing with them after he learns that they are stolen goods can be theft. But section 3(2), which so provides, does not explicitly protect against handling liability and cannot be read as impliedly doing so.[90] It seems that D, although innocent of handling by receiving when he buys the goods, may be guilty of handling by a later dealing with them for the benefit of E, a sub-purchaser (as by undertaking retention for E or assisting in E's sale to F). And if E knows that the goods are stolen when he buys from D, D may be guilty as a secondary party to the handling E commits by receiving them. It is doubtful whether these results were intended.   **14–35**

Proof of knowledge or belief

Where D has handled goods there may be little or no evidence tending to prove directly that he knew or believed them to be stolen; but the prosecution may be assisted in this proof by one or both of two principles, the first judge-made, the second statutory.   **14–36**

"Recent possession"[91]

If D is proved to have been in possession of goods which had recently been   **14–37**

---

[86] See Tunkel (1983) 133 New L.J. 844, for a diagram analysing the position of "the innocent receiver with subsequent *mens rea*."
[87] *Alt* (1972) 56 Cr.App.R. 457; *Grainge* (1973) 59 Cr.App.R. 3; *Smythe* (1980) 72 Cr.App.R. 8 (receiving is "a single finite act").
[88] "Undertakes" must be allowed to mean "conducts" rather than "takes on" or "embarks upon."
[89] As in *Pitchley* (1972) 57 Cr.App.R. 30 (subject to the special doubt about that case expressed in n. 60, above).
[90] Though it may influence the interpretation of the handling section: see § 14–27 at n. 67.
[91] A person's possession of recently stolen goods may alternatively be evidence that he was the thief or involved in the theft. See below, § 14–51.

stolen, and gives no explanation, or no credible explanation, of how he came by them, the jury are entitled, if they think fit, to infer that when he received them he knew that they were stolen. The jury are not bound to infer guilty knowledge from "recent possession," as it is strangely called. The principle that they *may* do so[92] is one of common sense,[93] although it is too often dignified with the title "the doctrine of recent possession."

The inference, if drawn, is drawn from the unexplained fact of recent possession—not (in a case where D offers no explanation at all) from silence viewed as tacit admission.[94] In particular, no adverse inference is to be drawn from silence after caution; the principle is not an exception to "the right of silence."[95] The lack of plausible explanation to which regard is to be had is that before caution and at trial.

14–38   The principle was originally stated as applying to a case of receiving, to which alone the corresponding offence under the old law was limited. But the Court of Appeal (rejecting an argument to the contrary in earlier editions of this book and disapproving an earlier dictum of its own[96]) asserted in *Ball*[97] that the principle now applies to all modes of handling. In that case D and E were found in a car at 2.45 a.m. with 30 citizen's band radios. E was not a dealer in such goods; yet D (on his own eventual story) was going to help E sell them. At his first interview with the police D told some damaging lies. It is plain that his knowledge that the radios were stolen might properly be inferred from these facts, whether the theft had occurred two days before (as was the case) or much less recently. The more there is of other evidence tending to justify a conclusion that the defendant knew the goods were stolen, the less relevant (it is submitted) becomes the fact that the theft was a recent one. The fact acquires true significance where there is no, or very little, other evidence from which guilty knowledge can be inferred. For it is, undoubtedly, alone enough to establish a case to answer against one who has received exclusive control of the goods. But section 22(1) covers, at the other extreme, one who briefly lends a casual hand with carriage of the goods. It remains, with respect, unclear why such menial involvement should inevitably raise a case to answer just because the goods were stolen two days before. Why should a casual porter, unlike other defendants, be virtually forced to give evidence? It is stubbornly submitted that whether it is proper to infer that the defendant knew the truth depends on the common sense of the individual case[98]; that "recent possession" has variable relevance to the commonsense judgment; and that the inference of knowledge was plainly justifiable in *Ball* irrespective of the time of the theft.

---

[92] With "the proper degree of assurance" (*Greaves, The Times*, July 11, 1987)—that is, beyond reasonable doubt.

[93] *D.P.P.* v. *Nieser* [1959] 1 Q.B. 254 at 266–267.

[94] *Bruce* v. *The Queen* (1987) 61 A.L.J.R. 602 (High Court of Australia).

[95] *Raviraj and Others* (1986) 85 Cr.App.R. 93; and see *Bruce* v. *The Queen*, above, at 603: "the absence of any reasonable explanation must not itself be explicable in a manner consistent with innocence."

[96] See 4th edition of this book, § 13–23; *Sloggett* [1972] 1 Q.B. 430 at 433.

[97] (1983) 77 Cr.App.R. 131.

[98] The nature of the goods is a relevant factor; see *Mason* [1981] Q.B. 881 (recent possession of antique silver wine coasters stolen five months previously); compare *Simmons* [1986] Crim.L.R. 397 (music centre; nearly a year: not "recent possession").

"Recent possession" should not be a shibboleth uttered unthinkingly without regard to the total facts.

Other goods or other conviction: s.27(3)[99]

The statutory aid to the proof of *mens rea* is to be found in section 27(3). **14–39**
This renders admissible, "for the purpose of proving that [D] knew or
believed the goods to be stolen goods," two classes of evidence:

"(*a*) evidence that he has had in his possession, or has undertaken or
assisted in the retention, removal, disposal or realisation of, stolen
goods[1] from any theft taking place not earlier than twelve months
before the offence charged[2]; and

(*b*) . . . evidence that he has within the five years preceding the date of
the offence charged been convicted of theft or of handling stolen
goods."

The subsection is to be strictly construed. It does not render admissible
the details of the transactions that it lets in: evidence of D's possession of
other stolen goods, admitted under paragraph (*a*), is not to include evidence
showing that he knew or believed them to be stolen[3]; and evidence admitted
under paragraph (*b*) is to be limited to the fact, and the time and place, of the
previous conviction for theft or handling.[4] It has been cogently objected that
what is thus excluded is evidence of the very fact that makes the admitted
transaction relevant to the issue of *mens rea* in the case being tried; that what
the subsection, so interpreted, permits is evidence from which, taken alone,
unsafe inferences of fault may be drawn; and that therefore "the fair prosecutor should be slow to rely upon it."[5]

Certain conditions must be satisfied before evidence becomes admissible **14–40**
under section 27(3): (i) D must be being proceeded against[6] only for handling stolen goods; (ii) evidence must first be given of D's having committed
an act of handling in relation to the goods the subject of the charge; and (iii)
a conviction can be proved under paragraph (*b*) only if D[7] has had seven

---

[99] See Munday [1988] Crim.L.R. 345 for a history and full consideration of this anomalous
provision.
[1] The words "stolen goods" have the same wide meaning here as they have in s.22: s.27(5).
[2] The evidence may relate to goods from a theft taking place after the offence charged: *Davis*
[1972] Crim.L.R. 431. Possession of articles from two thefts may under this paragraph
provide evidence of guilty knowledge in the receiving of each: *Simmons* [1986] Crim.L.R.
397. Evidence relating to possession of other stolen goods will also be admissible at common
law, whether or not it is within s.27(1)(*a*), if there is a substantial nexus between the offences:
ibid.; Cross, *Evidence* (6th ed.), p. 345.
[3] *Bradley* (1979) 70 Cr.App.R. 200; *Wood* (1987) 85 Cr.App.R. 287.
[4] *Fowler* (1988) 86 Cr.App.R. 219.
[5] J. C. Smith [1980] Crim.L.R. 174; see also *Wood*, above, at 292.
[6] This refers to the proceedings before the court at the time when the evidence is tendered; it is
immaterial that some other offence was charged in the same indictment but has been severed
and awaits trial: *Anderson* [1978] Crim.L.R. 223 (Judge Stroyan Q.C.).
[7] Or, no doubt, his solicitor: compare *Bott* [1968] 1 All E.R. 1119. It is not essential for the
notice to refer to the section: *Airlie* [1973] Crim.L.R. 310.

days' notice in writing of the intention to prove it. Subject to these conditions the evidence is admissible at any stage of the proceedings—that is, at committal proceedings as well as on trial.

14–41   Even if these conditions are satisfied the evidence should not be admitted automatically. Section 27(3) merely gives the judge a discretion to admit it, to be exercised only when the demands of justice warrant its admission.[8] It will be the judge's duty to exclude it if in the circumstances of the case it can be of only "minimal assistance" to the jury; the assistance it can afford must outweigh its prejudicial effect.[9] In exercising his discretion in a case involving a number of handling counts, the judge must bear in mind that the evidence will be relevant only where there is an issue as to D's knowledge or belief that the goods were stolen, and not relevant to any count in which, for example, the only or primary issue concerns D's alleged possession of the goods. If the evidence is admitted, the judge must take care to ensure that the jury realise that it is relevant only to the issue of guilty knowledge.[10]

Dishonesty

14–42   No one can be guilty of handling unless he acts dishonestly; and the dishonesty—like knowledge or belief that the goods are stolen—must coincide with the relevant act of handling. The test for dishonesty is that laid down in *Ghosh* with respect to deception offences and theft.[11] The question "Did D act dishonestly?" is one for the determination of the tribunal of fact; a conviction depends upon the tribunal's finding (i) that D's act was dishonest according to the ordinary standards of reasonable and honest people, and (ii) that D realised that it was dishonest according to those standards (but finding (ii) will normally be required only if there is evidence capable of raising a doubt about it[12]).[13]

14–43   The rule referring the judgment of dishonesty to the tribunal of fact must be subject to an exception where D intends, when he receives stolen goods, to do with them what the law requires—to seek their owner or inform the police. And it ought not to apply when D believes that he has in law the right to receive and retain the goods because he believes they are his own. As his receiving will not, as a matter of law, be dishonest for the purpose of theft (section 2(1)(*a*)), it would be absurd if D had to depend upon a jury to declare it not dishonest for the purpose of handling. Yet a *Ghosh* direction has been held to be required where a "claim of right" is relied upon in a case of obtaining by deception.[14] Perhaps the fact that deception somewhat taints

---

[8] *Rasini, The Times*, March 20, 1986.
[9] *Knott* [1973] Crim.L.R. 36; *Perry* [1984] Crim.L.R. 680. See *Herron* [1967] 1 Q.B. 107 and *List* (1965) 50 Cr.App.R. 81, for examples of a situation in which the discretion to exclude should be exercised.
[10] *Wilkins* (1975) 60 Cr.App.R. 300.
[11] [1982] Q.B. 1053; see above, § 2–127.
[12] *Roberts* (1985) 84 Cr.App.R. 117; and other cases cited above, § 2–128, n. 29.
[13] *Harvey* [1972] Crim.L.R. 213 reports an anonymous trial (before the modern cases on dishonesty) at which Shaw J. ruled that D does not *dishonestly* assist in the realisation by the thief of stolen goods where he acts as an intermediary between owner and thief for the payment of ransom money for the goods.
[14] See above, § 7–66.

the obtaining it achieves may serve to distinguish the deception and receiving cases. Certainly the pressure to treat D's act consistently as appropriation and as receiving feels peculiarly strong.

5. THE RELATIONSHIP BETWEEN HANDLING AND THEFT[15]

Handling can occur only "otherwise than in the course of the stealing"

If D1 and D2 are both parties to a theft, either or both of them may do acts   **14–44** generally prohibited as handling. D1 may take goods from P's house and hand them to D2 who is waiting outside: D2 thus "receives the goods." D1 and D2 may each carry some of the stolen goods away from the scene: then each "assists in their . . . removal . . . for the benefit of" the other. To avoid the liability of a thief for handling in such situations, it is provided that the acts prohibited by section 22(1) shall be handling only if done "otherwise than in the course of the stealing."

What is "the course of the stealing"?

The phrase will first be considered on principle. It seems clear that "the   **14–45** course of the stealing" must last for some time beyond the first moment of appropriation or obtaining: "the stealing" cannot simply mean "that which renders the goods stolen," for the goods must already be stolen if an offence of handling is to be in question at all. Presumably what is referred to is the total process of *effective* appropriation, including the "get-away." But it is not at all clear how long "the course of the stealing" lasts. If D1 and D2 take silver goods, drive them 50 miles, melt them down and contract over the telephone to sell the metal to E (without, as it were, pausing for breath), at what point does their "stealing" cease? It is suggested that its "course" must be over at the latest when they are "clean away," if not before—though this is, inevitably, to use one vague phrase to set a limit to the scope of another for the purposes of just one kind of factual situation. If the suggestion is correct, each of the thieves will be guilty of handling at least during the later stages of their journey and thereafter.

This view would be consistent with the robbery case of *Hale*,[16] according to which an appropriation (and therefore "the time of" the stealing) is not a mere momentary event but endures for some time, obviously varying with the circumstances. There must be a strong case for supposing that "the course of the stealing" within the meaning of section 22 and "the time of" the stealing within the meaning of section 8 are the same period. If they are, however, it seems that one who receives or relevantly deals with goods during the continuance of the appropriation must be guilty only of the original theft (as a secondary party) and not of handling. This conclusion would be embarrassing if such a person was charged only with handling, as he might easily be.

[15] A. T. H. Smith [1977] Crim.L.R. 517.
[16] (1978) 68 Cr.App.R. 415 (above, § 3–08).

14-46   *Pitham and Hehl*[17] is the only reported case directly raising the issue. One
M offered to sell to D the furniture of a man who was in prison. This offer
was an appropriation of the furniture. The rest of the facts are not quite
clear, but on one reading of the judgment it appears that D inspected the
furniture on two occasions before buying it and taking it away. His act of
handling was held to have occurred "otherwise than in the course of the
stealing"—that is to say, after the course of M's stealing was over. The Court
of Appeal referred to arguments such as that conducted above but found it
unnecessary to pass upon them. That seemed to confirm that the theft and
the handling were on separate occasions (though it did not explain why the
course of the stealing was not regarded as continuing until the offer for sale
was accepted; the acceptance, an arranging to receive, was surely D's first
act of handling). In a subsequent case, however, *Pitham* was said to be "a
case . . . of what might be called instantaneous appropriation."[18] This suggests that a theft of goods by offering to sell them lasts only as long as it takes
to speak the words and makes irrelevant the interpretation of the rest of the
facts in *Pitham*. It also tends to confirm that the principle of *Hale* applies to
the more common, physical taking, kind of appropriation.

Is this an ingredient for the prosecution to prove?

14-47   The Court of Appeal held in *Cash*[19] that the prosecution do not in the
ordinary case have the burden of proving that the alleged handler acted
"otherwise than in the course of the stealing." This was said to be true "at
least so far as 'recent possession' cases are concerned." But, as the court
observed, the inference in such cases that D "was a guilty handler, includes
the inference that he was not the actual thief"[20]; and since the former
inference must be drawn beyond reasonable doubt, that seems to amount to
proof that D was not the thief. So perhaps what is meant is this: first, that the
jury can draw the inference of handling without, for example, receiving
direct evidence that D was not present at the theft or that he had an alibi for
the occasion when it occurred (such evidence, as the court pointed out,
cannot be expected)[21]; secondly, that the jury need not be directed that they
must make a positive finding that D's receiving or other act of handling was
done "otherwise than in the course of the stealing." Not, that is to say, if no
issue as to this arises on the evidence, as it would if D testified that he was
indeed a party to the theft.[22]

The thief as handler

14-48   A former rule that a person could not be guilty both of stealing and of
receiving the same goods has not survived the combination of the Criminal

[17] (1976) 65 Cr.App.R. 45.
[18] *Gregory* (1981) 77 Cr.App.R. 41 at 46.
[19] [1985] Q.B. 801; compare *Koene* [1982] V.R. 916.
[20] [1985] Q.B. 801 at 804–805.
[21] *Ibid.* at 806.
[22] See *Griffiths* (1974) 60 Cr.App.R. 14.

Law Act 1967 (which abolished all rules peculiar to felony) and the Theft Act.[23] Once beyond "the course of the stealing," therefore, a person guilty of theft may commit an offence of handling the same goods or part of them. D, a thief, may, for example, the "course of the stealing" being over:

(i) "undertake" acts within section 22(1) for the benefit of E, an accomplice in the theft, or "assist" in the performance of such acts by E;

(ii) receive the goods or part of them from another party to the theft, or from a handler, or from an innocent party into whose hands they have come;

(iii) give or sell the goods to E, a handler, or to F, an innocent party, and then help E or F to dispose of the goods (or retain or remove them for E or F)[24];

(iv) be liable as a secondary party to a handling by E (whether that handling is a receiving from D himself[25] or from another person, or some other act within section 22(1)).

The handler as thief

Handling stolen goods requires an act done "otherwise than in the course of the stealing." But the "stealing" referred to is that by which the goods first acquire their stolen character. A person who subsequently deals with them may be guilty of theft as well as of handling.[26] Almost any act of handling is likely to be an appropriation of the stolen goods with the intention of permanently depriving their owner of them. The only illustrative case given by the Committee was that of a handling by receiving.[27] But an act of "retention, removal, disposal or realisation" may equally be an appropriation.[28] For the purposes of theft, the appropriation need not be made "for the thief's own benefit" (s.1(2)). And it cannot be said that, because the victim is already deprived, the handler has no intention of depriving him; for on that argument even a receiver would not steal—which, save exceptionally,[29] he certainly does.[30] It seems, therefore, that all handlers may also steal who actually deal with the goods themselves.[31]

14–49

Suppose that goods are "stolen" goods because they were obtained by deception or by blackmail.[32] Then the "thief" may have acquired a voidable title to them. If so, the victim's right "as regards those goods to . . . restitution in respect of the theft"[33] depends on a timely disaffirmation of the

14–50

---

[23] *Dolan* (1975) 62 Cr.App.R. 36.
[24] See *Eighth Report*, para. 131.
[25] Possibility admitted in *Bloxham* [1983] 1 A.C. 109 at 115; compare *Carter Patersons and Pickfords Carriers Ltd.* v. *Wessel* [1947] K.B. 849.
[26] *Sainthouse* [1980] Crim.L.R. 506.
[27] *Eighth Report*, para. 132.
[28] *Sainthouse*, above.
[29] Where he does not intend to deprive the victim permanently; and see § 14–50, below.
[30] *Stapylton* v. *O'Callaghan* [1973] 2 All E.R. 782; *Shelton* (1986) 83 Cr.App.R. 379.
[31] This would exclude one who only "arranges" to receive or to deal with the goods, and perhaps some who only "assist in," rather than "undertaking," an act within the section; but any of these might be a secondary party to someone else's theft. If the purpose or one of the purposes of an act of handling (*e.g.* retention or removal of the goods) is to assist the thief or another handler to escape apprehension or prosecution, the handler will also be guilty of assisting an offender under the Criminal Law Act 1967, s.4(1).
[32] See s.24(4).
[33] The language of s.24(3). When this right is lost, the goods cease to be "stolen goods."

transaction by which the "thief" obtained them. Only if this right of dis-affirmation and "restitution" is a "proprietary interest" in the goods within the meaning of section 5(1) will the goods for the time being continue to "belong to" the victim so that a handler of them can also be guilty of theft. It would not be wise to predict that a criminal court would be prepared to find a "proprietary interest" in this situation.[34]

Handler or original thief?

14–51   A person found in possession of stolen goods, and without a satisfactory explanation of his possession, may have acquired them as the original thief or may have subsequently received them as a handler. The circumstances, and particularly that of "recent possession,"[35] may justify either inference.[36] This can give rise to a difficulty to which the law has so far found no satisfactory solution: even though one offence or the other must have been committed, how is a conviction of either to be ensured? Two methods of proceeding require consideration.

14–52   *Alternative counts.* It is permissible to include in an indictment alternative counts for theft (or robbery, or burglary involving theft) and handling,[37] even though those counts are "factually mutually contradictory in the sense that proof of one charge destroys the other"[38]; and the judge may leave both counts to the jury if a prima facie case is made out in support of each.[39] The jury may have no doubt, in the light of all the evidence, that the defendant came by the stolen goods dishonestly—that he is indeed guilty of one of the offences charged. It was, however, clear to the Judicial Committee of the Privy Council in *Attorney-General of Hong Kong* v. *Yip Kai-foon*[40] that the jury may not be directed simply to convict of the offence that seems more probably to have been committed. Such a direction "detracts, or may be thought to detract, from the obligation of the jury to be satisfied beyond reasonable doubt that the accused is guilty of the particular offence" of which they convict him.[41] The course approved by the Judicial Committee is to direct the jury to consider first whether they are satisfied beyond reason-

---

[34] See above, § 2–28.
[35] See above, § 14–37.
[36] In *Cash* [1985] Q.B. 801 at 806–807, the Court of Appeal (referring to *Seymour* (1954) 38 Cr.App.R. 68) appeared to limit the possibility of an inference of D's being a party to the theft to cases where the theft occurred very shortly before D was found in possession. But it is clear that every case depends on its own facts (see, *e.g. Smythe* (1980) 72 Cr.App.R. 8 at 11–12; *Greaves, The Times,* July 11, 1987), including the nature of the goods. Possession of stolen money is said to suggest participation in the theft more strongly than possession of stolen chattels: see *per* Lord Denning M.R. in *Stupple* v. *Royal Insurance Co. Ltd.* [1971] 1 Q.B. 50 at 70, citing the direction of Phillimore J. in *Fallon* (1963) 47 Cr.App.R. 160 at 165. *Smith* (1984) 148 J.P.Rep. 216 discourages invocation of the "doctrine" of recent possession as relevant to theft where other evidence implicates D in the theft. *Sed quaere?* Does not recent possession more strongly justify an inference of guilt when aggregated with other evidence? See the discussion at § 14–38, above.
[37] *Shelton* (1986) 83 Cr.App.R. 379.
[38] *Bellman* [1989] A.C. 836 at 847.
[39] *Bellman,* above, for the general principle relating to "mutually destructive" counts.
[40] [1988] A.C. 642.
[41] *Ibid.* at 656.

able doubt of the defendant's guilt on the theft count; and, if they are not, to consider secondly whether they are satisfied "in relation to each of the ingredients of the alternative [offence] of handling."[42] One consequence may, of course, be a disagreement on each count, in which case the jury must be discharged.[43] But there must also be the possibility of an agreement *both* that the defendant's involvement in the theft has not been proved *and* that his receiving the goods subsequently (rather than as thief) has similarly not been proved[44]: an outcome strictly leading to a totally unmeritorious acquittal.[45]

One passage in the Judicial Committee's opinion in *Yip Kai-foon* can be taken to imply a different conclusion. The Committee rejected a submission that, because handling could only be committed "otherwise than in the course of the stealing," the trial judge must specifically direct the jury that they must be satisfied beyond reasonable doubt that the defendant did not receive the goods in the course of theft. In the Committee's opinion, the parenthesis in section 22(1) "called for no specific direction," because the jury's decision to acquit of theft (in which event only would they consider handling) rendered the question of his involvement in the theft "no longer a live issue. The presumption that he was innocent of the theft . . . was . . . never rebutted."[46] But this cannot legitimately mean that a decision to acquit of theft inevitably entails a conviction of handling where the jury are satisfied that it must be one or the other.[47] For, first, this would be to let in by another route a conviction, outlawed by the Committee's principal ruling, of the offence thought merely more probable—even (if theft was thought more probable but not proved) of the offence thought less probable! Secondly, it would contradict the Committee's approval of a direction to convict of handling if satisfied of "each of [its] ingredients"; for two of these ingredients are the receipt of (already) stolen goods and knowledge or belief that they are (already) stolen. If the jury are otherwise properly directed, an omission to mention the parenthesis ought not itself to produce a handling conviction of one who they think *may* have been the original thief. **14–53**

A widely-drawn theft charge. Suppose that goods are stolen on January 1st and found in D's possession on January 8th. He may have been the original thief; or he may have received the goods, knowing them to be stolen, between January 1st and 8th. Whichever is the truth, he stole the goods, because a handling by receiving is itself theft. It is accurate to say that on a day between January 1st and 8th he appropriated the goods by assuming **14–54**

---

[42] *Ibid.*
[43] *Ibid.; Shelton* (1986) 83 Cr.App.R. 379 at 385.
[44] Compare *Bellman*, above, at 847, considering mutually contradictory charges of supplying heroin (for payment) and obtaining by deception payment for a harmless substance proffered as heroin.
[45] In practice, one suspects, the jury are likely to avoid this outcome "pragmatically"—by convicting of the more probable offence.
[46] [1988] A.C. 642 at 658; applying the reasoning in *Griffiths* (1974) 60 Cr.App.R. 14 and *Cash* [1985] Q.B. 801 (see above, § 14–47).
[47] This meaning is extracted, but deplored, by Smith, *Theft*, para. 429.

possession of them. Can the dilemma be solved by obtaining a conviction of theft on a charge in such terms? The case of *Stapylton* v. *O'Callaghan*[48] first suggested that it can. D was tried on informations charging, respectively, theft and handling (by receiving) of a driving licence. It was clear that the licence had been stolen and that D, in whose possession it was found not long afterwards, had come by it dishonestly and intended to keep it. But the magistrate, not being satisfied as to which of the informations was appropriate, dismissed both. The Divisional Court directed a conviction of theft, because, on any view, D "dishonestly possessed himself of the licence and meant to keep it."[49] And in *Shelton*,[50] where D was in possession of a cheque book on the day it was stolen, the Court of Appeal upheld a theft conviction because, on any view, "on the day specified in the indictment [D] had dishonestly appropriated" the cheque book.[51]

14–55   But the court spoke with two voices in *Shelton*. On the one hand it asked: how could the problem of the ambiguous possessor "be solved by an indictment in sufficiently wide terms to cover both . . . appropriations . . . without breaching the rules against duplicity?"[52] On the other hand, it rationalised the conviction by, in effect, understanding the charge of theft to mean, "D appropriated the property *either* by taking it from the owner at such-and-such a time (and place) *or* by receiving it from the thief at such-and-such a later time (and, no doubt, other place)." The court seems in the end to have conquered its anxiety about duplicity. It is submitted that it was right to do so. The charge of theft by an assumption of possession on a named date, or between named dates, alleges only one offence, committed in an identified manner. The prosecution cannot further particularise but rely upon D's possession as evidence of an assumption of possession that, whenever it occurred, constituted the offence.[53] It is sufficient that the jury are satisfied that he took possession dishonestly and with the required intention; it is immaterial when and where he did so[54] and immaterial that different members of the jury may prefer different theories as to when he did so.[55]

14–56   There may be a case where it is desired to obtain a handling conviction as accurately reflecting D's apparent role, but in which it is feared that the whole of the evidence at the trial may make the case less clearly one of

---

[48] [1973] 2 All E.R. 782.
[49] See also *Gregory* (1983) 77 Cr.App.R. 41; *Devall* [1984] Crim.L.R. 428; *More* (1986) 86 Cr.App.R. 234 (in the Court of Appeal). The suggestion in *Devall* of a separate theft count giving particulars of an alleged "second appropriation" merely reproduces the difficulty discussed in the text above.
[50] (1986) 83 Cr.App.R. 379.
[51] *Ibid.* at 384.
[52] *Ibid.* at 383.
[53] *Tsang Ping-nam* v. *R.* [1981] 1 W.L.R. 1462 has been thought to present a difficulty (*Archbold* (43rd ed., 1988); J. C. Smith in commentary on *Bellman* [1989] Crim.L.R. 301 at 304) but appears to be distinguishable. D was charged with attempting to pervert the course of justice. He had either given false information to a criminal investigation or committed perjury by testifying that that information was false, so that (at 1465) "[h]ad particulars . . . been asked for, the Crown must have given alternative and mutually inconsistent particulars"—that is, particulars of acts of quite different characters.
[54] See *More* (1986) 86 Cr.App.R. 234 at 246; *Shelton* (1986) 83 Cr.App.R. 379 at 385.
[55] Compare J. C. Smith [1988] Crim.L.R. 335 at 343.

handling than it began. Such a case, it is suggested, is suitable for a widely-drawn theft charge (assuming that to be permissible) presented as an alternative to a handling charge. The judge could invite the jury to consider first whether they are satisfied that D was a handler and, if they are not, to consider secondly whether they are satisfied that he committed theft as alleged in the alternative count.[56]

6. INFORMATIONS AND INDICTMENTS

Section 22(1) creates a single offence[57] and an information simply alleging **14–57** handling contrary to the section is not bad for duplicity. But where D may be embarrassed by an absence of particulars as to the mode of handling alleged, the information should set out particulars or an application for particulars should be acceded to.[58]

Similarly, although a conviction may be had upon an indictment in which the particulars of offence allege simply that D dishonestly handled certain goods, knowing or believing them to be stolen,[59] the particulars ought to allege the mode of handling it is proposed to establish, with adequate detail.[60] Where a particular mode is alleged (*e.g.* receiving), there cannot be a conviction of a different species of handling (*e.g.* assisting in removal)[61] —or there cannot, at any rate, without amendment of the indictment. Where the mode is uncertain, there should be separate counts to cover different modes.[62] It is neither necessary nor helpful, however, to cover every possible alternative[63]; normally two counts are the most required, one alleging receiving, the other alleging an act within the second part of section 22(1).[64]

A count alleging an undertaking or assisting in the retention, removal, disposal or realisation of goods or an arranging to do so should include the words "by or for the benefit of another."[65]

---

[56] A passage in the judgment of Lord Widgery C.J. in *Stapylton* v. *O'Callaghan* [1973] 2 All E.R. 782, at 784, may appear to discourage this procedure by suggesting that whenever "the facts justify the conclusion that the offence of stealing was committed, the right . . . course is to convict of stealing" and not to consider handling "with the added penalty which might arise." Compare *Shelton* (1986) 83 Cr.App.R. 379 at 385: "handling is the more serious offence, carrying a heavier penalty because those who knowingly have dealings with thieves encourage stealing." But it is not thought that small-time handlers are in practice punished more severely than the thieves from whom they receive; and in any case a conviction clearly describing the offender's role seems desirable in principle.

[57] *Contra*, Lord Bridge in *Bloxham* [1983] 1 A.C. 109 at 113; but the dictum is inconsistent with the authorities cited below.

[58] *Griffiths* v. *Freeman* [1970] 1 W.L.R. 659; [1970] 1 All E.R. 1117.

[59] *Ikpong* [1972] Crim.L.R. 432; *Kirby* (1972) 56 Cr.App.R. 758; *Pitchley* (1972) 57 Cr.App.R. 30.

[60] *Alt* (1972) 56 Cr.App.R. 457.

[61] *Nicklin* (1976) 64 Cr.App.R. 205, in which the principles stated in this paragraph were reaffirmed.

[62] *Sloggett* [1972] 1 Q.B. 430; *Marshall* (1971) 56 Cr.App.R. 263.

[63] *Ikpong*, above.

[64] *Willis and Syme* (1972) 57 Cr.App.R. 1; *Deakin* (1972) 56 Cr.App.R. 841 at 849, where a formula is offered of particulars of a count alleging handling within the second part of s.22(1).

[65] *Sloggett*, above. (In some cases the words "by or" or "or for the benefit of" will strictly be inappropriate. See above, § 14–22.)

The particulars of a count for handling should include an averment of knowledge or belief that the goods were stolen.[66]

14–58 There are some cases in which it is necessary to name the owner of the stolen goods in the indictment—cases, that is to say, "where the property is of a common and indistinctive type" and "where, unless the ownership be assigned in the particulars of the charge, the accused may be at a loss to understand fully the nature of the charge which he has to meet."[67] But this certainly does not mean that whenever the goods are of a common type, the attribution of ownership will be a material averment so that the prosecution must fail if that ownership is not proved; on the facts it may be immaterial from whom the goods were stolen.[68]

14–59 There may sometimes need to be a compendious count covering a "hoard" of goods, possibly received over a period of time; this will be when particular goods are not identifiable as the proceeds of particular thefts. (Similarly, a single charge of receiving a sum of money between named dates, being the total of various unidentifiable sums received on unknown dates from the same person, is unobjectionable.[69]) But where some at least of the goods in a compendious count are shown to have been received on different occasions from different thefts, a single conviction on that count of handling all the goods cannot be substituted for defective convictions of the thefts. In such a case the indictment should have been differently drawn.[70]

14–60 Section 27 contains provisions permitting the charging in one indictment, and the trial together, of any number of persons alleged to have handled, whether at different times or at the same time, goods deriving from the same theft (s.27(1)); and the conviction of any of two or more accused indicted for jointly handling any stolen goods if he handled all or any of the goods, whether or not he did so jointly with any of the other accused (s.27(2)).[71] The latter provision permits the conviction of two persons jointly charged who are proved to have been guilty of successive handlings of the same goods.[72]

7. ADVERTISING REWARDS FOR RETURN OF GOODS STOLEN OR LOST

14–61 It is convenient to mention here that section 23 (which reproduces a pre-existing offence) prohibits the use of certain words—*e.g.* words to the effect "no questions asked"—in public advertisements of rewards for the return of

---

[66] *Amos* [1971] Crim.L.R. 352.
[67] *Gregory* (1972) 56 Cr.App.R. 441, where a late amendment of the assertion as to ownership was improper as giving rise to a risk of injustice.
[68] *Deakin*, above, referring to r. 6(1) of the Indictment Rules scheduled to the Indictments Act 1915, which had, however, been revoked by the Indictment Rules 1971 and not replaced.
[69] *Cain* [1983] Crim.L.R. 802 (citing cases referrd to at § 2–154, above). But a charge wrapping up several specified handling offences, with the intention of proving one as a sample, was bad.
[70] *Smythe* (1980) 72 Cr.App.R. 8.
[71] See *Eighth Report*, pp. 132–133 (notes on draft Bill).
[72] *French* [1973] Crim.L.R. 632.

stolen or lost goods. The offence, which carries a maximum fine on summary conviction of £400,[73] may be committed by the advertiser, the printer or the publisher.[74] It is an offence of strict liability; the printer or publisher (*e.g.* of a newspaper) will commit it although he does not know of the offending advertisement.[75]

---

[73] Originally £100; thus, level 3 on the standard scale (Criminal Justice Act 1982, ss.37, 38), currently £400 (S.I. 1984, No. 447).
[74] The advertising manager of a newspaper is one who publishes advertisements in it: *Denham and Scott* (1983) 77 Cr.App.R. 210.
[75] *Ibid.* For the fascinating history behind this provision and its forebears, see Hall, *Theft, Law and Society* (2nd ed.), pp. 70–76.

Chapter 15

GOING EQUIPPED

1. DEFINITION. ENFORCEMENT

15–01   SECTION 25(1) (read with subs. (5)) makes it an offence for a person to
have with him, when not at his place of abode, any article for use in the
course of or in connection with any burglary, theft (which includes for this
purpose an offence under section 12(1) of taking a conveyance other than a
pedal cycle) or "cheat" (that is, an offence of obtaining property by deception under section 15).

The offence is punishable on conviction on indictment with imprisonment
for three years (s.25(2)).[1] Where it is committed "with reference to the theft
or taking of motor vehicles" the offender may be disqualified for holding or
obtaining a driving licence.[2] An offence under section 25 may justify an
order under section 43 of the Powers of Criminal Courts Act 1973, operating
to deprive the offender of his rights, if any, in the article involved, on the
ground that it was intended by him to be used for the purpose of committing,
or facilitating the commission of, an offence.

Arrest and search

15–02   Although punishable with a maximum of only three years' imprisonment,
the offence created by section 25 is an arrestable offence (as is conspiring or
attempting to commit, or inciting, aiding, abetting, counselling or procuring
the commission of, such an offence).[3] The powers of arrest without warrant
provided by the Police and Criminal Evidence Act 1984, s.24(4)–(7), therefore apply; and one who does an act with intent to impede the apprehension
or prosecution of an offender may be convicted under section 4(1) of the
Criminal Law Act 1967, as amended by Schedule 6 to the 1984 Act.

Enforcement of the section is facilitated by the power given to constables
by section 1 of the 1984 Act to search persons and vehicles for prohibited
articles.[4]

---

[1] This remains so even where the intended offence is taking a conveyance, now a summary
offence punishable with no more than six months' imprisonment: see above, § 5–12.
[2] Road Traffic Offenders Act 1988, Sched. 2, Pt. II.
[3] Police and Criminal Evidence Act 1984, s.24(2)(d) and (3). Section 25(4) of the Theft Act has
been left unrepealed. It partially duplicates the 1984 provisions, at least as to a citizen's
arrest; as to constables, see the 1984 Act, s.26(1)(a).
[4] See the 1984 Act, s.1(7)(b) and (8), for relevant prohibited articles.

2. THE DETAILS OF THE OFFENCE

The articles covered by the section

The Committee offered a convenient list of typical articles covered by the section: **15–03**

> "The offence will apply, for example, to firearms and other offensive weapons, imitation firearms, housebreaking implements, any articles for the purpose of concealing identity (for example, masks, rubber gloves and false car number-plates) and ... car keys and confidence tricksters' outfits"[5];

and it will apply to a vehicle for use in getting to or from the place of a crime. Indeed it can be any article whatsoever so long as it is intended for a relevant criminal purpose.

"When not at his place of abode"

It is important to stress that the offence is limited to occasions when the possessor of the article is not at his place of abode. The professional burglar is safe in his possession of the tools of his trade as long as he keeps them at home. No doubt the possession at home of a burglar's kit or of a confidence trickster's outfit is some indication of a general intention to use that equipment; but when the intending offender takes his equipment with him away from home it will usually be safe to regard him as having a particular crime in contemplation or at least as intending to use the equipment on that occasion if an opportunity to do so presents itself, and it is at this point that the section becomes an acceptable and very important weapon in the armoury of crime control. The section in fact goes a little further than this. For D may, for instance, make his mask or skeleton key at his place of work, intending to take it home to add to his stock-in-trade. Nevertheless, if caught at work in possession of an article capable of being shown to have an intended criminal use covered by the section, he is clearly within the section. **15–04**

One is "at his place of abode" only if he is on a site where he intends to abide; so a person who has equipment for theft with him in a vehicle in which he lives commits an offence under the section except when the vehicle is on such a site.[6]

"Has with him"

The cross-heading above section 25 ("Possession of housebreaking implements, etc.") must be intended simply to indicate the provision of the old law that is here replaced.[7] The marginal note to the section ("Going equipped for stealing, etc.") seems to offer a brief hint of the mischief with which the **15–05**

[5] *Eighth Report*, para. 148.
[6] *Bundy* (1977) 65 Cr.App.R. 259.
[7] Larceny Act 1916, s.28(2).

section deals. The language of the marginal note, though not having the status of a definition,[8] is useful. Having an article with one, within the meaning of this section, is probably narrower than having it in one's possession. To adopt the language of a case decided under the Firearms Act 1968, it probably requires "a very close physical link and a degree of immediate control" over the article.[9] This test will be satisfied where D is carrying the article (about his person or in his vehicle) or where he is responsible for its being in a place where it is immediately available for his use—in a word, where he is "equipped" with it. We may add a further case—namely, that where D1 and D2 are in company and D1 has with him an article within the section; then, it seems, D2 also has it "with him" if, but only if,[10] he knows that D1 has it[11] *and* he is jointly with D1 a party to a relevant enterprise in which the article will be available for use.[12]

"For use in the course of or in connection with" an offence

15–06   D must have an article with him "for use in the course of or in connection with" one of the stated offences. He has an article "for use" if he intends it to be used (not necessarily by himself) for a relevant offence, whether one already determined upon—even one embarked upon by the performance of preparatory acts[13]—or one for which opportunity may present itself.[14] But if he has not decided whether he will use it, given the opportunity, he does not have it "for use."[15]

The use of the phrase "in connection with" widens the scope of the section by providing for a case in which an article is intended for use in preparation for a crime or, for instance, in escaping after it has been committed.[16] But an intended use of documents to obtain a job that will afford opportunities for theft is too remote from the proposed thefts to be "in connection with" them.[17]

The contemplated offences

15–07   The article may be intended for use in the course of or in connection with any:

(i) *burglary*

The offence of "possessing housebreaking implements"[18] by night was a

---

[8] *D.P.P.* v. *Schildkamp* [1971] A.C. 1, cited in *Kelt* (below).
[9] *Kelt* (1977) 65 Cr.App.R. 74 at 78; and see other cases cited above, § 4–43, n. 92. In *Kelt* the Court of Appeal pointed out that the terms of the Firearms Act 1968 plainly drew a distinction between having a firearm with one and having it in one's possession.
[10] Compare *Lester and Byast* (1955) 39 Cr.App.R. 157; *Harris* [1961] Crim.L.R. 256.
[11] Compare *Webley and Webley* [1967] Crim.L.R. 300.
[12] Compare *Thompson* (1869) 11 Cox C.C. 362; *Jones* [1979] C.L.Y. 411.
[13] *Minor* v. *D.P.P.* (1987) 86 Cr.App.R. 378 (possession of syphoning equipment after removing car petrol cap).
[14] *Ellames* (1974) 60 Cr.App.R. 7.
[15] *Hargreaves* [1985] Crim.L.R. 243.
[16] *Ellames*, above.
[17] *Mansfield* [1975] Crim.L.R. 101.
[18] See cross-heading above s.25. See latterly, Larceny Act 1916, s.28(2).

weapon of long standing in the armoury of preventive justice; and the main function of the broader generalisation achieved in section 25 no doubt remains the control of the intending burglar. Not that the section is used only when a criminal enterprise has proceeded no further than the stage of preparation. Sometimes it cannot be proved, although it is the case, that a person was involved in a burglary, and a conviction under section 25 is all that can be obtained. And a burglar (or a thief[19]) may sometimes be convicted of both the preparatory and the substantive offences; and in such a case, although it was all one criminal activity, it has been held, surprisingly, that consecutive sentences of imprisonment are not improper.[20]

(ii) theft

Taking a conveyance contrary to section 12(1) is treated as theft for this purpose (s.25(5)).

(iii) cheat—that is, an offence under section 15

All the authorities on this form of the offence concern a troublesome kind **15–08** of case in which D intends to sell the article in question in fraud of a third person (E). According to these authorities, the offence requires reference to the hypothetical state of mind of a notional person—namely, any unsuspecting customer. This approach may be misconceived (a matter considered below); but, as will be explained, there ought at least to be reference to D's state of mind as to a customer's likely state of mind. The offence of going equipped for cheat plainly requires careful handling.

Going equipped for cheat: the elements of the offence

E, the ultimate intended victim of D's fraud, has in most of the cases been **15–09** D's employer. D (a British Rail buffet car steward[21] or a waiter in a restaurant[22]) has food or drink of his own for sale to E's customers, with the intention of keeping the proceeds of sale for himself. He does not intend the customers to know that he is selling his own goods. It has authoritatively been said[23] that what has to be proved in a prosecution under section 25 is: first, "that there was an article for use in connection with the deception"— that is, the goods to be sold; secondly, "that there was a proposed deception"—"deception of [the customers] into believing that the proffered

---

[19] *Minor* v. *D.P.P.* above.
[20] *Ferris* [1973] Crim.L.R. 642, cogently criticised by D. A. Thomas at 643.
[21] *Rashid* (1976) 64 Cr.App.R. 201; *Corboz* [1984] Crim.L.R. 629; *Cooke* [1986] A.C. 909.
[22] *Doukas* (1977) 66 Cr.App.R. 228.
[23] *Doukas*, above, at 231; approved in *Cooke*, above, at 934; followed in *Corboz*, above; *Whiteside and Antoniou* [1989] Crim.L.R. 436 (selling pirated copies of cassette tapes on the street).

[goods were E's] and not [D's]"; thirdly, "an intention to obtain ... by means of the deception," and of course to keep, the money of the customers; fourthly, "dishonesty"—that is, "the lying to and misleading of [the customers] so that there is a deception of them"[24]; and fifthly, "that the obtaining would have been, wholly or partially,[25] by virtue of the deception." This way of summarising the offence, however, does not draw attention to a crucial aspect of the proposed deception: it must be "deliberate or reckless."[26] In one case a conviction was quashed because the jury were not told that, in order to convict, they must be satisifed that D believed that a prospective purchaser would decline to purchase if he knew the truth.[27]

The notional deceived customer

15–10   The cases treat as relevant the question whether a person to whom D might sell his own goods in fraud of his employer would be induced to buy the goods by an implied representation that they belong to the employer. Would customers buy if they knew the truth?[28] The answer to this question has been said to depend in any particular case on "the detail of the evidence, particularly that relating to the attitude and understanding of [the purchasers]."[29] But it is not necessary that any deceived person should give evidence[30]; indeed, there may have been no purchasers, D having simply had the articles with him but not used them. The offence does not require an obtaining by deception but only an intention to do so. The question must therefore rather be as to the effect that the intended deception would have on a notional purchaser.[31] One matter relevant to that question is the nature of the commodity being sold.[32] Another is the fact that a customer who was aware that the goods belonged to D would realise that D was practising a fraud on his employer. In the leading case the court was confident that a diner in a restaurant would be unwilling to participate in such a fraud.[33] But others have declined to assume that British Rail passengers would refuse to buy refreshments because they knew that the buffet staff were practising a

---

[24] Dishonesty vis-à-vis E is not a necessary element of the offence: *Cooke*, above, *per* Lord Mackay at p. 934.

[25] These words caused unnecessary difficulty in *Whiteside and Antoniou*, above. They appear to be redundant; it is axiomatic that the deception need never be the only factor inducing the victim to act as he does.

[26] s.15(4).

[27] *Rashid* (1976) 64 Cr.App.R. 201. Realisation that he *might* decline to purchase is surely enough for reckless deception.

[28] See above, § 7–42.

[29] *Cooke* [1986] A.C. 909, *per* Lord Mackay at 934; and compare the approach of the court in *Whiteside and Antoniou* [1989] Crim.L.R. 436.

[30] *Whiteside and Antoniou*, above.

[31] "[T]he question has to be asked of the hypothetical customer: ... if you had been told the truth, would you or would you not have bought the commodity?": *Doukas* (1977) 66 Cr.App.R. 228 at 232.

[32] *Rashid*, above, at 203 (contrasting food bought on a train with a watch bought in a jeweller's shop); *Doukas*, above, at 232 (jury may be expected to find that a diner is induced to buy wine in a restaurant by the supposition that it is the restaurant's wine).

[33] *Doukas*, above, at 233. (Compare *Lambie* [1982] A.C. 449; above, § 7–42.) This consideration justified the trial judge's leaving the matter to the jury.

"fiddle."[34] Such scepticism, however, does not mean that the question ought not to be left to a jury.[35]

Criticism of the case law

The case law, then, looks for an intention to obtain property by what would *in fact* be an operative deception. But it has been cogently objected, in effect, that a search for the state of mind of the notional person-to-be-deceived is misdirected.[36] The only relevant state of mind is that of D himself. What is necessary—but, equally, all that is necessary—is that *D intends* to obtain property by deception, that is, by behaving in a way that *he believes* will (or may) induce another to act otherwise than as he would if he knew the truth. Whether D's intended behaviour is capable of deceiving the other and thereby of inducing the desired transaction is not, substantively, to the point (although, of course, any view that the jury has on that matter may assist them in divining the view of it that D himself had). It is thought that this criticism is justified.

15–11

Proof of the criminal purpose

The fact that D intended the article to be used in the course of or in connection with one of the stated offences must be proved by the prosecution. Commonly that intention will be suggested forcibly enough by the nature of the article and the circumstances in which D had it with him; and then an explanation from D seems called for. This common sense proposition is rendered statutory in relation to a limited class of articles by section 25(3), which provided that:

15–12

"proof that [D] had with him an article made or adapted for use in committing a burglary, theft or cheat shall be evidence that he had it with him for such use."

Some comments may be made upon this provision.

First, it seems to do little if anything more than state the obvious. The subsection surely means merely that possession of an article of the kind to which it refers is in itself evidence from which a jury *may* infer the necessary criminal purpose. Even in the absence of a credible explanation consistent with innocence, possession of an article within the subsection is only "evidence" of such a purpose and is not necessarily conclusive. Still less does such evidence place on D a burden of positively persuading the jury of his innocent purpose.[37] No doubt he must come forward with some explanation

15–13

---

[34] *Rashid*, above 203 (*obiter*; prosecution regarded as misconceived); *Cooke* [1986] A.C. 909, *per* Lord Bridge at 921.
[35] And a conviction was upheld in *Corboz* [1984] Crim.L.R. 629.
[36] Smith, *Theft*, para. 385, and commentary on *Whiteside and Antoniou* [1989] Crim.L.R. 436 at 437–438; Parry, *Offences against Property*, para. 2.38.
[37] See on subs. (3), *Eighth Report*, paras. 151–153.

if he can; and perhaps subsection (3) will in some cases justify strong comment from the trial judge upon an accused's failure to give evidence. But, apart from this possible effect upon the judge, it is submitted that the position would have been the same without the subsection.

Secondly, the phrase "made ... for use ..." may be unfortunate. As noted earlier in the context of aggravated burglary, an article is to be regarded as "made" for a particular use if it was originally made for such use.[38] But there are many articles, which have long been known as "housebreaking implements" and are probably meant to be within the scope of subsection (3), which are not in the normal sense "made" for housebreaking. Assuming subsection (3) to have any substantial value at all, it may therefore be necessary to give the phrase "made ... for use ..." a special meaning here, and one different from that which we have assumed it to bear in section 10. This indeed seems to be implied by the Committee's reference in this context to skeleton keys, possession of which "in itself calls for explanation by the accused."[39] A locksmith may make a skeleton key for a perfectly legitimate purpose. If such a key is in D's possession when not at his place of abode, it is surely not the Committee's intention that the application of subsection (3) should depend upon whether D is a locksmith and, if he is, on proof of his purpose in making the key; or, if D is not a locksmith, on proof of the source of the key and of the original purpose of its making.

15–14   In summary, subsection (3) appears to distinguish needlessly and clumsily between different kinds of case. It is submitted that the question in all cases should be—and is—whether the circumstances taken together amount to evidence of a relevant criminal purpose. If three men are found late at night in a van with a torch and some carpenter's tools, and each man has a stocking in his pocket, there is clearly evidence of an intention to wear the stocking on the head. An explanation is called for—no less in this case than in a case within the terms of subsection (3), however interpreted. It is suggested that such a case will be dealt with in practice identically with a case within the subsection, except that it will not be proper to direct the jury in terms of subsection (3).[40]

---

[38] See above, § 4–39 on s.10(1)(*b*).
[39] *Eighth Report*, para. 151.
[40] *Harrison* [1970] Crim.L.R. 415.

Chapter 16

RESTITUTION AND COMPENSATION

1. TITLE TO PROPERTY

SECTION 31(2) provides that the title to property that has been stolen or **16–01** obtained by fraud or other wrongful means shall not be affected by reason only of the conviction of the offender. It was formerly the law that if goods were stolen and a title to the goods was acquired by a third party by purchase in market overt, the effect of a conviction of the thief after such purchase was to cause the property in the goods to revest in the original owner or his personal representative. There was no justification for the continuance of this rule in modern times. The relevant statutory provisions[1] were repealed by the Act. Section 31(2) ensures, if express provision for the purpose was required, that the title to property shall depend on the operation of civil law principles and not on the outcome of criminal proceedings.

2. RESTITUTION AND COMPENSATION[2]

Not only is the title to property which has been the subject of an offence to be **16–02** unaffected by criminal proceedings against the offender. It is also clear that disputes concerning the title to such property are not appropriate for litigation in those proceedings. Nevertheless it is desirable to make available to criminal courts procedures whereby, in cases where no dispute as to title appears to exist, they may make orders for the restoration of property or for the compensation of losers at the conclusion of their proceedings. Special provisions for this purpose are contained in section 28, as amended.[3]

The powers of the court under section 28 may be exercised where:

"goods have been stolen and either a person is convicted of any offence with reference to the theft (whether or not the stealing is the gist of his offence) or a person is convicted of any other offence but such an offence as aforesaid is taken into consideration in determining his sentence. . . ." (s.28(1)).

In this context, as in that of handling, the words "stealing," "theft" and so on refer to offences of obtaining property by deception and blackmail as well as to theft, and to such offences whether committed in England or Wales or

---

[1] Sale of Goods Act 1893, s.24(1); and see Larceny Act 1916, s.45.
[2] Hodgson *et al.*, *The Profits of Crime and Their Recovery* (Heinemann, 1980).
[3] See Macleod [1968] Crim.L.R. 577; Thomas, *Current Sentencing Practice*, J3.

abroad (s.28(6)). "Goods" means all kinds of property except land, but including things severed from the land by stealing (s.34(2)(*b*)). The exact scope of the phrase "any offence with reference to the theft" is not clear. It obviously includes handling. It may include offences such as conspiracy to steal, or assisting the thief contrary to the Criminal Law Act 1967, s.4(1). The phrase "taken into consideration in determining sentence" has in a related context been held to be the "well-known term of legal art" referring to the conventional procedure for the admission on conviction of further offences to which the offender invites the court to have regard in sentencing.[4]

The convicting court[5] may on the conviction, even if the passing of sentence is in other respects deferred, make any of a number of orders. These will be set out and briefly discussed; after which we shall deal with some matters relevant to the section as a whole.

Restoration of the stolen goods: s.28(1)(a)

16–03   Section 28(1)(*a*) empowers the court to order anyone having possession or control of stolen goods to restore them to anyone entitled to recover them from him.

Such an order can be made by the court of its own motion. But it is unlikely to be made in practice without an application. Most commonly that application will be made by the police, who may wish for their own protection to have the formal authority of a court order for the return of the goods to the victim of the offence. More commonly still, no doubt, the police will return the goods to the owner at the conclusion of the criminal proceedings without any order for that purpose being made. But this course can have its hazards.[6] Where the proceedings end in an acquittal the police, seeking judicial sanction for parting with the property to a particular claimant, must take separate proceedings for the purpose in a magistrates' court under the Police (Property) Act 1897.[7] Where there has been a conviction, an application to the convicting court under section 28(1)(*a*) is clearly more convenient. The paragraph may be of similar service to anyone other than the police who may have stolen property in his hands at the end of a trial.

16–04   Of course an application for restoration may be made by the victim of the offence or anyone else claiming to be entitled to recover the property. It is not appropriate to consider at length the problems of title that could theoretically arise on such an application. For the jurisdiction of the court under this section, which is entirely discretionary, should not be exercised in any case raising difficult questions of civil law. To embark upon such questions would be beyond the proper province of a criminal court. The court will make an

---

[4] *D.P.P.* v. *Anderson* [1978] A.C. 964 at 977.
[5] But where a magistrates' court commits an offender to the Crown Court for sentence, the power to make an order under s.28 passes to the Crown Court and is not to be exercised by the committing court: Criminal Justice Act 1967, s.56(5); *Blackpool JJ., ex p. Charlson and Gregory* (1972) 56 Cr.App.R. 823.
[6] See, *e.g. Winter* v. *Bancks* (1901) 84 L.T. 504.
[7] See below § 16–15. For an illustration of the value of such proceedings to the police, see *Bullock* v. *Dunlap* (1876) 2 Ex.D. 43.

order only in a clear case.[8] Normally such a case will be one in which it is apparent that neither the offence itself nor any subsequent dealing with the property by the offender has had any effect upon the title to the property.[9] It may be anticipated, therefore, that the vast majority of orders will be made in cases of theft in the narrow sense. But they may also be made in some cases of obtaining property by deception or blackmail in which the original offender is caught before disposing of the property obtained by the offence.[10] Where a person guilty of obtaining by deception or blackmail has transferred the property to a third person (other than a person convicted of handling) there is always liable to be an issue as to title between the transferee and the original owner; for the offender may have acquired a voidable title by his offence and, if he has, may have passed a good title to his transferee[11] before his own title was avoided by the act of the victim.

Goods representing the stolen goods: s.28(1)(b)

The convicted person (the thief or a handler) may be proved to have **16–05** property into which the stolen property or some part of it has been directly or indirectly converted, as by the spending of stolen money or the sale of stolen goods. A person entitled to recover such identifiable proceeds of the stolen property from the convicted person may obtain an order under section 28(1)(b) that those proceeds be delivered or transferred to him.[12] Such an order, in contrast to orders under paragraphs (a) and (c), requires an application by the person in whose favour it is to be made. He must be able to show a right under the civil law to "follow" the stolen goods into the goods that represent them. It must be clear that he can do this, for it will not be appropriate for the court to decide difficult questions of the law of tracing for the purpose of enabling itself to make an order.

---

[8] *Ferguson* (1970) 54 Cr.App.R. 410 (applying to s.28 the principles laid down in *Stamp* v. *United Dominions Trust (Commercial) Ltd.* [1967] 1 Q.B. 418, for the exercise of the corresponding jurisdiction under the Larceny Act 1916, s.45, and the Magistrates' Courts Act 1952, s.33); *Church* (1970) 55 Cr.App.R. 65. A possible reason for the refusing of an order even when the question of title is clear would be the claim of the possessor that, believing in his good title to the goods, he has improved them since acquiring them. On the making of an order under para. (a) he would not be able to obtain an allowance for the improvement, as he would in proceedings against him for wrongful interference: Torts (Interference with Goods) Act 1977, s.6(1).

[9] Mann, *The Legal Aspect of Money* (4th ed.), p. 4, says that "it is an open question whether money passed and accepted bona fide from hand to hand as currency is 'money' for the purpose of an order for restitution" (referring to "money" in the definition of "goods" in s.34(2)(b), and citing *Moss* v. *Hancock* [1899] 2 Q.B. 111). It is submitted that this is the wrong question. The question should be whether anyone is "entitled to recover" the money from its possessor; and the answer might well turn on the negotiable character of money as currency (compare coins as curios: *Moss* v. *Hancock*, above).

[10] See the situations in *George* (1901) 65 J.P. 729; *Cohen* (1907) 71 J.P. 190. In each of these cases property found in the possession of the prisoner was identifiable as the proceeds of property obtained by false pretences (see now s.28(1)(b), below). The prisoner's title to the property had been avoided, not by the conviction (cf. s.31(2)), but by the victim's disaffirmation of the transaction between himself and the prisoner. In *Cohen* the order was made against the opposition of the prisoner's trustee in bankruptcy.

[11] By virtue of the Sale of Goods Act 1979, s.23, or of corresponding common law principles.

[12] Orders may be made under both paragraph (b) and paragraph (c) of s.28(1), but not so that the person in whose favour the orders are made recovers in total more than the value of the stolen goods: s.28(2).

The court has no power under this paragraph to order a sale of goods and the distribution of the proceeds among different losers.[13]

Money taken out of convicted person's possession: s.28(1)(c)

16-06   The convicted person may not have been found in possession of the stolen goods, but it may be clear that had they been in his possession some person (usually the victim of the offence) would have been entitled to recover them from him. In such a case the court may,[14] under section 28(1)(c), order a sum not exceeding the value of the stolen goods to be paid, out of the convicted person's money[15] taken out of his possession on his apprehension, to any person who, if those goods were in the possession of the convicted person, would be entitled to recover them from him.[16]

The Criminal Justice Act 1972, s.6(2), provides that an order under paragraph (c) may be made "without any application being made in that behalf or on the application of any person appearing to the court to be interested in the property concerned."

D may be convicted of handling part only of a larger quantity of stolen goods. If all the goods the subject of the conviction have been recovered, it is an incorrect exercise of discretion to make an order under paragraph (c) for the payment to P of money found on D so as to compensate P for the loss of the other goods with which, so far as his conviction shows, D was not concerned.[17]

"Taken out of his possession on his apprehension"

16-07   For an order to be made against a person under paragraph (c) the money must have been "taken out of his possession on his apprehension." This does not mean that it must actually have been found on his person at the time of his arrest. First, it may be found elsewhere, though in his "possession." In *Ferguson*[18] it was in a safe deposit box at Harrods store, the box being in his name and he holding the key. Secondly, it may be found some time after the arrest. In *Ferguson* the Court of Appeal had no doubt that there was power to make an order under the paragraph in respect of money found and taken 11 days after the arrest. This reading—the result of "giving the words 'on his apprehension' a common-sense meaning"[19]—is quite strikingly expansive. Perhaps the decision stretches this far and no farther: that money will be "taken out of [D's] possession on his apprehension" if it is in his legal

---

[13] *Thibeault* (1982) 76 Cr.App.R. 201; 4 Cr.App.R.(S.) 375.
[14] With no obligation to have regard to the convicted person's means: *Lewis* [1975] Crim.L.R. 353.
[15] As to "money," see § 2–11, above. The limitation of para. (c) to money taken out of D's possession may have escaped attention in *Hammond* [1983] Crim.L.R. 571; see commentator's note at 572.
[16] See n. 12, above.
[17] *Parker* (1970) 54 Cr.App.R. 339. In fact there may be no power to make an order in these circumstances; the point was reserved in *Parker*.
[18] (1970) 54 Cr.App.R. 410.
[19] *Ibid.* at 412.

possession (on his person; in his house or his safe deposit box; in the keeping of his servant) both when he is arrested and when it is found and taken, he being still in custody when the latter event occurs.

Although the police may lawfully have taken money out of a person's possession on his apprehension, they do not have power to retain it pending trial solely in anticipation that the court may on his conviction make an order under paragraph (c).[20]

Offenders other than thieves or handlers

The operation of paragraph (c) depends upon the hypothesis that, *if* the **16–08** convicted person had possessed the stolen goods, the person in whose favour the order is to be made *would* have been entitled to recover them from him. But the victim of theft will usually be entitled to recover the stolen goods from almost anyone in possession of them. It does not seem right to make any convicted person liable to pay their value simply by notionally attributing possession to him. To be so liable he should surely be guilty either of the substantive offence or of a handling that amounts to the tort of conversion. Most convicted persons within the section will be so guilty, but not all. It is submitted that the paragraph should be interpreted (or at least applied, by virtue of the court's discretion) in this limited way.

Compensation for a bona fide purchaser or lender: s.28(3)

The person against whom an order for restoration of the stolen goods is **16–09** made under section 28(1)(*a*) may be one who has in good faith bought the goods from the convicted person or has in good faith lent money to the convicted person on the security of the goods. Section 28(3) provides that in such a case the court may order the payment of compensation to the purchaser or lender out of the convicted person's money taken out of his possession on his apprehension. The compensation is not to exceed the amount paid for the goods or the amount owed in respect of the loan. The Criminal Justice Act 1972, s.6(2),[21] applies to this subsection as to section 28(1)(*c*).

Summary procedure for use in clear cases

The point has been made several times above that the jurisdiction under **16–10** section 28 is only to be exercised in very clear cases.[22] The procedure is an essentially summary one, to be exercised as a matter of convenience at the tail-end of a criminal trial. No procedure is provided for giving notice to a person not already before the court that he may make a claim or that an order under section 28(1)(*a*) may be made against him. Such a person, even

---

[20] *Malone* v. *Metropolitan Police Commissioner* [1980] Q.B. 49; approved by a majority of the court in *Chief Constable of Kent* v. *V* [1983] Q.B. 34.
[21] See above, § 16–06.
[22] See cases cited in n. 8 above.

though not concerned in the criminal trial, may, of course, know of the proceedings and be present for the purpose of making or resisting an application; and there is no doubt that he may be heard in person or by counsel.[23] But a third party to whom, for instance, money found in the convicted person's possession might belong has no *locus standi* before the court and might be unjustly affected by an order for payment of that money to the victim of the theft. Nor does the criminal court have the necessary machinery (especially the process of discovery) for resolving issues as to title.[24]

Materials on which and time at which order to be made

16–11   The summary nature of the procedure is further emphasised by the provisions of section 28 as to the materials on which an order under the section is to be made and as to the time for making the order.

Section 28(4) provides that none of the powers conferred by the section is to be exercised

> "unless in the opinion of the court the relevant facts sufficiently appear from evidence given at the trial or the available documents,[25] together with admissions made by or on behalf of any person in connection with any proposed exercise of the powers. . . ."

For the purpose of section 28(4) the trial comes to an end when sentence is passed,[26] so that there is no power to make an order based on facts appearing from evidence given after that time. And an order under section 28(1) must be made "on the conviction," which has been said to mean "immediately after the conviction."[27] All in all, the intention seems to be that the court is not to resolve disputed questions of title upon the basis of the evidence, documents and admissions referred to in section 28(4), but rather that that material, to justify an order, should reveal that there is no dispute to be resolved.

Suspension of orders

16–12   There are provisions for the suspension of orders under section 28 to allow time for appeal.

Where any order under the section is made *by a magistrates' court*, it is automatically suspended unless (in the case of an order made under sub-section (1)(*a*) or (*b*)) the court directs otherwise because it is of the opinion

---

[23] Compare *Macklin* (1850) 5 Cox 216.
[24] See *Ferguson* (1970) 54 Cr.App.R. 410. And see *Church* (1970) 55 Cr.App.R. 65, suggesting questions as to the rights of an insurance company which has paid the victim of the theft under a policy covering the stolen goods.
[25] For the meaning of this phrase, see the full text of s.28(4) in Appendix 1.
[26] *Church* (1970) 55 Cr.App.R. 65.
[27] *Ibid.* The language of Lord Esher M.R. in *Justices of the Central Criminal Court* (1886) 18 Q.B.D. 314 at 318 remains appropriate; ". . . it seems that the order can, and what is more, ought to be, made practically at the time of the trial; I do not say that it must be made at the minute, but it must be made as one of the conclusions of the trial."

that title to the property affected by the order is not in dispute. The suspension is for the period for the time being prescribed by law for the giving of notice of appeal against a decision of a magistrates' court, or until the determination of an appeal of which notice was given during that period.[28]

There is similar automatic suspension of the operation of "an order for the restitution of property to a person" made *by the Crown Court.*[29] Any order under section 28 is to be treated for this purpose as an order for the restitution of property (section 28(5)). The suspension occurs unless the Crown Court[30] directs to the contrary for the reason mentioned above. It lasts until there is no further possibility of an appeal on which the order could be varied or set aside.[31]

Appeals

Orders made on conviction on indictment

The Court of Appeal may by order annul or vary any order made by the court of trial under section 28, although the conviction is not quashed.[32] A convicted person may also, with leave, appeal against an order under the section as a "sentence."[33] But a person who has been refused an order or a third party claiming to be prejudiced by an order has no right of appeal,[34] though in an appropriate case he may apply for judicial review.[35]

16-13

Orders made on summary conviction

A convicted person against whom an order under section 28 is made by a magistrates' court may appeal to the Crown Court against the order by way of an appeal against sentence.[36] And any person aggrieved by an order of a

---

[28] Criminal Justice Act 1972, s.6(5).
[29] Criminal Appeal Court 1968, s.30(1), as substituted by the Criminal Justice Act 1988, s.17(1), Sched. 15.
[30] s.30(1) of the Criminal Appeal Act says "the Court," which usually in that Act means the Court of Appeal but must here mean the Crown Court.
[31] Disregarding any possibility of leave to appeal out of time: *ibid.*
[32] Criminal Appeal Act 1968, s.30(2) (as substituted by the Criminal Justice Act 1988, s.170(1), Sched. 15), read with the Theft Act 1968, s.28(5).
[33] Criminal Appeal Act 1968, ss.9(1), 50(1); see also *Parker* (1970) 54 Cr.App.R. 339. For appeal against an order made in respect of an offence taken into consideration, see Criminal Justice Act 1972, s.6(4)(*b*).
[34] He cannot appeal either to the criminal division (*Elliot* [1908] 2 K.B. 452) or to the civil division (*Justices of the Central Criminal Court* (1886) 18 Q.B.D. 314) of the Court of Appeal. (But the Criminal Appeal Rules 1968 contemplate that the Court of Appeal may wish a person "immediately affected by an order of the judge of the court of trial" to be represented at the hearing of a convicted person's appeal: rr. 22(2)(*a*), 25(1). A clearer right to be heard was formerly provided: Criminal Appeal Rules 1908, r. 9, now revoked.) The absence of a right of appeal is another reason why an order should not be made under s.28 except in a clear case: see *Stamp* v. *United Dominions Trust (Commercial) Ltd.* [1967] 1 Q.B. 418 at 430.
[35] See, *e.g. London County JJ., ex p. Dettmer & Co.* (1908) 72 J.P. 513.
[36] Magistrates' Courts Act 1980, s.108(1)(3).

magistrates' court under section 28 may appeal to the Divisional Court by way of case stated on the ground that the order is wrong in law or is in excess of jurisdiction.[37]

Enforcement of orders under section 28

16–14   An order made under section 28 by the Crown Court will be enforceable by committal for contempt.[38]

Disobedience to an order made by a magistrates' court, other than an order for the payment of money, may be punished under the Magistrates' Courts Act 1980, s.63(3). The person in default may be ordered to pay a sum not exceeding £50 for every day during which he is in default[39] or a sum not exceeding £2,000,[40] or may be committed to custody until he has remedied his default[41] or for a period not exceeding two months.

Other procedures

16–15   There are some other procedures available either for the restoration of stolen property to its rightful owner or for the compensation by order of the criminal courts of the victims of offences under the Act.

Procedures relating to stolen property

It has already been mentioned[42] that the police often act quite informally by returning stolen property to the owner after the termination of criminal proceedings. Alternatively either the police or any person claiming the property can invoke the Police (Property) Act 1897, under which a magistrates' court may make an order for the delivery of the property to the person appearing to the court to be the owner.[43] If the owner cannot be ascertained the court may make "such order . . . as to the . . . court may seem meet."[44]

An order under the Police (Property) Act does not prevent a person taking proceedings for the recovery of property against any person in possession of it as a result of the order, but such proceedings must be brought within six months of the order.[45] In the case of property that has not been the subject of an order under section 28 or under the 1897 Act, a person

---

[37] *Ibid.* s.111.
[38] R.S.C., Ord. 52. Compare *Wollez* (1860) 8 Cox 337.
[39] But not more than £2,000 in all (see next note).
[40] Sum substituted by Criminal Penalties, etc. (Increase) Order 1984 (S.I. 1984, No. 447).
[41] But not more than two months in all.
[42] Above, § 16–03.
[43] "Owner" means owner in its ordinary popular meaning of the person entitled to the goods: *Raymond Lyons & Co. Ltd.* v. *Metropolitan Police Commissioner* [1975] Q.B. 321. The court should not make an order under the Act except in a straightforward case where there is no real issue of law or difficulty in determining whether a person is the owner: *ibid.* at 326.
[44] Police (Property) Act 1897, s.1(1). The Police (Disposal of Property) Regulations 1975 (S.I. 1975, No. 1474), made under s.2(1), provide for the disposal of property whose owner has not been ascertained and in respect of which no order of a competent court has been made.
[45] Police (Property) Act 1897, s.1(2).

claiming to be entitled to it is of course left to his civil remedies, which are unaffected by the fact that an order under section 28 has been refused or not applied for.[46]

Compensation

Under section 35 of the Powers of Criminal Courts Act 1973[47] a person **16–16** convicted of an offence may be ordered by the convicting court[48] "to pay compensation for any personal injury, loss or damage resulting from that offence or any other offence which is taken into consideration[49] by the court in determining sentence" (subs. (1)). The order may be made "instead of or in addition to dealing with [the offender] in any other way." In the case of an offence under the Theft Act, "where the property ... is recovered, any damage to the property[50] occurring while it was out of the owner's possession shall be treated ... as having resulted from the offence, however and by whomsoever the damage was caused" (subs. (2)).

Compensation orders made by a magistrates' court are subject to a maximum of £2,000 in respect of any offence of which the court has convicted the offender, and in effect, where compensation is ordered in respect of offences taken into consideration by a magistrates' court, the total compensation in respect of all offences may not exceed £2,000 multiplied by the number of offences of which the offender has been convicted.[51]

In determining whether to make an order, or the amount of compensation **16–17** to be paid, a court must have regard to the offender's means so far as they appear or are known to the court (subs. (4)). The court will decide what amount is "appropriate, having regard to any evidence and to any representations that are made on behalf of the accused or the prosecutor" (subs. (1A)).

Where both a fine and a compensation order would be appropriate, but the offender has insufficient means to pay both, the court is to give preference to compensation (subs. (4A)). A sentencing court must give reasons for not making a compensation order where it has power to do so (subs. (1)).

The principles governing the making of compensation orders are elaborated in a substantial case law, for which reference should be made to works on sentencing.[52]

[46] Compare *Ex p. Davison* (1896) 60 J.P. 808; *Scattergood* v. *Sylvester* (1850) 15 Q.B. 506.
[47] As amended by the Criminal Justice Act 1967, s.67, and the Criminal Justice Act 1988, s.104.
[48] But see n. 5, above, reading that note as applying to compensation orders as to orders under s.28.
[49] That is, is the subject of formal "t.i.c." procedure: compare *D.P.P.* v. *Anderson* [1978] A.C. 964 (above, n. 4).
[50] Not, in case of taking a car without consent contrary to s.12, other property damaged by the offender when driving the car: *Quigley* v. *Stokes* (1976) 64 Cr.App.R. 198 (see subs. (3)).
[51] This is the effect of the Magistrates' Courts Act 1980, s.40(1) (formerly Powers of Criminal Courts Act 1973, s.35(5)), as amended by the Criminal Penalties, etc. (Increase) Order 1984 (S.I. 1984 No. 447).
[52] *e.g.* Thomas, *Current Sentencing Practice*, J2.

APPENDIX 1

Theft Act 1968

(1968 c. 60)

ARRANGEMENT OF SECTIONS

Definition of "theft"

SECT.

Theft, robbery, burglary, etc.

Fraud and blackmail

Offences relating to goods stolen, etc.

264

Possession of house-breaking implements, etc.

Enforcement and procedure

General and consequential provisions

Supplementary

An Act to revise the law of England and Wales as to theft and similar or associated offences, and in connection therewith to make provision as to criminal proceedings by one party to a marriage against the other, and to make certain amendments extending beyond England and Wales in the Post Office Act 1953 and other enactments; and for other purposes connected therewith. [26th July 1968]

Definition of "theft"

Basic definition of theft

1.—(1) A person is guilty of theft if he dishonestly appropriates property **17–01** belonging to another with the intention of permanently depriving the other of it; and "thief" and "steal" shall be construed accordingly.

(2) It is immaterial whether the appropriation is made with a view to gain, or is made for the thief's own benefit.

(3) The five following sections of this Act shall have effect as regards the interpretation and operation of this section (and, except as otherwise provided by this Act, shall apply only for purposes of this section).

"Dishonestly"

2.—(1) A person's appropriation of property belonging to another is not **17–02** to be regarded as dishonest—

(*a*) if he appropriates the property in the belief that he has in law the right to deprive the other of it, on behalf of himself or of a third person; or

(*b*) if he appropriates the property in the belief that he would have the other's consent if the other knew of the appropriation and the circumstances of it; or

(*c*) (except where the property came to him as trustee or personal representative) if he appropriates the property in the belief that the person to whom the property belongs cannot be discovered by taking reasonable steps.

(2) A person's appropriation of property belonging to another may be dishonest notwithstanding that he is willing to pay for the property.

"Appropriates"

17–03 **3.**—(1) Any assumption by a person of the rights of an owner amounts to an appropriation, and this includes, where he has come by the property (innocently or not) without stealing it, any later assumption of a right to it by keeping or dealing with it as owner.

(2) Where property or a right or interest in property is or purports to be transferred for value to a person acting in good faith, no later assumption by him of rights which he believed himself to be acquiring shall, by reason of any defect in the transferor's title, amount to theft of the property.

"Property"

17–04 **4.**—(1) "Property" includes money and all other property, real or personal, including things in action and other intangible property.

(2) A person cannot steal land, or things forming part of land and severed from it by him or by his directions, except in the following cases, that is to say—

(*a*) when he is a trustee or personal representative, or is authorised by power of attorney, or as liquidator of a company, or otherwise, to sell or dispose of land belonging to another, and he appropriates the land or anything forming part of it by dealing with it in breach of the confidence reposed in him; or

(*b*) when he is not in possession of the land and appropriates anything forming part of the land by severing it or causing it to be severed or after it has been severed; or

(*c*) when, being in possession of the land under a tenancy, he appropriates the whole or part of any fixture or structure let to be used with the land.

For purposes of this subsection "land" does not include incorporeal hereditaments; "tenancy" means a tenancy for years or any less period and includes an agreement for such a tenancy, but a person who after the end of a tenancy remains in possession as statutory tenant or otherwise is to be treated as having possession under the tenancy, and "let" shall be construed accordingly.

(3) A person who picks mushrooms growing wild on any land, or who picks flowers, fruit or foliage from a plant growing wild on any land does not (although not in possession of the land) steal what he picks, unless he does it for reward or for sale or other commercial purpose.

For purposes of this subsection "mushroom" includes any fungus, and "plant" includes any shrub or tree.

(4) Wild creatures, tamed or untamed, shall be regarded as property; but a person cannot steal a wild creature not tamed nor ordinarily kept in captivity, or the carcase of any such creature, unless either it has been reduced into possession by or on behalf of another person and possession of it has not since been lost or abandoned, or another person is in course of reducing it into possession.

"Belonging to another"

5.—(1) Property shall be regarded as belonging to any person having   **17–05**
possession or control of it, or having in it any proprietary right or interest (not being an equitable interest arising only from an agreement to transfer or grant an interest).

(2) Where property is subject to a trust, the persons to whom it belongs shall be regarded as including any person having a right to enforce the trust, and an intention to defeat the trust shall be regarded accordingly as an intention to deprive of the property any person having that right.

(3) Where a person receives property from or on account of another, and is under an obligation to the other to retain and deal with that property or its proceeds in a particular way, the property or proceeds shall be regarded (as against him) as belonging to the other.

(4) Where a person gets property by another's mistake, and is under an obligation to make restoration (in whole or in part) of the property or its proceeds or of the value thereof, then to the extent of that obligation the property or proceeds shall be regarded (as against him) as belonging to the person entitled to restoration, and an intention not to make restoration shall be regarded accordingly as an intention to deprive that person of the property or proceeds.

(5) Property of a corporation sole shall be regarded as belonging to the corporation notwithstanding a vacancy in the corporation.

"With the intention of permanently depriving the other of it"

6.—(1) A person appropriating property belonging to another without   **17–06**
meaning the other permanently to lose the thing itself is nevertheless to be regarded as having the intention of permanently depriving the other of it if his intention is to treat the thing as his own to dispose of regardless of the other's rights; and a borrowing or lending of it may amount to so treating it if, but only if, the borrowing or lending is for a period and in circumstances making it equivalent to an outright taking or disposal.

(2) Without prejudice to the generality of subsection (1) above, where a person, having possession or control (lawfully or not) of property belonging

17–06

to another, parts with the property under a condition as to its return which he may not be able to perform, this (if done for purposes of his own and without the other's authority) amounts to treating the property as his own to dispose of regardless of the other's rights.

Theft, robbery, burglary, etc.

Theft

17–07 7. A person guilty of theft shall on conviction on indictment be liable to imprisonment for a term not exceeding ten years.

Robbery

17–08 8.—(1) A person is guilty of robbery if he steals, and immediately before or at the time of doing so, and in order to so, he uses force on any person or puts or seeks to put any person in fear of being then and there subjected to force.

(2) Any person guilty of robbery, or of an assault with intent to rob, shall on conviction on indictment be liable to imprisonment for life.

Burglary

17–09 9.—(1) A person is guilty of burglary if—

(*a*) he enters a building or part of a building as a trespasser and with intent to commit any such offence as is mentioned in subsection (2) below; or

(*b*) having entered any building or part of a building as a trespasser he steals or attempts to steal anything in the building or that part of it or inflicts or attempts to inflict on any person therein any grievous bodily harm.

(2) The offences referred to in subsection (1)(*a*) above are offences of stealing anything in the building or part of a building in question, of inflicting on any person therein any grievous bodily harm or raping any woman therein, and doing unlawful damage to the building or anything therein.

(3) References in subsections (1) and (2) above to a building shall apply also to an inhabited vehicle or vessel, and shall apply to any such vehicle or vessel at times when the person having a habitation in it is not there as well as at times when he is.

(4) A person guilty of burglary shall on conviction on indictment be liable to imprisonment for a term not exceeding fourteen years.

Aggravated burglary

17–10 10.—(1) A person is guilty of aggravated burglary if he commits any burglary and at the time has with him any firearm or imitation firearm, any weapon of offence, or any explosive; and for this purpose—

(*a*) "firearm" includes an airgun or air pistol, and "imitation firearm" means anything which has the appearance of being a firearm, whether capable of being discharged or not; and

(*b*) "weapon of offence" means any article made or adapted for use for causing injury to or incapacitating a person, or intended by the person having it with him for such use; and

(*c*) "explosive" means any article manufactured for the purpose of producing a practical effect by explosion, or intended by the person having it with him for that purpose.

(2) A person guilty of aggravated burglary shall on conviction on indictment be liable to imprisonment for life.

Removal of articles from places open to the public

11.—(1) Subject to subsections (2) and (3) below, where the public have access to a building in order to view the building or part of it, or a collection or part of a collection housed in it, any person who without lawful authority removes from the building or its grounds the whole or part of any article displayed or kept for display to the public in the building or that part of it or in its grounds shall be guilty of an offence.   **17–11**

For this purpose "collection" includes a collection got together for a temporary purpose, but references in this section to a collection do not apply to a collection made or exhibited for the purpose of effecting sales or other commercial dealings.

(2) It is immaterial for purposes of subsection (1) above, that the public's access to a building is limited to a particular period or particular occasion; but where anything removed from a building or its grounds is there otherwise than as forming part of, or being on loan for exhibition with, a collection intended for permanent exhibition to the public, the person removing it does not thereby commit an offence under this section unless he removes it on a day when the public have access to the building as mentioned in subsection (1) above.

(3) A person does not commit an offence under this section if he believes that he has lawful authority for the removal of the thing in question or that he would have it if the person entitled to give it knew of the removal and the circumstances of it.

(4) A person guilty of an offence under this section shall, on conviction on indictment, be liable to imprisonment for a term not exceeding five years.

Taking motor vehicle or other conveyance without authority

12.—(1) Subject to subsections (5) and (6) below, a person shall be guilty of an offence if, without having the consent of the owner or other lawful authority, he takes any conveyance for his own or another's use or, knowing that any conveyance has been taken without such authority, drives it or allows himself to be carried in or on it.   **17–12**

(2) A person guilty of an offence under subsection (1) above shall [be liable on summary conviction to a fine not exceeding level 5 on the standard scale, to imprisonment for a term not exceeding six months, or to both].

[(3) *Repealed by the Police and Criminal Evidence Act* 1984, *s*.18, *Sched.* 7.]

(4) If on the trial of an indictment for theft the jury are not satisfied that the accused committed theft, but it is proved that the accused committed an offence under subsection (1) above, the jury may find him guilty of the offence under subsection (1) [and if he is found guilty of it, he shall be liable as he would have been liable under subsection (2) above on summary conviction].

(5) Subsection (1) above shall not apply in relation to pedal cycles; but, subject to subsection (6) below, a person who, without having the consent of the owner or other lawful authority, takes a pedal cycle for his own or another's use, or rides a pedal cycle knowing it to have been taken without such authority, shall on summary conviction be liable to a fine not exceeding [level 2 on the standard scale].

(6) A person does not commit an offence under this section by anything done in the belief that he has lawful authority to do it or that he would have the owner's consent if the owner knew of his doing it and the circumstances of it.

(7) For purposes of this section—

    (*a*) "conveyance" means any conveyance constructed or adapted for the carriage of a person or persons whether by land, water or air, except that it does not include a conveyance constructed or adapted for use only under the control of a person not carried in or on it, and "drive" shall be construed accordingly; and

    (*b*) "owner," in relation to a conveyance which is the subject of a hiring agreement or hire-purchase agreement, means the person in possession of the conveyance under that agreement.

[*Subsections* (2) *and* (4) *were amended by the Criminal Justice Act* 1988, *s*.37(1). *Subsection* (5) *was amended by the Criminal Justice Act* 1982, *s*.46(1).]

Abstracting of electricity

17–13 13. A person who dishonestly uses without due authority, or dishonestly causes to be wasted or diverted, any electricity shall on conviction on indictment be liable to imprisonment for a term not exceeding five years.

Extension to thefts from mails outside England and Wales, and robbery etc. on such a theft

17–14 14.—(1) Where a person—

    (*a*) steals or attempts to steal any mail bag or postal packet in the course of transmission as such between places in different jurisdictions in the British postal area, or any of the contents of such a mail bag or postal packet; or

    (*b*) in stealing or with intent to steal any such mail bag or postal packet or

any of its contents, commits any robbery, attempted robbery or
assault with intent to rob;

then, notwithstanding that he does so outside England and Wales, he shall
be guilty of committing or attempting to commit the offence against this Act
as if he had done so in England or Wales, and he shall accordingly be liable to
be prosecuted, tried and punished in England and Wales without proof that
the offence was committed there.

(2) In subsection (1) above the reference to different jurisdictions in the
British postal area is to be construed as referring to the several jurisdictions
of England and Wales, of Scotland, of Northern Ireland, of the Isle of Man
and of the Channel Islands.

(3) For purposes of this section "mail bag" includes any article serving the
purpose of a mail bag.

Fraud and blackmail

Obtaining property by deception

15.—(1) A person who by any deception dishonestly obtains property   **17–15**
belonging to another, with the intention of permanently depriving the other
of it, shall on conviction on indictment be liable to imprisonment for a term
not exceeding ten years.

(2) For purposes of this section a person is to be treated as obtaining
property if he obtains ownership, possession or control of it, and "obtain"
includes obtaining for another or enabling another to obtain or to retain.

(3) Section 6 above shall apply for purposes of this section, with the
necessary adaptations of the reference to appropriating, as it applies for
purposes of section 1.

(4) For purposes of this section "deception" means any deception
(whether deliberate or reckless) by words or conduct as to fact or as to law,
including a deception as to the present intentions of the person using the
deception or any other person.

Obtaining pecuniary advantage by deception

16.—(1) A person who by any deception dishonestly obtains for himself or   **17–16**
another any pecuniary advantage shall on conviction on indictment be liable
to imprisonment for a term not exceeding five years.

(2) The cases in which a pecuniary advantage within the meaning of this
section is to be regarded as obtained for a person are cases where—

[(*a*) *any debt or charge for which he makes himself liable or is or may
    become liable (including one not legally enforceable) is reduced or in
    whole or in part evaded or deferred; or*]
  (*b*) he is allowed to borrow by way of overdraft, or to take out any policy
    of insurance or annuity contract, or obtains an improvement of the
    terms on which he is allowed to do so; or

271

(*c*) he is given the opportunity to earn remuneration or greater remuneration in an office or employment, or to win money by betting.

(3) For purposes of this section "deception" has the same meaning as in section 15 of this Act.

[*Subsection (2)(a) was repealed by the Theft Act 1978, s.5(5).*]

False accounting

17–17   **17.**—(1) Where a person dishonestly, with a view to gain for himself or another or with intent to cause loss to another,—

(*a*) destroys, defaces, conceals or falsifies any account or any record or document made or required for any accounting purpose; or

(*b*) in furnishing information for any purpose produces or makes use of any account, or any such record or document as aforesaid, which to his knowledge is or may be misleading, false or deceptive in a material particular;

he shall, on conviction on indictment, be liable to imprisonment for a term not exceeding seven years.

(2) For purposes of this section a person who makes or concurs in making in an account or other document an entry which is or may be misleading, false or deceptive in a material particular, or who omits or concurs in omitting a material particular from an account or other document, is to be treated as falsifying the account or document.

Liability of company officers for certain offences by company

17–18   **18.**—(1) Where an offence committed by a body corporate under section 15, 16 or 17 of this Act is proved to have been committed with the consent or connivance of any director, manager, secretary or other similar officer of the body corporate, or any person who was purporting to act in any such capacity, he as well as the body corporate shall be guilty of that offence, and shall be liable to be proceeded against and punished accordingly.

(2) Where the affairs of a body corporate are managed by its members, this section shall apply in relation to the acts and defaults of a member in connection with his functions of management as if he were a director of the body corporate.

False statements by company directors, etc.

17–19   **19.**—(1) Where an officer of a body corporate or unincorporated association (or person purporting to act as such), with intent to deceive members or creditors of the body corporate or association about its affairs, publishes or concurs in publishing a written statement or account which to his knowledge is or may be misleading, false or deceptive in a material particular, he shall on conviction on indictment be liable to imprisonment for a term not exceeding seven years.

(2) For purposes of this section a person who has entered into a security for the benefit of a body corporate or association is to be treated as a creditor of it.

(3) Where the affairs of a body corporate or association are managed by its members, this section shall apply to any statement which a member publishes or concurs in publishing in connection with his functions of management as if he were an officer of the body corporate or association.

Suppression, etc. of documents

20.—(1) A person who dishonestly, with a view to gain for himself or another or with intent to cause loss to another, destroys, defaces or conceals any valuable security, any will or other testamentary document or any original document of or belonging to, or filed or deposited in, any court of justice or any government department shall on conviction on indictment be liable to imprisonment for a term not exceeding seven years.   **17–20**

(2) A person who dishonestly, with a view to gain for himself or another or with intent to cause loss to another, by any deception procures the execution of a valuable security shall on conviction on indictment be liable to imprisonment for a term not exceeding seven years; and this subsection shall apply in relation to the making, acceptance, indorsement, alteration, cancellation or destruction in whole or in part of a valuable security, and in relation to the signing or sealing of any paper or other material in order that it may be made or converted into, or used or dealt with as, a valuable security, as if that were the execution of a valuable security.

(3) For purposes of this section "deception" has the same meaning as in section 15 of this Act, and "valuable security" means any document creating, transferring, surrendering or releasing any right to, in or over property, or authorising the payment of money or delivery of any property or evidencing the creation, transfer, surrender or release of any such right, or the payment of money or delivery of any property, or the satisfaction of any obligation.

Blackmail

21.—(1) A person is guilty of blackmail if, with a view to gain for himself or another or with intent to cause loss to another, he makes any unwarranted demand with menaces; and for this purpose a demand with menaces is unwarranted unless the person making it does so in the belief—   **17–21**

  (*a*) that he has reasonable grounds for making the demand; and
  (*b*) that the use of the menaces is a proper means of reinforcing the demand.

(2) The nature of the act or omission demanded is immaterial, and it is also immaterial whether the menaces relate to action to be taken by the person making the demand.

(3) A person guilty of blackmail shall on conviction on indictment be liable to imprisonment for a term not exceeding fourteen years.

Offences relating to goods stolen, etc.

Handling stolen goods

17–22 **22.**—(1) A person handles stolen goods if (otherwise than in the course of the stealing) knowing or believing them to be stolen goods he dishonestly receives the goods, or dishonestly undertakes or assists in their retention, removal, disposal or realisation by or for the benefit of another person, of if he arranges to do so.

(2) A person guilty of handling stolen goods shall on conviction on indictment be liable to imprisonment for a term not exceeding fourteen years.

Advertising rewards for return of goods stolen or lost

17–23 **23.** Where any public advertisement of a reward for the return of any goods which have been stolen or lost uses any words to the effect that no questions will be asked, or that the person producing the goods will be safe from apprehension or inquiry, or that any money paid for the purchase of the goods or advanced by way of loan on them will be repaid, the person advertising the reward and any person who prints or publishes the advertisement shall on summary conviction be liable to a fine not exceeding one hundred pounds.

Scope of offences relating to stolen goods

17–24 **24.**—(1) The provisions of this Act relating to goods which have been stolen shall apply whether the stealing occurred in England or Wales or elsewhere, and whether it occurred before or after the commencement of this Act, provided that the stealing (if not an offence under this Act) amounted to an offence where and at the time when the goods were stolen; and references to stolen goods shall be construed accordingly.

(2) For purposes of those provisions references to stolen goods shall include, in addition to the goods originally stolen and parts of them (whether in their original state or not),—

    (*a*) any other goods which directly or indirectly represent or have at any time represented the stolen goods in the hands of the thief as being the proceeds of any disposal or realisation of the whole or part of the goods stolen or of goods so representing the stolen goods; and

    (*b*) any other goods which directly or indirectly represent or have at any time represented the stolen goods in the hands of a handler of the stolen goods or any part of them as being the proceeds of any disposal or realisation of the whole or part of the stolen goods handled by him or of goods so representing them.

(3) But no goods shall be regarded as having continued to be stolen goods after they have been restored to the person from whom they were stolen or to other lawful possession or custody, or after that person and any other

person claiming through him have otherwise ceased as regards those goods to have any right to restitution in respect of the theft.

(4) For purposes of the provisions of this Act relating to goods which have been stolen (including subsections (1) to (3) above) goods obtained in England or Wales or elsewhere either by blackmail or in the circumstances described in section 15(1) of this Act shall be regarded as stolen; and "steal," "theft" and "thief" shall be construed accordingly.

Possession of housebreaking implements, etc.

Going equipped for stealing, etc.

25.—(1) A person shall be guilty of an offence if, when not at his place of   **17–25**
abode, he has with him any article for use in the course of or in connection with any burglary, theft or cheat.

(2) A person guilty of an offence under this section shall on conviction on indictment be liable to imprisonment for a term not exceeding three years.

(3) Where a person is charged with an offence under this section, proof that he had with him any article made or adapted for use in committing a burglary, theft or cheat shall be evidence that he had it with him for such use.

(4) Any person may arrest without warrant anyone who is, or whom he, with reasonable cause, suspects to be, committing an offence under this section.

(5) For purposes of this section an offence under section 12(1) of this Act of taking a conveyance shall be treated as theft, and "cheat" means an offence under section 15 of this Act.

Enforcement and procedure

Search for stolen goods

26.—(1) If it is made to appear by information on oath before a justice of   **17–26**
the peace that there is reasonable cause to believe that any person has in his custody or possession or on his premises any stolen goods, the justice may grant a warrant to search for and seize the same; but no warrant to search for stolen goods shall be addressed to a person other than a constable except under the authority of an enactment expressly so providing.

[(2) *Repealed by the Police and Criminal Evidence Act* 1984, *s.*18, *Sched.* 7.]

(3) Where under this section a person is authorised to search premises for stolen goods, he may enter and search the premises accordingly, and may seize any goods he believes to be stolen goods.

[(4) *Repealed by the Criminal Justice Act* 1972, *s.*64(2), *Sched.* 6.]

(5) This section is to be construed in accordance with section 24 of this Act; and in subsection (2) above the references to handling stolen goods shall include any corresponding offence committed before the commencement of this Act.

Evidence and procedure on charge of theft or handling stolen goods

17–27   27.—(1) Any number of persons may be charged in one indictment, with reference to the same theft, with having at different times or at the same time handled all or any of the stolen goods, and the persons so charged may be tried together.

(2) On the trial of two or more persons indicted for jointly handling any stolen goods the jury may find any of the accused guilty if the jury are satisfied that he handled all or any of the stolen goods, whether or not he did so jointly with the other accused or any of them.

(3) Where a person is being proceeded against for handling stolen goods (but not for any offence other than handling stolen goods), then at any stage of the proceedings, if evidence has been given of his having or arranging to have in his possession the goods the subject of the charge, or of his undertaking or assisting in, or arranging to undertake or assist in, their retention, removal, disposal or realisation, the following evidence shall be admissible for the purpose of proving that he knew or believed the goods to be stolen goods:—

(*a*) evidence that he has had in his possession, or has undertaken or assisted in the retention, removal, disposal or realisation of, stolen goods from any theft taking place not earlier than twelve months before the offence charged; and

(*b*) (provided that seven days' notice in writing has been given to him of the intention to prove the conviction) evidence that he has within the five years preceding the date of the offence charged been convicted of theft or of handling stolen goods.

(4) In any proceedings for the theft of anything in the course of transmission (whether by post or otherwise), or for handling stolen goods from such a theft, a statutory declaration made by any person that he despatched or received or failed to receive any goods or postal packet, or that any goods or postal packet when despatched or received by him were in a particular state or condition, shall be admissible as evidence of the facts stated in the declaration, subject to the following conditions:—

(*a*) a statutory declaration shall only be admissible where and to the extent to which oral evidence to the like effect would have been admissible in the proceedings; and

(*b*) a statutory declaration shall only be admissible if at least seven days before the hearing or trial a copy of it has been given to the person charged, and he has not, at least three days before the hearing of trial or within such further time as the court may in special circumstances allow, given the prosecutor written notice requiring the attendance at the hearing or trial of the person making the declaration.

(5) This section is to be construed in accordance with section 24 of this Act; and in subsection (3)(*b*) above the reference to handling stolen goods shall include any corresponding offence committed before the commencement of this Act.

Orders for restitution

28.—(1) Where goods have been stolen, and either a person is convicted **17–28**
of any offence with reference to the theft (whether or not the stealing is the
gist of his offence) or a person is convicted of any other offence but such an
offence as aforesaid is taken into consideration in determining his sentence,
the court by or before which the offender is convicted may on the conviction
[(whether or not the passing of sentence is in other respects deferred)]
exercise any of the following powers—

    (*a*) the court may order anyone having possession or control of the goods
        to restore them to any person entitled to recover them from him; or
    (*b*) on the application of a person entitled to recover from the person
        convicted any other goods directly or indirectly representing the
        first-mentioned goods (as being the proceeds of any disposal or
        realisation of the whole or part of them or of goods so representing
        them), the court may order those other goods to be delivered or
        transferred to the applicant; or
    (*c*) the court may order that a sum not exceeding the value of the
        first-mentioned goods shall be paid, out of any money of the person
        convicted which was taken out of his possession on his apprehension,
        to any person who, if those goods were in the possession of the
        person convicted, would be entitled to recover them from him.

(2) Where under subsection (1) above the court has power on a person's
conviction to make an order against him both under paragraph (*b*) and
under paragraph (*c*) with reference to the stealing of the same goods, the
court may make orders under both paragraphs provided that the person in
whose favour the orders are made does not thereby recover more than the
value of those goods.

(3) Where under subsection (1) above the court on a person's conviction
makes an order under paragraph (*a*) for the restoration of any goods, and it
appears to the court that the person convicted has sold the goods to a person
acting in good faith, or has borrowed money on the security of them from a
person so acting, the court may order that there shall be paid to the
purchaser or lender, out of any money of the person convicted which was
taken out of his possession on his apprehension, a sum not exceeding the
amount paid for the purchase by the purchaser or, as the case may be, the
amount owed to the lender in respect of the loan.

(4) The court shall not exercise the powers conferred by this section unless
in the opinion of the court the relevant facts sufficiently appear from
evidence given at the trial or the available documents, together with admissions made by or on behalf of any person in connection with any proposed
exercise of the powers; and for this purpose "the available documents"
means any written statements or admissions which were made for use, and
would have been admissible, as evidence at the trial, the depositions taken at
any committal proceedings and any written statements or admissions used as
evidence in those proceedings.

(5) Any order under this section shall be treated as an order for the restitution of property within the meaning of [section 30 of the Criminal Appeal Act 1968 (which relates to the effect on such orders of appeals)].

(6) References in this section to stealing are to be construed in accordance with section 24(1) and (4) of this Act.

(7) An order may be made under this section in respect of money owed by the Crown.

[*Subsections* (1) (*other than the words in square brackets*), (2) *and* (3) *are printed as substituted by the Criminal Justice Act* 1972, *s.*64(1), *Sched.* 5. *The words in square brackets in subsection* (1) *were added by the Criminal Law Act* 1977, *s.*65(4), *Sched.* 12. *The words in square brackets in subsection* (5) *were substituted by the Criminal Justice Act* 1988, *s.*170(1), *Sched.* 15. *Subsection* (7) *was added by ibid. s.*163.]

Jurisdiction of quarter sessions, and summary trial

17–29   **29.**—[(1) *Repealed by the Courts Act* 1971, *s.*56, *Sched.* 11.]
          [(2) *Repealed by the Criminal Law Act* 1977, *s.*65(5), *Sched.* 13.]

General and consequential provisions

Husband and wife

17–30   **30.**—(1) This Act shall apply in relation to the parties to a marriage, and to property belonging to the wife or husband whether or not by reason of an interest derived from the marriage, as it would apply if they were not married and any such interest subsisted independently of the marriage.

(2) Subject to subsection (4) below, a person shall have the same right to bring proceedings against that person's wife or husband for any offence (whether under this Act or otherwise), as if they were not married, and a person bringing any such proceedings shall be competent to give evidence for the prosecution at every stage of the proceedings.

[(3) *Repealed by the Police and Criminal Evidence Act* 1984, *s.*18, *Sched.* 7.]

(4) Proceedings shall not be instituted against a person for any offence of stealing or doing unlawful damage to property which at the time of the offence belongs to that person's wife or husband, or for any attempt, incitement or conspiracy to commit such an offence, unless the proceedings are instituted by or with the consent of the Director of Public Prosecutions:
          Provided that—

   (*a*) this subsection shall not apply to proceedings against a person for an offence—
      (i) if that person is charged with committing the offence jointly with the wife or husband; or

(ii) if by virtue of any judicial decree or order (wherever made) that person and the wife or husband are at the time of the offence under no obligation to cohabit [*and*

(*b*) *Repealed by the Criminal Jurisdiction Act* 1975, *s.*14(5), *Sched.* 6.]

(5) Notwithstanding [section 6 of the Prosecution of Offences Act 1979] subsection (4) of this section shall apply—

(*a*) to an arrest (if without warrant) made by the wife or husband, and
(*b*) to a warrant of arrest issued on an information laid by the wife or husband.

[*Subsection* (5) *was added by the Criminal Jurisdiction Act* 1975, *s.*14(4), *Sched.* 5. *The words in square brackets were substituted by the Prosecution of Offences Act* 1979, *s.*11(1), *Sched.* 1.]

Effect on civil proceedings and rights

31.—(1) A person shall not be excused, by reason that to do so may incriminate that person or the wife or husband of that person of an offence under this Act— **17–31**

(*a*) from answering any question put to that person in proceedings for the recovery or administration of any property, for the execution of any trust or for an account of any property or dealings with property; or
(*b*) from complying with any order made in any such proceedings;

but no statement or admission made by a person in answering a question put or complying with an order made as aforesaid shall, in proceedings for an offence under this Act, be admissible in evidence against that person or (unless they married after the making of the statement of admission) against the wife or husband of that person.

(2) Notwithstanding any enactment to the contrary, where property has been stolen or obtained by fraud or other wrongful means, the title to that or any other property shall not be affected by reason only of the conviction of the offender.

Effect on existing law and construction of references to offences

32.—(1) The following offences are hereby abolished for all purposes not relating to offences committed before the commencement of this Act, that is to say— **17–32**

(*a*) any offence at common law of larceny, robbery, burglary, receiving stolen property, obtaining property by threats, extortion by colour of office or franchise, false accounting by public officers, concealment of treasure trove and, except as regards offences relating to the public revenue, cheating; and

279

(*b*) any offence under an enactment mentioned in Part 1 of Schedule 3 to this Act, to the extent to which the offence depends on any section or part of a section included in column 3 of that Schedule;

but so that the provisions in Schedule 1 to this Act (which preserve with modifications certain offences under the Larceny Act 1861 of taking or killing deer and taking or destroying fish) shall have effect as there set out.

(2) Except as regards offences committed before the commencement of this Act, and except in so far as the context otherwise requires,—

(*a*) references in any enactment passed before this Act to an offence abolished by this Act shall, subject to any express amendment or repeal made by this Act, have effect as references to the corresponding offence under this Act, and in any such enactment the expression "receive" (when it relates to an offence of receiving) shall mean handle, and "receiver" shall be construed accordingly; and

(*b*) without prejudice to paragraph (*a*) above, references in any enactment, whenever passed, to theft or stealing (including references to stolen goods), and references to robbery, blackmail, burglary, aggravated burglary or handling stolen goods, shall be construed in accordance with the provisions of this Act, including those of section 24.

Miscellaneous and consequential amendments, and repeal

17–33
33.—(1) The Post Office Act 1953 shall have effect subject to the amendments provided for by Part I of Schedule 2 to this Act and (except in so far as the contrary intention appears) those amendments shall have effect throughout the British postal area.

(2) The enactments mentioned in Parts II and III of Schedule 2 to this Act shall have effect subject to the amendments there provided for, and (subject to subsection (4) below) the amendments made by Part II to enactments extending beyond England and Wales shall have the like extent as the enactment amended.

(3) The enactments mentioned in Schedule 3 to this Act (which include in Part II certain enactments related to the subject matter of this Act but already obsolete or redundant apart from this Act) are hereby repealed to the extent specified in column 3 of that schedule; and, notwithstanding that the foregoing sections of this Act do not extend to Scotland, where any enactment expressed to be repealed by Schedule 3 does so extend, the Schedule shall have effect to repeal it in its application to Scotland except in so far as the repeal is expressed not to extend to Scotland.

(4) No amendment or repeal made by this Act in Schedule 1 to the Extradition Act 1870 or in the Schedule to the Extradition Act 1873 shall affect the operation of that Schedule by reference to the law of a British possession; but the repeal made in Schedule 1 to the Extradition Act 1870 shall extend throughout the United Kingdom.

Supplementary

Interpretation

34.—(1) Sections 4(1) and 5(1) of this Act shall apply generally for **17–34**
purposes of this Act as they apply for purposes of section 1.
(2) For purposes of this Act—

(*a*) "gain" and "loss" are to be construed as extending only to gain or loss
in money or other property, but as extending to any such gain or loss
whether temporary or permanent; and—
(i) "gain" includes a gain by keeping what one has, as well as a gain by
getting what one has not; and
(ii) "loss" includes a loss by not getting what one might get, as
well as a loss by parting with what one has;
(*b*) "goods," except in so far as the context otherwise requires, includes
money and every other description of property except land, and
includes things severed from the land by stealing.

Commencement and transitional provisions

35.—(1) This Act shall come into force on the 1st January 1969 and, save **17–35**
as otherwise provided by this Act, shall have affect only in relation to
offences wholly or partly committed on or after that date.
(2) Sections 27 and 28 of this Act shall apply in relation to proceedings for
an offence committed before the commencement of this Act as they would
apply in relation to proceedings for a corresponding offence under this Act,
and shall so apply in place of any corresponding enactment repealed by this
Act.
(3) Subject to subsection (2) above, no repeal or amendment by this Act
of any enactment relating to procedure or evidence, or to the jurisdiction or
powers of any court, or to the effect of a conviction, shall affect the operation of the enactment in relation to offences committed before the commencement of this Act or to proceedings for any such offence.

Short title, and general provisions as to Scotland and Northern Ireland

36.—(1) This Act may be cited as the Theft Act 1968. **17–36**
[(2) *Repealed by the Northern Ireland Constitution Act* 1973, *s.*41(1),
Sched. 6.]
(3) This Act does not extend to Scotland or ... to Northern Ireland,
except as regards any amendment or repeal which in accordance with section
33 above is to extend to Scotland or Northern Ireland.
[*The words omitted in subsection* (3) *were repealed by the Northern Ireland
Constitution Act* 1973, *s.*41(1), *Sched.* 6.]

SCHEDULES

Section 32   ## SCHEDULE 1

OFFENCES OF TAKING, ETC. DEER OR FISH

Taking or killing deer

17-37   [1. *Repealed by the Deer Act* 1980, *s.*9(2). *For s.*1 *of the Deer Act* 1980, *see above,* § 2-08.]

Taking or destroying fish

17-38   **2.**—(1) Subject to subparagraph (2) below, a person who unlawfuly takes or destroys, or attempts to take or destroy, any fish in water which is private property on which there is any private right of fishery shall on summary conviction be liable to a fine not exceeding fifty pounds or, for an offence committed after a previous conviction of an offence under this subparagraph, to imprisonment for a term not exceeding three months or to a fine not exceeding one hundred pounds or to both.

(2) Subparagraph (1) above shall not apply to taking or destroying fish by angling in the daytime (that is to say, in the period beginning one hour before sunrise and ending one hour after sunset); but a person who by angling in the daytime unlawfully takes or destroys, or attempts to take or destroy, any fish in water which is private property or in which there is any private right of fishery shall on summary conviction be liable to a fine not exceeding twenty pounds.

(3) The court by which a person is convicted of an offence under this paragraph may order the forfeiture of anything which, at the time of the offence, he had with him for use for taking or destroying fish.

(4) Any person may arrest without warrant anyone who is, or whom he, with reasonable cause, suspects to be, committing an offence under subparagraph (1) above, and may seize from any person who is, or whom he, with reasonable cause, suspects to be, committing any offence under this paragraph anything which on that person's conviction of the offence would be liable to be forfeited under subparagraph (3) above.

Section 33(1)(2)   ## SCHEDULE 2

MISCELLANEOUS AND CONSEQUENTIAL AMENDMENTS

PART I

Amendments of Post Office Act 1953

17-39   1. The Post Office Act 1953 shall have effect subject to the amendments provided for by this Part of this Schedule (and, except in so far as the contrary intention appears, those amendments have effect throughout the British postal area).

2. Sections 22 and 23 shall be amended by substituting for the word "felony" in section 22(1) and section 23(2) the words "a misdemeanour," and by omitting the words "of this Act and" in section 23(1).

3. In section 52, as it applies outside England and Wales, for the words from "be guilty" onwards there shall be substituted the words "be guilty of a misdemeanour and be liable to imprisonment for a term not exceeding ten years."

4. In section 53 for the words from "be guilty" onwards there shall be substituted the words "be guilty of a misdemeanour and be liable to imprisonment for a term not exceeding five years."

5. In section 54, as it applies outside England and Wales,—

    (a) there shall be omitted the words "taking, embezzling," and the words "taken, embezzled," where first occurring;

    (b) for the words "a felony" there shall be substituted the words "an offence" and the word "feloniously" shall be omitted;

    (c) for the words from "be guilty" to "secreted it" there shall be substituted the words "be guilty of a misdemeanour and be liable to imprisonment for a term not exceeding fourteen years."

6. In sections 55 and 58(1), after the word "imprisonment," there shall in each case be inserted the words "for a term not exceeding two years."

7. In section 57—

    (a) there shall be omitted the words "steals, or for any purpose whatever embezzles," and the words from "or if" onwards;

    (b) for the word "felony" there shall be substituted the words "a misdemeanour."

[8. *Repealed by the British Telecommunications Act* 1981, *s.*89, *Sched.* 6.]

9. Section 69(2) shall be omitted.

10. For section 70 there shall be substituted the following section—

"Prosecution of certain offences in any jurisdiction of British postal area.

70.—(1) Where a person—

    (a) steals or attempts to steal any mail bag or postal packet in the course of transmission as such between places in different jurisdictions in the British postal area, or any of the contents of such a mail bag or postal packet; or

    (b) in stealing or with intent to steal any such mail bag or postal packet or any of its contents, commits any robbery, attempted robbery or assault with intent to rob;

then, in whichever of those jurisdictions he does so, he shall by virtue of this section be guilty in each of the jurisdictions in which this subsection has effect of committing or attempting to commit the offence against section 52 of this Act, or the offence referred to in paragraph (b) of this subsection, as the case may be, as if he had done so in that jurisdiction, and he shall accordingly be liable to be prosecuted, tried and punished in that jurisdiction without proof that the offence was committed there.

(2) In subsection (1) above the reference to different jurisdictions in the British postal area is to be construed as referring to the several jurisdictions of England and Wales, of Scotland, of Northern Ireland, of the Isle of Man, of the Channel Islands; and that subsection shall have effect in each of those jurisdictions except England and Wales."

11. In section 72 there shall be added as a new subsection (3)—

    "(3) In any proceedings in England or Wales for an offence under section 53, 55, 56, 57 or 58 of this Act, section 27(4) of the Theft Act 1968 shall apply as it is expressed to apply to proceedings for the theft of anything in the course of transmission by post; and in the case of proceedings under section 53 of this Act a statutory declaration made by any person that a vessel, vehicle or aircraft was at any time employed by or under the Post Office for the transmission of postal packets under contract shall be admissible as evidence of the facts stated in the declaration subject to the same conditions as under section 27(4)(a) and (b) of the Theft Act 1968 apply to declarations admissible under section 27(4)."

12. In section 87(1), the definition of "valuable security" shall be omitted but, except in relation to England and Wales, there shall be substituted:—

" 'valuable security' means any document creating, transferring, surrendering or releasing any right to, in or over property, or authorising the payment of money or delivery of any property, or evidencing the creation, transfer, surrender or release of any such right or the payment of money or delivery of any property, or the satisfaction of any obligation."

PART II

Other amendments extending beyond England and Wales

Act amended	*Amendment*

17–40 [*Entry relating to the Extradition Act* 1973, *Sched.: repealed by the Extradition Act* 1989, *s.*37, *Sched.* 2.]

The Public Stores Act 1875 (38 & 39 Vict. c. 25)	For section 12 (incorporation of parts of Larceny Act 1861) there shall be substituted:—

"(1) Any person may arrest without warrant anyone who is, or whom he, with reasonable cause, suspects to be, in the act of committing or attempting to commit an offence against section 5 or 8 of this Act.

(2) If it is made to appear by information on oath before a justice of the peace that there is reasonable cause to believe that any person has in his custody or possession or on his premises any stores in respect of which an offence against section 5 of this Act has been committed, the justice may issue a warrant to a constable to search for and seize the stores as in the case of stolen goods, and the Police (Property) Act 1897 shall apply as if this subsection were among the enactments mentioned in section 1(1) of that Act."

The Army Act 1955 (3 & 4 Eliz. 2, c. 18)	For section 44(1)(*b*) there shall be substituted—

"(*b*) handles any stolen goods, where the property stolen was public or service property, or".

For section 45(*b*) there shall be substituted—

"(*b*) handles any stolen goods, where the property stolen belonged to a person subject to military law, or".

In section 138(1) for the words from "receiving" to "stolen" there shall be substituted the words "handling it".

In section 225(1) after the definition of "Governor" there shall be inserted—

" 'handles' has the same meaning as in the Theft Act 1968";

and for the definition of "steals" there shall be substituted—

" 'steals' has the same meaning as in the Theft Act 1968, and references to 'stolen goods' shall be construed as if contained in that Act".

The Air Force Act 1955 (3 & 4 Eliz. 2, c. 19)	The same amendments shall be made in sections 44, 45, 138 and 223 as are above directed to be made in the corresponding sections of the Army Act 1955, except that in the amendment to section 45(*b*) "air-force law" shall be substituted for "military law".

The Naval Discipline Act 1957 (5 & 6 Eliz. 2, c. 53)	For section 29(*b*) there shall be substituted—

"(*b*) handles any stolen goods, where the property stolen was public or service property, or".

In section 76(1) for the words from "receiving" to "embezzling" there shall be substituted the word "handling".

In section 135(1) the same amendments shall be made as are above directed to be made in section 225(1) of the Army Act 1955.

The Army and Air Force Act 1961   Section 21 shall be omitted.
(9 & 10 Eliz. 2, c. 52)

[*Entry relating to the Road Traffic Act* 1962, *Sched.* 1, *Part II; repealed by the Road Traffic Act* 1972, *s*.205(1) *Sched.* 9.]

PART III

Amendments limited to England and Wales

Act amended	*Amendment*	
The Gaming Act 1845 (8 & 9 Vict. c. 109)	In section 17 (punishment for cheating at play, etc.) for the words "be deemed guilty of obtaining such money or valuable thing from such other person by a false pretence" and the following words there shall be substituted the words—	**17–41**

"(*a*) on conviction on indictment be liable to imprisonment for a term not exceeding two years; or
(*b*) on summary conviction be liable to imprisonment for a term not exceeding six months or to a fine not exceeding two hundred pounds or to both".

[*Entry relating to the Pawnbrokers Act* 1872, *s*.38: *repealed by the Consumer Credit Act* 1974, *s*.192(3)(*b*), *Sched.* 5.]

[*Entry relating to the Bankruptcy Act* 1914, *s*.116: *repealed by the Insolvency Act* 1985, *s*.235, *Sched.* 10.]

The House to House Collections Act 1939 (2 & 3 Geo. 6, c. 44)   In the Schedule (offences for which a conviction is a ground for refusing or revoking a licence under the Act to promote a collection for charity) for the entry relating to the Larceny Act 1916 there shall be substituted:—
"Robbery, burglary and blackmail".

[*Entry relating to the Magistrates' Courts Act* 1952, *Sched.* 1, *para.* 8: *repealed by the Criminal Law Act* 1977. *s*.65(5), *Sched.* 13.]

The Visiting Forces Act 1952 (15 & 16 Geo. 6 & 1 Eliz. 2, c. 67)   In the Schedule there shall be inserted in paragraph 1(*a*) after the word "buggery" the word "robbery", and in paragraph 3 there shall be added at the end—
"(*g*) the Theft Act 1968, except section 8 (robbery)".

The Finance Act 1965 (1965 c. 25)   In Schedule 10, in the Table in paragraph 1, for the words "Sections 500 to 505" there shall be substituted the words "Sections 500 to 504".

The Finance Act 1966 (1966 c. 18)   In Schedule 6, in paragraph 13, for the words "Sections 500 to 505" there shall be substituted the words "Sections 500 to 504", and the words from "together with" to "the said section 505" shall be omitted.

[*Entry relating to the Criminal Law Act* 1967, *Sched.* 1: *repealed by the Courts Act* 1971, *s*.56, *Sched.* 11.]

The Firearms Act 1968 (1968 c. 27)   Schedule 1 (offences in connection with which possession of a firearm is an offence under section 17(2)) shall be amended, except in relation to a person's apprehension for an offence committed before the

285

commencement of this Act, by substituting for paragraph 4—
     "4. Theft, burglary, blackmail and any offence under
     section 12(1) (taking of motor vehicle or other con-
     veyance without owner's consent) of the Theft Act
     1968":
          by omitting paragraph 7: and by substituting in
          paragraph 8 for the words "paragraphs 1 to 7" the
          words "paragraphs 1 to 6".

SCHEDULE 3

REPEALS

17–42   [*This Schedule repealed penal enactments superseded by this Act and obsolete and redundant
enactments and effected certain consequential repeals.*]

APPENDIX 2

Theft Act 1978

(1978 c. 31)

An Act to replace section 16(2)(*a*) of the Theft Act 1968 with other provision against fraudulent conduct; and for connected purposes.
[20th July 1978]

Obtaining services by deception

1.—(1) A person who by any deception dishonestly obtains services from another shall be guilty of an offence.   **18–01**

(2) It is an obtaining of services where the other is induced to confer a benefit by doing some act, or causing or permitting some act to be done, on the understanding that the benefit has been or will be paid for.

Evasion of liability by deception

2.—(1) Subject to subsection (2) below, where a person by any deception—   **18–02**

(*a*) dishonestly secures the remission of the whole or part of any existing liability to make a payment, whether his own liability or another's; or

(*b*) with intent to make permanent default in whole or in part on any existing liability to make a payment, or with intent to let another do so, dishonestly induces the creditor or any person claiming payment on behalf of the creditor to wait for payment (whether or not the due date of payment is deferred) or to forgo payment; or

(*c*) dishonestly obtains any exemption from or abatement of liability to make a payment;

he shall be guilty of an offence.

(2) For purposes of this section "liability" means legally enforceable liability; and subsection (1) shall not apply in relation to a liability that has

287

not been accepted or established to pay compensation for a wrongful act or omission.

(3) For purposes of subsection (1)(*b*) a person induced to take in payment a cheque or other security for money by way of conditional satisfaction of a pre-existing liability is to be treated not as being paid but as being induced to wait for payment.

(4) For purposes of section (1)(*c*) "obtains" includes obtaining for another or enabling another to obtain.

Making off without payment

18–03   **3.**—(1) Subject to subsection (3) below, a person who, knowing that payment on the spot for any goods supplied or service done is required or expected from him, dishonestly makes off without having paid as required or expected and with intent to avoid payment of the amount due shall be guilty of an offence.

(2) For purposes of this section "payment on the spot" includes payment at the time of collecting goods on which work has been done or in respect of which service has been provided.

(3) Subsection (1) above shall not apply where the supply of the goods or the doing of the service is contrary to law, or where the service done is such that payment is not legally enforceable.

(4) Any person may arrest without warrant any one who is, or whom he, with reasonable cause, suspects to be, committing or attempting to commit an offence under this section.

Punishments

18–04   **4.**—(1) Offences under this Act shall be punishable either on conviction on indictment or on summary conviction.

(2) A person convicted on indictment shall be liable—

   (*a*) for an offence under section 1 or section 2 of this Act, to imprisonment for a term not exceeding five years; and
   (*b*) for an offence under section 3 of this Act, to imprisonment for a term not exceeding two years.

(3) A person convicted summarily of any offence under this Act shall be liable—

   (*a*) to imprisonment for a term not exceeding six months; or
   (*b*) to a fine not exceeding the prescribed sum for the purposes of [section 32 of the Magistrates' Courts Act 1980] (punishment on summary conviction of offences triable either way: £1,000 or other sum substituted by order under that Act),

or to both.

[*The words in square brackets in subsection* (3) *were substituted by the Magistrates' Courts Act* 1980, *s.*154(1), *Sched.* 7.]

Supplementary

5.—(1) For purposes of sections 1 and 2 above "deception" has the same **18–05** meaning as in section 15 of the Theft Act 1968, that is to say, it means any deception (whether deliberate or reckless) by words or conduct as to fact or as to law, including a deception as to the present intentions of the person using the deception or any other person; and section 18 of that Act (liability of company officers for offences by the company) shall apply in relation to sections 1 and 2 above as it applies in relation to section 15 of that Act.

(2) Sections 30(1) (husband and wife), 31(1) (effect on civil proceedings) and 34 (interpretation) of the Theft Act 1968, so far as they are applicable in relation to this Act, shall apply as they apply in relation to that Act.

[(3) *Repealed by the Extradition Act* 1989, *s.*37, *Sched.* 2.]

(4) In the Visiting Forces Act 1952, in paragraph 3 of the Schedule (which defines for England and Wales "offences against property" for purposes of the exclusion in certain cases of the jurisdiction of United Kingdom courts) there shall be added at the end—

"(*j*) the Theft Act 1978."

(5) In the Theft Act 1968 section 16(2)(*a*) is hereby repealed.

Enactment of same provisions for Northern Ireland

6. An Order in Council under paragraph 1(1)(*b*) of Schedule 1 to the **18–06** Northern Ireland Act 1974 (legislation for Northern Ireland in the interim period) which contains a statement that it operates only so as to make for Northern Ireland provision corresponding to this Act—

(*a*) shall not be subject to paragraph 1(4) and (5) of that Schedule (affirmative resolution of both Houses of Parliament); but
(*b*) shall be subject to annulment by resolution of either House.

Short title, commencement and extent

7.—(1) This Act may be cited as the Theft Act 1978. **18–07**
(2) This Act shall come into force at the expiration of three months beginning with the date on which it is passed.
(3) This Act except section 5(3), shall not extend to Scotland; and except for that subsection, and subject also to section 6, it shall not extend to Northern Ireland.

INDEX